Late Colonial Sublime

FLASHPOINTS

The FlashPoints series is devoted to books that consider literature beyond strictly national and disciplinary frameworks, and that are distinguished both by their historical grounding and by their theoretical and conceptual strength. Our books engage theory without losing touch with history and work historically without falling into uncritical positivism. FlashPoints aims for a broad audience within the humanities and the social sciences concerned with moments of cultural emergence and transformation. In a Benjaminian mode, FlashPoints is interested in how literature contributes to forming new constellations of culture and history and in how such formations function critically and politically in the present. Series titles are available online at http://escholarship.org/uc/flashpoints.

A complete list of titles begins on page 279.

Late Colonial Sublime

Neo-Epics and the End of Romanticism

G. S. Sahota

NORTHWESTERN UNIVERSITY PRESS | EVANSTON, ILLINOIS

THIS BOOK IS MADE POSSIBLE BY A COLLABORATIVE GRANT FROM THE ANDREW W. MELLON FOUNDATION.

Northwestern University Press
www.nupress.northwestern.edu

Printed in the United States of America

10 9 8 7 6 5 4 3 2 1

Library of Congress Cataloging-in-Publication Data

Names: Sahota, G. S., author.
Title: Late colonial sublime : neo-epics and the end of Romanticism / G. S. Sahota.
Other titles: FlashPoints (Evanston, Ill.)
Description: Evanston, Illinois : Northwestern University Press, 2018. | Series: FlashPoints
Identifiers: LCCN 2017022781| ISBN 9780810136496 (cloth : alk. paper) | ISBN 9780810136489 (pbk. : alk. paper) | ISBN 9780810136502 (e-book)
Subjects: LCSH: Hindi literature—India—19th century—History and criticism. | Hindi literature—India—20th century—History and criticism. | Urdu literature—India—19th century—History and criticism. | Urdu literature—India—20th century—History and criticism. | Romanticism—India. | Sublime, The, in literature.
Classification: LCC PK2037 .S24 2018 | DDC 891.4309—dc23
LC record available at https://lccn.loc.gov/2017022781

The paper used in this publication meets the minimum requirements of the American National Standard for Information Sciences—Permanence of Paper for Printed Library Materials, ANSI Z39.48-1992.

For Siddhartha S. Sahota

τὸν δ' αὖτε προσέειπε συβώτης, ὄρχαμος ἀνδρῶν:
'ξεῖν', ἐπεὶ ἂρ δὴ ταῦτά μ' ἀνείρεαι ἠδὲ μεταλλᾷς,
σιγῇ νῦν ξυνίει καὶ τέρπεο, πῖνέ τε οἶνον
ἥμενος. αἵδε δὲ νύκτες ἀθέσφατοι: ἔστι μὲν εὕδειν,
ἔστι δὲ τερπομένοισιν ἀκούειν: οὐδέ τί σε χρή,
πρὶν ὥρη, καταλέχθαι: ἀνίη καὶ πολὺς ὕπνος.

"My friend," the swineherd answered, foreman of men,
"you really want my story? So many questions—well,
listen in quiet, then, and take your ease, sit back
and drink your wine. The nights are endless now.
We've plenty of time to sleep or savor a long tale."

—Homer, *Odyssey*, 15.389–94 (trans. Robert Fagles [New York: Penguin, 1999], 331–32).

The epic is not merely a *genre* but a way of life.

—Harry Levin, preface to *The Singer of Tales*

E riportiamo anche la conclusione poco confortante: noialtri europei, e sopratutto noialtri francesi, abbiamo la tendenza all'*egocentrismo*. Ci crediamo centro dell'universo e immaginiamo appena che fuori di noi, fuori della nostra vecchia sfera continentale, vi siano dei grandi movimenti d'attività umana, dove stanno elaborandosi già degli avvenimenti che potranno avere delle ripercussioni decisive sui nostri destini. Alla guerra europea non potrà molto tardare la guerra delle colonie.

And we arrive at this hardly comforting conclusion: We Europeans, and especially we French, have a tendency toward *egocentrism*. We believe ourselves the center of the universe and we can barely imagine that beyond us, beyond our old continental sphere, there are huge upsurges of human action such that there are events already developing which can have decisive repercussions on our destiny. It is only a matter of time before the war in the colonies becomes the European war.

—Antonio Gramsci, "La Guerra e Le Colonie," in *Nel mondo grande e terribile: Antologia degli scritti 1914–1935* (my translation)

Contents

Acknowledgments *xi*

Introduction: Aporias of Modernity 3

PART I. FRACTURED FRAMES: IMPERIAL PARALLAX AND DISJOINTED TIME

1. Commodity and Sublimity: Mimesis of the Immaterial 29
2. Romanticism's Horizons, or The Transmission of Critique 54
3. Atmospherics of Imperialism: Benjamin's Sublime 96

PART II. NEO-EPIC CONSTELLATION: OUT OF BRITISH INDIA

4. Hali's Transvaluation of Modernity: Allegories of *Marsiya* 127
5. Iqbal, or the *Sturm und Drang* of Late Colonial India: Resemblances of Pure Content 143
6. Utility and Culture: Modern Subjectivity and Neotraditional Aesthetics 172

Epilogue: Melancholic Ornament: TV *Ramayana*, Nostalgia, and Kitsch as Counter-Enlightenment 209

Appendix A. Translation of Muhammad Iqbal's Preface to *Payam-e Mashriq* (Message of the East) 233

Appendix B. Translation of Sumitranandan Pant's "The Usefulness of the Epic Form in the Modern Age" 242

Notes 247

Index 273

Acknowledgments

“And is the life of a thinking person anything more than a steady inner symphilosophy?” Thus asks rhetorically the German romantic Novalis, borrowing fittingly a term coined by his fellow Jena school theorist of *die Romantik*, Friedrich Schlegel. The present work may be considered an investigation into a “symromanticism” involving ever more complicated borrowings and exchanges of thought forms across imperial divides for which no accounting or settling of debts is possible or necessary. Not only was independent invention always a potentiality on all sides of this literary history, but whatever was borrowed was elaborated with such ardor that its value exceeded what it had been initially—each paying back thus an indebting, requiring a cycle of compensation in turn. It would be better to see the dynamics of indebtedness in any symphilosophy in absolute terms as a borrowing of energies that sustain a critical life-thought with no reduction to a zero balance ever again possible or even desirable. Eternal gratitude is the flip side of the luck of happy indebtedness.

It has been my good luck to have accrued manifold debts in the process of completing this book. Susan Gillman was assigned to me as the FlashPoints series editor very early in the process and stayed with the project even during its least promising moments, always offering boundless enthusiasm and penetrating criticisms through her diamond-sharp sparkle and anarchic wit. An ever more explicit engagement with translation in the course of revising this work is due to her reasoned urgings. Gianna Francesca Mosser, editor in chief at Northwestern University Press, facilitated rounds of anonymous external reviews of the manuscript with unwavering integrity and efficacy. I also thank the two anonymous readers: their comments were aimed at improving the work down to the last detail; if it still needs improvement, the fault is mine alone.

It was also my good fortune to have skated happily through a public education system right into the midst of some of the most illustrious scholars and intellectuals the world has recently known in the humanities and social sciences. If the work displays any modicum of philological rigor, it is not least for attempting to mimic the scholarly discipline and synthetic intelligence of Sheldon Pollock and Muzaffar Alam. For its critical apparatus I owe a great deal to the Social Theory Workshop at Chicago, especially its stewards, Moishe Postone and William Sewell, for generating widely ramifying and relevant discussions. The earlier guides into the disparate bodies of knowledge that make up this book, Dilip Basu, Jonathan Beecher, Edmund Burke III, James Clifford, Robert Goldman, and Hayden White, all from my deeply impressionable undergraduate days, have left an indelible mark on many of its main contours. Dilip is no longer with us. I had waited too long to share with him the sections on Tagore and Datta, which were written with his adage always in mind: to give priority to the primary sources in any account; that is what I attempted in these parts, despite the risks. It is to his memory now that those sections are dedicated.

This book has taken me to, and in turn reflects, various locations around the world. In these diverse places, colleagues and loosely affiliated members of distinct universities and institutions have provided a rich and challenging intellectual climate in which to think. I would like to thank the entire Literature Department at the University of California in Santa Cruz for providing a hospitable environment for this work. Among those connected to UCSC, the following are deserving of special mention: Jordi Aladro, Gopal Balakrishnan, Karen Bassi, Hunter Bivens, Christopher Chen, Christopher Connery, Nathaniel Deutsch, Dion Farquhar, Carla Freccero, Wlad Godzich, Martin Devecka, Sean Keilen, Sharon Kinoshita, William Ladusaw, H. Marshall Leicester, Tyrus Miller, Loisa Nygaard, Mary Scott, Daniel Selden, Juned Sheikh, Deanna Shemek, Tyler Stoval, Richard Terdiman, and Rob Wilson. At the Wissenschaftskolleg zu Berlin, which hosted me in the "Europa im Nahen Osten—der Nahe Osten in Europa" over 2010–11, I would like to thank Georges Khalil and Reinhart Meyer-Kalkus as well as the other fellows of that year. A professorial appointment at the University of Minnesota (Twin Cities) allowed me to enter into productive dialogues and friendly relations with a number of colleagues of that institution as well as neighboring ones: Joseph Allen, Timothy Brennan, Giancarlo Casale, Keya Ganguly, Chris Isett, James Lane, Silvia López, Christine Marran, Jason McGrath, Arun Saldanha, Simona Sawhney, Ajay Skaria, Hoon Song, and Ann Waltner. Evelyn Davidheiser and Klaas van der Sanden of the Institute for Global Studies helped fund and facilitate a four-year workshop, Dialectics and Society, which allowed us to engage with renowned thinkers such as Raymond Geuss, Neil Larsen, and Susan Buck-Morss, among others mentioned earlier. The members of Theorizing Early Modern Studies—Juliette Cherbuliez, J. B. Shank, and Michael Gaudio—must be thanked for organizing a semester-long reading group around Walter Benjamin's *The Origin of German Tragic Drama.*

A number of foundations, libraries, and collections deserve mention for making their materials accessible to me. The librarians at Woodstock School in Mussoorie (Uttarakhand, India) gave me access to their Hindi collection and provided a most august environment—in the Himalayas—for beginning my research on Jayashankar Prasad's *Kamayani.* The University of Chicago Library (especially James Nye and Bronwen Bledsoe, now at Cornell University) as well as the Staatsbibliotek, the Berlin Graduate School in Muslim Cultures and Societies, and the libraries of Freie Universität in Berlin must be mentioned for what they offer a foreign scholar. In India, I frequented the libraries of Delhi, especially Nehru Memorial and Museum Library and the collections of Jawaharlal Nehru University, and of Lucknow, mostly the Amir-ud-Daula Public Library and the collections of the Indian Council of Philosophical Research. In London, the British Library's Oriental and India Office collection was critical in innumerable ways. In Minneapolis, I was fortunate to have the Ames Library of South Asia at the University of Minnesota. I made use of materials from the University of Michigan and the University of California collections, especially the latter's indispensable interlibrary loan system. While visiting family in the Bay Area, I was always delighted by the multilingual collection made available via the Pearl Avenue branch of the San Jose Public Library System. Generous support from the University of Chicago, the American Institute for Indian Studies, the Fulbright Foundation in India, the University of Minnesota, UC Santa Cruz, the Institute for Humanities Research, and the Wissenshaftskolleg zu Berlin allowed me to delve into these collections and write much of this book.

I am grateful for all of the venues in which this work has been presented over the years, and their respective hosts and audiences. These include UC Santa Cruz, UC Berkeley, the University of Chicago, the University of Minnesota, the University of Michigan, Columbia University, Macalester College, the Wissenshaftskolleg zu Berlin, Jawaharlal Nehru University, and Delhi University. The American Comparative Literature Association meetings at Harvard University and New York University allowed for especially productive seminars in 2016 and 2014, respectively. A part of chapter 5 and appendix A were published in the *Journal of Postcolonial Studies*, and I would like to thank the editors for permission to reprint that material here, slightly revised. I have deep gratitude for the editors of Rajkamal Prakashan in Delhi for permission to publish the translation (appendix B) of Sumitranandan Pant's essay on epic in modern Hindi. The Mellon Foundation's Modern Language Initiative funded the excellent copyediting and production oversight of Judith Hoover and Tim Roberts.

This work would not have been possible without the succession of numerous language instructors over the years. For their patience, I wish to thank Aftab Ahmad, Elena Bashir, Fauzia Farooqi, Sally Sutherland Goldman, Gildas Hamel, Ursula Kohler, C. M. Naim, and Zeba Parveen. The friendship of Laura Brueck, Sarika Chandra, Jessica Jacobs, Amy Kim, Jesse Knutson, David Lau, and Laura Martin provided essential refuge. Several people in graduate school sustained my educational pursuits in memorable ways: Whitney Cox, Rajeev Kinra, Riaz Khan, Nikhil Rao, Ajay Rao, Andrew Sartori, and Ananya Vajpeyi, among many others. Sami Khatib, Ryaz Latif, Philip Lutgendorf, and Angela Thalis, each in their own way, provided much needed assistance with a charitable touch. This project could never have gotten off the ground were it not for the largesse of my late father, Sardar Darshan S. Sahota, and the care of my mom, Harjinder Kaur, and brothers, Gurbir and Gurkanwal.

Late Colonial Sublime

Introduction

Aporias of Modernity

I. APORIA AND FORM: RUINATION/MODERNIZATION IN THE GARDEN

Every form is the resolution of a fundamental dissonance of existence.
—Georg Lukács, *Theory of the Novel*

Whereas the Prophet Muhammad takes on the guise of a Victorian taskmaster in Altaf Husain Hali's Urdu neo-epic *Musaddas: The Ebb and Flow of Islam* (1879), the demotic masses and their old aristocratic superiors, now remnants of the recently ruined empire of the Mughals, acquire the romantic luster of life lived off the clock of capitalist time.[1] The Prophet made the barbarous tribes of pre-Islamic Arabia "realize the value and worth of time, and imparted to them the keen desire and urge to work."[2] Yet today, as the poem's narrator points out, the decadent aristocrats and the broader Indo-Islamic community as a whole seem no better in their ways than these legendary reprobates. Just as there was then "pleasure-seeking, there was obliviousness, there was madness, in short, their condition was iniquitous in every respect," today the same decadence continues to resurface, despite the new Victorian imperatives. "Some have the vice of flying pigeons, others have a mania for quail-fighting. / Some are addicted to hemp and cannabis, others are addicted to the delight of opiates."[3] Hali surveys the fairs, wrestling pits, and local hangouts left over from precolonial times.

"Here," Hali elaborates in reference to his contemporary Indians, "the life of all is filled with wild passion. Whoever you see here is a Qais or a Farhad," referring to the archetypal lovers of the Indo-Persian literary tradition. As much as Hali is set explicitly against it, the lavish, carefree, even extravagant lifestyle of the old aristocrats and their motley emulators receives embellished description in his work. What gives them a peculiarly ambivalent charge is the alternative imposed by the imperial powers of the West, with all their prizing of efficiency and thrift, but to no apparent end:

They [the people of Europe] never sleep their fill, they are
 never sated by hard work,
They do not squander their substance, they do not waste an instant
 uselessly,
They do not tire or get weary of going along. They have advanced a
 long way and keep on advancing.[4]

The frisson that results from these ambivalent juxtapositions—these disparate temporalities and the vexed desires underlying them—as the South Asia scholars Christopher Shackle and Javed Majeed remark, "emerges from the intertwining of moral disapprobation with the fecund possibilities of pleasure in the text."[5] This frisson—a momentary yet sublime shattering of the immanent subjectivity of the *Musaddas*—has as its fundamental source an aporia within late colonial society, that is, a general predicament that made imperative the formal aesthetic experimentations that I will analyze over the following chapters. As is the case with Hali's *Musaddas*, the works assembled here indexed urgent questions: how to tether together the disparate temporalities that had begun to tear apart, as in Hali's depictions, the social fabric of everyday society; how, in other words, to face the instrumental-rational norms governing modern civil society without sacrificing past inheritances or the horizons of an alternative existence; how, indeed, to rescue pasts or futures without bringing them to ruination in the process. How, for instance, to avoid releasing in their stead the neotraditional monstrosities—reifications par excellence—which, like those of early twenty-first-century India, confound Independence with the reimplementation of colonial laws, thereby threatening to return one to a perpetually late colonial present (or otherwise reminding one that perhaps the "post" is too soon).

I invoke Hali's neo-epic here for it serves as a map into the very general aporia that formed after the passing of the Act for the Better

Government of India, which vested the sovereignty of India in Queen Victoria just a year after the Mutiny of 1857. This book indexes the ongoing and ever-penetrating reconfiguration of sociocultural codes according to market norms since the last decades of the nineteenth century. Shackle and Majeed's pioneering research on Hali's neo-epic—my own coinage, about which I will have occasion to say more below; for them it is simply an "epic"[6]—retraces the new imperial spatial and temporal vectors that began to penetrate the core of Indo-Islamic poetic tropes as much as it did other cultural forms such as visual representation, or indeed, the very grammar of modern Hindi. Not even that celestial inner recess, the Islamicate garden, was spared in this intrusive reconfiguration of motifs in accordance with the commodity-form, which in their totality redefined the scope of the modern aesthetic imagination in vernaculars like Urdu and Hindi, making them less allegories of merely local or national phenomena (as might be habitually imagined in imperial metropoles) than bearers of a contradictory dynamic that continues to characterize late modernity as such: the crisis of value.

We will return to the garden. For now, allow Shackle and Majeed to elucidate the problem, for they realize that what is operative in Hali's neo-epic is a new "economic nexus" premised on an emergent system of value. Hali is emphatic that his fellow community members understand that the new system is universally binding and reorganizes the temporal imperatives that ought to govern one's life. Indeed, as Shackle and Majeed observe, the new value form penetrates the colonial subject's psychosomatic core: "Even the very rhythms of the body are measured in accordance with an economic scale of value," they note, for Hali writes, "If we reckon all the breaths of day and night, then very few will be left to be gathered for the next day. / Our days and nights are continually spent for nothing." Bodily rhythms are assimilated to clock time; they must be employed.[7] For Hali, wealth or capital (*daulat*)—his terminology is not yet able to mark the crucial distinction[8]—is now an index of time, which lends itself to standard measure. "Wealth becomes, as it were, a synecdoche of time, or put another way, wealth becomes" for Hali, as Shackle and Majeed note, "a manifestation of time." Some suprasensible power—Could it be Adam Smith's ghostly hand of the market?—has reestablished the scales and redetermined the scope of value. Now its measure is unitary and can extend across all spatial and temporal horizons, including those of a distant past: "That plain of Sanjar and of Kufa, in which the geometers of the age assembled. / They deployed their apparatus for surveying the globe. The value of the whole became apparent from the part." The totality depicted here, in which parts are unified into spherical wholes bearing the sum of market prices, though associated anachronistically with the scientific discoveries of classical Islam, has its contemporary correlate in the new infrastructure allowing for free trade and mobility of peoples at a quicker and wider pace in Hali's very midst. In a section titled "The Blessings of British Rule," Hali remarks that government "has completely opened up the roads to progress."[9] Time, space, material wealth, and value are all imagined as commensurate in this neo-epic; in becoming mutually constitutive, they enforce a new routine, which his fellow Indian Muslims neglect to espouse to their own future detriment, as Hali is at pains to press upon them, having himself become a member of the Victorian Indian establishment.

The underlying social dynamic that gives rise to this new temporality and that produces novel forms of value and unprecedented regimes of productive activity will be discussed in chapter 1. Suffice it to say for the moment that what Hali alights upon in his own fashion in the *Musaddas* is the very aporia produced by the processes unleashed by the British in their Indian colony, namely commodification and reification, or, to put it simply, the imperative to make all values accord with the market. The pressures this new economic nexus placed on his aesthetic and general intellectual activity are remarkable. Having obliterated the old regime, scrambled customary patterns, and devastated the swaths of hapless peasantry with artificial famines of unfathomable sizes—all judged necessary and binding by the administrative custodians of the new value form—the new economic nexus began to leave indelible signatures in the very material texture of the *Musaddas*. It gave a negative, indeed a transgressive outline to the kinds of attitudes, aesthetic practices, and modes of existence that will take on the auras and names of romanticism in Hindi and Urdu literary spheres in subsequent decades, facets of which will be covered over the course of *Late Colonial Sublime*. Moreover, as Shackle and Majeed observe, "poetry was now being fashioned in terms of transmitting information, rather than as highlighting those non-falsifiable, non-informative aspects of language captured by the predominantly metaphorical modes of classical poetry." Adopting the traits of a mechanical art "created for the purpose of conveying information," the *Musaddas* could not help but give the Prophet's message a Victorian inflection. Yet, if one looks carefully at the *Musaddas*'s fundamental message of moral reform—alloyed, as mentioned, with the alluring image of freedom from clock time—it becomes possible to see how it is at odds with the very form chosen, given that the *Musaddas*, a stanza of six half-verses, is "particularly associated with the suffering of Imam Husain and his companions at the battle of Karbala" in 680 C.E.[10] Grounded thus in Shi'a Islamic theology, the choice of form threatens to radically exceed the secularity of the new Victorian morality, producing yet another occasion for the frisson of which Shackle and Majeed speak. In other words, a peculiarly compensatory antimodern valence is given in the very form of the work. It is as if after having acknowledged the new instrumental-rational logic of modernity and the shrinking of subjectivity to materialist-narcissistic ends for which no breath can be wasted, a hesitation is registered at the level of form. The widest formal dimension of the work reasserts incommensurate imaginary frontiers. Modeled on the sublime laments, or *marsiya*, Hali's *Musaddas*, somber and melodic like the threnodies upon which this stanzaic form (*musaddas*) is based, reverse the secularity of the new Victorian morality and produce a neo-epic chronotope of cosmic ebbs and flows of imperial power, apparently impenetrable to human agency, as we will see in greater detail in chapter 4.

Thus a neo-epic in late colonial India took form directly in response to the aporias—crises of value—produced by the new dispensation premised on the commodity-form. The disturbances sent shudders through the creatures of the garden. The poet himself has departed from the company of the nightingale: "From poets and recitals now I quail." Like other works examined in *Late Colonial Sublime*, Hali's *Musaddas* reveals deep misgivings about life under both temporalities. It marks as unlivable the harrowing imperatives of clock time and as infeasible the carefree attitude of an emergent romantic nostalgia. Yet, the very fact that old religious categories must be reconstructed to accord with the new imperatives of utility and progress meant that traditional authority had lost its moral autonomy. Hali berates his immediate community members for having "not made use of intelligence and faith," as if both reason and faith (*aql o din*) were now like ordinary implements to be manipulated at will. The implication is that the logic of the commodity-form has assumed powers previously reserved for transcendent entities, such as the divine cosmological structure to which Hali elsewhere takes recourse. This sublime material force respects no preestablished boundaries: "To a certain extent," observe Shackle and Majeed, "the nexus of economic values" has entered into the garden of the nightingale—the very *bulbul ki chaman* with which the *Musaddas* begins. This nexus of economic values "overlaps with the imagery of cultivation and irrigation, given that the transformation of agriculture and the changes in social structure in parts of British India which were wrought through irrigation, were a significant aspect of the colonial state's public works." Such public works are indeed praised in the *Musaddas*. Yet, given that, it is now no longer clear what is to be cultivated in the garden. "Although the spring-garden of my youth [*bagh-e jivani ki bahar*] was indeed a sight to behold, I was granted no respite from the most odious aspects of worldly existence," shares Hali in his first introduction of 1879.[11] Will the archetypal garden of classical Indo-Islamic culture need to incorporate the hydraulic engineering of the colonial regime to flourish, and if so, what will take root there now? Will the garden retain some autonomy from the imperatives of utility, progress, markets, and the vast world shaped now by the logic of commodities? Have things already begun to change irrevocably?

II. NEO-EPICS AND ROMANTICISM IN LATE COLONIAL INDIA: LITERARY PARALLAXES OF EMPIRE

In epic naivety lives the critique of bourgeois reason.
—Theodor W. Adorno, "On Epic Naivety"

The epics in India do not belong to the past alone—they are also part of the contemporary consciousness.
—Meenakshi Mukherjee, "Epic and Novel in India"

Hali's *Musaddas* signals for the literary historian not merely the aporias that defined the new dispensation of late colonial India, but the cultural forms and activities they generated as well.[12] At the core of *Late Colonial Sublime* is an investigation into the puzzles these aporia generated, especially at the level of cultural form. Literary form, given my own intellectual formation, appears throughout as the privileged medium for registering and proliferating the immanent social contradictions cleaving imperial capitalism as a whole. Yet, the form in question—the neo-epic—was itself thoroughly riven from within and generally charged with the contradictory currents of modern instrumentality, on the one hand, and romantic mitigations, if not negations, of clock time (among other constraints), on the other. The form never appeared merely on its own but rather entangled with competing ideologies for and against progress. As with Hali's *Musaddas*, traditionalism was always alloyed with modern learning; conversely, modern challenges were often imagined to be curbed by the imposition of familiar formal schemes, such as the haloed narrative of epic martyrdom of the *Musaddas* itself. Despite being a recent renovation of auratic elements of a quickly receding past, the neo-epic thus often displayed a deep distrust of modernity as a whole. The affinity to varieties of romantic self-fashioning becomes apparent in myriad ways across distinct linguistic and cultural spheres. Under the auspices of a revitalized romanticism, now translated and giving new valences and added pressures to a moment of imperial crisis, writers as diverse as Michael Madhusudana Datta (1824–1873), Muhammad Iqbal (1877–1938), Jayashankar Prasad (1889–1937), and Sumitranandan Pant (1900–1977), to name a few prominent figures, experimented with epic forms and got their bearings within the imperial arena through a translated and transmuted romanticism. The untimeliness of the epic combined readily with the general romantic disregard for bourgeois norms and capitalist clock time.

By analyzing the nature of this form in juxtaposition against modernist aesthetics in the metropolitan domains, the significance of these late colonial developments comes into sharp relief. Specific countervalences of the neo-epic can be seen in broad strokes as the emphasis on the reactivation of religious cosmologies (rather than "the utilitarian impatience with the mythic imagination"),[13] the consolidation of civilizational narrative (against the processes of its eclipse in the metropolitan West), the historical content of the colonial experience (rather than its mere formalisms),[14] solemnity of the didactic lesson (against the modernist taboo on the educative motive), and the possibility of a neotraditional subjectivity based on articles of faith (rather than speculative flexibility offered by secularist assimilationism). In refusing to construe neo-epics as the anomalous hangover from a previous era evincing the difficulties a "traditional" society has in modernizing, this work asks: What would it mean to imagine these neotraditional developments as indices of the manner in which capitalist modernity, rather than being "an unfinished project," *pace* Jürgen Habermas, constitutes a peculiar sociocultural logic whose culmination is ever its own undoing?[15] Such a realization, however intuited or fully elaborated, is the motivating force, I argue, behind late colonial "antimodern" modernism magnetized by the neo-epic. Rather than modernity's inexorable movement forward, as was once universally expected, neotraditionalism sets back the historical clock, resituating large stretches of the global into a late colonial temporal rut, bringing, as it were, dialectics to a standstill. Given their countervailing cultural energies, metropolitan and colonial forms require a fracturing of ready-made hermeneutical frames—hence the title "Fractured Frames" for part I—in order to sound the parallactic gaps they too often obscure. Historical movement in dialectical standstill, awaiting resolution: the aporias that open up and define the late colonial period prevent easy progress and passage forward. One grasps through this temporal parallax—between metropolitan and colonial times—the manifold ambivalences arising everywhere vis-à-vis the newly imposed discipline of capitalist clock time and the directionality of Enlightenment.

All those slow to comply, like Hali's decadent aristocrats, take on the tinge of transgression. Violating the new norms by which time as commodity ought to be managed, they are out of the times. In marking a peculiar anachronism, they draw out immanent possibilities for negating the modern imperatives of thrift, efficiency, and temperance, shifting thereby the ground of valuation beyond the measures afforded by the imperial order. A peculiar space, in other words, is negatively established within the imperial dispensation. This space will foster various forms of late romanticisms within British India, which here is understood to merely be one among many arenas across a decolonizing Asia that formed "schools" dubbed "romantic," translating, reframing, and elaborating this term on uncharted terrains: the Japan Romantic School, the Creation Society in China, Chayavad or "Shadowism" in Hindi, and a newly articulated *rumaniyat* in Urdu (see chapter 2). Each of these formations slowly accrued resonances with each other as well as English, French, and German romanticisms, as one can reveal, for instance, through a sojourn with Iqbal into Goethe's Islamic imaginary or Bergson's recuperative intuitionism (see chapter 5).

Just a few general points need be noted here regarding the argument that unfolds. First, in tracing the intermediation and even interpenetration of utilitarian norms and romantic aesthetics, especially the neo-epic dimension, across Bengali, Hindi, and Urdu cultural spheres, this work makes no claim to comprehensiveness. The chapters merely draw out these persistent negations (of imperial reification) in the form of neo-epic—however imaginary they may be—in order to fathom the shape of the aporias to which they speak. Second, romanticism, however loosely conceived, most often frayed the instrumental-rational normativity of bourgeois society. In *The Literary Absolute*, Phillipe Lacoue-Labarthe and Jean-Luc Nancy remark on how early romanticism spoke to the crises into which European society had been plunged. It opened "not a crisis *in* literature, but a general crisis and critique . . . for which literature or literary theory will be the privileged locus of expression." Their citation of Dorothea Schlegel's aphoristic remarks concerning romanticism affirms their general theory that "die Romantik" always maintained an agonistic relationship to emergent bourgeois norms, attaining its allure from the fact that "the *romance* languages were the vulgar languages, thought of as derived from the vulgar *romance* tongue as opposed to the *Latin* of the clergy." Not surprisingly, romanticism came immediately under moral condemnation as it spread in the seventeenth century in England and Germany: "Since it is altogether contrary to bourgeois order and absolutely forbidden to introduce romantic poetry into life, then let life be brought into romantic poetry; no police force and no educational institution can prevent this."[16] Romanticism will continue over the long uneven course of its movement eastward to maintain a critical perspective over and against the emergent nexus of value and its sublime corrosive power. Third, romanticism was always situated as a world literary phenomenon, emerging as it did between languages more than within any single one; this in itself indicates the need to conceptualize it within broad interstitial planes of production, circulation, reception, and translation. I saw no reason to impose upon the languages covered here, whether metropolitan or subaltern, any of the hierarchies that conditioned their historical existence; rather I have allowed them, as much as my skills permit, a spontaneous interplay, allowing them to reveal in their own way their internalization of the silver rib of the other language's presence.[17] "Epic" itself was now firmly implanted in Indian vernaculars.

What is thus implied is that romanticism is imbricated in imperialism over its entire historical durée. Only by shifting the literary-historical focus to its late colonial moment (after it is presumably all over), in, say, the relatively understudied colonized languages of British India—Hindustanee!—can romanticism really be understood for what it was all along: an evolving critique, generated by yet ultimately antagonistic toward imperialism. (See the allegorical reading of Conrad's *Lord Jim* in chapter 2, for instance.) Fourth, and finally, by putting these Eastern arenas on an analytical plane equal to the Western romantic traditions, it appears that late romanticism in the Asian sphere was not merely treading yet again on long familiar "romantic" turf but rather spoke to the simultaneity of the nonsimultaneous, of the antimodern within the modern, forming thereby a peculiar literary parallax. In elaborating a critique of modern or Western civilization, late colonial romanticism predicated itself no longer upon the appearance of nature to men "as [a] completely alien, all-powerful and unassailable force, with which men's relations are purely animal and by which they are overawed like beasts," as Kant's sublime is depicted somewhat tongue-in-cheek in Marx and Engel's *German Ideology*.[18] Rather in late colonial times the entire dispensation of imperial capitalism—the interconnected totality between metropole and colony—substitutes for and eviscerates old romantic landscapes, revealing underneath an imperial skeleton, as argued in chapter 3 with reference to Walter Benjamin's early experiments with poetic *Landschaften.* The force of this most striking stage of imperialism works every bit as vehemently, disastrously, and inscrutably as nature—perhaps even more so, considering how much of its energies are unleashed beyond the immediate space of coherent representation within any particular location of the modern imperium. What was a diffuse impersonal force mediating metropolitan and colonial worlds attained concentrated manifestation in the event that marked the end of classical imperialism: the bombing of Hiroshima and Nagasaki in August 1945.[19] Famously, J. Robert Oppenheimer commemorated the atomic test at Alamogordo, New Mexico, just a month earlier with reference to a *shloka* from the Bhagavad-Gita:

kalo'smi loka-kshaya-krt-pravrddho
lokan samahartum iha pravrttah

Time am I, wreaker of the world's destruction, matured,—
[grimly] resolved here to swallow up worlds.[20]

Oppenheimer's choice—"Now I am become death, destroyer of worlds"—is worth noting for it dramatizes the uncanny affinity between the sublime material powers of modernity and the metaphysical imagination of classical epic. It is through this very crucible of modernity's material and immaterial force that a neotraditional aesthetics was forged. Given the prevalence of epic narrative in Indian literary cultures since antiquity, the neo-epic was perhaps as significant as the usual cultural products of modernity, including the novel. By indexing the forms of life that had been wiped out and by revalorizing modes of existence that had been savaged by imperial power, a new kind of traditionalism by nontraditional means had come slowly to fruition. The neo-epic in late colonial India, a British Indian constellation of which makes up part II of *Late Colonial Sublime*, speaks as much to the internal dynamics of modernity as any canonical work of Western literature; indeed, they may, in many cases, be deciphered to bear the brunt of the cultural logic that will slowly descend upon the core metropolitan cultures over capitalism's longue durée, demanding universal acquiescence to the instrumental imperatives of the commodity-form in our neoliberal present; they simultaneously demonstrate an effort to distance oneself from reification and imagine a resubstantialization of reason.

These claims, all bundled here, receive distended argumentation over the chapters that follow. "The nights are endless now. / We've plenty of time to sleep or savor a long tale."[21] What does it mean, then, for method to be *Umweg*, a roundabout way, as Benjamin remarked ironically in the *Trauerspielbuch*? Unhurried reflection has been given here to the challenges of composing literary histories in the form of metropolitan-colonial parallax. The book contends that constellational form helps to reframe fractured realities and their temporal-material determinants. Datta's Bengali *The Slaying of Meghanad* (Meghanadvadhkavya, 1861), Prasad's Hindi *The Daughter of Kama* (Kamayani, 1936), Iqbal's Indo-Persian *Book of Eternity* (Javid Nama, 1932), and even Sagar's TV *Ramayana* of the late 1980s evince not only the endurance, malleability, and salience of the epic in modern India but also the strange critical—indeed, deteriorative—powers the neo-epic as form continues to wield vis-à-vis the imperatives of reified society. The obstinacy of the epic is perhaps more attributable to the persistence of a need to critique bourgeois reason, following Adorno, than it is to any "traditional" cultural reflex.[22] In the case of the TV *Ramayana*, this resulted in a nearly collective self-distancing from the clock time of the workaday world and deep immersion in the temporality of dream kitsch, despite the troubling political fallout of it all for the secular modern inheritance of the Indian nation-state (see the epilogue). Romanticism, in any case, always displayed a peculiar affinity toward the epic, even if, as in Wordsworth's attempts at the *Prelude*, it was not always able to get it fully launched. In India, though, the story reflects distinctly powerful narrative inheritances. Here the epic has long predominated and established an interface with, even a definition of demotic collectives on an ongoing basis. It is perhaps for this reason that the neo-epic became the epicenter for the expression of the aporia that had begun to tear apart the social fabric underlying different long-standing life-worlds.[23]

In these neo-epics' attempts at re-creating wholes where they no longer exist and articulating antimodernism where it is no longer feasible, they reveal deep fissures in the social totality. Rather than thinking of them as mere national allegories—as forms manipulated for merely national or proto-national mobilization (which is itself an uncritical perspective at best for reflecting too little on the normative instrumentality by which it is guided)—*Late Colonial Sublime* accords them broader allegorical reach by noting the pervasive, if not fundamentally constitutive contradictions that inhere within them as quintessentially modern products. More perhaps than any other genre, the neo-epic in late colonial India gave dynamic expression to the underlying aporias of modern society as a whole and a yearning to get once again beyond them. As the form long associated with temporal continuity, oral presence, and an enduring reckoning with nature, the scope of reason, and the moral shape of collective existence, the epic form appeared for the writers explored in this book as a vehicle for imagining, at the very least, a turn toward future livability. Grasping for the immanence of aesthetic forms in late colonial India has resulted thus in the neologism "neo-epic," for none of the usual categories of literary analysis—epic, novel, short story, or lyric—proved quite adequate for either the textual forms discussed here or the neotraditional dynamism they display. This is not to downplay the other genres for these are important in their own right and still require more research in the South Asian as well as other colonial and postcolonial contexts. Rather it is to deposit into the hegemonic register of English a vestige of its colonial past through a process of translation. Emerging from within colonial modernity's aporia, the neo-epic promised to take one and all back home from its malaise. A paradox often noted, new beginnings seem to require a return to traditional civilization structures; in the neo-epic, the return is often simultaneously a mimesis of future civilizational possibilities. Thus the neologism "neo-epic" proved necessary as a means of conveying a peculiar neotraditionalism premised upon the malaise that followed colonial ruin. (The category may prove illuminating in more canonical arenas of Western modernism. Think, for instance, of the mélange of epic idioms in the *Cantos* of Ezra Pound or the sweeping visions and totalizing moves of William Carlos Williams's *Patterson*.)[24]

III. POSTCOLONIAL MARXISM? RECONSTELLATING THE DIALECTIC OF ENLIGHTENMENT

343. All *forms*, even the strangest, must *come again* and receive *new meaning*.
—Friedrich Schlegel, "Fragments on Literature and Poesy"

Late Colonial Sublime wishes to avoid unnecessary polemic.[25] It simply urges a move beyond current disciplinary and theoretical impasses via methodological inquiry (instead of the usual rehearsal of tired debates that may no longer even inform the current state of critical theory, given how quickly trends shift in the current marketplace of ideas). Nevertheless it owes the astute reader an overview of some of the challenges a literary history working through categories of Marxist criticism and processes of decolonization must necessarily face. The challenges are manifold, as becomes clear when taking into stock just a few of the questions posed by the work: How does one present the fundamental aporia informing the social, political, and cultural imaginations across imperial divides? What form ought a literary or intellectual history adopt in order to bring out the historical period in question—given that the "late colonial" may by no means be a mere figment of the past? (Questions such as these point out as well the parallaxes within disciplinary norms themselves. For instance, in English literary studies, expertise in the Victorian period requires no necessary reflection on the imperial expanse or the experience of the colonized, let alone any expertise in their languages or literatures; on the other hand, literary histories of Hindi and Urdu reveal the deep imprint of Victorian imperial power [sometimes down to their very grammars and lexica] but are organized according to modernizing national agendas and thus downplay accordingly their imperial conditions of possibility, despite the occasional encounter of a eulogy [*qasida*] composed by a Hali or a Ghalib addressed to Her Majesty.)[26] How can one sound out the wider social totality constituted by imperial capital through the precise configuration of a constellation, interconnecting material and immaterial realities all at once? How can one assemble distinct languages and literary traditions such that the usual cultural and regional hierarchies stemming from the imperial past are undermined and new kinds of categories can emerge in their stead? These somewhat abstract theoretical questions receive further elaboration in chapter 1. All that need be mentioned here is that *Late Colonial Sublime* neither aims at securing a theoretical method that can be "applied" elsewhere unproblematically, nor does it endeavor to reconcile the disparate theoretical formations—Marxism and postcolonial criticism primarily—that inform its analytical framework. Rather an attempt is made to strike these now hardened schools of thought against each other so that a spark might illuminate zones of imperial darkness that still linger with us. By extending Marxist categories into colonial spheres and, reciprocally, postcolonial inquiry into metropolitan conceptual structures, it becomes possible, I claim, to reframe the dialectic of Enlightenment that undergirded Frankfurt School Critical Theory and disclose the wrenching contradictions common to situations across the imperial totality. The exiled philosopher and literary critic Walter Benjamin—whose intellectual legacy is woven through the entirety of *Late Colonial Sublime* and whose somewhat cryptic yet ubiquitous theory of the sublime is dilated upon in chapter 3 to reveal its wide social underpinnings—mediates the theoretical divide and provides indices for resituating questions of universalism in light of imperial exclusions. His technique of constellational form is reworked to speak to a decolonizing Asia, with a focus on British India. By reconstellating the dialectic of modernity from a postcolonial vantage point it becomes possible to recapture critical, egalitarian, and indeed redemptive currents lost to Adorno and Horkheimer's iteration of this problematic.

The parallax between Adorno and Horkheimer's problematic *Dialectic of Enlightenment* (*Dialektik der Aufklärung*, 1944) and various histories of decolonization is discussed at some length in chapter 2. Thus I will here take a shortcut to the main points, which are given much less apologetic treatment than absorption into the method and *Darstellung* for what follows. The first point is that this work takes the political and cultural processes of decolonization and the assertion of postcolonialism into the very writing—that is, into the very mode of presentation—of a necessarily widely configured literary history of the imperial age. That is to say, the work itself asserts parity between the different levels of an imperial structure of power and thereby attempts to de-reify the persistent presence of imperialism in our highly toxic racialized forms of capitalism. I began by imagining that whatever might be called "romanticism," for instance, in the late colonial Asian sphere may not necessarily amount to some paltry mimicry of hegemonic Western models (a stereotype as much colonial as "postcolonial" at this point). Rather than assuming that this history could be no more than a mere addendum to an already concluded history of the imperial West, I granted that these materials may be speaking to modernity's very core aporia and that, in doing so, they may be revealing a profound and original elaboration of translingual concepts (such as romanticism itself) within a distinct historical conjuncture. Far from corresponding to patterns preestablished by Western hegemons, the Asian interventions marked out salient strategies of cultural renewal. New forms—the neo-epic!—occasionally present themselves as struggling to redeem the corrupted rationality of Enlightenment, including its pressured clock time, in ways that might allow for the reconfiguration of pasts ruined and traditions unsettled by the imposition of imperial capital. Through the broad conceptualization of the late colonial as a historical period marked profoundly by "the simultaneity of the non-simultaneous" and spatial disjuncture of a radical sort (hence parallaxes), the present work posits a wide totality permitting movement from one extreme to another of a variegated yet socially cohering imperial order, however marked by political divisions and unequal terrains.[27] Indeed, the theoretical framework offered here necessitates such movement across hegemonic and subaltern spheres. For only through experiments with distinct constellational patterns made up of disparate fragments from a singular imperial modernity does it become possible to represent this past without falling into the twin traps of a reductive positivist method and the surface phenomena of reification. (These points will be further spelled out in chapter 1.)

In his celebrated essay on epic and novel, "The Storyteller," Benjamin explained that narrative "does not expend itself." In sharp contrast to information, which "does not survive the moment in which it was new," a story "preserves and concentrates its energy and is capable of releasing it even after a long time."[28] In the present work, the narrative regarding the dialectic of Enlightenment is released once again from the late colonial era of its original articulation. This narrative retains the germinative powers of which Benjamin speaks, for it now extends out into regions that appeared foreign to its original authors, Adorno and Horkheimer. That is to say, in its current iteration the dialectic of Enlightenment spills beyond the Euro-American purview originally conceived for it, and in doing so helps to historically contextualize the limitations that beset these critical theorists' efforts, preventing them from grasping the metropolitan-colonial grounding the theory fundamentally required. By shifting the geographical frame, it becomes possible to see the horizon of egalitarianism—that other legacy of Enlightenment—forming against reified imperial hierarchy and its self-suiting structures of historical time. This other legacy remains obscured and should not be confused with liberal equality. It demands a dislocating look beyond the Marquis de Sade, Hollywood, Nazi antisemitism, Odysseus, as these all orbit within a Eurocentric universe. Like Benjamin himself, who long wished to escape and was eventually exiled, this work guarantees no easy return to narrow confines of national or civilizational canons. In *Late Colonial Sublime*, it is not the case that these familiar points of reference are erased; rather, they are subsumed within a wider and more dispersed imperial geography. The coordinates of the new constellation allow for a more precise gauging of modernity's aporia—their extent and depth—opening up possibilities for translation across disparate colonial and metropolitan domains. What is offered here necessarily exceeds reified boundaries of all sorts—linguistic, disciplinary, and theoretical. This is evident in the very pregnant possibilities of political solidarity given in the interplay of what are too often sharply segregated cultural fields in scholarly conventions—such as Hindi and Urdu literary cultures, for instance—an interplay and potential solidarity little imaginable under imperial capitalist or nationalist auspices.

IV. AN ARGUMENT OF ASSEMBLED FRAGMENTS

> 116. The romantic genre is, however, still in the process of becoming; indeed, this is its essence: to be eternally in the process of becoming and never completed. No theory can exhaust romantic poesy, and only a divinatory critique might dare attempt to characterize its ideal.
>
> —Friedrich Schlegel, "Athenäum Fragments"

If, despite the disparate nature of the phenomena constellated over these chapters, a running argumentative thread is perceptible through them, it is less on account of any agenda of my own than what inheres in these things themselves.[29] It would be perversely contrary if it were otherwise. A project that brings into question instrumental reason must itself refrain from adopting a utilitarian approach to materials at hand. Instead of forging texts into preconceived theoretical frames, marshaling data for purposes for which they are rarely suited, cataloging things only to assert a domineering will over them, ventriloquizing dead voices for the points of view already adopted—modalities to which contemporary academic culture in neoliberal society is all too often inured—the chapters that follow seek rather to assimilate themselves to and mimic the ideational and material structures of the phenomena with which they deal. They do so by attempting to shed interpretive intention and instead translate into somewhat ill-equipped theoretical registers a language that would resemble the simple existence of things. "Truth is not an intent which realizes itself in empirical reality," remarks Benjamin. "It is the power which determines the essence of this empirical reality." Thus it requires an approach not so much of "intention and knowledge, but rather a total immersion and absorption in [the object]." Absorption into the texts making up the body of *Late Colonial Sublime* was an act of love that, as such, always lost its temporal bounds as a way to acknowledge the autonomy of the thing loved: "And so it is with human love," Benjamin reminds us, for "a person is beautiful in the eyes of his lover, but not in himself, because his body belongs in a higher order of things than that of the beautiful."[30] The allusion to the sublime in Benjamin's formulation should not be lost. It cannot be approached except by way of constellation, lest the researcher be scorched like the moth in the flame of truth. The late colonial sublime can reveal itself only through the interplay of fragments brought together as wholes that demand larger spheres of semblance for their understanding than they can possibly offer in their limited natures. Their constellational patterning allows a dialectical interplay of unity and disunity, part and whole, presence and absence. Ventures Benjamin in "On the Mimetic Faculty," "For if words meaning the same thing in different languages are arranged about that signified as their center, we have to inquire how they all—while often possessing not the slightest similarity to one another—are similar to the signified at their center" (II: 721).[31]

Before orbiting around the late colonial sublime through a tour of the fragmentary shards assembled here, a few key points must be kept in mind. First, this constellation attempts to index something infinite—the value form of imperial capital and its abstract powers—and thus always beyond the reach of a comprehensive intention. As captured in the nature of the fragment itself, no claim to completion is made for any of these studies. As pieces, they can only determine negatively what they were once a part of; though absent, that whole of which they are a missing part fills them with a degree of unfathomability. The texts analyzed shall surely reward further inquiry with more insights than can be garnered and put on display here (especially around questions of gender and sexuality) and are by no means depleted of their truth-content.[32] Second, if some topics fall beyond the scope of the bits and pieces covered here, it is certainly not because they lack equal importance; rather only so much could be achieved by one conatus, itself struggling under the compulsions of capitalist clock time. The fact that the materials led me into their internal dynamics more than I led the materials to any pregiven intention doubtless means that many disciplinary, linguistic, and cultural boundaries have been crossed. This has occurred more often than not without official documents. In any case, credentials were as soon earned as willingly abandoned in this process whenever they proved cumbersome or impeded any intellectual latitude. Indeed, this is the work of intellectual exile: it finds no possibility of rest within any of our tightly policed disciplinary boundaries but rather assumes that risking illegal status in all of them is better for critical perspective than complacency within any of these gated communities. This work thus stands in solidarity with those who suffer the brunt of the unjust legal regimes of our times, if only analogically. The risk is legion, but the gamble essential. For the "factor of danger"—alongside the pleasure, Benjamin reminds us—"arises not so much from the threat of losing as from that of *not winning*."[33]

Part I, "Fractured Frames: Imperial Parallax and Disjointed Time," comprises three chapters that unearth the key categories of *Late Colonial Sublime*: reification, romanticism, and sublime. The parallax in question is between metropolitan modernism and late colonial romanticism, wherein the same fleeting moment is characterized by endings and renewals, fits and starts, pulls and pushes palpable on opposite ends of the imperial order. Chapter 1, "Commodity and Sublimity: Mimesis of the Immaterial," provides glosses on "commodity" and "reification" in order to orient readers to concepts that have been generally obscured over the neoliberal era of "high theory" but that are central, indeed immanent, to the phenomena presented over the course of this book. By retracing Benjamin's own efforts at devising a materialist literary history that would avoid the pitfalls of reification, this chapter lays out the general theoretical premises for the dialectical capture of "nonsensuous similarity" across disparate fields and the advantages of constellational form for breaking the deluding surface sheen of capitalist materiality. The second chapter, "Romanticism's Horizons, or The Transmission of Critique," assembles a series of vignettes—photographs really—marking the shifting terrain of romanticism over the late nineteenth and early twentieth centuries. Beginning with Conrad's *Lord Jim*, which allegorizes the waning of romanticism in metropolitan culture, this chapter demonstrates how the critical potentials of this aesthetic ideology were renewed and actualized in the wake of its adoption in influential Asian arenas. Its critical lens was focused not merely on bourgeois normativity but on the reifications of imperial capitalism and increasingly modernity as a whole. The chapter argues that late romanticism was crucial for the processes of decolonization in Asia and, further, that a better understanding of this very diffuse and elusive aesthetic category emerges through an investigation of the contradictory political energies it fostered and that eventually devoured it. Part I ends with chapter 3, "Atmospherics of Imperialism: Benjamin's Sublime." By reading Benjamin as a late colonial thinker on the perilous margins and interstices of imperial Europe, this chapter goes beyond the usual Eurocentrism of Benjamin scholarship to demonstrate that his thought bears as much relation to the aporias of the late colonial world as to the predicaments facing Europe under fascism. They become one and the same in his exile. This chapter uncovers the processes that allowed him to shed the idealist Kantian premises of his theory of the sublime and to reconfigure it instead in light of the peculiar materialism of the commodity-form. Benjamin's late work evinces the powerful affinity between this conception of the sublime and the possibilities for a renewed epic form for the collective narration of widely dispersed but interconnected masses.

Part II, "Neo-Epic Constellation: Out of British India," offers three separate historical accounts of the material processes and cultural imperatives that led to the fashioning of canonical neo-epics in Hindi and Urdu literary cultures. By juxtaposing them in the following fashion, it becomes possible to fathom the common aporia to which neo-epics forged by the likes of Hali, Iqbal, and Prasad were imaginary counterpoints, allegorizing within themselves the contradictions governing social life over the last decades of British rule in India. Chapter 4, "Hali's Transvaluation of Modernity: Allegories of *Marsiya*," centers primarily on the *Musaddas* with which I began this introduction. For Hali, an allegory set in the mold of classical epic—in this case, *marsiya*—becomes the means for bringing rhetorical resolution to the contradictory currents shaping Victorian India, occasionally threatening to bring entire communities such as Hali's Indo-Muslim one to collective shipwreck: "The shore is far away, and a storm is raging. At every moment there is the apprehension that it is just about to sink."[34] The recourse taken to traditional metaphysics in Hali's magnum opus is an index of the contradictions out of which romanticism in the Urdu literary culture will later emerge, and Hali's writings give emphatic expression to the contrapuntal, antagonistic, even desecularizing dynamics that unfold over the late colonial period. Whereas we encounter Hali in the ruins of post-Mughal India, when we turn to Muhammad Iqbal in chapter 5, we find ourselves in the remaining fragments of a legacy torn apart by competing nation-states—in this case, India, Pakistan, and Iran. Titled "Iqbal, or the *Sturm und Drang* of Late Colonial India: Resemblances of Pure Content," this chapter attempts to read the fashioning of Iqbal's characteristically sublime aesthetics in his magnum opus, *Javid Nama*, in light of engagements with German romanticism, Bergsonian intuitionism, and the crisis-ridden politics of the late imperial world. In a close reading of *Javid Nama*, the final fragment retraces the means by which a language of the absolute was recovered in an Islamicate idiom. The third and final point in this constellation turns to the overlapping world of Hindi via colonial Bengal. Chapter 6, "Utility and Culture: Modern Subjectivity and Neotraditional Aesthetics" is an investigation into how neotraditional culture was forged in modern India through the crucible of utility and instrumental reason—or, more generally, processes of reification under imperial capitalist hegemony. The chapter works through the historical conditions of possibility that led to the making of the celebrated neo-epic *Kamayani* by the Hindi romantic (Chayavadi) Jayashankar Prasad. Along the way, the chapter uncovers the manifold possibilities of culture once it had become an object of political utility. The consequence is a peculiar restlessness in the protagonist of *Kamayani*, a new Manu for the present age, embodying all the conflictual energies of the new masses.

Late Colonial Sublime rounds out and closes with an epilogue, "Melancholic Ornament: TV *Ramayana*, Nostalgia, and Kitsch as Counter-Enlightenment," and two appendixes. The epilogue analyzes the mass aesthetics that surrounded the phenomenal TV *Ramayana* serial in the late 1980s by connecting it to the processes of massification instigated by British imperial policies and magnified by universal adult franchise and political party machines in independent India. Against the imperatives of reification and clock time, the masses entered into the Counter-Enlightenment logic of dream kitsch through a temporal break allowed by the TV *Ramayana*'s profane illumination. Despite the current political turmoil, this break, I suggest, marks an opening out of the world ruled by the commodity-form through the surface sheen of that form itself.

Two translations are given as appendixes: the first from the Urdu (Muhammad Iqbal's preface to his Persian collection *Payam-e Mashriq* [Message of the East, 1923]), and the second from the Hindi (Sumitranandan Pant's short essay, "The Usefulness of the Epic Form in the Present Age," n.d.). Each of these is situated in its historical context in the preceding translator's preface, yet what lies at the level of implication in these works (and in translating and juxtaposing them) deserves a brief indication here. Each brings out in its own way the interconnection between late romanticism and neo-epic as a form. Iqbal's preface and *Payam-e Mashriq* as a whole show how dialogue and translation between Eastern and Western horizons, across the temporal divide of *Goethezeit* and Iqbal's own troubled late colonial moment, generated the prophetic emphasis of Iqbal's reading of Goethe's *West-östlicher Divan* (West-Eastern Divan, 1819). This translational energy helped forge a neo-epic idiom, as in the miniature epic "Conquest of Nature," central to Iqbal's literary assemblage. In the case of the Chayavadi or "Hindi romantic" Pant, neo-epic is also given a particularly central role in defining the modern age, with Prasad's *Kamayani* given pride of place as ushering in a new era for the Hindi sphere. Pant's essay replays the cosmopolitan egalitarianism embedded in the trope of Indian and European authors having interchangeable status with each other in their seriality. The essay also indicates the degree to which utility had begun to penetrate the discussion of aesthetic form, giving rise to new literary languages such as the Hindi neo-epic itself. These translations are put in juxtaposition here not merely to put into constellational interplay their internal themes and ways of capturing the late colonial moment; they also serve to betoken the fundamental practice—translation—that underlies this entire project. It is through this practice that a consistent yearning to maintain an otherwise declining faculty—the mimetic one—attains expression.

V. A NOTE ON THE LATE COLONIAL: PERIODIZATION FROM BELOW

Can one recognize that which is past if one does not even understand that which is present? And who can conceptually appraise what the present is without knowing what is to come in the future? What is to come determines what is present, and this determines what is past.

—Johann Georg Hamann, "Cloverleaf of Hellenistic Letters"

"We cannot not periodize."[35] Even those well-intentioned critics of historicism, such as Dipesh Chakrabarty, who, when it was opportune, wished to present history as a mere representational "artifice" devised to keep "not-yet modern" subjects always subaltern and lacking before the standards of the European Enlightenment, cannot avoid taking recourse to historical categories, protocols, and periodization schemes themselves.[36] Given its inevitability, the question is thus not whether to periodize, but rather how. That is, how is one to conceptualize experienced time in a critically reflective fashion, and not merely disavow what are revealed, often in the posthistoricist's next breath, to be deeply embedded disciplinary habits, including conventional historical periods? (The irrationality surreptitiously fostered in this manner hardly furnishes critical self-awareness.) However much one may wish to relinquish these habits and espouse others in their stead (whatever they may be), the task is not so easy, and in disregarding the challenge, trite periodization schemes continue to crop up. In any case, grasping conventional disciplinary practices prove necessary for any effective intervention into contemporary fields of knowledge and politics. Despite this, the present work does not shy away from an attempt to rethink critically the inheritance of metropolitan literary-historical periodizing schemes—realism, modernism, and postmodernism, for instance—from the vantage point of colonial subordination, as well as ways of deforming methodological common sense in literary history. But the point here is merely to convey what defines the late colonial.

Emanating from the center of the constellation that follows is the crisis-ridden aporia generated by the abstract powers of the commodity-form underlying the imperial formations encircling the world by the end of the nineteenth century. If there is any "spiritual" homogeneity holding together the late colonial, as in a Zeitgeist, it is one riven by contradiction, fundamentally in agonistic tension with a material order premised on coercion and radical unfreedom. As I write in chapter 2, the late colony is the sphere in which reason, having transvalued all values in tandem with the compulsions of the imperial capitalist market, verges on self-destruction and dissolution into the Unreason of self-made unsurvivability: a sacrifice of world into the abyss of a dubious secular process. Elaborations such as this one convey the aporia that ensued as historically necessary bouts with reification, or the reduction of reason to bare instrumentality, a process that unfolded in conflictual patterns across the era, bringing in its train negations of history as "progress" and various methods, however "romantic," for decelerating the pull of the modern into a harrowing clock time. These abstract conflictual patterns find their expression in aesthetic domains such as the neo-epics sampled over the pages ahead. In light of their undergirding aporia, the late colonial leaves a lingering shadow over the so-called postcolonial world in that these conflicts remain fundamentally unresolved. The possibilities generated through dream kitsch regarding possible ways forward are explored in the reading of the TV *Ramayana* in the epilogue.

Though this work does not pretend to be a social history, it nevertheless invokes widely ramifying categories such as "capital" in its formulations regarding the particular shape of literary and aesthetic works over the late colonial and post-Independence periods. It thus owes the reader a glimpse into the social processes that were initiated by the financial imperatives of the British imperium, came to a head at the turn of the nineteenth to the twentieth century, and continue to penetrate and expand into the cultural fabric of contemporary India. Though imperialism and capitalism should not always be considered synonymous, they nevertheless display an internally reinforcing dynamism over the course of British colonial rule over India. With new industrial capacities realized by the late nineteenth century, the vast expansion of commodity production for export in the metropolitan sector accelerated market integration between India and Britain, generally on the latter's terms. The historians Michael Geyer and Charles Bright recognize that "Britain utterly dominated Indian domestic markets, which remained the largest single outlet for British exports" over the period in question.[37] The period witnessed some modest advances in the way of modernization. For instance, large-scale factory industry, one of the biggest railway and telegraphic systems, some of the best banks, ports, universities, and hospitals in the hemisphere began to see the light of day in late colonial India.[38] Yet, as seen from below, the "accelerating forces of global integration," as Geyer and Bright realize, resulted in the "disintegration of autonomy among subordinated people": "Across the colonial and semicolonial world, the elements of production, power, and social reproduction whose articulation in the past had produced the capacity for autonomous histories were pulled apart, sometimes violently, often quietly, but always in ways that destroyed autonomy."[39] The present work indicates the extent to which the diminishing of autonomy coincided with the imposition of instrumental-rational normativity across diverse cultural planes. Moreover, it is worth noting that the social processes that characterized the late colonial period did not come to an end with colonial rule in the subcontinent. Instead, as examined by the journalist Harish Damodaran, the cultural logic of capitalist entrepreneurship has shifted onto broader swaths of Indian society and penetrated new demographic tiers, most remarkably traditionally non-merchant castes. This process has only accelerated since the liberalization of the economy under Rajiv Gandhi in the 1980s.[40] The internally generated contradictions of the post-Independence dispensation signify that neither scapegoating foreign powers for intractable social problems that unfold inevitably nor finding solutions solely within (neo)traditional formations is a possible alternative.

The words of the late eighteenth-century German esoteric Johann Georg Hamann in the epigraph to this section capture an orientation toward the future that is writ large over nearly all of the aesthetic media into which the following chapters became absorbed. It is often from the very materiality—down to the very sound structures—of the literary works read over the coming pages that peculiar possibilities became palpable: possibilities that preserve themselves only, for the moment, for future time. It is most immediately through the aesthetic dimension (such as that of the neo-epic) that the past can be seen to carry with it "a secret index by which it is referred to redemption," as Benjamin mentions in his second thesis, "On the Concept of History" (IV: 390). In a penetrating essay titled "'Now': Walter Benjamin on Historical Time," the literary theorist Werner Hamacher connects this "secret index" to happiness as a political affect that structures the temporality of history: "Happiness is never experienced in a present without this present relating to that which has been (*Gewesene*)"; likewise, as the envy kindled by the failure to seize a course toward one's own happiness when it was possible, happiness "preserves itself for another time." Indeed, as Hamacher notes, "the temporality of the cognition of possible happiness" demands a jumping out of "traditional categories of time and history."[41] As a risky attempt to seize in the present the missed opportunities for happiness in the past and to alert one to future states of general contentment before it is too late, *Late Colonial Sublime* makes one such leap.

PART I

Fractured Frames

Imperial Parallax and Disjointed Time

CHAPTER I

Commodity and Sublimity

Mimesis of the Immaterial

I. COMMODITY-FORM AND CULTURAL FORM: TOWARD A MATERIALIST LITERARY HISTORY

The sputtering of the global economy since the financial crisis of 2008 has coincided with the resurrection of fundamental theoretical categories, including "commodity" and "reification," not to mention "capitalism" itself.[1] This chapter aims to provide a gloss on "commodity" and "reification," two key terms that together mediate material existence and cultural forms in modernity. The very fact that this exercise is required at this moment of widespread crisis is testimony to the deep erosion of the conceptual and practical bases for grasping epochal historical shifts in the wake of the neoliberalization of much of global society and culture over the past four decades. The consequences are most dire for imagining, let alone generating, transformative crises in response. Even the most astute Marxist critic of the American imperial epicenter, Fredric Jameson, affirmed late capitalist "postmodernism" as a "permanent because more thoroughgoing and all-pervasive" state rather than "anything so silly as the ultimate senescence, breakdown, and death of the system as such."[2] The fall from the indeterminate vagaries of a postmodern theoretical stratosphere to the hard objectivity of capitalism's terminal crisis—with all the threats it poses to human habitation on the planet—has been sharp. For those disoriented by this uncanny object-world—writhing under logics of scientific disenchantment yet "abounding in metaphysical subtleties and theological niceties" attributable to nothing other than the worldly processes of capital self-valorization—the following is meant as a short guide.[3] Those already familiar with the ramifications of generalized commodification and the socially necessary illusion that it inevitably secretes—something like objective hallucination on a systemic scale—should expect little more than a connecting of key dots. The conceptual picture that forms from such an exercise spells out distinct possibilities and challenges for grasping sublimity as a materially grounded phenomenon. Further, what would a materialist literary history seeking to give constellational form to metropolitan and colonial culture look like? What would be its theoretical ground and, moreover, its source of social critique?

Given how much Walter Benjamin sought to connect in nonreductive ways disparate relations between commodity-form and cultural form in his own crisis-ridden imperial-capitalist reality, his fragmentary works may serve as indices for fashioning a new literary history. The unfinished nature of his methodological reflections allows them to be reconfigured in other times and places with extraordinary potential. Stemming from the intellectual uncertainties that followed the destruction of World War I, Benjamin aimed increasingly at tracking the dialectic of material and immaterial "truth contents" in the wake of commodification. The particular representational form philosophical truth would need to adopt for the articulation of its fundamental insights was an ongoing concern of Benjamin's. "Darstellung ist der Inbegriff ihrer Methode" was his dictum for signifying that presentation becomes the inevitable incarnation of philosophical method.[4] Such a formulation had obvious relevance to the representational form literary history would need to acquire in order to give embodiment to aesthetico-historical truth contents. The representational form was especially significant in this case, considering that for Benjamin aesthetic forms took the shape of hieroglyphs exceeding the bounds of contemporary intelligibility and thereby intimating possible futurities. The challenge of giving adequate shape to truth contents that nearly always burst through the material moments of signification was most acute for Benjamin in the wake of his engagement with Marxism. Over a series of theoretical fragments Benjamin explored the inherited disciplinary limits of literary-historical scholarship and the radical, messianic breaks implied by Lukács's widely influential and strikingly controversial *History and Class Consciousness* (*Geschichte und*

Klassenbewusstsein, 1923), as well as Adorno's notion of "shrinkage" as "the entrance of truth-content into material content" (II: 292). In taking this course into the specificities of capitalist materiality, Benjamin aimed at formulating a program for literary study that would tie all truth claims to a commodity-ridden material world, including those involving revelation, divine power, or messianic time. The problematic that subsequently unfolds in his work is premised on "a detour through materialist aesthetics" and is invested in grasping the relations between commodity-form and cultural form (II: 415–16). In his *dérive* through "Central Park," which would take Benjamin ultimately to the Parisian arcades, where consumer society served the "reactivation of mythic powers,"[5] Benjamin begins to translate his conceptual vocabulary into the dynamics of commodification and reification: "The commodity has taken the place of the allegorical mode of apprehension" (IV: 188).

If so, what does the commodity-form signify from the mold left by allegory? How do metaphysical categories find peculiar resonance in the material structuration of capitalist society? What is it about the particular interpenetration of material and immaterial forms within commodities that allows them to take on a quasi-religious existence, even make capitalism into a religion? Benjamin's engagement with Marxism culminated in the experimental literary montage of the *Arcades Project*, with "Convolute X" devoted to Marx. Assuming what Howard Eiland and Kevin McLaughlin describe as "epic proportions," the *Arcades Project* is littered with citations regarding processes of commodification and suggestive commentary on the dream world that takes shape with the generalization of commodity-based production.[6] "Only a thoughtless observer," claims Benjamin, "can deny that correspondences come into play between the world of modern technology and the archaic symbol-world of mythology."[7] The new phantasmagoria generated by consumerist capitalism reactivate quasi-timeless myth images, becoming the internal condition of possibility for a logic of world decomposition, unfolding over secular and transcendental frames simultaneously. That is, for Benjamin, as he states in "Capitalism as Religion," "Capitalism is entirely without precedent, in that it is a religion which offers not the reform of existence but its complete destruction. It is the expansion of despair, until despair becomes a religious state of the world in the hope that this will lead to salvation" (I: 289). Benjamin's engagements with capitalism as a social form always corresponded with the articulation of a political theology. Capitalism indicated that the former referent of the divine had become immanent in the secular sphere: "God's transcendence is at an end. But he is not dead; he has been incorporated into human existence" (I: 289). Revelatory illumination was to be found within the profane, just as revolutionary possibilities were now harbored in the commodity-form. Numerous studies have shown how these various threads of Benjamin's thinking come together in the *Arcades Project*. Yet very few have attempted to clarify the analogies he ventures between capitalism and theology or between the material operations of capital's process of infinite accumulation and reconfiguration of sublimity as a secularly grounded phenomenon. Even less attention has been given to what the implications might be of this shift to the commodity-form for forging a materialist literary history.

II. COMMODITY: CELL STRUCTURE OF WORLD DEFORMATION

Ranajit Guha's essay "The Advent of Punctuality" provides an entryway into the patterns of spatiotemporal transformation premised on the logic of capital accumulation—a logic tied inextricably to the commodity-form, for reasons that will become clearer shortly. In order to secure financial solvency and satisfy "capital's urge to invest money into commodity in order to make more money"—an infinite drive that the company official Phillip Francis simply understood as "our necessities"—it was imperative by the end of the eighteenth century that the English East India Company assimilate the land tax of the recently conquered province of Bengal to its commercial aspirations. This conjoining of taxation of the land to its "utmost abilities" with the drive for capital's self-valorization was critical for "capital's self-realization in its mercantilist phase," according to Guha, and it thus "counted as an authentic moment of its drive to conquer space by time." Especially noteworthy for present purposes is the extent to which the imposition of capitalist time functioned almost immediately as "an engine of expropriation" and spelled the imminent demise of "the age-old system of the semi-feudal type" maintained by the Mughals in Bengal. Under the pressures of capitalism's abstract temporal compulsions guiding the "blunt and rigid fiscal routine" imposed by the colonial power, the rhythms of precapitalist modes of agriculture were dislodged. Severed irrevocably were the ties the old system maintained to flexible intervals required by the soil, and displaced radically were the traditional calibrations of work suspensions to the movements of the heavenly bodies and passage of the seasons. The disruption of Bengal's indigenous farm calendar by an "alien mercantile-fiscal timetable" had, Guha notes, "an unmistakably spatial correlative": "nowhere was that spatial connection elucidated more clearly than in the drama of seizure and auction enacted in thousands of villages with the bailiff's hammer coming down on the defaulter's properties with clockwork regularity."[8] The unrelenting burden of the tax regardless of drought or other natural contingencies combined with the rigidity of the fiscal calendar. Together they created the conditions for the vast famines that characterized British colonial rule in India from beginning to end.[9]

The following chapters track related patterns of world deformation in the wake of subsumption under the commodity-form. The ensuing disorientation finds myriad expressions in the colonial context. For instance, in the Indo-Islamic idiom we find the late Victorian intellectual Altaf Husain Hali's admission "We still do not have even the slightest idea as to what sort of carrion bitch [*murdar kuttiya*] progress is."[10] The sentiment was followed up more emphatically by Muhammad Iqbal's reflection on the obliteration of agency under the oppressive reason of modernity in his famous neo-epic, *Javid Nama* (1932): "Reason is a chain fettering this present age: / where is a restless soul such as I possess."[11] For the moment, what is needed is sharper clarification of the dynamic of commodification, for it is this, as Guha recognizes, that destabilizes and corrodes precapitalist forms of existence and thus informs neotraditional responses.

The locus classicus for any such discussion is Marx's famous chapter "The Commodity" in volume 1 of *Capital: A Critique of Political Economy*, published in 1867. The theory of the commodity-fetish in which the first chapter culminates is immediately remarkable for the poetic energy it commands vis-à-vis what Marx calls alternately the "sublime" (*sublime Wertgegenständlichkeit*) or "phantom-like" (*gespentige Gegenständlichkeit*) objectivity of commodity-based society in previous sections of the chapter.[12] The French philosopher Étienne Balibar has recognized the theory of fetishism as "not only one of the high points of Marx's philosophical work, completely integrated into his 'critical' and 'scientific' oeuvre, but a powerful [*grand*] theoretical construction" that tests the bounds and redetermines the field of philosophy in becoming "an alternative to philosophy, a non-philosophy, indeed an anti-philosophy." Balibar's own insights into the interplay of material and immaterial realities in Marx's writings will inform my discussion, especially since the "permanent oscillation between being short of and going beyond philosophy" that Balibar detects running throughout Marx's career helped give shape to a critical theory grounded not in philosophical, or pure, speculation but in the concrete abstractions embedded in the commodity-form.[13] Far from being ordinary lifeless things, commodities appear to have a will of their own as they leave the hands of their producers and enter the sphere of the market. These things, "far from being under [the producers'] own control, in fact control them."[14] In calling this relation in which human agents come under the spell of objects of their own making a form of "fetishism," Marx was undercutting the self-aggrandizing claims of Enlightenment and reason that characterized liberal bourgeois societies of the imperial-capitalist epicenter from which he was writing, London. Far from being "progressive," Marx was suggesting with his terminology, societies premised on the commodity-form were no better than those sad remnants of primitive human existence in the planetary recesses of the newly encroaching global society. Rather, modern societies were worse off. Operating under illusions of equal market exchange and liberal freedoms that they generated automatically, these societies were subject to machinations of their own creation, which, far from taking on the guise of something alterable, adopted instead the appearance of quasi-natural necessity.

Though the notion of commodification implies that not all commodities are necessarily produced by the human hand or even by machinery, it also signifies that whatever is being commodified has been transformed into an object with a price and can now be potentially sold on the market. It has, in other words, adopted a social form congruent with capital. The process of commodification presumes a society in which the production of commodities for exchange has been, or is becoming, universalized. This would have to be a society where one's labor power is itself a commodity that can be exchanged for wages, which would in turn be used to purchase other commodities, such as groceries, for one's everyday survival. Such a society is by definition capitalist for Marx in that it presumes both sellers and buyers of labor power and therefore a sharp division of labor. This division is as essential for social reproduction, given the advanced state of social interdependence that evolves with commodity-driven specialization, as for the accumulation of more capital, which would be the sole rationale or necessity for the purchase of labor power in the first place. As Gopal Balakrishnan has noted, "Marx's theory of the capitalist mode of production attempts to explain the totality of an exchange-mediated economic process by isolating the part of it whose historically cumulative dynamic of development determines the fate of the whole."[15] For bourgeois society, Marx writes in the first preface to *Capital*, "the commodity-form of the product of labour, or the value-form of the commodity, is the economic cell-form" (90). It is therefore the commodity that Marx isolates in his analysis of capital, for it is from the tensions immanent to this most crucial cell form that the entire dynamic of capital accumulation unfolds with all of its internally generated crises and potential for self-demolition.

By grounding his entire analysis of capitalism on any given thing up for purchase in market society, Marx displaces abstract philosophical speculation and brings center-stage the material entities critical for everyday sustenance; yet it must be recalled that the commodity is, despite appearances, no ordinary thing. Being exchangeable with other commodities at equitable ratios—seven nails for a coffee mug, and so on—the ordinary commodity reveals an underlying value as its "phantom-like objectivity." The commodity, given its very existence as a good (or "use-value") made for exchange (and not immediate consumption), oscillates between the extreme polarities of concretion and abstraction. On the concrete end of the spectrum, the use-value of a commodity consists in nothing other than its usefulness, as Michael Heinrich states, and as such points to a frontier beyond exchange: "The use-value is independent [*unabhängig*] of whether or not an object is exchanged"; a chair has use-value in being sat upon, for instance.[16] In its qualitatively distinct and physically singular form, use-value reveals an immediate interconnection between human and natural entities—air, water, trees, and so on—and thus harkens to an ongoing metabolic interaction between society and nature. "Use value is therefore quality; it is the life of the body, of existential or phenomenological experience, of the consumption of physical products, but also the very texture of physical work and physical time," writes Jameson in *Representing* Capital.[17] And, as such, the qualitative dimension indexes a "deep existential constant that justifies that Utopian strain in Marxism which anticipates the transformation of work into aesthetic activity."[18] (I will return to this dimension of the commodity-form—or rather commodity-based society—in the concluding discussion on the presentation or *Darstellung* of a materialist history of romanticism.) On the other extreme of what the commodity beholds is its "supra-natural property," or value, which Marx describes as "something purely social." This pure social substance—what will turn out to be abstract human labor time (impossible to generate except under conditions of universalized commodification)—constitutes the value dimension of all commodities and thus allows for their commensurability and mutual exchangeability. The uniform and thus quantifiable dimension opened up by exchange with other commodities—precisely what value makes possible—stands in opposition to the qualitative and heterogeneous side of sold goods. Whereas use-values do not depend on exchange, exchange-value cannot do without use-values. The latter are, Marx specifies, "the material bearers [*Träger*] of . . . exchange value" (126). That is, under capitalist conditions the very materiality in which commodities present use-value is charged with an immaterial objectivity, value, whose driving aim is to be converted into another commodity—ultimately, the money form—through exchange.

This contradictory interplay between the two polarities of use- and exchange-values generates a wide developmental dynamic resulting in a social totality marked by material interdependence through commodity exchange yet riven by social antagonisms of all sorts (including those stretching across imperial orders, as discussed over the course of this work). The entire range of the implications of the tensions and oppositions found in the commodity-form cannot be adequately covered in the space given here. Yet in order to grasp the engine-like propulsion of the process of capital accumulation—what helps explain the interchange between material and immaterial forms in the commodity—a few key points must be made regarding what the tensions within the commodity-form imply. These will ultimately lead us to the fetish dimension of commodity-based societies—that is to say, to the way in which the very products of human activity under capitalism fashion a hard objective world that takes on the appearance of immutable nature, compelling its own creators to the vicissitudes of the commodity world's seemingly independent existence and making apparently inevitable a hard reality of market-based bottom lines. These tendencies consolidate and propel ever further an abstract form of domination consonant with what Guha's account illustrates regarding peasants being shunted off the land in tandem with the precise ticks of the East India Company's financial clocks, having failed to instrumentalize their land assets to the satisfaction of mercantile capital's temporal imperatives.

The commodity-fetish comes into sharpest relief through an investigation into the predicament of labor when subsumed by commodification. As a commodity, labor power, like any other, consists of use- and exchange-value and thus is given to the same play of dualisms observed earlier: concrete and abstract, qualitative and quantitative, material and immaterial dimensions. As a concrete use-value, Marx notes in a crucial passage in the first volume of *Capital*, labor power "possesses the peculiar property of being a source of value," deducing from the apparently equal exchange of commodities the necessity for at least one that would be productive of value if accumulation were to obtain in capitalist society (270). ("Capital cannot . . . arise from circulation, and it is equally impossible for it to arise apart from circulation. It must have its origin both in circulation and not in circulation," which is to say that a commodity must exist on the market that can be bought for production [268].) In its concrete realization, the use-value of labor opens a threshold to the manifold universe of activities that constitute useful labor, for "as the creator of use-values, as useful labour, [labor as such] is a condition of human existence which is independent of all forms of society; it is an eternal natural necessity which mediates the metabolism between man and nature, and therefore human life itself" (133). In its immediate concreteness, labor opens outward toward extinct and future worlds where it does not have to adopt the form required by the capitalist mode of production—that is, commodified labor power, available for purchase like any other commodity. This at once residual and adumbrative dimension of labor in its concrete state is distinct from labor power for it has no necessary connection to exchange and, despite being "the substance, and the immanent measure of value," it itself has no value (677). This free, purposeful and self-sustaining activity remains ever the "substance of value," though bearing no value itself, for it is ontologically separate from its own reduction to labor power. This shading of labor lurks in weak messianic form beyond the wage and other necessary appearances of bourgeois society in Marx's *Capital*. It hints at the possibility of a society in which labor power is not a commodity, where the social dispensation that allows for the accumulation of value no longer obtains, and where labor itself may no longer be necessary. The very fact that it has no value means that it is free of the compulsions to which value-bearing commodities are subject under capitalism.

These compulsions reveal their starkest contours when one examines what is implied by the exchange dimension of labor power as a commodity. The article labor power is a bearer of has a value determined, as is the case for all other commodities, by the socially necessary labor time required for its production: "the labour-time necessary for the production of labour-power is the same as that necessary for the production of those means of subsistence" on which the bearer of labor power must depend (274). I will turn to the temporal dynamic of capitalism later, for that will make up an especially hard facet of the commodity-fetish and allow for the reification of abstract power (and help us return to Guha and his account of the unrelenting punctuality introduced by capital and initially administered by the British colonial establishment in India). For the moment, the exchange-value of labor power reminds one of the peculiar, if not completely unprecedented character of labor in capitalist society: both abstract and concrete simultaneously. In being the bearer and the producer of value, abstract labor is the modality by which all producers connect with one another, and it is in this sense general labor. In becoming general, it is "abstracted," as Moishe Postone notes, "from all material specificity as well as any overtly social particularity."[19] This abstract quality of labor power under capitalism lends itself to quantification and measure. It is nothing other than the "pure social substance" underlying commodities, or what Marx otherwise calls "value." Giving them an abstract objectivity in capitalist conditions that is no less effective than their empirical qualities, value allows for the commensurability of and thus exchangeability between commodities, as noted earlier. This sublime charge underlying the concrete use-value of a commodity is what propels it toward self-valorization, drawing it magnetically toward exchange, for it is only through this medium that valorization is possible. The value of the commodity labor power allows it to be exchanged for wages, which are in turn exchanged for commodities, uncovering the form of simple circulation C—M—C, where C stands for "commodity" and M for "money." When labor power is exchanged for wages (M), what is necessarily occluded is the fact that the capitalist has purchased no ordinary commodity but the one privileged in being productive of value, thus making possible surplus-value, the sine qua non of the capitalist mode of production (M—C—M', where M' is the original sum advanced plus an increment). The necessary illusion of fair and equal exchange embedded in mere conversion of labor power into money "extinguishes," Marx notes in the chapter "Wages," "every trace of the division of the working day into necessary labour and surplus labour, into paid and unpaid labour" (680). He elaborates: "All the notions of justice held by both the worker and the capitalist, all the mystifications of the capitalist mode of production, all capitalism's illusions about freedom, all the apologetic tricks of vulgar economics, have as their basis the form of appearance discussed above, which makes the actual relation [between capital and labor] invisible, and indeed presents to the eye the precise opposite of that relation" (680). The ensuing social logic cannot be covered here in all its momentousness, yet it must be emphasized that the commodification of labor power and its deployment for the production of surplus-value entails for Marx the absorption of human powers into things and the thingification of human subjectivity.

It must be kept in mind that labor power attains a quasi-thing-like quality in the conditions presumed by classical political economy. In selling it, the bearer of labor power realizes its exchange-value but simultaneously alienates (*veräussert*) its use-value, for now this peculiar value-producing power, labor, "belongs just as little to its seller as the use-value of oil after it has been sold belongs to the dealer who sold it": the "owner of the money has paid the value of a day's labour-power; he therefore has the use of it for a day, a day's labour belongs to him," including whatever it amounts to in products (301). The capitalist has disposal over the use of this capacity, and like any other article he might purchase, he wishes to obtain its full utility. This immediately brings about a conflict between the buyer and seller of labor power that plays out on a number of planes all at once, for instance safety and health standards in the workplace. The disputes around work conditions can be arbitrated only by a state apparatus, which must establish and enforce standards. In doing so, the state is inevitably drawn into the struggle on the temporal plane, forcing management to limit the hours of the workday. Attention must be paid to the struggle over time, as it is through the temporal dimension, as Postone has argued most effectively, that the force of abstract domination with which capitalism is coterminous attains full expression. The temporal dynamic that unfolds with the employment of labor power for the purposes of producing surplus-value is complicated yet fundamentally contradictory, and thus relatively easily depicted in broad strokes. It is a dynamic that underlines the overall primacy given to utility in the capitalist mode of production, for whatever can be instrumentalized for the sake of surplus-value must necessarily be instrumentalized, if only under the compulsion of competition with other independent capitalists. These systemic conditions encourage the reduction of all phenomena, including nature itself, to the status of instrument. Yet the process aiming at the maximization of labor power for the accumulation of surplus-value ultimately threatens to render obsolescent this very essential entity. Postone clarifies the point: "What underlies the central contradiction of capitalism, according to Marx, is that value remains the determining form of wealth and of social relations in capitalism, regardless of developments in productivity; however, value also becomes increasingly anachronistic in terms of the material wealth-producing potential of the productive forces to which it gives rise."[20]

To see how this is so is to encounter simultaneously the logic of mechanization under capitalism and the production of homogeneous, empty time—a form of temporality abstracted from calendrical events and cyclical shifts of the seasons or the days and nights and thus turned into "an independent framework within which motion, events, and action occur," which is to say, a form of temporality that is "divisible into equal, constant, nonqualitative units."[21] The universalization and normalization of abstract time is a function of the general systemic tendency toward the full utilization of labor power for the production of commodities. Abstract time becomes the measure of productivity, establishing the social average time required to make any particular good intended for exchange. Market competition and the endless drive for virtually infinite accumulation make it imperative for each independent capitalist to maximize surplus-value, which is now measurable as the quantity of value produced exceeding the amount required to cover wages. Nature as well as moral agency, generally taking the form of legal restriction, will impose their separate constraints on absolute surplus-value by restricting the length of the workday. A day is only so long and a worker can be worked only so much if one wishes for the return of labor power the following day. The only option is to make each unit of time more productive by "completely revolutioniz[ing] the technical processes of labor and the groupings into which society is divided," in other words by producing "relative surplus-value" (645). That is, the instrumentalization of scientific knowledge coupled with capital investment in the productive apparatus makes for a specifically capitalist mode of production, one that constantly revolutionizes itself in tandem with each individual advance in rationalizing and automating the production process and thereby reducing labor costs. "If the production of absolute surplus-value was the material expression of the formal subsumption of labour under capital," elaborates Marx in the first volume of *Capital*, "then the production of relative-surplus value may be viewed as its real subsumption" (1025). With real subsumption and the advent of machinery, "it is not the worker who employs the conditions of his work, but rather the reverse, the conditions of work employ the worker" (548). The temporal imperative imposed by competition suborns all other temporalities. It is to this machine-like rhythm of the Taylorized production process that the worker must submit himself or herself. Likewise, it is the demands for greater efficiency, higher productivity, and ever larger profits that the captains of industry must face, and if those are not met, the stewards of capital know who will need to be sacrificed to keep the books balanced. Though the production process must throw out all employees rendered unproductive by its constantly revolutionized and expanded capacities, unproductive labor is not so easily able to relinquish its dependency on commodities.

The hardening of this temporal logic and the shrinking, if not imperiling of collective human prospects on account of it is all the more astounding given that it is in itself not necessary but only apparently so given the conditions of commodity society and the levels of illusion it generates as a natural excrescence of its internal functioning.

The apparently uncontrollable drive for self-valorization embedded in the commodity-form deforms time by making its own temporality binding and normative, regardless of geographical location, spatial context, or cultural orientations, all of which are reconfigured to accommodate its force, becoming mere facets of a world transformed into a mere means for capital accumulation. The commodity-form penetrates and restructures the social hardware according to its instrumental logic. "Production for the sake of production," remarks Postone, "signifies that production is no longer a means to a substantive end but a means to an end that is itself a means, a moment in a never-ending chain of expansion. *Production in capitalism becomes a means to a means*."[22] The emptying of the world and its reason of all substance is but one reflection of its world-dissolving force, proceeding according to an abstract logic of value under capitalism. As we saw in Guha's powerful essay on the abstract temporal modality of colonial power, the empty homogeneous time that began to tick according to the financial necessities of the East India Company's annual schedule swept over the famine-stricken lands of colonial India with a force that made the past deprivations of mere nature seem slight in comparison. The modern times imposed by the colonial power spared no time in trashing all vestiges of a civilization that did not accord with its instrumental logic, whether these took the guise of sacred traditions or mere empathy for the victims of its destruction. Little did the petty barbarisms of traditional culture compare with the inexorable compulsions and nonnegotiable temporality of the commodity-fetish in its pure abstraction, however great were the fantasies of a Rudyard Kipling or a Captain William H. Sleeman or the ghoulish lore of thuggee, feudal cruelty, ritualized sex, and demonic deities.[23]

I offer an analysis of the cultural encoding of the abstract temporality and its embedded instrumental rationality in late colonial society, focusing primarily on the northern Indian literary and intellectual sphere. While concentrating on the twin vernaculars of Hindi and Urdu, my frame of reference is the imperial order that had long mediated romanticism, allowing for a translatability of motifs and forms, including the epic across language and regions. A cultural pattern anchored directly or indirectly on the spatiotemporal logic of the market, on the one hand, yet expressive of immanent wariness, dissent, and contradiction, on the other, poses the problem of culture shaped, if not hardened, to accord with the dynamics of commodification and the value form, or in other words, the problem of reification.

III. REIFICATION: SUBLIME THING-WORLD

Unlike the neologisms Marx was compelled to invent to distinguish his critical approach from the misleading surface categories deployed by bourgeois economists or philosophers such as David Ricardo and John Stuart Mill, the widely current notion of reification (*Verdinglichung*), as the late British philosopher and critic Gillian Rose notes, has "no canonical source."[24] Liberal political economists and social commentators would generally be loath to speak of surplus-value (*Mehrwert*) or labor power (*Arbeitskraft*) and would prefer "profit" or "labor market" instead, yet when it comes to "reification" such political anxiety barely obtains. The wide acceptance of this term in liberal society is in part attributable to Marx's very spare usage of it in his own writings, a fact that in itself allowed the term to range widely among philosophers, sociologists, and literary critics as diverse as Nietzsche, Simmel, Weber, and Lukács in fin de siècle Central Europe. This legacy is reflected in Axel Honneth's recent removal of all vestiges of a Marxist Critical Theory from the category itself and Timothy Bewes's insistence that reification is an expression of a generalizable social decadence that gives rise to acute cultural anxieties in late capitalism.[25] The term's uncertain status between liberal social science and Marxist cultural criticism reflects how easily reification and critiques premised on it can go from engaging with the processes of surplus-value production that necessarily give rise to the commodity-fetish to the obscuring of these very processes, including all their ties to class conflict, the state, and violence.[26] Yet what is indicated by these regular slippages between facile and critical deployments of reification is just how much it alludes to—or is itself symptomatic of—a broad social totality built upon, but never immediately reducible to, capitalist social relations. In Lukács's influential essay "Reification and the Consciousness of the Proletariat" in his *History and Class Consciousness* (1923), the question of totality was put so powerfully as to attain a quasi-theological dimension. Lukács's theory of reification unified the disparate iterations in the works of Simmel and Weber and grounded it fundamentally in Marx's categories of commodity and commodity-fetish. Nevertheless, the notion of reification displaced the centrality of "class struggle" as a means of political mobilization advanced by the Communist International, and thus spilled beyond the guarded boundaries of orthodox Marxism, drawing its author under the charge of ultraradicalism. The quasi-theological dimensions of the notion of totality Lukács advances are thus worth examining, if only because they take us into the strangely evolving materiality of imperial and late capitalist society. That is to say, the prescient and messianic qualities of Lukács's essay come into sharper relief as the processes of atomization and the general subsumption of material existence under the abstract powers of global capital become ever more pronounced, if not normalized. For the destructive force of capital's self-valorization process erodes the very planetary resources upon which it relies, exhausting human potentials, and therefore necessitating the standpoint of a revolutionary subjectivity as absolute as the very subsumption of global objectivity by market fundamentalism.

We can bracket for the moment the subjectivity that could possibly occupy this historically pressing role of socio-ecological salvation and merely note the renewed relevance of Lukács yet again. It behooves us to turn first to the sociocultural problematic Lukács sought to address—the emerging gap between proletarian consciousness and the role Marx assigned to it—and the ramifications that his notion of reification opened up, including the political ones that have long shaped the complicated and uneven reception of *History and Class Consciousness* to the present moment. By the time Lukács published this work in 1923, he had already led an eventful and controversial path into the political struggle that would define the twentieth century: internationalist communism against capitalist imperialism. The immediate context was one of revolutionary tumult that followed in the wake of World War I. The epicenter of this political storm was the Russian Revolution, or more precisely the Bolshevik Revolution of October 1917. The son of a prominent banker of noble status in turn-of-the-century Budapest, Lukács joined the Communist Party in his native Hungary a year later, after long experimentation with mixes of apocalyptic aesthetics and late romantic vitalism. Given his youthful messianic yearning for a real *Gemeinshaft* that would lead to "a reawakening of German philosophy and religiosity," and his failed efforts in the short-lived Hungarian Revolution of 1918–19, which left him a Leninist in exile, Lukács had great affinity for the ultraradicalism that defined certain strains of revolutionary politics in the wake of October 1917.[27] Though *History and Class Consciousness* retains vestiges of these earlier political phases, it nevertheless marks a turn beyond what the political commentator and activist John Rees calls "the unstable intellectual amalgam of Marxism and romantic anti-capitalism." This classic work constitutes for Rees "a fundamental break with his philosophical past under the impact of the experience of the Russian and Hungarian revolutions."[28] Lukács's recapture of reification extended praxis beyond the restricted purview of class politics and thus inevitably inspired sharp condemnation among Party officials at a moment of inner Party struggle between Lenin's revolutionary legatees and Stalin's *Machtpolitik*.

The controversy around *History and Class Consciousness* cannot be covered in all its details here; it will suffice to make a few immediately relevant observations. First, the fissures that formed largely mapped the separation between Soviet and Western Marxisms. The tendencies of the former were already taking shape in the rebukes that met Lukács's efforts: the reduction of praxis to labor, which could now be instrumentalized by the Party apparatus, all under the authority of dialectical materialism and its stagist understanding of human progress. Though Lukács ultimately recanted his views and capitulated to Stalinism, his initial spirited defense in *Tailism and the Dialectic* (c. 1925) set the pattern for an anticapitalist politics not necessarily aligned with the Party form of organization and open to absorbing the challenges of capitalist innovation, including the co-optation of working-class populations into its structure of domination—all of which characterized the Western Marxism unaligned with the USSR. Ironically, it must be noted too, both Eastern and Western forms of Marxism were suspected after the rise of 1960s radicalism for having equally shunted the question of revolutionary praxis, allowing a return of abstracted epistemologies putatively covering both natural and social development, on the Eastern end, and what the critic Slavoj Žižek has described as a "shift from concrete socio-political analysis to philosophico-anthropological generalization," most predominantly in the Frankfurt School, on the Western end. Just as philosophical categories vouched for abstractions of future human emancipation in the East, in the West the tendencies were equally distanced from immediate realities of capitalist social relations. Žižek elaborates: "the reifying 'instrumental reason'" of *Dialectic of Enlightenment* was "no longer grounded in concrete capitalist social relations" but instead became "their quasi-transcendental 'principle' or 'foundation.'"[29] Banned in the Soviet bloc and grudgingly referenced in Western Marxist contexts, whether connected with the Frankfurt School or the French philosopher Louis Althusser, Lukács's *History and Class Consciousness* acquired cachet with its "underground spectral existence of an 'undead' entity," as Žižek notes, circulating in pirated editions and rare translations, retaining contemporary relevance despite efforts to contain it in the historical past, including those of its own author in the 1967 reprint.[30]

The point of departure for Lukács was the theoretical deficiency of Second International Marxism in explaining what was in evidence all around in advanced capitalist societies: the ever-widening divergence of working-class consciousness from the revolutionary role imputed to it in Marx's writings. Lukács's brilliant response to this problematic was to ground the contradictory consciousness among workers in the totality of relations, both illusory and real, premised on the commodity-form. That is, no direct or immediate connection could be assumed any longer between class position and class consciousness. Rather, the commodification of labor power and universalized interdependency through commodity production meant that "the actual make-up of social phenomena is *not immediately* apparent" but must be understood against the quasi-natural surface appearances of fragmentation and atomization, processes that undermine in themselves the radicalization of struggles over labor power and work time.[31] "That is to say," Lukács elaborates at the beginning of "Reification and the Consciousness of the Proletariat," "the problem of commodities must not be considered in isolation or even regarded as the central problem in economics, but as the central, structural problem of capitalist society in all its aspects."[32] Capitalist social conditions both constitute and are constituted by everyday practice, encompassing subject and object, but in a manner that is ridden with class contradiction and unequal power relations, thereby rendering the connection between subjective and objective realms opaque and any notion of unity abstract so long as society is founded on class division. In what Postone calls a "materialist appropriation of Hegel," Lukács makes explicit "the idea that Marx's categories represent a powerful attempt to overcome the classical subject-object dualism."[33]

At the crux of Lukács's brilliant essay is an analysis of the transmutation of the processes of capital accumulation into the hardened bureaucratic logic that conforms to nothing more than the instrumentality of commodity exchange. "Reification requires that a society should learn to satisfy all its needs in terms of commodity exchange," he clarifies, alluding to the "pretense" embedded in the commodity-form "that society is regulated by 'eternal, iron' laws which branch off into the different special laws applying to particular areas," including the culture industry and educational institutions.[34] The ramifications of this recasting of reification as the materialized objectification, standardized quantification, and rationalized bureaucratization all in accord with the commodity-form are multiple. That the emerging Stalinist orthodoxy expressed reservations about the extension of revolutionary praxis beyond the immediate sphere of labor has already been mentioned. It itself alludes to the wide theoretical implications of totality, where "all social problems cease to transcend man and appear as the products of human activity," including those of suffering and death.[35] The apparently implacable and inscrutable logic of the laws that abstractly govern market society is itself the result of constituted practices of capitalist society and thus has the immanent potentiality of being reconstituted otherwise. In dissolving these practices the fatalism before the alien objectivity of market society itself loosens. Socially reconstitutive practices must necessarily break through the one-dimensionality of reified structures, indicating how "the possible determinate negation of the existent order cannot be rooted in the categories that purportedly grasp it," as Postone notes.[36] For Lukács, "the essence of praxis consists in annulling that indifference of form towards content that we found in the problem of the [Kantian] thing-in-itself."[37] All of this is to suggest that in Lukács a dialectical interplay between subject and object unfolds through revolutionary praxis such that the rigid opposition between form and content is overcome, thereby avoiding the reductionism and determinism that characterized Second International Marxism. Reflecting back in his preface to the

1967 edition, he writes, "It is undoubtedly one of the great achievements of *History and Class Consciousness* to have reinstated the category of totality in the central position it had occupied throughout Marx's works and from which it had been ousted by the 'scientism' of the social-democratic opportunists."[38]

Spilling beyond fixed political boundaries and occasionally calling forth an absolute subject of history to match the absolute subsumption of the world by the commodity-form, the vast sublime thing-world indexed by the concept of reification is not easily exhausted. Rather it remains generative of quasi-archaic spirits and mythical figments from a capitalist ether, as Benjamin asserted. Their reappearance in epic form will be retraced across the late imperial span between metropolis and colony by picking up where Benjamin had to abandon his materialist theo-philology. All of the ramifications of Lukács's theoretical intervention cannot be adequately addressed here. Other commentaries elaborate in greater detail on the implications of his recasting of Hegel's identical subject-object into the material context of the commodity-form and capitalist social relations; others on the problems of a lingering humanism or the question of praxis and the various arenas in which it may be actualized; still others have explored the question of standpoint and its relation to contemporary political categories, including the formation of national, ethnic, or other "cultural" identities. As a segue back to the methodology for a materialist literary history around the late colonial sublime, I want to explore the ambiguities that emerge in recent dismissals of Lukács as a theologian of totality when combined with his understanding of a necessarily material mediation in capitalist social formations. Is this peculiar theology necessarily materialist? Does it now find itself curiously embedded in a market-driven world "peculiarly without transcendence and without perspective," as Jameson once observed with the looking glass of neoliberal economics?[39]

The point is that if there is a quasi-theological core within capitalism—if capitalism harbors qualities that betray an inner religiosity—this core cannot be accessed except by reference to the materiality of the commodity-form and the sharp political tensions to which it gives rise. In counterpoint, if there is no materiality in modernity that is not already shaped and alloyed by the propulsive movement of capitalist accumulation, then it is a materiality imbued with contradictions and generative of forms that mark their horizon of overcoming. "Every form is the resolution of a fundamental dissonance of existence,"

Lukács famously writes in his pre-Marxist *Theory of the Novel*.[40] The notion finds its Marxist translation in the following manner: There is no materiality that is not secularized theology; there is no theology that is immaterial except through the forms generated by capital's internal dissonance. The following chapters trace the dynamic interrelations of historical truth content and aesthetic form in the context of the late colonial moment, a period characterized by the sharp antagonism between an increasingly reified utilitarianism tied to the commodity-form and a late romanticism that mediated it as a wide-ranging and generative internal critique. But first, given the tendencies toward reification under conditions of ever-increasing commodification, the theoretical and practical implications of constellated colonial literary history must be spelled out. How to reference and mimic the immaterial propulsions of a sublime thing-world is the primary question of the following section.

IV. COLONIAL LITERARY HISTORY IN CONSTELLATIONAL FORM: RIDDLES OF THE INCOMMUNICABLE

> Today the philosopher is confronted with a deteriorated [*zerfallenen*] language. His material is the ruins of the words to which history binds him: his only freedom is the possibility of configuring them in accordance with the coercion of truth within them.
>
> —Theodor W. Adorno, "Theses on the Language of the Philosopher"

Adorno's coruscating yet tortured words give expression to the predicament that an antipositivist literary history must inevitably face: how to grasp the intangible social processes and dynamics belying the objective thing-like structures and entities these processes themselves have generated?[41] How, in other words, to employ a tainted, critically compromised language in ways that resist its own illegitimacy? This difficulty characterized Marx's own writings, which sought to reference simultaneously the fetishistic surfaces in which capitalist realities come inevitably wrapped as well as the underlying social relations that "have absolutely no connection with the physical nature of the commodity and the material [*dinglich*] relations arising out of this" (165). The critical demands that this social reality places on language force it to adopt a variety of rhetorical strategies, from irony, paradox, chiasmus, and personification in the work of Marx, to parataxis, parallax, inversion, and ultimately configurational form in Benjamin and Adorno. These efforts were meant to evade the ideological trappings of facile languages that turn humans into instruments for the consolidation of abstract power. In their stead the dialectical interventions stemming from Marx's Critical Theory sought to make language supple enough again so as to allow for mimesis of the referent itself, even if this referent is not necessarily sensuous or even necessarily communicable in its entirety. Considering it was Benjamin who advanced the practice of constellational form for configuring a materialist literary history attentive to the "nonsensuous similarity" (*unsinnliche Ähnlichkeit*) of the commodity-form, it is to him we return in this concluding section. Through a reconstruction of his doctrines of similarity, mimesis, and translation—which were closely connected to and informed his concepts of theology and history—it will be possible to spell out the advantages of depicting late colonial literary history in the form of a constellation. Constellational form's underlying trope of parataxis indexes "the unity of the whole [that] is composed of the dissociations between the discrete parts as well as their associations," as Sherry Weber Nicholson has observed. Furthermore, its implications of the "discontinuity and lack of linear or cumulative order" allow for the allegorization of contradiction, dissonance, and redemptive form. As fundamental contradictions took hold across the imperial sphere, they demanded the disjunction of parallax, uniting thereby the metropolitan West and colonial territories.[42]

For the moment, let us return to Benjamin. We left him at the point where he was in the process of translating a late romantic idealist inheritance into a materially grounded critical method for composing a literary history attuned to the dynamics of the commodity-form and able to emerge as a literary genre in its own right. "What is required now," he wrote in a fragment entitled "Program for Literary Criticism," dated to 1929 or 1930, "is a detour through materialist aesthetics, which would situate books in the context of their age. Such a criticism would lead to a new, dynamic, dialectical aesthetics," one that would affirm that "everything must be possible at every moment" (II: 294). These writings foreshadowed the methodological orientation that would lead eventually to the *Arcades Project*, the theater of what Benjamin describes in a letter to Gershom Scholem as "all my conflicts and all my ideas." In this letter, Benjamin writes that he must bring into conversation the two problems that have bedeviled him in preparation: "on the one hand, the problem of documentation and, on the other hand, . . . that of metaphysics." The solution requires a return to the dialectic: "I now see that I will at least need to study some aspects of Hegel and some parts of Marx's *Capital* to get anywhere and to provide a solid scaffolding for my work."[43] This materialist detour was consequential for the valences his romantically saturated critical vocabulary would acquire as it got reworked, translated, and allegorized. The jaunt through the arcades would result in a consolidation of constellational form, reanimating the nearly defunct field of literary history by sweeping it against the grain of a reified world order and the positivist method it supported. By retracing a variety of fragments from Benjamin's corpus of surviving works, it becomes possible to grasp constellational form as a translational medium, distilling diverse strains of Benjamin's writings around similarity, mimesis, the absolute, now-time, and translation. These all become overlapping modalities for grasping nonsensuous similarity and the riddle of a capitalist materiality that contains "a symbolic core, beyond the meaning communicated in it, a core that is the symbol of noncommunicability" (I: 267–68).[44] The materialist philological method Benjamin advanced aimed "to open up the material content, from which the truth content can then be plucked off historically like petals," as he put it to Adorno in a sharp exchange of views (IV: 108). Benjamin made a note in 1930 reminding himself that the theory of criticism he was advancing "as a manifestation of the life of works has a connection with my theory of translation" (II: 372–73). Though Benjamin himself never systematically connected his theory of translation with his theory of a literary history that refused to judge, it is nevertheless possible to glean the transmutations through which an early language theology became the basis for constellated materialist literary history.

The task is akin to following gravitational waves as they compress and elongate space and time. This is because Benjamin's thought patterns moved across disparate fields and media, leaving in their wake nothing like a system per se but rather what appear as bodies draped in patterns of nonsensuous similarity, themselves assemblable as constellations. That is, despite fits and starts, lags and leaps, resumptions and repetitions, retracings and elaborations in new materials, what we discover is how many of Benjamin's works appear as mimeses of the other's intention. This oeuvre is characterized by repeated attempts at redemption of eventual ruination, no matter the material form in which the signature of sublimity is inscribed. In this manner, it engraves the precarity of life under fascism into its thematic texture. This very process of slow and subtle shifts in emphases can be detected across Benjamin's writings on language and translation, resulting in experiments with constellational form. This form is the culmination of a search for a noninstrumental medium for the mimesis of an immaterial sublimity—precisely what Marx discovered under the thing-like surfaces of the commodity world. At the core of Benjamin's evolving materialist theology is the doctrine of similarity, whose canon is an original language and whose possible recovery in the present state involves testing the referential powers of constellational mimesis. "For if words meaning the same thing in different languages," ventures Benjamin in "On the Mimetic Faculty," "are arranged about that signified as their center, we have to inquire how they all—while often possessing not the slightest similarity to one another—are similar to the signified at their center" (II: 721). Weber Nicholson observes how such configurative language "effectively alters the words used," creating, in the words of Adorno, a "unity of concept and thing that is dialectically intertwined and cannot be disentangled through explication."[45]

At the core of constellational form is an attempt to redeem language from its fallen state as mere instrumental medium through a resuscitation of the "increasing fragility of the mimetic faculty" (II: 721). This process of resuscitation involves nothing less than bringing back into play an original tendency of bodily mimicry of the child in which the divide between subject and object is momentarily dissolved and the mute signature of things presents itself as a medium of communication in its own right. In other words, it involves nothing less than translation. For Benjamin, the translational process is quintessentially one of ephemeral release of philosophical truth content (*Wahrheitsgehalt*) from the material content (*Sachgehalt*) in which it finds itself deposited, for only the conceptual truth content "could in the last analysis," observes the Benjamin scholar Beatrice Hanssen, "ensure the work's endurance, located on the other side of ephemeral beauty."[46] Translation, in other words, becomes the medium of revelation: it destroys the original form in which content appears, returning it to its originary chaotic force. And yet in mimicking this content in a new medium, translation potentiates a counterinstrumentalist tendency: instead of subjecting language to the status of a tool for the expression of content apparently abstracted from it, now the reverse is the case: the materiality of language is made to accommodate the original content. Contents thus open through language's immanent translatability. The hard materiality of language itself—much in the manner of onomatopoeia—becomes a communicative medium in its own right, re-creating for itself a process of transmutation and thus falling into identity with originary correspondences. Language in this moment becomes an absolute in miniature: "God is inexpressible except in the form of his pure expression; he is identical with his being expressed."[47] That is, manifesting a quasi-divine power in the destruction of form and through the release of a sublime inner content, translation also transforms the medium of the target language, turning it into an allegory of the absolute. Its force is at one with its mode of transformative expression. These doctrines are of course founded on the concept of spontaneous (and not necessarily sensuous) similarity. As Benjamin elaborates in "Doctrine of the Similar," a fragment composed in 1933, such translational processes work through the modality of mimesis, becoming themselves one with a nature that produces similarities since time immemorial. Human beings thus become vehicles for the production of nonsensuous similarities for natural correspondences assume the role of "stimulants and awakeners of the mimetic faculty," beckoning responses in human form (II: 695). "The perception of similarity is in every case bound to a flashing up. It flits past, can possibly be won again, but cannot really be held fast as can other perceptions. It offers itself to the eye as fleetingly and transitorily as a constellation of stars" (II: 695–96).

Lending itself to none of the standards of positivist epistemology and thus avoiding the pitfalls of reified objectivity, Benjamin's unfinished methodology offers itself instead to myriad critical elaborations. I will detail through the constellated chapters that follow a lingering late colonial moment, all the while translating into wider circumferences of the capitalist imperial system Benjamin's cues for resisting reified time and space. Enough perhaps has been said for the moment about his elaborations of a literary-historical method that would inhere in a mode of presentation. It would nevertheless be helpful to retrace some of these ramifications and indicate what they spell out for the chapters ahead. In trying to hold fast to the late colonial as a lingering moment, my presentation is neither linear nor even necessarily bound to narration but rather conglomerative and recursive. Through its own mimetic powers, constellation helps to capture the aporias, such as those facing Hali in the introduction. These aporias cannot be captured except as refracted across different languages and literary traditions as British imperial statecraft in the subcontinent entered terminal crisis. It is the grappling with the imposition of a reason reduced to bare instrumentality that unites the topics of the chapters ahead. What gave some historical unity to the neo-epic itself as a distinct genre was the response it gave to reification in immediately recognizable epic forms, however novel. Part II explores the rise of this form in tandem with the imposition of utilitarian norms in different social spheres across northern India, with an emphasis on Hindi and Urdu literary cultures. Whether Hali and Iqbal on the Urdu-Persian scene or Datta, Dvivedi, or Prasad on the Bengali-Hindi tract, the neo-epics they generated all sought to give form to the historically generated dissonance of late colonial times. The epilogue aims to read the kitschy materiality of the TV *Ramayana* phenomenon of the late 1980s as a hieroglyph of a future mass departure from the temporality of clock time and a recapturing of lost temporalities for forging future times. Let us take leave of Benjamin for the moment. We return in any case to decipher his material imperatives anon over the course of *Late Colonial Sublime*. We turn instead to the ebbs and flows of romanticism under the high noon of empire. The agonistic shifts of this period fashioned Benjamin's own notions of epic on the outskirts of imperial Europe, as will be covered in chapter 3, as well as the Hindi and Urdu works arising out of British India, readings of which make up the entirety of the second part of this work.

CHAPTER 2

Romanticism's Horizons, or The Transmission of Critique

I. CONRAD ON IMPERIALISM AND THE SHIFTING SANDS OF ROMANTICISM

Introduction

If one takes Joseph Conrad's fin de siècle fiction as a historical cue, a peculiar cultural logic of the late colonial era becomes faintly visible. Whereas in metropolitan spheres this period witnessed the withering of romantic ideology, betrayed as it was by the less than honorable imperatives of imperial domination, in colonial and semicolonial realms there seems to have occurred, however briefly, an attempt at translating and redeeming this aesthetic. These two moments of the history of romanticism—the metropolitan and the colonial—are connected, I suggest, but in the disjunctive way of parallax. In the process of romanticism's reconstruction across the imperial divide, many valences were transformed, reconfigured, even reversed. Through an interaction, indeed identification of hypostatized "Eastern" and "Western" romanticisms, a powerful critique of imperialism or, more specifically, Western modernity attained profound articulation over the late colonial period.

W. H. Auden has asserted that romanticism signified the slow gestation of a revolutionary change in human sensibility and outlook, constituting a distinct "complex of attitudes and styles" but not necessarily doctrines, dogmas, or blueprints.[1] Ready-made definitions based on a search for common academic reductions miss the point of what romanticism is about. Arthur O. Lovejoy once remarked with reference to romanticism that the "singular potency which the subject has from the first possessed to excite controversy and breed divisions has in no degree diminished with the lapse of years."[2] One might suppose that with the spatial expansion of this aesthetic ideology into non-Western spheres, the expressions are multiplied and definitions further complicated. Yet I will argue that with the widening of the circumference and through the transfer of romantic tropes into a slowly decolonizing Asia, certain determinate qualities can be faintly retraced and a peculiar critical logic distilled. To grasp certain contradictory tendencies that attain acute expression in this aesthetic, the field of investigation must be expanded beyond canonical materials and historical periodizations, and attention must be brought to the point where romanticism dissolves into competing political agendas. The literary-historical task is to maintain an interface between the level of specific utterance of or about romanticism in particular moments and places and the trajectory it cuts across metropolitan and colonial spaces temporally. Alongside the formal decoding of literary works must be included the analysis of specific practices, such as the stroll or adventure, particular geographical affinities, such as the ocean, certain media, such as folk songs or woodcuts, and a multiplied set of orientations toward the sublimities of imperial power and the question of what may lie beyond its rule of measure. As a recognizable attitude and style more than a clear-cut politics, romanticism may itself be likened to a medium: through its concrete practices and materiality a dissatisfaction with emergent bourgeois utility and market civility in metropolitan domains got elaborated in the late colonial world into a critique of modernity per se.

Postcolonial studies have shown repeatedly that the most vulnerable members of the imperial order experienced modernity's self-justifying slogans of progress and freedom as lies. Metropolitan verities are lived in the colony as falsities, or what is but another way of saying the same thing: the colonial condition is the truth behind metropolitan illusions. In other words, the truth and illusion of imperial capitalist society become confounded in the colony, for here illusion is revealed to be socially necessary.[3] "Some such truth or some such illusion," remarks Marlow in Conrad's *Lord Jim*, "I don't care how you call it, there is so little difference, and the difference means so little."[4] As Conrad understood, one essential condition for imperial domination is the illusion that it generates of itself. As the colony becomes the site in which the truth of capital's illusion is contradicted yet revealed to be socially necessary, late colonial romanticism takes on dialectical valences. The late colony is the sphere in which reason, having transvalued all values in tandem with the compulsions of the imperial capitalist market, verges on self-destruction and dissolution into the Unreason of self-made unsurvivability: a sacrifice of world into the abyss of a dubious secular process. It is no surprise that romanticism in such conditions wishes to redeem for the new times all that has been dismissed or destroyed by the onslaught of modernity in the colonial hinterland: tradition, nature, love, collectivity, autonomy, truth, faith, creativity, and selfhood in their autonomy. This is perhaps overly schematic. But it does help point out how romanticism, however momentarily, attempted to put Reason itself on the path to redemption from its general fallen state as instrumental rationality.[5]

As with imperialism, the ocean is the key mediating entity between the metropolitan zone and the colony. As becomes apparent in Conrad, the ocean becomes the crucible, as it were, that turns metropolitan modernity into its colonial other. Moving toward those rejections and reversals worked out in the attitudes and styles of late colonial romanticism, our journey begins upon the seas with Conrad's fictionalization and allegorization of the waning of romantic ideology in *Lord Jim*. To cross the ocean means in this case to move beyond the experiential limits and worldview of Western imperialism.

Allegorico-Historical Tangent on Conrad's Lord Jim

When Jim finally makes it to Patusan, he leaves the vagaries of the seas behind and is finally grounded again. At this moment of the narrative, an intriguing passage puts land and sea into an antagonistic, even contradictory relationship to one another: "At the first bend he lost sight of the sea with its labouring waves for ever rising, sinking, and vanishing to rise again—the very image of struggling mankind,—and faced the immovable forests rooted deep in the soil, soaring towards the sunshine, everlasting in the shadowy might of their tradition, like life itself" (*LJ*, 147). Once upon land, Jim can finally escape the humiliation of dishonorable discharge from the imperial service for abandoning a ship, the *Patna*, full of Muslim pilgrims to Mecca as it was believed to be sinking. Through the intervention of Marlow, the narrator of Jim's story and the one who orchestrates Jim's departure to Patusan with Stein, a revolutionary romantic turned imperial merchant, Jim was able to escape the shame of past shortcomings. He is now allowed to redeem his romantic fantasy of imperial chivalry as a minor potentate on an obscure island in the far southeastern seas, far away from the *Patna* controversy that had socially enveloped him. At this central turning point in a notoriously sprawling narrative, all of the internal doubts corroding the ideological foundations of imperial domination and dissolving the link between romantic naïveté and imperial expansion—all of which were expressed over the first half of the narrative in Marlow's skeptical reconstruction of Jim's story—are finally put aside. From this point forward, as Benita Parry has recognized, the tendency of the novel's tone "to interrogate a range of assumptions fundamental to the official ethos" is arrested, and *Lord Jim* ultimately "legitimises imperialism's formal suppositions by locating the source of moral consciousness in obedience to the spirit of a mystically conceived homeland and seeking to identify the saving impulses redeeming a heartless and conscienceless project."[6] And thus, land and sea, dirt and water, become no longer neutral natural substances sustaining Jim's destiny in the novel. Instead they are elements fashioned by imperial possibilities and impediments into potent symbols mediating immanent contradictions of the imperial order. The ocean becomes the mysterious presence into which all romantic aspiration may sink and all imperial legitimacy may flounder. The ocean's sublime potency as symbol in the novel allows for the focalization of a dispersed, distant, and subaltern otherness: through its symbolism of death and mystery as well as life-sustaining dream, the dialectical underside of modernity is mediated in the novel. The sea "with its labouring waves for ever rising, sinking, and vanishing to rise again—the very image of struggling mankind" (*LJ*, 147)—channels mutely the suffering behind the colonial rejection of modernity, its formidable yet unsuccessful attempts, whether imaginative or practical, at overcoming imperialism. Summoning the experiences and truths that belie the legitimizing illusions of imperial rule and worldview, the ocean intimates danger, overflow, and drowning. The transformative powers of this ocean-as-crucible both attract and repel. They present a phenomenology of the late colonial sublime from the position of imperial inevitability, which is, by default, the perspective of *Lord Jim* shared by Conrad's other novels. The ocean is the site of a certain kind of civilizational surrender and suicide: "on that exact spot in the midst of waters he had suddenly perceived the gates of the other world flung open wide for his reception" (*LJ*, 39). On another occasion, "a silence of the sea, of the sky, merged into one indefinite immensity still as death around these saved, palpitating lives" (*LJ*, 71). Ultimately, it is from this sense of danger that the novel recoils such that Jim's destiny can be lived out in the reified conventions of obsolete and no longer credible colonial adventure narratives, but this time without any grandeur or redemptive valence.

What has made Conrad compelling for readers for more than a century is the way the illusions of modern imperialism are thickened in his masterpieces into a presence that breaks through the fiction; the illusory ideals in Conrad become a site of collective self-reflection on the historical meaning of these experiences. Imperialism is a presence that can be summoned more easily than it can be banished, ignored, or redeemed. This is no less the case for *Lord Jim*, where the eponymous antihero embodies the obsolescence of romanticism as a viable creed or attitude and the *Patna* incident serves as a metaphor for the emptiness of imperial ideals of honor and charity, let alone heroism. It is as if Conrad brings into concentrated presence what has no empirical or objective dimension but merely dispersed and diffuse existence as doubtful attitudes, bad faith, and a certain miscoloration in outlook. Such historical realities attain presence through the device of fiction—and thus can be decoded as the kinds of historical realities that require allegorical address in order to come into view. What crystallizes as a literary theme in *Lord Jim* is what is already untimely—what is dead yet lingering. The untimely allows that which is so obvious in other times as to be virtually imperceptible to finally appear.

In *Lord Jim* the untimely is nothing other than the faith in imperial beneficence and romantic innocence shared by Jim. Thus the work as a whole may be understood as an attempt to meditate upon the demise of the Western moment of romanticism in the faltering of imperial ideology. In the end, romanticism's life appears to have depended upon imperial expansion, to have been embedded within its structure of domination, conveniently sustaining its myths, irrationalities, and structures of feeling. Though tarnishing the soul of Western subjectivity, the rejection and undoing of imperialism appear unimaginable in Conrad. That limit point is, again, marked by the ocean in *Lord Jim*. As the postromantic figure of Stein asserts, "A man that is born falls into a dream like a man who falls into the sea. If he tries to climb out into the air as inexperienced people endeavor to do, he drowns—*nicht wahr*?" (*LJ*, 129). "Dream" in this case merely expresses the wish to redeem imperialism for the homeland, though its ugliness always threatens to awaken the dreamer. The sleep-sustaining dream from this perspective is lived as a nightmare on the other end of the imperial divide. To awaken from such a nightmare requires breaking through the limits of conscious imaginative powers of the likes of Conrad and his characters. This was the critical or negative task of late romanticism in the colonial world: to at least imaginarily produce a vision of the world that does not take Western imperial presuppositions as the starting point. If it was redemptive, it had to pass through diremption.

The erosion of faith in empire and civilizational malaise marked the beginning of the end of classical imperialism. This slow historical shift attains expression allegorically in *Lord Jim* through murky limit figures, generally dream and nightmare metaphors. The work begs for inquiry into all that which is intimated, figured powerfully as the ocean, but that remains utterly eclipsed from analysis. What underworld is the ocean's surface covering? What negative mystery or imagination lurks in this beyond of Conrad's narrative?[7] In the tale of Jim's fall from imperial grace and his attempt to redeem himself one learns how imperial ideology entered into a state of malaise and misgiving as it came into contradiction with imperial realities and just how much romanticism as a specific attitude and style, but also as a certain structure of feeling and belief, swam or sank with imperial ideology in metropolitan society. Both Conrad and his colonial counterparts on the other side of the imperial divide entertain strategies for redeeming imperial failings. The conventional imperialist strategy maintained by default by Marlow over the course of the narrative proves unsatisfying and is ultimately haunted by other anti-imperial or postimperial possibilities, such as Marlow's affected Eastern mysticism. These absences will be further conjured by the end of this chapter.

"Trust a boat on the high seas to bring out the Irrational that lurks at the bottom of every thought, sentiment, sensation, emotion," encourages Marlow (*LJ*, 75). Yet, as Marlow understands, a sinking boat on the imperial seas does even more: it draws out of the submerged realities and the disturbing truth elements behind seemingly inevitable structures of illusion. Such is the case with the *Patna* incident in *Lord Jim*. As Thomas C. Moser has made abundantly evident in the "Sources" section of his critical edition of *Lord Jim*, the central *Patna* incident of the novel is a fictionalization of a controversial historical event: the abandonment of the steamship *Jeddah* by its English captains and officers while carrying nearly a thousand Muslim pilgrims to Mecca in 1880.[8] As the *Jeddah* was flying under the British flag, the incident symptomatized for the metropolitan public a general breakdown of the imperial system, for here the duties and codes of the imperial order were betrayed by its highest representatives on the seas. It is certain that Conrad read the reports in the London papers during his stay there in August 1880, and the buzz of this sensational event became ever thicker as he made his way by sea to Sydney via Singapore. (Incidentally, this trip would itself require Conrad's abandonment of a ship, the *Palestine*, with the rest of the crew and passengers as well as make possible a direct encounter with the infamous *Jeddah* at port in Singapore.)

Key for our purposes is not the veracity of this historical event but the metaphorical resonance and allegorical depth that Conrad brings to his fictionalization of it. A "hint of a destructive fate ready for us all" connected to the hopelessness of any really viable alternative lingers everywhere in *Lord Jim.* Such apprehension is concentrated in "the doubt of the sovereign power enthroned in a fixed standard of conduct" (*LJ*, 35). The voice of Marlow captures the ambivalences and impasses of thinking through the problem of the imperial divide from the metropolitan angle, yet the murky oceanic depths that this voice seeks to fathom give negative shape to the pervasive doubts about imperial power and Western Civilization as such by the fin de siècle. As Parry notes, "the fears expressed by Conrad's contemporaries, optimistic socialists and authoritarian pessimists alike, that the West was embarking on a course that would lead to its own destruction," attains immediate expression through Marlow's voice.[9] Yet this voice's most diabolical utterances mediate the vast shift of allegiance from metropolitan centers of the imperial system to its peripheries and the rise of social, cultural, and political imaginaries that did not observe the sanctity of the imperial project. Jim's abandonment of the faithful pilgrims on the *Patna* signifies the lie of imperial chivalry and the impossibility of actualizing romantic ideals within imperial structures. Within the diamond in the crown of the British Empire, India, of which the name Patna is a metonym, the emergent dissident critique of "un-British" rule suggested that the violation of the empire's liberal promises had become routine. Bureaucratic exercises such as the inquiry into the *Patna* disaster reveal only the degree to which imperial power can disavow its darker nature and shift it imaginarily across the imperial divide. The object of the inquiry, "held on the appointed day to satisfy the law," as Marlow observes, "was not the fundamental why, but the superficial how, of this affair" (*LJ*, 37, 38). In order to grasp what the true implications of this event are, Marlow realizes that he must step out of the official imperial blindnesses and disavowals, but in doing so he risks compromising his allegiance to the empire. Intimations of dark dialectical movement and muted possibilities of other modes of existence surface in his speech. But such intimations require for their full actualization the dissolution of territorial identifications that ground nation and race. This proves unimaginable for Marlow. They require, in other words, dissolution into the oceanic otherness symbolizing the wretched of the imperial system: "the sea with its labouring waves for ever rising, soaring, sinking, and vanishing to rise again—the very image of struggling mankind" (*LJ*, 147). The way to truth takes shape in such allegorizations, yet the way is not devoid of obstacles. The fortunes of the metropolitan moment of romanticism, Conrad seems to suggest, rode on the success or failure of imperialism to fulfill desires and dreams that exceeded the constraints and compromises of metropolitan domesticity. The critical dimension of romantic ideals are frustrated by the spiritually tainting iron-clad quasi-bureaucratic logic of imperial domination. Imperialism itself is no progression of the human collective but rather the inexorable return to the scene of primal sacrifice: the renunciation of the alienated self for the preservation of imperial society's illusion: "The conquest of the earth, which mostly means the taking it away from those who have a different complexion or slightly flatter nose than ourselves, is not a pretty thing when you look into it too much. What redeems it is the idea only. An idea at the back of it; not a sentimental pretence but an idea; and an unselfish belief in the idea—something you can set up, and bow down before and offer a sacrifice to."[10] As Parry observes, "Imperialism itself is perceived as the dark within Europe."[11] Its shadow darkens the future, obscuring the possibilities of redemption.

It is on the question of redemption that *Lord Jim* reveals itself, Parry writes, as "a fiction which discovers the ultimate sanctions for moral consciousness to reside in the indwelling essence of the nation and the race."[12] The unfulfilling resolutions that Marlow wishes to force upon the story of Jim require gathering the entirety of Jim's divided experience under the fold of the imperial West. Thus it becomes clear that the imperial allegiance is chosen over the deterritorializing allegiance of oceanic belonging once the imperial divide is experienced. The social body to which Marlow relegates Jim's story is the empire, and it is imperial territory that welcomes back all those who have gone outward to expand imperial glory. Though "going home must be like going to render an account" and "one must return with a clear conscience," the imperial territory is welcoming even to the most wayward of its faithful subjects so long as the otherness of oceanic dissolution and cultural death is given up for the life-sustaining traditions of the imperial nation. "At the first bend he lost sight of the sea with its labouring waves for ever rising, sinking, and vanishing to rise again—the very image of struggling mankind,—and faced the immovable forests rooted deep in the soil, soaring towards the sunshine, everlasting in the shadowy might of their tradition, like life itself" (*LJ*, 147). This very terrestrial homecoming for Jim is but a step to the ultimate homecoming Marlow has in store for Jim's legend: "We return to face our superiors, our kindred, our friends—those whom we obey, and those whom we love; but even they who have those for whom home holds no dear face, no familiar voice,—even they have to meet the spirit that dwells within the land, under its sky, in its trees—a mute friend, judge, and inspirer" (*LJ*, 134). In the end, Conrad remarks in the author's note that accompanied the republication of the novel seventeen years later, Jim is "one of us" (*LJ*, 6).

Marlow's default choice of reterritorialization within the heart of the imperial tradition sits uncomfortably with his erstwhile dramatization of, in Parry's succinct rendering, a "radical critique of imperialist ideology that is directed against a spiritually repressive culture demanding unreflexive obedience to the laws of order and progress, misrepresenting social utilities in the definition of knowledge to exclude meditations on alternative human conditions."[13] (*LJ*, 97).

And thus occurs a splitting of the central subjectivity in *Lord Jim* between the territorial and the oceanic, between the self-sacrificing subject of the empire and his sacrificed self, between the compromised ideals of the imperial order and the dream of self-fulfillment through the experiencing of life's intensities. The full unraveling of Jim's subjectivity into a quasi-collective historical spirit whose boundaries become indistinguishable from the expanse and depth of the ocean and the limits of dreams occurs through the figural externalization of the self sacrificed by the self, in this case, Stein. As an erstwhile revolutionary but now successful imperial merchant who has long since given up his romantic dreams, Stein understands perfectly the tragic dialectic of Enlightenment's normative subjectivity. Horkheimer and Adorno economically relay this same contradiction: "The nimble-witted man survives only at the cost of his own dream, which he forfeits by disintegrating his own magic along with that of the powers outside him."[14]

Recognizing in Jim his own renounced self, Stein diagnoses Jim's condition as romantic. "But *is he*?" Marlow queries.

> "*Gewiss*," he said. . . . "Evident! What is that by inward pain makes him know himself? . . ."
>
> At that moment [continues Marlow] it was difficult to believe in Jim's existence—starting from a country parsonage, blurred by crowds of men as by clouds of dust, silenced by the clashing claims of life and death in a material world—but his imperishable reality came to me with a convincing, with an irresistible force! I saw it vividly, as though in our progress through the lofty silent rooms amongst fleeting gleams of light and the sudden revelations of human figures stealing with flickering flames within unfathomable depths, we had approached nearer to absolute Truth, which, like Beauty itself, floats elusive, obscure, half-submerged in the silent waters of mystery. (*LJ*, 131)

Oceanic Interlude

> From the point of view of epic, existence is an ocean. Nothing is more epic than the sea. One can of course react to the sea in different ways—for example, lie on the beach, listen to the surf, and collect the shells that it washes up on the shore. This is what the epic writer does.
>
> —Walter Benjamin, "The Crisis of the Novel"

> I will show you the measures of the resounding sea, being altogether unskilled in seafaring and in ships . . . but even so I will tell the thought of aegis-bearing Zeus; for the Muses have taught me to sing unlimited song.
>
> —Hesiod, *Works and Days*

> The Pacific is the end of the UNKNOWN which Homer's and Dante's Ulysses opened men's eyes to. END of individual responsible only to himself. Ahab is full stop.
>
> —Charles Olson, "Call Me Ishmael"

> We are forced, now, to confront the ocean not as myth element, as figure of transcendence of imperial sublime, of imagined cross-cultural commons, but in its biological, microbiological, and chemical materiality, all of which have been and are being transformed by human activity in the Capitalocene.
>
> —Christopher Connery, "Thalassophilia and Its Discontents"

In Hugo, the crowd enters literature as an object of contemplation. The surging ocean is its model, and the thinker who reflects on this eternal spectacle is the true explorer of the crowd, in which he loses himself as he loses himself in the roaring of the sea.

—Walter Benjamin, "The Paris of the Second Empire in Baudelaire"

The existence of Mickey Mouse is . . . a dream [to make up for the sadness and discouragement of the day—a dream that shows us in its realized form the simple but magnificent existence for which the energy is lacking in reality] for contemporary man. His is [a] life full of miracles—miracles that not only surpass the wonders of technology, but make fun of them. For the most extraordinary thing about them is that they all appear, quite without any machinery, to have been improvised out of the body of Mickey Mouse, out of his supporters and persecutors, and out of the most ordinary pieces of furniture, as well as from trees, clouds, and the sea.

—Walter Benjamin, "Experience and Poverty"

Brecht spoke of a "worker's monarch"—and I drew an analogy between such an organism and the grotesque freaks of nature which, in the shape of horned fish or other monsters, are brought to light from out of the deep sea.

—Walter Benjamin, "Diary Entries, 1938"

II. CRITICAL REPRISIONS: ASIAN REARTICULATIONS OF ROMANTICISM UNDER IMPERIALISM

No idea can seize a people's soul unless, in some sense, it is the people's own. External influences may wake it up from its deep unconscious slumber; but they cannot, so to speak, create it out of nothing.

—Muhammad Iqbal, *The Development of Metaphysics in Persia*

Introduction: Three Images in the History of Romanticism in the East

Whereas in Conrad's *Lord Jim*, romanticism is given thick description to make palpable its vanishing presence as an abstract governing ethos of empire, in the Asian spheres to which Conrad's imagination had little access, romanticism simultaneously attained a distinctly embodied concreteness.[15] That is to say, in a range of non-Western locations, romanticism had sedimented into a demeanor one could

Figure 1. An iconic portrait of Muhammad Iqbal "in a characteristic pose as the romantic poet, lost in thought." Paris, 1933. Photograph by Umrao Singh Shergill.

adopt while posing for one's portrait. The famous photograph of Muhammad Iqbal plaintively resting his head on his hand, with his eyes lightly closed in reverie, demonstrates along with other photographs from across Asia in the interwar period how much romantic aesthetics had attained a consciously adoptable form. "Muhammad Iqbal photographed in a characteristic pose as the romantic poet, lost in thought," is the caption of a recent publication of this portrait.[16]

At the beginning of a comparable formation of romantic self-positioning in China—in the Creation Society—Tian Han and Guo

Moruo could also appropriate an unmistakable romantic air. Admiring together the verses of Goethe and Heine, exploring nature's sights, improvising poetry inspired by wine and spirits into the night brought them ineluctably to self-portraiture. A photograph taken in the early 1920s shows them standing side by side holding a wreath in the likeness of Goethe and Schiller memorialized in the Weimar Theaterplatz statue.[17] Likewise, Rabindranath Tagore and Okakura Tenshin embodied the mystique of Eastern seers for the camera, presaging the formations of self-styled romantic schools of thought in northern India and Japan, respectively, just a few years later. Despite the modern medium in which romanticism was being reproduced in twentieth-century Asia, with its distinct surface nature, photographic portrayals of Tagore as a romantic artist index a deeper temporal connection between Asia and Europe in the history of this aesthetic.

This is the famous history of Europeans fashioning themselves as Orientals and thus as all the more romantic. Portraits of Tagore especially reflect earlier images, such as those of a turbaned Lord Byron or the sepia tones of Sir Richard Burton in religious costume. These earlier self-portrayals of romantic thought predate the Asian versions by roughly a century. At that moment, Europe was awash in the new discourses and poetics of an enchanted East. This classical Orient was where Friedrich Schlegel and many others thought one must look to find the ultimate romanticism, *le romantisme suprême*, as Raymond Schwab puts it.[18] Yet just as historians of Western romanticism justly consider the Orientalist motifs to be merely faddish and superficial, one wonders if there is not equally an autonomous logic behind the glossy black-and-white surfaces framing romantic self-fashioners in Asia.

The modern mediations of the Asian moment of late romanticism—not simply photography but broad swaths of aesthetic ideology as well—occlude complicated past interactions. Moreover they obscure the internal historical logic indexed by Asian romanticism (or neoromanticism). The circle of appropriations has a gravitational pull. The magnetism of this circular poetics itself structured the acts of poets like Iqbal, who self-consciously chose those literary styles, genres, and devices borrowed earlier by Europeans from the Orient as a sign of their own romantic ethos.[19] Yet confinement to the circle threatens to analogize the superficiality of the mechanically reproduced image. It leaves undisturbed the modern commonsensical rendering of the Asian moment of this history of romanticism especially: as belated imitation. This, ostensibly, is just the history of an East belatedly receiving a modernity it is always trying to catch up with, coming to romanticism only once Europe has turned to the stark future of modernism.

Recent research on Asian articulations of romanticism, I suggest, delineate another kind of historical trajectory that would remain obscure by this rather trite account. Just as European romanticism was pregnant with a historicity that digested Eastern motifs—such as Blake's "Brama in the East"[20]—into an internal local logic, Asian neoromanticism can arguably be seen as metabolizing troubling dynamics of an even more globalized late modern culture in crisis. When the celebrated cultural historian Wang Hui gave an interview titled "Contemporary Chinese Thought and the Question of Modernity," he may as well have been describing much of Asia in the early twentieth century: "Modern Chinese thought is characterized by an anti-modern modernity."[21] The devolution of the critical, deeply negative moment in romanticism led beyond the critique of bourgeois norms and instrumental rationality in early European romanticism to a critique of modernity as such. To summarize, the target of the Asian schools of romanticism I will survey was nothing less than a reified notion of the modern as a whole. The crosshairs of the Asian critical weaponry focused initially on the Western powers imposing the new dispensation as a standard, leading to the disintegration of the life-worlds of the colony, semicolony, and informal spheres of influence, or India, China, and Japan, respectively. Yet it turned out that simply targeting a foreign power was not an adequate solution, for the sovereignty that the compromised powers of the Asian sphere wished to reestablish required the implementation of the very kinds of modernization programs that undermined the customary *Lebenswelt* these powers wished to secure. The bind in which the Asian world found itself concentrated the logic of an aporia of modern reason: the elixir of political hope amounted to a poison for one's cultural ambitions. I will uncover how influential intellectuals from key locations of a highly pressured if not totally subjugated Asia responded to this aporia by airing sharp critiques of a cold, formalistic scientism and expressing a keen desire for a new (anti)mythology to replace the obsolete one of yesteryear and help assert equality with the imperial West in the present. By tracing the mutually contradictory political programs into which romanticism eventually dissolved in China, Japan, and India, it becomes possible to detect what were perhaps long-standing disparate political tendencies grinding against each other under the cover of an appealing and apparently innocuous, apolitical romanticism.

The Dialectic of Reason, or Myth after Modernization

What is it about the unfolding of modernity—in other words, capitalism—that gives rise to myth? At the core of romanticism in the late colonial world is this question. While the parameters of this problematic are wider than the critical compass of anyone anywhere, the insights of Benjamin, Adorno, and, to a lesser extent, Horkheimer help us grasp the transmogrification of reason into the rebirth of myth under specifically imperial capitalist conditions. Whereas many of their contemporaries presented speculative accounts for a decline of the West, these key figures of the Frankfurt School interconnected their theories of a paradoxical rise of myth in modernity on the sociocultural dynamics of the commodity-form itself. Their immediate precarity in Nazi Germany lent validity to their theories of the potential for capitalist social relations to consolidate into structures of manipulation, domination, and encampment. When Adorno and Horkheimer observed the activation of totalitarian apparatuses of social repression in liberal polities such as the United States, they speculated on the dystopic state of consumerist distraction extending unchanged into oblivion, eclipsing memories of the past and damaging the prospects of livability in the future.

Yet the potential dynamism implicit in imperial capital's social relations was often dimmed for them on account of a nearly institutionalized theoretical neglect of the extra-European world. Thus, with the benefit of hindsight, the critical task becomes one of illuminating their blind spots by inscribing their insights into a wider geography and a more precise historical picture than was generally possible from a late imperial European perspective. Overcoming these historically imposed limitations helps to situate the dialectic of Enlightenment at the heart of the Frankfurt School's critique of modernity as part and parcel of a late colonial aporia wherein Enlightenment always only completes itself as quasi-mythical beast.[22] Turning one's attention to late romanticisms in the Asian world allows for the reframing of this barbaric dynamic from the perspective of those ruined in the process. In other words, it helps when reconsidering the collective—though highly differentiated and fragmentary—experience of a singular historical phenomenon. Through a radicalizing shift toward the politics of modernism, especially the relationship between Marxism and modernism, Raymond Williams made the acute observation that the modernism being institutionalized and canonized in his day was merely "a highly selected version of the modern which then offers to appropriate the whole of modernity." For Williams, modernism had already become a fixed, frozen form abstracted from its lived content. In order to break out of this attenuated yet normalized version of the modern experience, Williams suggests, "we must search out and counterpose an alternative tradition taken from the neglected works left in the wide margin of the century" for the sake of "a modern *future* in which community may be imagined again."[23] In taking up Williams's suggestion and extending the circumference of analysis into the late colonial sphere, the possibility obtains for reconfiguring the critical potentialities of Enlightenment, especially the notion of equality; furthermore, the kind of mythologies to which Enlightenment oddly gives rise, including those that are critical of the constriction of reason to forms of domination and control unleashed by imperial power, can be grasped within a singular historical constellation.

The seemingly common encounter with modernity as a generator of new myth-laden phantasmagorias such as that of the pure ethnos and the observation that "correspondences are at work between the modern technical world and the archaic symbol world" perplexed many the world over by the early twentieth century.[24] Horkheimer and Adorno's controversial *Dialectic of Enlightenment* (*Dialektik der Aufklärung*, 1944) undertakes the difficult project of explaining this phenomenon bequeathed to them, most immediately, by their late colleague Benjamin in dispersed writings.[25] In "Walter Benjamin's Theory of Myth," the literary historian Winfried Menninghaus redraws the deeply rent terrain upon which the critical theorist was operating. On the one hand, Enlightenment dismissed myth as a prescientific explanation of nature and a hindrance before truth; on the other, romanticism called for the resuscitation of myth as an antidote to the destabilization of "binding horizons of justification or legitimation" precipitated by the capitalist social form, racked as it is by division and antagonism.[26] Between a privative notion of reason in Enlightenment and a reactionary reactivation of myth in romanticism there was no choosing for Benjamin. As each option was unpromising on its own and exclusive of the other, Benjamin aimed to push toward a horizon in which the two would find unintended reconciliation. As Adorno reflects in "A Portrait of Walter Benjamin," "The reconciliation of myth is the theme of Benjamin's philosophy."[27] This reconciliation involved the dissolution of the ideological containments of each term: against romantic conservatism, Benjamin launched a critique that appropriates the *topoi* of

Enlightenment while leaving out its contents (scientism, progress, etc.); against the attenuated reason of Enlightenment, Benjamin presents the dialectic of intoxication (*Rausch*) as a means of freeing reason from all constraints and releasing new modes of human solidarity and connection with nature.[28]

Menninghaus's mimetic retracing of Benjamin's notion of myth, however thorough it may be, leaves unanswered the antimythic apocalypticism in his thought. Nevertheless his intervention does help gauge how his successors in the Frankfurt School elaborated the problematic. The redemptive urge underlying some of Benjamin's attempts at undoing the antinomian—either/or—structuration of the relation between Enlightenment and romanticism gives way in Horkheimer and Adorno's *Dialectic of Enlightenment.* There are nevertheless several points of convergence between Benjamin's work and that of his Frankfurt School survivors. Readers may refer to the next chapter for a survey of key moments of Benjamin's own dialectic of modern rationality and intoxication by "colonial" substances. I will here concentrate on Horkheimer and Adorno's magnum opus, distilling what might be considered the lesson (*Lehre*) that Benjamin left for them to ponder, and drawing out those theoretical points that illuminate the impetus behind Asian romanticisms' efforts to restitute (anti)myth against bare instrumentality. Much of the brunt of what Horkheimer and Adorno call "Enlightenment" fell on the colonial world. In this sphere, the implementation of "reason" took the guise of fated necessity and became synonymous with the destruction of old life-worlds and the perishing of genus and species, the rendering of everything, human and otherwise, small, as if before an absolute sovereign. It thus provoked responses aimed at forging a new subjectivity that could, as the nearly ubiquitous trope goes, re-create a new dwelling, in other words, a new myth (*muthos*) and home (*nostos*), a new "everyday" premised on an epochal overcoming of modern dystopia.

Horkheimer and Adorno pitch their narrative regarding what has befallen modern civilization on the plane of historical epic and in terms of tragedy. Speaking from the aftermath of Enlightenment's devastation—from post-Nazi ruin and exile—the authors reconstruct a singular Western narrative of an agonistic struggle with nature in which human beings' increasing technical mastery over physical forces is "purchased," as the philosopher Raymond Geuss puts it, "at a very high price which we have come systematically to underestimate: at the cost of self-repression, alienation, and the exploitation of inferiors in a social system divided into classes."[29] Reason, in the process of its unfolding, undermines itself. Though there is "an increasing distantiation from Marxian terminology" over the course of its making, *Dialectic of Enlightenment* does at the very least make its argument for reason's self-destruction intersect with the culture industry, in other words, with Marx's concept of the commodity-form and commodity-fetish.[30] The commodity-form is predicated on and generative of control and technical advancement, yet the rationality it fosters differentiates itself fundamentally for Horkheimer and Adorno from reason's originally immanent potentials. It loses these in becoming indistinguishable from bare instrumentality. The process of commodification reveals essential axioms of Enlightenment: just as the process of commodification must subordinate the use-value of the commodity, which becomes increasingly contingent, to exchange-value (for the accumulation of value), the norms of Enlightenment knowledge are reduced to "identifying" knowledge, that is, knowledge that distinguishes objects and identifies general concepts under which individual things can be subsumed and, furthermore, to reduce the meaning of anything to mere utility.[31]

Thus, the story that Horkheimer and Adorno tell is one in which one concept of reason—predicated initially on a harmony between subjective consciousness and a totality considered to encompass both the self and the phenomenal world as "the good life"—is eroded from within. Rising against the myth that subtends classical reason, Enlightenment suborns the technical control that reason allows to the imperative of domination. So great is the will to domination in Horkheimer and Adorno's Enlightenment rationality that reason itself falls under its tracks, releasing myth again as if from the genie's magic lamp. In the world governed by the classical notion of reason, the value and rationality of one's actions can be judged with reference to how much they harmonize with the social collectivity and the natural environment, whose health in turn is assessed by the liberty they lend to human potential. In contradistinction, the rationality associated with Enlightenment dismisses the notion of totality itself as a remnant of crude superstition or metaphysics. Enlightenment fuels capitalism's propensity to break up integrative wholes into separate realms of external and internal nature, both of which are differentiated and abstracted from society in the process of categorization. As the classical notion of reason as integrative harmony and spontaneous self-fulfillment is dismissed as antiquated fancy, reason is reduced to utility, calculation, and objectification. These all buttress the modern self-determining subject, becoming his or her means for the suborning of empirical substances to human control and predictability. Yet as this ability becomes the primary standard by which to judge a system of beliefs rational or not, those forms of thought that do not hold instrumentality as their sole aim—and thus prove technically deficient in comparison—are rendered superstitious and dismissed by Enlightenment. Enlightenment rationality thus supplants the sovereignty of classical reason while betraying itself as one-dimensional, inflexible, and narrow. Having the technical upper hand over all competing knowledge systems, Enlightenment becomes vampire-like. Sucking the authority out of all that it deems merely superstitious, Enlightenment reveals itself ultimately as a totalitarian creature in Horkheimer and Adorno's eyes: "Any intellectual resistance it encounters merely increases its strengths."[32] In reverting to mythic creatureliness, Enlightenment formalizes all value, but in doing so it begins to eat away at the very properties of reason it initially offered. (In the negative dialectic of modernity's impending global ecological crisis, universalized instrumentality too will be measured by its utility.)

These moments of modern reason's self-destruction give inadvertent birth to myth as the revenge of nature in Horkheimer and Adorno's elaboration of a humanly entwined *Naturgeschichte*. At its natural extremes, Enlightenment reverts to myth. Thus, in its emptying of time and spatialization of power, Enlightenment reproduces unwittingly fundamental features of classical metaphysical thought. Following in the tracks of Benjamin, the authors point out a peculiar fatalism on the horizons of Enlightenment: "The arid wisdom which acknowledges nothing new under the sun, because all the pieces in the meaningless game have been played out, all the great thoughts have been thought, all possible discoveries can be construed in advance, and human beings are defined by self-preservation through adaptation—this barren wisdom merely reproduces the fantastic doctrine it rejects: the sanction of fate. . . . Whatever might be different is made the same. That is the verdict which critically sets the boundaries to possible experience."[33] The thoroughly surveyed and controlled world created by Enlightenment imposes limits to innate potentials given in modernity itself. Total bureaucratization makes for a self-limiting existence in a world increasingly divested of critique. The elimination of all exits from a world of one's own making is but one of the many ways in which Enlightenment undermines its pretentions of self-mastery and self-determination and finds itself absorbed back into a new, evermore overwhelming mythic nature.

This brief retracing of Horkheimer and Adorno's steps on a theoretical foray beyond the limits of Enlightenment and onto the threshold of myth is but one of several instances in which modernity proves generative of new structures of phantasmagoria and allegorizations of antiquity. Mythical fear reappears, for the authors, when, for instance, positivism makes a taboo of any "outside" to its empiricist immanence. Science itself is abstracted of all motives that may have guided it. It emerges as pure as any formalist aestheticism: "a system of isolated signs devoid of any intention transcending the system."[34] In its artificiality, the world Enlightenment furnishes is the modern counterpart to the ancient Greek *muthos* (what is said): an unchanging universe that can be taken as inexplicably given. The commodity-fetish is taken to emanate a distracting dream world as powerful as any narcotic for coping with the deeply disturbing mechanisms of domination and exploitation. Its prevalence over the media results in the slow erosion of the classic bourgeois public sphere and communicative rationality; instead it produces a conformism that compromises the critical function of culture and the autonomy of the individual intellect. As Adorno later specifies, previously "culture, in the true sense, did not simply accommodate itself to human beings"; in contrast to the contemporary culture industry's full affirmation of all things existing, "it always simultaneously raised a protest against the petrified relations under which they lived, thereby honouring them."[35]

Between the fragments that make up *Dialectic of Enlightenment* emerges a faintly recognizable ambivalence regarding the category of myth. In one of its guises, myth is containable and made compatible with Enlightenment; in another it emerges as pure Dionysian force. The problematic is left unresolved, undercutting the argument of the work from within its own negativity, as if expressly. The contradictory tendencies Horkheimer and Adorno manifest in the category of myth, I argue, can be seen as markers of divergent political valences that informed romanticism all along and came into relief in the political sphere as romanticism came apart as an ideological terrain. That is to say, seen from the vantage point of non-Western spheres such as their own contemporary Asia, Horkheimer and Adorno's endless seesaw of Enlightenment and myth appears simultaneously replete with translatable insights and peculiarly bereft of any historical sense of a sociopolitical dynamic that could break the deadlock. In abstracting itself from the politics of imperialism, their analysis is unable to gauge new dialectics of Enlightenment and myth under decolonization. The fact that Horkheimer and Adorno were unable to register the historical dynamism fomented by the global spread of the concept of equality—a key pillar of the Enlightenment—had a crippling effect on their diagnosis of these key categories and of their larger sociohistorical context as well. Nevertheless, their pessimism implicitly resonated with anticolonial views of Enlightenment progress. The extended temporality of epic in their excursus "Odysseus or Myth and Enlightenment" undercut the Enlightenment notions of a civilizing mission, just as decolonization heaped skepticism on the rhetoric of improvement and the temporality of the "not-yet" that it implied for self-rule. Yet it is worth pointing out how they diverge from Benjamin on this front as well. Whereas Benjamin intimates in his late work how the deterioration of the progress narrative would go hand in hand with immediate revolution in the colonial spheres, Horkheimer and Adorno seemed impervious to the kind of temporality that was thus emergent in their midst.[36] The result is a limited perspective on the ensuing dynamics of twentieth- and twenty-first-century systemic and antisystemic movements that were already under way. Horkheimer and Adorno's narrative concludes in stasis: their stunted dialectic erroneously depicts their historical moment as stuck at a standstill. In this respect, the authors depart from their late colleague perhaps fundamentally: nothing that issues from the dour *Dialectic of Enlightenment* has the futural charge of *Sprengung* that Benjamin had intimated beyond the antinomy of Enlightenment and romanticism and that decolonization manifested in this very historical moment.[37]

The wider perspective needed to gauge both the insights as well as blindnesses of classical Critical Theory is provided by the vantage point of the revolt against the West and the onset of decolonization in the Asian world over the early decades of the twentieth century. In China, Japan, and India, imperial economies had already begun to reconstitute the cultural sphere in the reflection of the commodity-form, with just the same potentialities for phantasmagoric politics and consumerist distraction. The alterations in the cultural spheres that imperial pressures and capitalist social relations had precipitated were abrupt and enormous. "Because of the pressure this new civilization exerts on us," wrote the influential Japanese novelist Natsume Soseki, "we have no choice but to develop in unnatural ways."[38] Alongside the slow erosion of Mughal hegemony over the subcontinent, India witnessed in Bengal the rise of "the first Asian social group of any size whose mental world was transformed through its interactions with the West," according to the Indian historian Tapan Raychaudhuri.[39] Simultaneously China experienced, according to Wang Hui, "the disintegration of the axiomatic world outlook of the late Qing period" and the defeat of "the heavenly principles of worldview."[40] Considering its aggressive cultural policies premised on Enlightenment disregard for all that could be deemed superstitious, it is not surprising to hear echoes of a culture of homelessness across the differentiated political terrains of China, Japan, and India after the rise of Western imperialism. Thus, "it is a fact that ours is a literature of the lost home," wrote Kobayashi Hideo in 1933. Likewise in Bengal, explains the neoconservative subalternist academic Dipesh Chakrabarty, "a haunting desire on the part of poets to return in their future lives to the land of Bengal" attained popular expression in the last years of colonial rule. On the tongues of the Bengali masses was a song with these opening lines: "In a hundred years, may you and I return to a home in this very land."[41]

The situation naturally generated widespread and diverse efforts to secure modes of dwelling in the ruins of the old civilizations, however much they would or would not resemble the integrated *Lebenswelt* imagined of classical antiquity. I turn now to the disintegration of romanticism in its final Eastern moment to register the cultural dynamism with which the Enlightenment principle of equality was elaborated in the moment of decolonization, anti-Westernism, and critiques of modernity—how, in other words, critique was transmitted and transformed, how romanticism came undone by generating divergent, mutually incompatible political energies.

The Formation of Asian Schools of Romanticism: China, Japan, India

CHINA

Lu Xun's quirky yet deeply penetrating "On Photography," published in 1925, has been translated by Kirk Denton, who correctly takes the work to be an "allegory" but restricts its allegorical scope immediately, and oddly, to the lesson of a different piece of writing altogether.[42] Despite Lu's presentation of photography as *the* marker of an entirely new epistemological, material, and social logic in contemporary Chinese society, photography is reduced in Denton's hands to merely the question of mimesis. Photography for Denton "symbolizes the Western aesthetic of representation."[43] As cultural representative of the foreign West, photography is immediately contrasted with an equally self-evident Chinese artistic sensibility. These reductive assumptions allow for the allegory to be restricted to that of "the reception of mimesis in the Chinese cultural context."[44] Lu's own rich set of reflections on this particular medium, especially how it is incorporated into Chinese cultural practices with unexpected, even uncanny results, is ignored. Instead, Denton unfairly substitutes the generative and deeply problem-laden qualities of the photographic medium in Lu's essay with a citation from another of his works: "'What a pity,' Lu Xun wrote elsewhere[!]," which is Denton's way of ventriloquizing Chinese authenticity while controlling it, "'that the moment foreign things reach China they change their color as if they had fallen into a vat of black dye.'"[45]

What follows is an alternative reading of "On Photography," working from Denton's own very serviceable translation. This reading asks first what Lu's essay itself has to say about this medium and to what extent it allegorizes not merely a cultural collision between East and West, demonstrating some unshakeable intransigence of both, but also a fundamental aporia of modernity, the very aporia to which late romanticism in China was a direct response. Like Wang Hui, I see Lu as a thinker of the paradoxes that modernity generates on the imperial fringes, an explorer of historical predicaments whose expositions, he says, "break . . . away from that simplistic China-West comparative representation, but also contain . . . doubts about the common belief of that age—in evolution, or progress."[46]

From a vantage point fluctuating constantly between that of scientism and superstition, "On Photography" reflects back on the period when the presence of "the foreign devils" of Western imperial powers had become palpable as a fundamental shift in the perceptual apparatus itself; in other words, when Enlightenment science and utilitarianism had reached hegemonic status in Chinese society, initiating a process of reconfiguring traditional worldviews through the lens, literally, of modern categories. The accounts Lu gives are patently absurdist but capture a fundamental truth of the new dispensation unfolding over the breakup of the Qing dynasty. This is that the modern technoscientific order imposed by the imperial powers is ruthless and vehemently reconstitutive of all relations according to an instrumental logic: at that time, "one often heard in S City men and women of all ages discussing how the foreign devils would pluck out people's eyes." This plucking of eyes, the narrator intimates, marks a fundamental shift in the relations between humans and their environment imposed as the new Enlightenment. The indexical powers of photography and linked technologies now mediate a natural environment dramatically opened to new uses. Everything, even "the hearts they tore out of people," is put to a practical use. The plucked eyes are pickled, according to one villager, so that they can be turned into wire: "Every year the foreigners would add some to the fence they were constructing to keep the Chinese from escaping on the day the foreign soldiers arrived." This sense of capture and enclosure is then embodied in the next practical use to which the "foreign devils" subject these eyes: photography. "Here the reason is clear enough," remarks the narrator, making oblique reference to the transparency of the medium just when its meaning is most obscure, "and there is no need to elaborate, for one has only to be face to face with someone and a little photograph of oneself is bound to appear in their pupils."[47] This enigmatic statement brings out a peculiar paradox, which I elaborate on later. Paradox upon paradox: as unfounded as the Chinese notions regarding the "foreign devils" and their machinations may appear, they nonetheless penetrate the bewildering logic of reification in their midst. But for the moment, a scientific perspective, which understands the human visual apparatus to have properties akin to the camera, now sees the reflection in the eye as a photograph. The plucked-out eye, steeped in the new techno-instrumental rationality of Enlightenment, is reinstalled in the modern Chinese subject, reflecting back to him or her the world's now obvious scientific structure and the utility of what always already existed.

What is beguiling about this new, technologically grounded "witchcraft" in Lu's essay is how it straddles all at once the presentation of reality "as it is," on the one hand, and allows for the staging of quasi-mythic illusion, on the other. Photography is taken ultimately to mediate the conditions of possibility as well as senescence of romanticism in late colonial Asia: the new technoscientific hegemony demands the reconstruction of traditional forms in new media, seeking to prolong the illusion of an "eternal" Asia and the stability of cultural values, however ethereal they may be, in media that themselves grow frail and obsolete by the day. As the narrator surveys the various ways in which photography was becoming incorporated into newly commoditized and retraditionalized cultural practices in Chinese spheres, he sees how mass commercial photography captures perfectly, innocently the new contradictory duality of modern Chinese subjectivity. This is most evident in the phenomenon of the "picture of two selves," in which two pictures of oneself are juxtaposed, each with a different costume and expression: "two selves, like a guest and a host, or a master and a slave." A peculiar truth is revealed in the illusion that is staged and re-presented in these photographs: photography, as it were, allows for illusions to be generated on the back of its realism; it can merely re-present what is staged for the camera as reality. At this point, Lu's essay enters into the very complicated terrain in which what is transparent is opaque and what is illusory is real, in other words, the very new reality of traditional aura decaying in the media of modern technology. In this way, "On Photography" helps situate the final moments of romanticism in Asia. This becomes more clear as the essay concludes with some ironic comments on the illusion of permanence and eternality produced through the photographic medium—how, in other words, the aura of Asian tradition, whenever it is meant to be frozen for all time, is always entering a state of decrepitude and old age. This leitmotif of false eternality culminates with a satirical take on Tagore's controversial visit to Beijing in 1925: "When the Indian saint of poetry, Tagore, visited China, he aromatized like sweet perfume several of our gentlemen of letters with his literariness and mysticism." After the newly christened "Zhu Cathay"—Tagore as the uniter of Asian civilization in its ideality—"took leave of his all-but-ideal country of Cathay, the sage-poets of Cathay no longer much wore their Indian turbans, and the newspapers only very rarely reported news of Tagore." Yet in Tagore's wake linger the auratic images of an essential Asia, "pictures of the 'Celestial Maiden Scattering Flowers' and 'Daiyu Burying Flowers,'" which hang, the narrator says, "so imposingly in the windows of the photography studios."[48]

More can be said of Lu's richly nuanced reading of the photographic medium under imperial conditions than can be covered here. For our purposes, it should be noted that he insinuates a connection between the technoscientific hegemony of which the photograph is but a metonym, and the peculiar social predicament from which a Chinese romanticism, or neoromanticism, emerged over the interwar period. We may also ask what in turn issued from this school of thought as it entered into the period of demise that Tagore's visit marked indelibly on the dynamic and deeply splintering Chinese cultural scene.[49] A body of scholarship has grown around the phenomenon of a specifically "romantic generation" of writers over these years. Leo Ou-fan Lee's 1973 *The Romantic Generation of Modern Chinese Writers* introduced key figures such Yu Dafu, Xu Zhimo, and Xiao Jun to an English readership in a series of informative vignettes.[50] More recent research, particularly on the Creation Society, the epicenter of Chinese neoromanticism from 1921 to 1930, but also more generally on the reception of Enlightenment scientism (i.e., social Darwinism) and modernist aesthetics (e.g., futurism), has given sharper political and historical definition to romanticism in interwar China. Two general tendencies assert themselves: first is the discovery of analogies between modern and premodern cultural forms; second is the elaboration of a new revolutionary subjectivity on the basis of these perceived analogies and continuities between premodernity and the imperial present. The dissolution of romanticism after the founding of the League of Left-Wing Writers and the collapse of the Creation Society in 1930 released certain long-incubating potencies of late romanticism. (It is as if what Carl Schmitt detected as a subjective "occasionalism" from romanticism's earliest German phase entered onto the very different political terrain of anti-imperialism and Maoist revolution in its late Chinese phase.)

The relation between the self-avowedly modernist cultural production of the May Fourth movement and certain uncannily prescient features of premodern culture has posed numerous interpretive problems for literary and cultural historians. Central to these problems is understanding the kinds of predicaments in which the proponents of cultural renewal found themselves by the early twentieth century, and how these predicaments shaped their cultural proclivities and lent them political significance. The affinity various schools spawned by the May Fourth movement betrayed for premodern forms such as late Qing quasi-symbolist lyric or the rudimentary technology of the woodcut image seem to either cast doubt on the modernist aspirations of these schools or to call for a very different understanding of what these reclaimed remnants of the past were meant to perform in the new context. A recent article titled "Chinese Modernisms" by Stephanie Hemelryk Donald and Yi Zheng advance our understanding of this "anti-modern modernity" (following Wang) unfolding over twentieth-century China. By focusing on the ways key figures of the May Fourth movement read, translated, and canonized or dismissed European currents such as futurism and symbolism, Donald and Zheng illuminate the kinds of imperatives that were at work in their aesthetic-literary practice. Neoromanticism for these critics "operated as a cultural inoculation against the overweening imperial power derived from European modernism, and thus especially as a riposte to the imperialism and sub-imperialism of China's own governance in the long period of humiliation leading up to the First World War and its immediate aftermath."[51] That is to say, influential writers of the period such as Guo

Moruo, Tian Han, and Mao Dun selectively imbibed those aspects of European modernism that helped strengthen them against the imperial onslaught. Thus, Guo dismissed futurism, with its glorification of the industrial machine, as a "freak birth out of extreme materialism" and therefore unfit to meet China's needs. Symbolist currents, on the other hand, especially those carried over from France, were welcome. From 1919 onward, Chinese intellectuals of various persuasions systematically translated and introduced symbolist poetry and aesthetic tracts to the literate public. Symbolist "emphasis on suggestion and ambiguity, and its reliance on the use of evocative subjects and images rather than explicit analogy or direct description" opened a fresh vista onto those very traditional Chinese forms that beheld similar qualities.[52] "It now appeared that Chinese poetic practice," such as strands of Ming mannerism, "had been modernist centuries before the event"; thus, a bridge to the Chinese past could now be forged with the materials borrowed from the European present.[53]

The paradox is not simply that neoromantics in interwar China forged a connection with remnants of their ruined past through modern symbolist aesthetics borrowed from contemporary Europe. The paradox extends in the other direction as well: the appropriation of European metaphors to challenge Western imperial hegemony and revitalize Chinese traditions for forging a non-Western future. For instance, in his preface to Goethe's *The Sorrows of Young Werther*, Guo emphasizes that Goethe is "a great subjective poet." He is one who "seeks to forget himself not in quietude but in activity. With the energy of a lion assailing a rabbit, with his whole heart and soul, he seeks the fulfillment of each moment and the enlargement of his Self, with his entire spirit he seeks to devote himself to everything."[54] The agency that had made the linkages between past and future through the mediation of modernist symbolist aesthetics now identified itself as "an unexpected eruption of an unknown army."[55] Guo himself asserted a thoroughly modernist subjectivity. "An artist," he wrote, "should not be the grandson of nature, not even her son, but should become the father of nature."[56] Amplified in proportion to how much it was frustrated by a society disintegrating under imperial pressure and dynastic inertia, the Creation Society embodied a new subjective turn in Chinese thought, one that could mobilize the powers of the emergent masses through the projection of a sovereign Chinese selfhood. The mythic self that neoromantics fashioned countered the cold logic, calculation, and determinism of Enlightenment with a new Philosophy of Life. A famous public address by Zhang Junmai, a fellow traveler of the Creators, highlighted "subjectivity, intuitiveness, synthesizing power, free will, and personal unity" as the distinguishing points of the new doctrine.[57] At the core of the Creators' project was the concept of expression. Beginning with a commitment to an inner meaning or depth beyond verisimilitude and to giving voice to one's emotions, the concept of expression (*biaoxian*) ultimately amounted to a reformulation of the question of reason and concomitantly revolutionary praxis. Romantic aesthetic expression sought to actualize a renewed harmony between the subjective and the objective realms and to suture divisions imposed by Enlightenment. This harmony could only result, Feng Naichao affirmed, from a liberation of art from the shackles of commodification, held to be the source of the social inequalities that alienated classes from one another, made art mere ornamentation, and naturalized the social domination of capital.[58] This was but one step that took this new Chinese subjectivity beyond the ideological constraints of imperial capitalism and Western hegemony altogether.[59]

As Chinese neoromanticism quickly faded in the tracks of widely espoused collective revolutionary aesthetics and politics over the 1930s and 1940s, it is curious that what issued from its old shell was a new kind of "occasionalism." In *Political Romanticism*, the Nazi legal scholar and political philosopher Carl Schmitt opined that in eighteenth-century Germany, romantic poetry "lives off cultic and liturgical aftereffects and reminiscences that it squanders away into the profane." As a postsecular practice seeking to conserve the structures of a quickly fading past against its own immanent tendencies, romanticism for Schmitt finds its concept in the romantic subject. "Instead of God, however, the romantic subject occupies the central position and makes the world and everything that occurs in it into a mere occasion."[60] For Schmitt, romantic occasionalism ultimately supports a politically neutralizing "private priesthood" in counterrevolutionary Europe. Given the very different exigencies in early twentieth-century China, is it any surprise that romantic subjectivity would fashion a future that outstrips any limitation imposed on it by Western imperial hegemony; that, rather than a shriveled religiosity of individuated subjectivity, what obtained from Chinese experiments with romantic occasionalism are massive revolutionary experiments, whose objective results reverberate in our present and shape to a great extent our collective future?

JAPAN

In 1934, the very year the Japanese romantic school (*Nihon romanha*) was founded, Tanizaki Jun'ichiro finished his famous essay "In Praise of Shadows." Though there is no immediate connection between the two events, the situation Tanizaki describes gives a sense of the modern malaise that pervades nearly the entire corpus of Japanese romanticism up to the point of its dissolution over the U.S. Occupation following World War II. Tanizaki's essay gives compelling expression to a sentiment that can be widely detected across a Japanese public fitfully assuming the role of a modern militaristic empire over the 1930s. The "evils of excessive illumination" that the adoption of modern technologies has cast over Japan scare away the atmospheric aura that Tanizaki associates with the shade that had long sheltered Japanese traditions.[61] "It was not that I objected to the conveniences of modern civilization, whether electric lights or heating or toilets," explains Tanizaki, "but I did wonder at the time why they could not be designed with a bit more consideration for our own habits and tastes." The alienating glare of Enlightenment is unmistakable in the sheen of the new gadgetry on the market and makes Tanizaki wonder "how different everything would be if we in the Orient had developed our own science." For Tanizaki the logic of this borrowed Enlightenment is indistinguishable from a shaft of artificial light piercing through the enclosed and intimate zones of Japanese culture, leaving people bereft of the comforts once provided by "a pensive luster . . . a murky light that, whether in a stone or an artifact, bespeaks a [glow] of antiquity." So widespread is the discomfort that Tanizaki can adopt the plural first-person pronoun and express the intensity of the estrangement: "Now we must travel to such small cities as Nishinomiya, Sakai, Wakayama, or Fukuyama for the feel of Japan."[62]

We will follow Tanizaki and others into this difficult quest. I will especially explore those moments when his essay discloses what might be thought of as the spatial and temporal dimensions of the traditional sublime. But at this point it is worth pointing out that the nostalgia Tanizaki has named "In Praise of Shadows" culminated in the aporetic melancholia and malaise of the Japanese romantic school (JRS). Led by Yasuda Yojuro (1910–1981) and taking in luminaries such as Mishima Yukio (1925–1970) and Dazai Osamu (1909–1948) in their youth,[63] the JRS affected a wistful, ironic distance before a rabidly modernizing and militarizing Japan, while simultaneously grasping ideally for the centripetal security of Japan's past traditions. Japanese romantics realized that the price of Asian autonomy from the West was becoming modern, or Western. It would, in other words, be at best a Pyrrhic victory. This very aporia, which was thought synonymous with modernity at this time, was what burdened members of the JRS and culminated in the discourse "Overcoming Modernity" in the early 1940s. Yet so much did the cultural agenda of the JRS coincide with the imperial aims and militaristic mobilizing efforts of Emperor Hirohito that Yasuda Yojuro contemplated after the war, "Did my past writing really send young men to their deaths? It's not that I made them die; it's that I opened their hearts to the eternal, living beginnings of creation, in which it does not matter that Japanese literature might die."[64] I will briefly analyze the rhetoric through which tradition was valorized in the aesthetics of the JRS and how that valorization informed the politics of romanticism in its Japanese phase of dissolution.

The string of judgments and reflections that make up Tanizaki's "In Praise of Shadows," despite their associational surface patterns, condense an aesthetic philosophy that became increasingly entrenched and politicized under the stewardship of the JRS. Thomas J. Harper and Edward G. Seidensticker's highly regarded translation of this essayistic masterpiece conveys something of the elegance with which Tanizaki met the arid communicational rationality to which Japanese culture had capitulated over its pressured course of self-modernization since the Meiji Restoration: "The Westerner has been able to move forward in ordered steps, while we have met superior civilization and have had to surrender to it, and we have had to leave a road we have followed for thousands of years." Tanizaki evokes the passing of a traditional habitus whose modes of existence, forms of art, and styles of communication find no traction and thus are practically obliterated by the modern media adopted from the West. He is worth citing at length on the erosion of auratic experience in the wake of modernization:

> Japanese music is above all a music of reticence, of atmosphere. When recorded, or amplified by a loudspeaker, the greater part of its charm is lost. In conversation, too, we prefer the soft voice, the understatement. Most important of all are the pauses. Yet the phonograph and radio render these moments of silence utterly lifeless. And so we distort the arts themselves to curry favor for them with the machines. These machines are the inventions of Westerners, and are, as we might expect, well suited to

the Western arts. But precisely on this account they put our own arts at a great disadvantage.

Along with the passing of the old media and their material substratum occurs the quick obsolescence of traditional techniques and skills, and therewith the fearful vanishing of entire shared modes of being. "Western paper is to us no more than something to be used, while the texture of Chinese paper and Japanese paper gives us a certain feeling of warmth, of calm and repose," Tanizaki explains, preserving an iota of "affection for the old system."[65] This latent mix of fear and fatalism in Tanizaki's vision brings into relief the traditional sources of sublime affect just when they are decaying.

There are two moments in particular worth concentrating on that bring out the traditional sublime on temporal and spatial plains, respectively, in Tanizaki's essay. These two moments are crucial in establishing the fundamental binaries that subtly structure Tanizaki's aesthetic theory and inform the intellectual agenda of the JRS. Each of these moments is connected with the essential materiality of the old media and reveals the ways in which traditional aura once spontaneously constituted itself through them. In sharp contrast to electric light, which effectively blots out aura for Tanizaki, darkness remains "an indispensable element of the beauty" of numerous remnants of the traditional past, for instance lacquerware: "The lacquerware of the past was finished in black, brown, or red, colors built up of countless layers of darkness, the inevitable product of the darkness in which life was lived." The "inexpressible aura of depth and mystery" created by the innumerable layers on lacquerware evokes the presence of enduring generations, speaking to each other, making their presence felt through media shared over millennia. This sense of elongated time is again experienced with a peculiar frisson as Tanizaki reflects on the interplay of light and shadow allowed by old temple architecture: "Have you never felt a sort of fear in the face of the ageless, a fear that in that room you might lose all consciousness of the passage of time, that untold years might pass and upon emerging you should find you had grown old and gray?" The absorption into an ageless temporality is matched by a loosening of one's sense of self into shadowy spaces produced by antique puppets on the traditional stage: "But in the dim lamplight, the hard lines of the puppet features softened, the glistening white of their faces muted—a chill comes over me when I think of the uncanny beauty the puppet theatre must once have had."[66] Just as the sense of elongated time captured in the endless layers of lacquerware provokes in Tanizaki's subject a sense of temporal infinitude, the chill that comes over Tanizaki before the puppets is one of wide spatial extension, captured in the metaphor of lines "softening." The uncanny beauty harbored by traditional puppet theater demands a comparable beauty of the contemporary imagination. Though Tanizaki's work strays from the workaday world of state building and empire, the "absolute harmony" that is imagined of the past world would require something on the order of the Greater East Asia Co-Prosperity Sphere as its contemporary sociopolitical counterpart.

Just months after the outbreak of the Pacific War, members of the JRS stood alongside the official intelligentsia of Kyoto Imperial University and select stewards of the Japanese public sphere to discuss what had for years been a pressing intellectual problem: "overcoming modernity." "Designed to provide ideological justification for Japan's involvement in the war," as Masakazu Yamazaki has recognized, the "Overcoming Modernity" conference brought to light the predicaments that befell the intellectual scene of early Showa.[67] These very predicaments brought the JRS into a state of fracturing and erosion in tandem with the imperial state itself. Having advanced for years an anti-Western aesthetics in light of Tanizaki's interventions, the JRS was now drawn inexorably into sanctioning an expansionist military policy for a state modeled on Western authoritarian powers. It is not surprising that the conference took on a recognizably desultory character, as the famous critic Takeuchi Yoshimi emphasized. It did, however, highlight the opposing imperatives that eventually broke romanticism in late imperial Japan.

The now abundant scholarship on the JRS allows one to track some of the contradictory currents that dogged romanticism from the moment it emerged on the Japanese scene. In "Japan's Revolt against the West," Harry Harootunian and Tetsuo Najita provide an excellent account of the rise of the JRS and the position it staked out in the "Overcoming Modernity" conference. Other works, such as Kevin Michael Doak's *Dreams of Difference: The Japan Romantic School and the Crisis of Modernity*, Harootunian's own *Overcome by Modernity: History, Culture, and Community in Interwar Japan*, and Alan Tansman's *The Aesthetics of Japanese Fascism* have enriched our understanding of romanticism's historical trajectory, political proclivities, and philosophical underpinnings. What upholds romantic aesthetics is an edifice of binaries that were secured in Tanizaki's essay.

These may be organized in the following manner: Depth : Surface :: Tradition : Modernity :: Collectivity : Individuation :: Harmony : Dissonance :: Intransitive : Transitive :: Unintentional: Instrumental. In each binary, the first member is privileged over the second, securing a source for an idealistic scheme of valuation increasingly cut off from the conditioning mechanisms of imperial capitalism, as Harootunian especially has emphasized. The historical situation in which the JRS found itself, in other words, led to the implosion of the binary scheme upon which it advanced its culturalist agenda.

To conclude, let me point out the contradictions that ate away at the JRS over its short career, leaving it in ruins by the time of the U.S. Occupation. These contradictions are either explicitly pinpointed, as in Harootunian's work, or surface implicitly through the various strands of scholarship. Though premised on a critique of reification and Western cultural imperialism, the JRS's founding moment was a collective break with Marxism. Its defining program was the purification of Japanese culture of foreign influences and the reconstruction of an authentic literary tradition, yet it could not abandon the new media. Though the members of the school premised their work on a "general condemnation of literary modernism," many of them ended up falling into recognizably modernist tendencies, including the confabulation of a pure language, people, and origin, yet on this occasion as preparation for a new unfolding of a different, that is, non-Eurocentric, universal history. The JRS affected a melancholic, fatalistic, and even nihilistic stance toward the modern world while affirming, at least implicitly, the modern capacities of the imperial state. "Deeply influenced by modern Western culture, the participating intellectuals [in the 'Overcoming Modernity' conference] were in no position," Masakazu Yamazaki recognizes, "to turn their backs wholly on the entire spectrum of modern civilization, ranging from rationalism to more tangible mechanical conveniences."[68] This internal stunting of capacities for the overcoming of modernity became apparent over the course of the conference proceedings. For instance, Harootunian comments that "despite its intense concern for the status of history," the JRS "managed only to mount a displaced critique of the imperial claims of its grand narrative, setting its sights only on the level of representation and not on the political economic system that authorized it or the contradictions it produced."[69] The destruction of Hirohito's Japan and the end of the World War II proved fatal for the cultural program the JRS had been leading.

NORTHERN INDIA

As is the case with Japan and China, the phenomenon of romanticism in India covers so wide a range of media with so many distinct valences as to allow here only a telescopic view of its most overt forms of expression and most general political tendencies in the north. In part II, "Neo-Epic Constellation: Out of British India," I concentrate on one prominent genre, the neo-epic, that cropped up in the furrows left on Indian culture by various lines of romantic aesthetic ideology. These furrows crossed the divides between the colonial educational system and various unofficial venues, allowing for a cross-pollination of forms and contents and a proliferation of new expressive possibilities. Over the late nineteenth and early twentieth centuries, versions of romantic self-fashioning were on display across distinct literary and cultural arenas, giving rise to groups such as Chayavad and to institutions such as the Halqah-ye Arbab-e Zauq (Circle of Literary Connoisseurs) in Hindi and Urdu, respectively.[70] As facets of these developments will be covered in some detail in later chapters, what I want to point out here are some general dynamics that allowed for romantically inspired neotraditional forms to emerge, often with mutually exclusive agendas, generally employing religious language in reciprocally alienating ways. In this way, reifying and dereifying tendencies were brought into collision. The emergence of these broad culturalist tendencies fashioned in turn the nationalist politics that led to the partition of British India along broadly religious lines. A long history of competing epic forms was given new significance and political charge by those advocating communal sovereignty in the crisis-ridden end game of empire. Muhammad Ali Jinnah's famous words from his 1940 address to the Muslim League are germane: "The Hindus and Muslims belong to two different religious philosophies, social customs, literatures. They neither intermarry nor interdine together and, indeed, they belong to two different civilizations which are based mainly on conflicting ideas and conceptions. Their aspects on life and of life are different. It is quite clear that Hindus and Mussalmans derive their inspiration from different sources of history. They have different epics, different heroes, and different episodes. Very often the hero of one is a foe of the other and, likewise, their victories and defeats overlap."[71] Jinnah is reifying what had been for several decades an unconscious recourse to traditional icons, imagery, and languages on the part of varying religious identities, Hindu and Muslim, for idealizing past traditions and imagining postcolonial futures. To illustrate this, I turn to Tagore and Iqbal, who present the predicament of romantic thought in the moment of imperial dissolution in two distinct idioms, one mythic, the other iconoclastic—both struggling with belatedness, which is to say, an enmeshment with logics of reification.

RABINDRANATH TAGORE

In his letter to the English poet Thomas Sturge Moore, penned a year after receiving the Nobel Prize for Literature, Tagore described what he saw as the role of Western literature in India: the creation of "a bifurcation" in Indian civilization. Despite the violent undertone of being cut in two, the bifurcation Western literature performs on the "mental system" of Indian civilization is "needful for all life growth." Indeed, Tagore goes on, it is essential for "bringing into our life elements some of which supplement and some contradict our tendencies." What Indians are beginning to experience now is what has strengthened Westerners for millennia, for "absorbing the spirit of the East through the medium of the Bible," a thoroughly Eastern phenomenon in Tagore's mind, "has added to the richness of your life because it is alien to your temperament." Just as the West benefited from the bifurcation performed on it by the Bible, India is just now beginning to experience a similar bifurcation. "That is what we need," continues Tagore:

> It is not enough to charm or surprise us—we must receive shocks and be hurt. Therefore we seek in our writings not simply what is artistic but what is vivid and forceful. That is why Byron had such immense influence over our youths of the last generation. Shelley, in spite of his vague idealism, roused our minds because of his fanatic impetuosity which is born of a faith in life. . . . We look for your literature to bring to us the thundering life flood of the West, even though it carries with it all the debris of the passing moments.[72]

There is something prophetic about "the debris" in this passage, for Tagore would occasionally find himself unknowingly entangled in fascist politics over the following two decades, in Italy as well as in Japan. (There is also something slightly prophetic about the violent imagery he employs to describe India's encounter with English romanticism, given what political impact would follow upon the romanticization of religious communities.) Of immediate interest is how Tagore's account describes the jolting effect reading about modern romance had on his generation. Having witnessed the popularization of nationalism during the Swadeshi movement (1905–9), Tagore is well aware of the catalytic power of romanticism in the Indian context in unleashing, as if spontaneously, an idealized image of Hindu tradition among Bengali elites, leaving the question of the massive Muslim population of united Bengal unaddressed and deferred. As one who helped foster a romantic image of Bengali rural life, Tagore would also realize the dangerous life such images could take on their own, overpowering even himself on occasion and drawing him into the gambit of politics he did not consciously identify with. Yet undoubtedly the politics in question—fascism—identified with him. So appealing was Tagore's traditional mystique among Europe's hard political Right circles that an invitation was finally issued, and he landed in Mussolini's Italy in 1926.

The affinities betrayed in this instance between a particular neotraditionalist aesthetics and a fascist politics are intriguing. Looking into them provokes questions: How did Tagore's fascist admirers, including Il Duce, see him, and what were they identifying with? What does it mean that Tagore preferred to ignore the political strife in fascist Italy and began to turn mildly critical of it only when his visit started bringing him bad press and criticism from key supporters? Considering that Tagore had identified fascism as the "exact counterpart" of extreme Hindu orthodoxy, what does his acceptance, even affirmation of fascist politics in Italy imply about his views of the Hindu Right?[73] Though he stated, "I had neither the qualifications nor any inclination to dabble in the internal political issues of the European countries,"[74] he did express his "admiration for Mussolini as possessing the personality which alone can effect the miracles of creation in human history."[75] In an interview for the *Tribuna*, the leading organ of fascism under Mussolini, Tagore exalted in some sublime rhetoric, now verging on the banal, in his vision of Italy: "Let me dream that from the fire-bath the immortal soul of Italy will come out clothed in quenchless light."[76] Considering how Mussolini had just cleansed Italian politics of all political detractors, including figures Tagore admired, such as Benedetto Croce (who had to be taken out of house arrest for his meeting with "the mystic poet of the East"), the praise was misplaced. Nevertheless, an important question stands behind the description given of Tagore's speech the next day: "When the sonorous voice of the poet mingled with the pealing of bells from a nearby church, the audience, perceiving a symbolic blending of the voice of Rome with that of mystic India, was deeply moved and broke into warm and persistent applause."[77] What is the underlying connection between Indian neotraditionalist romanticism and a widely prevalent fascism?

An angle on some of these questions is provided by recent research into how the Bengali espousal of Enlightenment rationalism, especially positivism, gave way by the early twentieth century to what Raychaudhuri has called "a profound emotionalism," the very romantically induced emotionalism to which Tagore alludes in his letter to Moore.[78] To capture the nature of this change, one must register the profound discomfort produced, albeit in different ways, by Enlightenment and romanticism in elite Bengali culture. The rationalism of the former always threatened to push the colonial pupil toward an atheism where few dared and fewer were sanctioned, provoking in reaction attempts on the part of cultural authorities to keep Western materialism in check. "Hindus had nothing to learn from the West," as Raychaudhuri summarizes a widely espoused position, "except their knowledge of the external world and their skill in practical matters."[79]

The mores of Western romance could be just as destabilizing for the individual as Enlightenment was destabilizing for inherited systems of social hierarchy, yet romanticism did not allow such simplistic separations between internal and external worlds. "The yearning of romantic love" derived from the literature assigned in the colonial educational apparatus "apparently could not be satisfied within the institutional framework of child marriage and the extended family," giving rise to the frustrated lover as "a central figure in Bengali fiction of the late-nineteenth and early-twentieth centuries."[80] This situation fueled what Chakrabarty has called a "desperate search for a romanticized 'tradition' that would make room for the new individual, both male and female, while allowing the pursuit of happiness in a land in which the past did nothing to validate the European-humanist ideal."[81] What was called for in light of these hampered arenas for Western theory and practice was the sublimation of both rationality and romanticism toward the ideal of constructing a modern Hindu culture.[82] The new Hindu culture aimed to respond to the shrinking metaphysics under Enlightenment rationalism by providing a new mythology that proved useful for mobilizing peasant masses against a foreign power. This new mythology worked equally well in validating inherited institutions, idioms, and customs and channeling romantic energy into a new nationalist devotionalism easily sanctioned by traditional Hindu authorities.[83]

This historical backdrop sheds light on the competing imperatives in Tagore's work that came to a head over the course of his controversial sojourn through fascist Italy. On the one hand, there was the imperative to establish the notion of an Eastern civilization superior to the West, a notion aimed at keeping intact inherited codes of Indian kinship, religiosity, and social hierarchy, nurturing all the while aspirations of autonomy on a strictly spiritual level. On the other hand, it was imperative to keep in check the radical potentials of anti-Enlightenment and anticolonial tendencies in India, making sure these could be harnessed to an anodyne cosmopolitan idealism rather than an atavistic authoritarianism. Mussolini obviously saw parallels between Tagore's mystical neotraditionalism and Italian fascism. He saw how he could leaven his internationally troubling domestic agenda of "armed reaction," as Gramsci described it, with a visit from a blithely oblivious yet influential cosmopolitan mystic. Gramsci, who was imprisoned by Mussolini the very year Tagore was making his way through Italy and the rest of fascist Europe, points out what likely attracted Tagore to Mussolini's politics: its capacity to do the job of neotraditionalism. In 1925 Gramsci had noted how fascism in Italy aimed to disorganize working-class advances and fit the elements back into "the framework of traditional Italian ruling-class policies"; fascism "replaces the tactic of agreements and compromises by the project of achieving an organic unity of all the bourgeoisie's forces in a single political organism under the control of a single centre."[84] Yet Tagore remained unaware. A frustrated Romain Rolland observed about Tagore's Italian journey, "He had seen nothing, heard nothing, learnt nothing, he washed his hands of it."[85] Instead, Rolland regretted, "our great Tagore, after his visit to Mussolini, has once again been ill advised to have himself received and patronised by the criminals who are torturing Bulgaria and Romania."[86] Some days later, writing from Hungary, Tagore reflected, "In places like Budapest the attitude of the people towards me is so clingingly personal, so full of tender solicitude that I forget to ask myself what price I had ever paid for it. It only reveals a spontaneous attraction of a mysterious feeling of kinship. I cannot help thinking that in spite of my numerous deficiencies my providence has found in me an instrument which he can use for his own great purpose, though it is a matter of perpetual puzzle to the instrument itself."[87]

Let us leave Tagore in his tool-like self-perplexity. His puzzlement, it might be said, reflected the political muddle of romanticism after its moment had already passed. He himself was dimly aware of this much. Just before departing Italy, he said to the Leonardo da Vinci Society in Florence, "I wish I had not been preceded by my fame. I could then have come close to you, like the English poets, Browning, Shelley, Byron and Keats."[88] Romanticism was already a stereotyped entity, marking a lapse from original spontaneity and, thus, timeliness. Its lingering presence in the figure of Tagore disclosed some of its political colors with unmistakable clarity.

MUHAMMAD IQBAL

Iqbal's reconfiguration of romanticism in an Islamic idiom very much countered, implicitly if not explicitly, the mythology of neotraditional Hinduism. Chapter 5 focuses on interpreting Iqbal's encounter with German romanticism and the evolution of his magnum opus, the neo-epic *Javid Nama* (1932); here I will restrict the discussion to how Iqbal came to grapple with Enlightenment rationality from the Islamic theological vantage point. One of Iqbal's couplets from this magnum opus is "asar-e hazir ra khirad zanjir-e pa-ast / Jan-e be-tabe ki man daram kuja-ast?" (Reason is a chain fettering this present age: / where is a restless soul such as I possess?)[89] This is how the venerable Orientalist A. J. Arberry translated these lines from the opening prayer to *Javid Nama*, but the *kuja* of the second line may just as easily sustain translations suggestive of alternative readings: Whither a restless soul such as my own? That is, where can it possibly go? Or, is a restless soul such as I possess even possible, that is, able to survive in the world of reason, for as Iqbal elaborates, "without revelation life is a mortal sickness, / reason is banishment, religion constraint" (*be-tajalli zindagi ranjvari ast / 'aql mohjuri o din majburi ast*).[90] In order to grasp the answer Iqbal gave to this question, we must place him as an interlocutor between the modernizing trends in Muslim theology (*'ilm-e kalam*) and the reification of a social world sundered by Enlightenment's abstract domination yet teeming with new powers of distraction.

In contradistinction to the neo-Hindu world represented by Tagore, I would like to emphasize how Iqbal fashioned a modern iconoclastic and apocalyptic vision in keeping with long-standing traditions of Islamic thought while diverting sharply from them at the level of content. Working off the modern premises established for Islam in post-Mutiny India by the prominent reformer Sir Sayyid Ahmad Khan, Iqbal sought to supersede both traditionalist religion and the attenuated form of reason that was pitted against it. This conflict and the theme of superseding it got deeply encoded in the forms and idioms Iqbal chose for his vastly popular aesthetic expression. His poetry, for instance, attained a higher, chiseled, and unadorned style and sought ever larger frames of reference, leading ultimately to *Javid Nama*. Here I want to point out briefly how this reconfigured iconoclasm and apocalypticism in Iqbal's oeuvre are fully conditioned—or mediated—by Enlightenment. Through it, he sought to counter the limited though tyrannical version of reason that characterized it. Religious orders of the time sought either to accommodate themselves to the reign of Enlightenment (such as Sir Sayyid's loyalist school) or to fend off its deflating logic for as long as possible (such as Deoband).[91] Iqbal responded strongly to both positions. He was especially moved by the fearless naturalist theology of Sir Sayyid and its austere rationalist vision of Islam, but he wished to again imbue meaning into the hard lifeless materiality it exposed. Unlike those who clung desperately to the comfortable amalgam of received traditions, Iqbal turned to the renewed sublimity of iconoclasm in modern Islamic reformism. He realized early on that the new task was to reinhabit the blank, hard, and arid spaces to which the phenomenal world was reduced in Enlightenment. The strategy he adopted was one of apocalyptic allegoresis (further elaborated in chapter 5).

To grasp the underlying logic of this allegorical turn, consider the original articulation of the problematic in the Indo-Islamic sphere. In a series of publications that came out in the decades after the Mutiny, Sir Sayyid rethought scripture through the trope of *ta'vil*, or allegory, and in doing so issued what Islamicists would readily recognize as neo-Mu'tazalite theology. In the 1870s, he took the allegorical mode of interpretation further and constructed an Islam that was devoid of miracles. Sir Sayyid thought supernatural occurrences should be considered not merely contrary to reason and the laws of nature but also to the Qur'an. Christian Troll, in his informative study of Sir Sayyid, writes, "Where Sayyid Ahmad Khan makes rudimentary remarks about the process of knowing, they remain primitively empiricistic. At no point does Sayyid Ahmad Khan enter upon a critical consideration of the capability of the human mind to reach a knowledge of essence and metaphysical principles."[92] The austere religious landscape being depicted here is meant to substitute for the one imbued with spiritual significance, marked by shrines and reclusive memorials, as scattered across the Indian landscape. Further, the subject that is becoming normative is one reduced to material senses. The new religious *Weltanshauung* of neo-Mu'tazalite Islam put into question the most basic of dogmas: the special nature of prophethood and the miraculous nature of Islam itself. Explanations and justifications ensued. With respect to the former, Sir Sayyid constructs a habitus of cultivated natural gifts and skills to be most operative. With respect to the latter, what is most miraculous about Islamic revelation is that it accords so much authority to a natural science and rational investigation. "I firmly believe that there is no religion, except Islam, which when compared with former or contemporary research, with philosophy and natural philosophy, emerges in all respects true and valid."[93] Sir Sayyid's efforts to make the Muslim public amenable to Enlightenment placed a great deal of pressure on nature, a term that had begun to acquire a wide range of connotations. Ultimately, whatever may have been his intentions, the concept of nature begins to reveal religious ambiguity. Deposited now in the rigid law-like structure of its workings is the sublime and oracular mystery of divine agency.

The imputation of quasi-spiritual values onto the phenomenon of nature implies more generally pantheism, a question deflected in the writings of Sir Sayyid. But for Iqbal such values are the point of departure. For Iqbal, Sir Sayyid was the "first Muslim to catch a glimpse of the positive character of the age that was coming."[94] Though only the earliest moments of Iqbal's poetic oeuvre thematize nature, the spirit of Sir Sayyid's naturalism is consistently developed. In *Javid Nama* especially, but across a range of late works as well, there is a desire to reconfigure the sublime imputed to Sir Sayyid's nature as means for the resuscitation of faith. The initial point of departure is the realm of poetry and sphere of sound, but ultimately for Iqbal, the presuppositions, conventions, and constraints of secular literary culture must themselves be transcended for a new kind of apprehension of the sublime as appropriate to the age. For Iqbal, romanticism was a means as well as an end: as a means, for the revival of metaphysics against the positivist cage of modernity; as an end, romanticism was the calming of the *Sturm und Drang* of a world torn in contradictions. For him, this could only be accomplished through the securing of a different order of reason than that of a merely instrumental kind. Attempting the impossible, Iqbal wished to lift Islam out of its minority status under British colonialism and cleanse it of all its particularity, while employing and affirming the inevitable particularity of the forms and idioms employed. This predicament characterized the situation of Islam vis-à-vis Western imperial power: resistance to modernity meant a reconfiguration and resuscitation of a suborned spiritual force (however easily dismissed or threatened by the standards of modern science); such a resuscitation would allow for a reanimation of the meaning of reason and a new open mystical approach to nature, both essential moves toward a post-Enlightenment notion of selfhood.

We will turn in later chapters to the particular aporias that enveloped our legatees of Islamicate literary cultures in the wake of Sir Sayyid's rationalism. We will see that the contradictions that ultimately roiled Hali and Iqbal gave shape to new experiments with the epic form that marked the end of romanticism in its British Indian moment. But now some remarks are due to help unravel—if not cut through—the knots formed by all the argumentative threads woven together over this two-part chapter. First, a note on aura, a notion penetrating the pores of these late romantic formations, lending anachronistic coloring even to Lord Jim's sanguine imperial-romantic worldview. The incorporation of new media (such as the photograph or mass-produced paper) brings into acute relief the waning of cultic value embedded in traditional materials. Through the discrepancy running between new forms and old contents (or vice versa) emerges the possibility for an unstable neotraditionalist aesthetics premised on these auratic remains. Itself no longer able to evade Enlightenment's steady evisceration of traditionalist cultic value, romanticism ultimately revealed its underlying telos in its moment of historical demise. All of these vignettes of late romanticism—the Creation Society in China, the Japan romantic school, Tagore's Hindu mystique, and Iqbal's anguished iconoclasm—evince a pervasive conflictual pattern contra Enlightenment (even to the point of identification with fascism), and occasionally against the West as such. The assertion of equality with Western powers that largely characterized late romanticism came at the cost of the West's own imperial grandeur, portending instead its imminent dissolution.

From this vantage point at the edges of the colonial world, it becomes possible to grasp a logic by which critiques of European modernity were radicalized and cultural forms such as epic were reconstellated. It becomes possible, in other words, to detect parallels—or, rather, nonsensuous similarities—at the edges of Western imperial peripheries.[95] The following chapter expands on the problematic of Enlightenment rationality and the materialization of critical energies by following Benjamin into exile on the edge of Europe. The experience drew Benjamin ever closer to a renewed theory of epic as a way out of the temporality of imperial modernity, beyond the spatiality of reified categories, and, with its infusion of Marxist critique, over and above the idealistic impasses of romanticism.

CHAPTER 3

Atmospherics of Imperialism

Benjamin's Sublime

atmospherics, n. Atmospheric disturbances of electrical origin causing interference with communication in wireless telegraphy, television, etc. Also occas. without final *-s*.

—*Oxford English Dictionary*

I. ROMANTICISM'S RUIN, IMPERIAL SKELETON

Jedes weltgeschichtliche Moment verschuldet und verschuldend. (Every world-historical moment is in guilt and is making guilty.)

—Walter Benjamin, "Zur Geschichtsphilosophie, Historik und Politik"

Like a glare piercing through the protective layers of a fading dreamworld, the reality of imperial Germany obtrudes abruptly upon the scene in Benjamin's *One-Way Street*.[1] The kaiser—or imperial—panorama in which one unexpectedly finds oneself departs from the poetic ruminations of earlier fragments and drags one on "a tour through the German inflation." Here the devastation pervades the material as well as spiritual dimensions of German society. Benjamin's assessment aims to add to the wreckage and to render irredeemable the entire civilization that brought it about: "Again and again it has been shown that society's attachment to its familiar and long-since-forfeited life is so rigid as to nullify the genuinely human application of intellect, forethought, even in dire peril. So that in this society the picture of imbecility is complete: uncertainty, indeed perversion, of vital instincts; and impotence, indeed decay, of the intellect" (I: 451). Not only is this society incapable of rectifying itself; it is unable to recognize the deep-seated problems that generate its own miseries, let alone those of its colonial victims and imperial rivals. Such innate limitations undermine Germany's conceits of civilizational superiority. Benjamin's excoriating critique strips Germany of its most self-satisfying racist claims, for "in dealing with the Germans," other nations "are dealing with Hottentots (as it has been aptly put)" (I: 452). So great is the violence of this society that it is "incomprehensible to outsiders and wholly imperceptible to those imprisoned by it" (I: 453). And so powerful are the pressures of conformity that the Germans are no better than the savage races they hold in low regard. The "squalor . . . and stupidity here subjugate people entirely to collective forces, as the lives of savages are alone subjected to tribal laws" (I: 453). The drawing of parallels between "civilized" Europe and its conveniently more "savage" other suggest just how much Benjamin's intellectual and political outlook had begun to take shape, as one insightful critic has put it, "upon the horizon of a sharp critique of European civilization and the search for a new system of values."[2] Indeed, after reading "A Tour through the German Inflation," Gershom Scholem wondered how Benjamin could go on living in Germany.[3]

Such a search would begin for Benjamin by detecting certain uncanny connections and overlaps between the near (*Nah*) and the far (*Ferne*). This strong inclination toward the barely perceptible yet ever present trace of the distant within everyday metropolitan society allowed Benjamin to situate his critical apparatus upon the ambiguous dividing lines between metropolitan and colonial spaces. Thus, in another of Benjamin's *Denkbilder*, or thought-images, of the "Kaiserpanorama," written over a decade later as an autobiographical fragment, one is taken not on a tour through the devastation of inflation but rather to obsolete imperial entertainment. In this case, one is drawn into the phantasmagoria of old circular image projectors, which would display travel scenes of the distant world to metropolitan audiences. Benjamin had an intimate connection with such panorama projectors and witnessed their obsolescence as a child. The imperial panorama serves as a metaphor of the totality of the social field, for "it did not matter where you began the cycle. Because the viewing screen, with places to sit before it, was circular, each picture would pass through all the stations; from these you looked, each time, through a double window into the faintly tinted depths of the image."[4] The depths of these images leave an imprint on the historical unconscious of the audience,

Benjamin seems to suggest; their memory leaves a deposit in the collective's natural history. Such images of the distant allow for everyday experiences, faint memories, and unconscious associations to condense around them. They in turn illuminate previously unperceivable dimensions of the metropolitan everyday: "I went inside and found in fjords and under coconut palms the same light that illuminated my desk in the evening when I did my schoolwork."[5] It is significant that the experience of this remnant of a slowly passing age is that of a child, for Benjamin had spoken of the very different set of relations toward the powers of perceiving that children possessed: "In waste products they recognize the face that the world of things turns directly and solely to them. In using these things, they do not so much imitate the works of adults as bring together, in the artifact produced in play, materials of widely differing kinds in a new, intuitive relationship" (I: 449–50).

Coming of age under the wing of Gustav Wyneken's *Wandervögel*, Benjamin from childhood on would seek to make sense of the uncanny presences and unaccountable ellipses within the modern field of vision—but through the eyes of a child or, at the very least, through the reawakened eyes of vigorous youth. The spontaneous assemblages of which the child is most readily capable are significant for Benjamin because they potentially dissolve the hardened perspectives of adults as well as the oppressive norms maintained by prevailing political powers. Throughout his entire, ever peripatetic career Benjamin experimented with the "pure seeing" that he attributed early to "a child's view of color" (1914–15). The child's vision is able to glimpse the paradisiacal dimension of art, for in the fullness of color obtains "a state of identity, innocence, harmony."[6] Yet it is possible to discern how this romanticism in which he staked his initial claims was slowly dissolving and giving ground in his own thinking over the 1930s to the penetrating *Aussichtspunkt* of the machine-based optical unconscious. The edges of the romantic landscape to which the youthful Benjamin drew his reader's imagination—the edge of life, language, time and space (the limits of intelligibility itself)—revealed themselves in the negative exposure of his more mature technical apparatus to be the skeleton of imperial space. A rhetorical economy of the hidden and the manifest, the distant and the far, would play an increasingly vibrant, and thus intriguing, role in Benjamin's depictions of frontiers between the developed and undeveloped worlds, frontiers he himself would cross time and again over the course of his life. Upon the ruins of romanticism is exhumed, ultimately, the skeleton of imperial geography. In other words, the demise of romanticism reveals, as if in negative, its conditions of possibilities: the apocalyptic vision Benjamin brings to landscapes does not rest assured with surfaces. This is especially apparent in his travels into the peripheries of imperial Europe. "In such a town," he writes of Capri, "there is hardly anything that does not lie concealed and would not be worth the trouble of discovering" (II: 475).

Benjamin was often depicting in his *Denkbilder* the hidden imperial spatiality of metropolitan modernity. In these ekphrastic "thought-images," which verge as often on landscape as on the realm of what Benjamin called "nonsensuous similarity" (II: 722), he became the instrument, as it were, for indexing the sea change that had occurred in everyday spheres of metropolitan central Europe in the wake of imperial expansion. Born into a reformed Jewish bourgeois family just four years after Wilhelm II was crowned kaiser of the German Reich, Benjamin's experiences would be conditioned in innumerable ways by the imperial situation. Not only would he find himself in the exilic no-man's land between imperial rivals—happy in the end to have at least refugee papers as World War II started—but he would also come under the lethal forms of power that conjoined colonial aggression abroad with ever-deepening race politics on the domestic front. The push for colonial expansion had culminated under Bismarck with the founding of the German Colonial Society in 1887. The founding of the Pan-German League in the following decade, the pioneering efforts of the likes of Carl Peters and Gustav Nachtigal into Africa, and an ardent desire to catch up with the British lent the imperial agenda greater momentum under the new kaiser. As the grandson of Queen Empress Victoria, Kaiser Wilhelm II presented himself before a united Germany as an inheritor of the imperial mantle. By the time Benjamin would begin to collect the memories that make up his *Berlin Childhood around 1900*, the everyday world had already been inflected by the fact of imperialism, as Germany had acquired Southwest Africa (present-day Namibia), East Africa (Tanzania), Togo, and Cameroon directly; Tsingtao (Qingdao) in China and a part of New Guinea and surrounding islands as protectorates; and was actively drawing up blueprints for expansion into zones already occupied by European imperial rivals.

Recent scholarship aids in specifying how the new imperial situation abroad altered perceptions of space at various levels of everyday life in central Europe. Stabilization of German rule over East Africa by the end of the nineteenth century gave rise to aspirations on a British scale. The idea of turning this colony into a "German India in Africa" hints at the jarring spatial juxtapositions that imperialism was producing. Germany as an ideational space became attached to very unexpected physical geographies. Walter von Ruckteschell's 1914 landscape *Mt. Kilimanjaro in German East Africa* (shown on this book's cover), for instance, presented to his metropolitan countrymen the natural wonder that was now dubbed the highest "German" mountain. Popular journalism and travel writing, such as that of Paul de Lagarde, expressed a notion of the "Germanic" that was becoming increasingly messier and harder to experience coherently, as symptomatized in Kris Manjapra's gloss, where the "Germanic" is "not primarily a nation-state designation, but a composite of territorial, imperial, and traveling identities . . . not a fixed, but a traveling, category."[7] Wilhelm Raabe's novel of 1890, *Stopfkuchen: Eine See- und Mordgeschichte*, illustrates through allegory the difficulties such spatial incongruities presented for organizing coherent cognitive maps of a quickly shifting physical and ideational terrain. In her essay "Germany's Heart of Darkness," Judith Ryan deftly points out how Raabe's colonial novel signifies an impending erosion of conventional temporality under its questioning of the validity, let alone feasibility, of narrative continuity. The foregrounding of spatial discontinuity as immanent to the structures of everyday metropolitan life occurs in the novel's presentation of disparate fragments as pieces of a unitary world: "The complex nature of an expanding world where interconnections can only be understood through a prodigious leap of the imagination is precisely what makes traditional storytelling impossible. The involvement of familiar people and places with overseas events that seem remote and almost unintelligible is a recurrent theme in the novel."[8] The unmooring of Germany from a fixed geography went hand in hand with a jumbled sense of space in metropolitan spheres. In *Denkbilder* Benjamin expressed this parallax in the imperial spatiotemporal economy as the interweaving of disparate modalities of temporal experience. In "Spain, 1932," published posthumously, he writes that the "leveling of the globe through industry and technology has made such great strides" that it is only "a matter of time and study" before "even the most distant lands appear immediately familiar." In light of this, the task is to make sure that "the truly strange incommensurability of the near at hand" stands out sharply (II: 643–44). The effect is that of an intertwined time in Benjamin's writings—the totality effect that summons hidden presences in the force fields of the everyday metropolitan. The intertwining of spatial and temporal distances and proximities in Benjamin weave a sublime aura.

This summoning of distant realities within the imperial spatiality of everyday metropolitan life would come to have wide geosocial significance only once the ground of a powerful romantic inheritance had given way to the technologically enhanced visions characterizing his later writings. Whereas the youthful Benjamin affirmed in 1912, "We are still living deep within the discoveries of Romanticism" (in the voice of the "I" in "Dialogue on the Religiosity of the Present"), the mature Benjamin reflected back to Adorno in 1935 on the withering effect a conversation with him and others had on his romantic sensibility: "It was the conversations with you in Frankfurt . . . and then the . . . ones around the table with you, Asja, Felizitas, and Horkheimer, which brought that period to an end. Rhapsodic naïveté had had its day. The forced development of this Romantic mode made it more quickly obsolete, but at that time, and for years afterward, I had no inkling of any other" (III: 51).[9] The accelerated obsolescence of romanticism in Benjamin's outlook draws attention to the kinds of insights that the earlier romantic "forced development" had made possible (or impossible), and what kind of reconfiguration the romantic mode would undergo over subsequent years. That is, the mutation he mentions in his outlook poses these questions: What strata in his thinking remained continuous? Where did the fault lines begin to form? Where exactly did significant breaks and separations begin to surface, and with what consequences?[10]

This chapter will ultimately lead to the conjunction of Brechtian epic theater and Benjamin's notion of the *Lehre* (lesson) on narrative in order to begin addressing these demanding questions. I trace Benjamin's final passage into exile on the remote Spanish island of Ibiza and his drug and other thought experiments on the peripheries of the imperial system over the 1930s. Yet the distinct preconditioning patterns of this key historical shift are discernible in his writings from the earliest years. The relation these bear to the wider German sociohistorical milieu are intriguing, as recent scholarship suggests. For over the long nineteenth century, as the historians Mark Cioc and David Blackbourn have each narrated, nature was being tamed and reutilized for human purposes, secularized through the lens of modern science and technology, and framed, paradoxically, as a potent force in the depiction of landscape in the art and literature of the same period.[11] Simultaneously an elaboration of the tradition as much as an implicit critique of it, Benjamin's early writings betray just how moored he was to this most weighty of German romantic traditions in revealing landscapes pregnant with unmistakably sublime intimations. For instance, in his 1911 sketch, "The Pan of Evening," he indicates how much is concentrated in his landscapes: "Everything particular became landscape, outspread image."[12] In his nearly contemporary short poem "Estranged Land," it is the point of intersection of time and space that landscape captures for reflection on experience:

And where you fall, eons become space;
Glaring figurality will surge round me.
Gnawing thoughts.[13]

Landscape is the mediating point between quasi-autonomous temporal and spatial intuitions, a reflection of an intuition of the nonsensuous beyond the very phenomena represented. It is the encompassing objectivity that recalls to the subject the loss of wholeness and connection as much as it is the framing of the limiting nature of all phenomenal reality. "Things see us; their gaze propels us into the future, since we do not give them an answer but step among them." Rather than being what is expressed in the sunlit image of nature, as may have been the case for earlier moments in the history of German romanticism, the young Benjamin says of romanticism, "We are indebted to its powerful insight into the night side of the natural. At bottom, the natural is not good; it's strange dreadful, frightening, repugnant—crude." Romanticism and landscape unite early on as a purchase on all that lies beyond the edge of bourgeois normativity of fin de siècle Europe: together they produce "the radiance refracted in the nocturnal." This dark radiance illuminates for the young Benjamin, who wrote under the pseudonym "Ardor," alternative modes of grasping time, space, love, and property. In presenting the indeterminate zone between the natural environment and human activity, between the power of the naturally given and the force of historical agency, Benjamin's landscapes and reflections on landscape call for "the sublimity of a sovereign knowledge." The bearer of this knowledge often figures forth in Benjamin's diary, and it is to this bearer that he addresses himself, for "he sends landscape and beloved toward us and is the tireless thinker of thoughts that come only to us."[14]

What remains in the form of Benjamin's landscapes after the erosion of his romantic grounding is thus worth pondering. The tension-ridden and deeply haunted visions of his youth followed in the wake of a new melancholic sense of the fungibility and precariousness of cherished natural environments. Widespread peat digging, moorland drainage, and dam construction opened the gaping threat of ecological degradation, destruction, and pollution. Combined with the peculiar "sense of pathos for lost worlds," characterizing, as Blackbourn has noted, late nineteenth-century writings by the likes of Adalbert Stifter, Theodor Storm, Wilhelm Raabe, and Theodor Fontane, was an inkling of being caught inexorably in processes that were being celebrated simultaneously for making "the reasonless forces [of nature] subservient to the moral purposes of humanity," as Hermann von Helmholtz once put it before a wide German public.[15] Thus it is worth noting that in Benjamin's meditations just quoted, though draped in the romantic exuberance of youth, the landscape is already become mere form, a hangover from a romantic past that is fading, a skeletal language. For within this trope, so exactingly named (*Landschaft*), all flushness and intrinsic nature has been emptied, and the refracted presence of a sovereign appears as a radiance "refracted in the nocturnal."[16]

Like the angelic, allegorical, redemptive and other recurring figures in Benjamin's kaleidoscopic oeuvre, the messianic appears early and has its own quasi–natural-historical evolution. The messianic landscape—in which nature is rendered the mere artifice through which human powers take on refracted appearance, a landscape that only ever evokes the now-deadness of romanticism's once spontaneously vibrant tropes and the question of authorship at its edges—has a peculiar longevity in Benjamin's career. Considering this, it is instructive to observe how the messianic landscape becomes infused with new kinds of significance in step with Benjamin's political trajectory and wider exposure to the deeply divided geographies of imperial capitalism. The landscape form and the political commitment align as if on a split-focus screen in Benjamin's "Marseilles," published in the *Neue schweizer Rundshau* in April 1929. He presents here a panoramic view broken under the pressure of imperial capitalism's contradictions and reassembled in a constellational *Denkbild* in which disparate moments of the imperial totality are brought into a series of frames in the manner of double-exposed negatives. Marseilles is the infamous port city in which the different pieces of the imperial puzzle are in direct juxtaposition and where all the social strata of the French Empire, from the prostitute to the businessman, from the porter to the tourist, intermingle—and not only intermingle but become parts of an ever-functioning diabolical machine. (Benjamin was not averse to spiraling roulette tables of the casino and the street.) By the time he ended up surveying its offering, Marseilles had sealed its reputation as the "capital of the French colonies" by holding two colonial expositions, one in 1906 and the other in 1922. "Marseilles," begins the first fragment, "the yellow-studded maul of a seal with salt water running out between the teeth. When this gullet opens to catch the black and brown proletarian bodies thrown into it by ship's companies according to their timetables, it exhales a stink of oil, urine, and printer's ink" (II: 232). In the red-light district, bashfully referred to as *Les Bricks* by the locals, the "vast agglomeration of steps, arches, bridges, turrets, and cellars" coalesces with "invisible lines" that "divide up the area into sharp, angular territories like African colonies" (II: 232). The disequilibrium experienced in the quasi-colonial prostitutes' quarter is part and parcel of imperial traffic in bodies and services, fluids and appetites, and hints at dealings with the netherworld of imperial spheres—spheres that colors one inevitably in shame: "The whores are strategically placed, ready at a sign to encircle hesitant visitors, and to bounce the reluctant guest like a ball from one side of the street to the other. If one forfeits nothing else in this game, it is his hat" (II: 232). For this city, after all, "the palette itself is pink, which is the color of shame here, of poverty" (II: 232). Shame is the affective magnet of the late colonial city, the sensation at the heart of imperial capitalism: it tinges exploiter and exploited alike in this economy: "The pressure of a thousand atmospheres under which this world of images writhes, rears, piles up, is the same force that is tested in the hard hands of seamen, after long voyages, on the thighs and breasts of women; and the lust that, on the shell-covered caskets, presses from the mineral world a red or blue velvet heart to be pierced with needles and brooches is the same lust that sends tremors through these streets on paydays" (II: 234–35). The landscape that corresponds to the shame economy of Marseilles under this atmospherics of imperialism is that of the outskirts. Here a state of emergency is permanent. Benjamin stayed on this particular journey on the domestic side of what had a colonial counterpart: "the terrain on which incessantly rages the greater decisive battle between town and country" (II: 235).

In the parallaxes produced by the ten fragmentary thought-images that make up "Marseilles" is indexed the late colonial sublime. Benjamin, working as if with the exoskeletal remains of romantic landscapes, produces a vast imperial body of intense libidinal charge, of wide circulation, crosscutting city and country, extending over oceans, joined in the affect of shame. In shame is concentrated the state of emergency holding in place the contradictory relations of imperial society. Its source is discovered in the manner of a divining rod, which is nothing less than the form the *Denkbilder* is in effect: ways to tap into atmospherics that defy detection on phenomenal surfaces, except when it comes to shame, where what needs interpretation is displaced. "The phenomenon of shame is not therefore one phenomenon among others," the Benjamin scholar Peter Fenves has recognized; "it is the phenomenon that discloses a sphere of outwardness that runs counter to the immanence of absolute consciousness."[17] Shame as the alteration of bodily color or outward appearance in general is the sign flush with all the corporeal and libidinal contradictions and desires of empire in "Marseilles." Receiving the unfathomable of the world into itself, the coloration of shame shows simultaneously "how the world would appear if there was nothing in the world to be ashamed of."[18]

II. KENOSIS OF THE KANTIAN SUBLIME

kenosis, n. Theol. The self-renunciation of the divine nature, at least in part, by Christ in the incarnation.

—*Oxford English Dictionary*

A few years into his exile from Germany and long after his rejection from the German academic establishment, Benjamin had occasion to attend the third Conference of the International Congress for Unified Knowledge, held in Paris in July 1937. Of particular interest to him were the proceedings in philosophy, which he was attending with Adorno, the official representative of the Institute for Social Research in exile. Marking the three-hundredth anniversary of the publication of Descartes's *Discours de la méthode*, the event was a virtual spectacle for Benjamin, evoking some hilarity, nausea, and a jarring sense of impossible nostalgia. In a letter to Scholem of August 5, 1937, Benjamin could not help poking fun at the Viennese logistical school, writing that Molière's satire on "debating doctors and philosophers pales in comparison with these 'empirical philosophers,'" meaning Rudolf Carnap and company. In contrast, the presence of the German delegation brought him under the weight of the very academic establishment that had ostracized him: "Its products were sitting before me in the flesh." The Nazi sympathizer Alfred Bäumler "is impressive: his posture copies that of Hitler down to the last detail, and his bull neck perfectly complements the barrel of a revolver." Yet the editor of the journal *Kant-Studien*, the German idealist Arthur Liebert, "had hardly uttered his first words when I found myself carried back twenty-five years into the past, into an atmosphere, to be sure, in which one could have already sensed all the decay of the present."[19] In 1912, exactly twenty-five years earlier, Benjamin had attended Heinrich Rickert's lectures on Kant in Freiburg and attained his first exposure to the Kantian establishment of the new imperial Germany. As the Benjamin translator Howard Eiland has recently observed, Rickert's attempt "to overcome theoretically the antinomies of spirit and nature, form and content, subject and object, and thus to go beyond Kant, would exert a not inconsiderable influence on Benjamin."[20] The closeness and yet alienation—the deep ambivalence—with which Benjamin remembers these years is an index of the *unheimlich* presence of Kantian categories, structures, and contents, however revised, reversed, or transmogrified they became in Benjamin's thought over the intervening years.

With their constant referencing of Kant's moral theories and phrases such as "only in the inexperienceable can we ground all courage and meaning," Benjamin's earliest writings make unmistakable how deep, if not indelible, was the impression that the early exposure to Kant left on his mind.[21] Even toward the end of his career, when describing his historical method as a "Copernican turn in historiography," Benjamin deploys Kantian metaphors and works within recognizably Kantian structures of thought, despite how little accord there may be between the revolutionary tilt of his apparatus and the status quo maintenance of institutionalized Kantianism. I wish to argue not that Benjamin was "Kantian" but that he took advantage of certain indeterminacies and tensions around the question of the sublime in Kant and by doing so turned the entire Kantian system upside down: upon that new upturned basis the Benjaminian constellation of messianism, aura, profane illumination, and a critique of progressive teleology found support. "God's transcendence is at an end. But he is not dead; he has been incorporated into human existence" (I: 289).[22] The philosophical course upon which Benjamin eventually alighted took him from the transcendent sphere of Kantian metaphysics to the immanent potentialities of imperial capitalism. Kant furnished the young Benjamin what he called the "sublimity of a sovereign knowledge" and established the epistemological and critical structure for the central concepts of his late work: from his messianic political theology to the teleologically unhinged quality of now-time (*Jetztzeit*), from the return of aura in the phantasmagoria of the new commodity world to the loosening of categories of near (*Nah*) and far (*Ferne*) from the sphere of measure; from shadowy realms of the imperial totality Benjamin's work summons the redemptive-destructive power of a new collective agency. Much is premised, in other words, on Benjamin's contrapuntal elaboration of Kant's sublime.

When the young Benjamin sees youth as "the capacity for experience that exceeds the rational framework of life" and wishes to make of it the basis for launching a new humanity, he is indexing his indebtedness to the peculiar place of the sublime in Kant's system.[23] Without going too far afield, the aspects of Kant's sublime of greatest relevance to Benjamin's development must be pinpointed: these are to be found in the sublime's nearly unhinged position vis-à-vis the system that Kant is seeking to establish for a priori aesthetic judgment. Further, what is implied by this quasi-autonomy of the sublime is of paramount significance for Benjamin: rather than coming into harmony with the ends of nature, the sublime assumes a position elevated over external forces and an indifference to innate urges, including even those of bodily survival, for the sake of something higher. This "something higher" is essentially what Kant believes is being actualized in moral practice: as Kant marveled at the end of *The Critique of Practical Reason*, "Two things fill the mind with ever new and increasing admiration and awe the more often and more enduringly reflection is occupied with them: *the starry heavens above me and the moral law within me*."[24] Yet the sublime itself as an aesthetic judgment comes with no guarantee that the deep resolution with which, say, a soldier faces death is guided by a morally permissible end. In this moral vacuity is reflected the abyssal risks that the sublime presents for Kant. In his reconstruction of the philosophical system underlying Kant's theory of taste, Henry E. Allison delineates the tensions subsisting in the sublime and the paradoxes that unfold from it. Allison detects Kant's "deeply ambivalent attitude" toward this category, which appears as if included at the last minute. Circulating widely over eighteenth-century discussions on the *sensus communis*, the possibility of a universally shared moral sensibility, the sublime's intrinsic significance, Allison demonstrates, is ultimately ill-suited for the systemic aspirations of the *Critique of the Power of Judgment*. The implications ripple like trouble over the entirety of Kant's critical philosophy. It is perhaps for this reason that Kant speaks of his theory of the sublime as "a mere appendix to our aesthetic judging of the purposiveness of nature."[25]

The category of the beautiful, Kant's primary concern, accords with this "purposiveness of nature." This is because enjoyment of the beautiful, as opposed to the sublime, involves, in Allen Wood's succinct formulation, "a freedom of the imagination that is nevertheless in conformity with understanding, which is analogous to what occurs in a morally good action, where our faculty of desire is in free conformity with laws of reason."[26] Whereas beauty is a reminder that nature "favors us," the sublime is the inexplicable liking for that which hardly lends itself to form, a content Kant refers to as "crude nature," "nature insofar as it does not bring with it the thought of determinate purposes."[27] That is to say, the sublime is counterpurposive (*zweckwidrig*) for our faculty of judgment. Whereas the category of beauty accords with morality, the sublime does not necessarily. Whereas beauty establishes through its display of easily intelligible forms a harmonious interplay between the imagination and understanding, the sublime is charged with negativity and exceeds what can be understood. So beggared is the imagination before the sublime that Kant can only describe its relationship as violent (*gewaltthätig*): "It [the sublime] is an object of (nature) *the representation of which determines the mind to think of nature's inability to attain to an exhibition of ideas.*"[28]

Allison captures all of the implications of the category of the sublime that troubled Kant yet entranced the young Benjamin. At the very center of the sublime for both Benjamin and Kant is the severing of the link between moral duty and nature. In an important *Reflexion*, Kant distinguishes between the kinds of duties the beautiful and the sublime each entail. The beautiful provides an intimation of nature's cooperation if not amenability to moral ends, and thus the moral practice it enjoins is dependent upon what nature itself has to offer, such as, for instance, the cultivation of a spontaneously felt sympathy for suffering others. Because it is dependent upon and complementary to nature's telos, Kant calls the duties beauty enjoins "imperfect." In contrast, the duties connected with the sublime do not require the cooperation of nature to attain some end. Instead, as duties to refrain from doing anything that is inconsistent with humanity's self-legislating capacities, they are "perfect" for being independent, if not thoroughly negative vis-à-vis nature. As Allison realizes, the fulfillment of such perfect duties enjoined by the sublime is entirely "up to us," which means that "the whole teleological dimension that is so important to imperfect duties does not come into play."[29] The sublime is for this reason at odds with Kant's commitment to harmonization of aesthetic judgment, morality, and nature into one overarching teleology. Instead, it suggests a sovereign will not subject to what Benjamin early on calls "developmental time." The absolute sovereign evolves a countertemporality from within the intervals of a teleological process.[30] The young Benjamin grasps as well how Kant's moral philosophy is as much premised on worldly action as on anything supersensible: "Religion is recognition of our duties as divine commands, according to Kant. Which is to say, religion guarantees us something eternal in our daily labors, and that's what we need above all."[31] Already faintly visible through these very early explorations of Kant's metaphysics is a consistent tendency in Benjamin's thought toward the worldly and profane without any of the questions of the absolute being put in abeyance or canceled out. Rather what you have through this language of the absolute is the detection of immanent potentials of the emerging mass society: reflected in the aura of new media machines and dream-like realities of a commodity universe is the possibility of a new revolutionary sovereign creator-destroyer. As we will see, Benjamin in many ways invents a phenomenological language through which one can grasp the late colonial moment in its unbounded totality, a language that separates the categories of proximity (*Nah*) and distance (*Ferne*) from physical measure in what he calls a "colportage phenomenon," the curious phenomenon that is fundamental to the experience of, say, the flâneur "in which far-off times and places interpenetrate the landscape and the present moment."[32]

It is for good reason that the "decay of the present" that Benjamin felt all around him as he listened to the philosophical proceedings of the International Congress for Unified Knowledge took him back to the heyday of neo-Kantianism. By then his encounter with this institutional philosophical behemoth was inevitable. The military metaphors employed by one proponent of neo-Kantianism to describe its ascendancy were neither accidental nor misleading: "the diverse columns of neo-Kantianism had joined together [*schlugen vereint*] and marched out separately" into all of the various institutions of higher learning.[33] As Klaus Christian Köhnke observes in his *Entstehung und Aufstieg des Neukantianismus* (The Genesis and Advance of Neo-Kantianism), by the 1880s "neo-Kantianism had attained the form in which it would be passed down to the present day and in which all of the formulations of its theories—as foreseeable from its internal development and early history—got tacitly laid out and made foundational."[34] Scholem's recollections of his days with Benjamin just as they were both beginning to find their philosophical bearings in the *Universitätsphilosophie* of Wilhelmine Germany in the wake of this development illuminate a key dynamic of Benjamin's reading of Kant: his appreciation of exactly those sublime edges of Kant's system came into collision with the narrowness to which Kant's philosophy had been reduced. Both Scholem and Benjamin recognized these patterns as part and parcel of the rigid conformity and cultural shallowness of institutional philosophy under imperial conditions. The situation as a whole unleashed a series of attempts to resituate the underlying arguments around the sublime in Kant according to alternate cultural norms and social formations as a whole.

Scholem's reminiscences in *Walter Benjamin: The Story of a Friendship*, the correspondence between them, and Benjamin's earliest writings provide glimpses into the ambivalences from which Benjamin worked out his own early critical theory. Scholem recollects that from their first encounters, Benjamin took a special interest in Kant, going so far as to regard Kant's unadorned and rebarbative style as "sublime" (*sublim*).[35] Both Scholem and Benjamin pursued their studies of Kant despite their critical attitude toward the university environment in which neo-Kantianism reigned supreme and despite what Scholem refers to as the "mild but unmistakable anti-Semitic orientation on the part of certain neo-Kantians."[36] Benjamin's 1913 essay "Der Moralunterricht" (Moral Education) already demonstrates how those very unhinged categories of Kant's thought I have discussed could be brought into a critical engagement with the institutional environment in which philosophy was being taught. For instance, Benjamin here grounds "the possibility of a moral education as an integral whole" upon the legislative autonomy of a "pure will."[37] What the Benjamin scholar Beatrice Hanssen has recognized as his "markedly complex, even divided" engagement with Kant would continue over many years, involving a consistent purification of Kant's system through the shedding of antinomian encumbrances and the radicalization of the transcendental and absolute dimensions outlying Kant's system.[38] This kind of appropriation of Kant *contre lui même* was already in full effect in 1918, when Scholem and Benjamin took the opportunity to read together *Kants Theorie der Erfahrung* (Kant's Theory of Experience) by the leading neo-Kantian of their generation, Hermann Cohen. Scholem remembers, "Benjamin had no use for the rationalistic positivism that occupied us during this reading, because he was seeking 'absolute experience.'"[39] The problem fundamentally for Benjamin was that Kant had made foundational for the neo-Kantians an experience of "minor value" (*minderwertige Erfahrung*), making urgent in turn an alternate accounting of faculties and categories on the basis of another conception of experience altogether. The response to this urgency was Benjamin's programmatic statement "On the Coming Philosophy," a transcendental account, that is, "one that presupposes the actuality or existence of its object and seeks to discover the conditions of its possibility," premised on the indeterminacies of hallucinatory experience. Fully presumed are the very unbounded totalities and unbridled powers of an absolute subject underlying Kant's sublime.[40]

The irony of neo-Kantianism was clear: at the very historical moment when human experience had become exponentially expanded and enriched through modern technologies and their incorporation into everyday modes of apperception, neo-Kantianism had constructed its theories of experience as if operating within the confines of a scientific laboratory and upon the principles of a dry mechanistic worldview. Benjamin understood that a reconfiguration of the category of experience would have consequences for all the other central categories of a philosophical system that aimed to be adequate for modern times. Rethinking the category of experience, including the proper subject of such experience, would impact fundamentally the conception of knowledge, including the object of such knowledge: "The task of the coming philosophy can be conceived as the discovery or creation of that concept of knowledge which, by relating experience exclusively to the transcendental consciousness, makes not only mechanical but also religious experience logically possible" (I: 105). Benjamin intends by this "not that knowledge makes God possible but that it definitely does make the experience and doctrine of him possible in the first place" (I: 105). What must be reckoned with are the moments of phenomenal experience that help explain a new need for philosophy: "Eine Philosophie, die nicht die Möglichkeit der Weissagung aus dem Kaffeesatz einbezieht and explizieren kann, kann keine wahre sein."[41] Benjamin goes from merely adumbrating to taking the first steps toward such a future philosophy when he states that its foundations will be akin to religious doctrine, or *Lehre*. Moving from system to the absolutely—that is, ethically, aesthetically, and epistemologically—binding doctrine, Benjamin bases his epistemology not on the stringent logic of neo-Kantianism but on the infinity of language: "The great transformation and correction which must be performed upon the concept of knowledge, oriented so one-sidedly along mathematical-mechanical lines, can be attained only by relating knowledge to language" (I: 107–8).

III. THE ABSOLUTE: LANGUAGE, TRANSLATION, NAME

In July 1916, just when he was beginning to recognize the impoverished understanding of language, experience, and history at the heart of Kant's metaphysics and the constraints these austere foundations put on neo-Kantian thought, Benjamin composed a well-known letter to Martin Buber. With his background in Talmudic scholarship and deep initiation into Hebraic scripture, Buber had already established himself as an authority in biblical studies and as a linguistic virtuoso of sorts. His journal, *Der Jude* (The Jew), sought to bridge the codes of post-Enlightenment European civility with the scriptural languages and orthopraxy of Eastern Jewry in the interest of formulating a renewed Judaism, or what he later called a "Hebraic humanism." Benjamin had reservations about such a project and never in earnest took up Buber's invitation to collaborate on the journal. Yet Benjamin's response reflects an engagement with language and a turn toward the Oriental spheres with which Buber had envious facility, but not, as it were, correct orientation. In contradistinction to the reformist mindset of *Der Jude* Benjamin pointed out where he would follow what he earlier called "the oriental, mystical principle, the one that overcomes limits" (I: 34). In a sketch of what these principles might be, Benjamin provides sharp insight into enduring elements and fundamental patterns of his more mature theory of language. (Considering how Benjamin stalls in replying to the invitation to join *Der Jude*, expresses his intense dislike for many of the contributions to the first issue, and then goes on to draw out his own thoughts on language—"the reason is that what is foremost in my mind is their fundamental relevance to and necessity for my own practical behavior"—it is not without reason that Buber later expressed unhappiness with Benjamin's *chutzpah*).[42]

Much of Benjamin's audacity can be located in his struggling for the foundations of a theory of language that, far from secularizing, would return even "an impotent language, degraded to pure instrument," to its originary divine magic.[43] Benjamin insinuates that he is critical of the linguistic philosophy implicit yet thoroughly operative in *Der Jude* and bourgeois reformism more generally. The fundamental presupposition is one shared and normalized in modern bourgeois society for it establishes an absolute divide between word and deed, that is, between moral motivation (thought to precede language) and the linguistic means (reduced to mere empty code) employed to fulfill it.

Benjamin wishes, in other words, to rescue the linguistic medium from the zeal of the reformer and the norms of market society at the point where they intersect: instrumentality. This requires first of all reducing the distance that the instrumental relation always threatens to increase to the point of total separation of what was originally for Benjamin a magical unity. Undoing the modern sundering of action and language requires first taking into account what language is by momentarily eschewing any relation of potential force with respect to it. In this way, language can appear "as such." The linguistic medium in its purity allows for the maximization of the immanent powers of the present age, in Benjamin's estimation, for pure language on its own becomes a "mechanism for the realization of the true absolute." Against the "widespread tendency to string words together" as if they were mere lifeless objects, he adumbrates a new linguistic practice that would instead be responsive to the magic (*Magie*) and mystery (*Geheimnis*) of language. This depends on the awakening of "interest in what was denied to the word." As the word "is incapable of leading into the divine in any way other than through itself and its own purity," the task is to grasp fundaments of language whose immanent potentials are buried in the modern moment.[44]

A number of critical implications follow from the ruminations ventured in this inspired letter to Buber. Central among them are those Benjamin fashioned over the course of his career and that receive special treatment in his writings on language. One sees a fundamental departure from the narrow grounds of neo-Kantian conceptions of experience in favor of those experiences that correlate with sublime moral commandments, for example, moral autonomy and "pure self-activity" at the heart of such acts as self-sacrifice. Against the sharp divisions in Kant between mind and matter that justify modern control and exploitation of nature, Benjamin's position of noninstrumentality helps to reestablish unforced and originary harmonies of opposites. That is to say, through its unintentional turning of oneself into a tool for language's own self-expression, the noninstrumental disposition reverses and undoes modernity's compulsion to objectify and subjugate the external world and other selves, thereby serving to reveal the alternate ground of an equally intentionless reality. The forming of the absolute through the nonintentional relation between subject and object (or self and other) is thus coincident with the making of language whole again. Language is no longer the subservient bearer of a human will but rather the magical force that allows for a spontaneous harmony to obtain between human effort and creaturely existence, or, to adopt the ancient Greek terminology Benjamin often employs, a spontaneous harmony between the givenness of raw *phusis* and the innateness of human *poeisis*. Language absorbs the human, is entangled with materiality, reflects all historical experience, and yet, despite all the interplay, remains distinct. Key to bringing a harmony with language back into existence is a concerted linguistic policy that aims to keep this distinctness alive, the policy of the "elimination of the ineffable in language." That is, to free language from our own historical constraints with its structuring blindnesses is the essential task, for this goal is "the most obvious form given to us to be effective within language and, to that extant, through it. This elimination of the ineffable seems to me to coincide precisely within linguistic magic."[45] What Benjamin has reestablished in this apocalyptic understanding of language is that the ultimate speaker is the social totality and not an individuated "I" of bourgeois normativity—and, further, that the language in which the infinite social speaks is language as such, that is, the quintessential medium of epic narrative, which lends itself to the spontaneous singing of the absolute collective.[46]

Considering how inconclusive yet suggestive these ruminations on language remained in his letter to Buber, Benjamin returns to them and composes over subsequent months "On Language as Such and the Language of Man" (Über Sprache überhaupt und über die Sprache des Menschen, 1916), an inquiry into the central linguistic phenomenon of naming, and later "The Task of the Translator" (Die Aufgabe des Übersetzers, 1921), a seminal investigation into the processes of translation and their potential for forging a future universalism. These essays are remarkable for fusing a variety of intellectual currents that could take on articulation—such as the stronger absolute to which they give expression—only through the sloughing off of strictly Western, not simply Kantian, metaphysical frames of reference. Acting as a critical reminder of the limitations of Western metaphysics was an emerging body of work stemming from Judaism; like Benjamin's, this Judaic tangent in fin de siècle Germany aimed to surpass both the existing religious orthodoxies and secular premises of modern epistemology. The years immediately before, during, and after World War I are characterized by a series of encounters with significant religious thinkers in German Jewish circles, among whom, apart from Scholem, Erich Gutkind and Erich Unger will prove to have shaped Benjamin's intellectual direction in lasting ways. This interface with non-Western forms of experience and knowledge will establish for Benjamin an increasingly critical vantage point: that of "pessimism all along the line," as he puts it in "Surrealism: The Last Snapshot of the European Intelligentsia" (II: 216). The "organization of pessimism" in Benjamin's political vocabulary is nothing other than an expression of a larger pessimism about and self-distantiation from the fate of European civilization and humanity as such, as a matter of principle.[47] Equally fused into the substance of these essays, though, are the grounds for a redemptive urge. Between 1914 and 1915, Benjamin undertook a major translation of Baudelaire's poems. Working simultaneously with the concept of language and the materiality of communicative media, with foreign and familiar words, the experience of translation would prove decisive for producing an apocalyptic and redemptive form of criticism. Thus, in "Announcement of the Journal *Angelus Novus*," Benjamin claims that true translation "as the strict and irreplaceable school of language-in-the-making" develops new from old languages and responds to "the challenge to abandon superannuated linguistic practices" (1: 294). In other words, he fused together some essential elements of a language-theology, in which creative, redemptive, and fully generative potentials are given emphasis.

It is worth noting how micro- and macrological scales of Benjamin's *Sprachtheologie* find their point of intersection in this very generative element in language: from the ephemeral and microscopic manifestation of pure language between old idioms and new communicative media in the act of translation he deduces a theory of language that operates on the scale of the Genesis story in the Hebrew Bible. The generative dimension of language found in translation is but one facet of an ongoing creative vitality: creation as such. A remark Scholem makes in *Walter Benjamin: The Story of a Friendship* reveals the role translation played in shaping Benjamin's engagement with Jewish inheritance, including biblical narratives, over the longue durée. Scholem set up a meeting between Benjamin, himself, and the chancellor of the Hebrew University in Jerusalem, Rabbi Judah L. Magnes, when they all happened to be in Paris in the summer of 1927. He recalls that Benjamin on this occasion "laid stress on his translation work as a stimulus to philosophical and theological reflections, whose resolution was to be found in Hebrew. These things, he said, had made him ever more clearly conscious of his being Jewish [*jüdisches Wesen*]."[48] He spoke as well of how deeply the Bible had spoken to him in the context of ongoing translation work. Theological reflection is occasioned in his thought by the gap between different languages in which pure language speaks. Between this gap and God a reciprocity is ventured: Benjamin's notion of *Sprachmagie* finds its basis in the creative force of language to be found in the act of translation, and the act of translation, in turn, no matter how trivial it might appear, provides the conceptual apparatus for grasping "the frontier between the finite and infinite" (I: 69). This frontier is marked by the act of naming. Naming, in other words, is the translational moment or mediating point between the created world in its infinity and the infinity given to human creativity in language.

"On Language as Such and the Language of Man" points out how creative vitality is generated through an ongoing interaction between the contents of communication (the world that is communicated through language) and the medium of communication (what is communicated in language itself). This latter Benjamin calls "Das Mediale," for it is "the immediacy of all mental communication" (I: 64). "What is communicated *in* language—that is, in the medium itself—cannot be externally limited or measured, and therefore all language contains its own incommensurable, uniquely constituted infinity" (I: 64). What is communicated in the medium itself is a reflection of pure language, for in this instance no distinction between form and content, signifier and signified, or vehicle and tenor obtains. Thus language allows for a movement between what is measurable and what is not, between finite and infinite moments of thought. The recognition that mediation (language) is given immediately (i.e., as a spontaneous capacity) signifies, as Hanssen has noted, the possibility of "a language movement encompassing different centers, stadia of being or existence, which [are] infinitely completed and consummated in the Absolute."[49] Translation is simply the movement through these different, nearly incommensurable scales of language-existence, what brings them together and marks their separation. Translation as movement passes necessarily through "the decay of the blissful Adamite spirit of language" in which the word of God, indistinguishable from his creative act, gives way to the naming of things by Adam, which in turn collapses to the mere proper name in human society after the Fall (I: 71).

The referencing of Genesis throughout the essay is in keeping not with any institutional canon but with esoteric circles of predominantly Jewish intellectuals—Buber, Gutkind, and Cohen—who were turning to Hebrew scripture to grasp possibilities in the contemporary moment. The biblical narrative, with its affirmation of "a special relationship between man and language resulting from the act of creation," must be seen as a general longing for a paradisiacal state in futurity. This state of absolute beatitude is evoked in the pure language that God is known to speak in Genesis, in which there is perfect coincidence between speaking and creation, word and thing, meaning and form, speech and intention, motivation and result. The phenomenon in the fallen human world that allows for interface and participation with this order of language is to be found in the act of naming. "The proper name is the communion of man with the *creative* word of God," writes Benjamin, and the "theory of the proper name is the theory of the frontier between finite and infinite language" (I: 69). Reflected in the very act of naming is an index of a wide-open freedom of self-determination that is hidden in the figure of God, for in the very act of naming is reflected what is gifted by natural agency to the human: the potential "to give birth to the language of things themselves" (I: 69). The mystical appreciation of the name is translational of the quasi-divine for in it there is full coincidence between word and thing, and through it an impossible ideal is established by which modernity's fallen state can be measured. The act of naming is the "language of language" (*Sprache der Sprache*) for here one is in accord with the linguistic nature of the human (*Das Sprachliches Wesen des Menschen*). In naming, one is participating in spontaneous and intentionless creativity with the medium that is given and, in doing so, giving expression to language as such. This trajectory toward an absolute linguistic state in Benjamin verges on the loss of intelligibility, as if before blinding refulgence. As Shierry Weber Nicholssen has expressed it, "when language itself begins to speak, when it moves farther from meaning and closer to mimesis, even briefly, it comes closer to names and thus to things as well."[50]

This erasure of the ineffable within the materiality of a reflective medium—in this case, language—gives expression to the Absolute in a historical moment characterized by increasing fragmentation, normalized instrumentality, distortions of freedom, rampant relativism, and spiritual impoverishment.

IV. EPIC AND INTOXICATION: VEILS OF THE ABSOLUTE SUBJECT

Sie stehen im Zentrum; ich promenierte bestenfalls auf einer Tangente. (You're standing in the center; I'm at best traveling on a tangent.)

—Walter Benjamin, letter to Alfred Kurella, June 2, 1933

Composed during the unique Ibizan experience of "the most inhospitable and most untouched of any habitable landscapes" he had yet witnessed, these lines from Benjamin's letter to the Soviet Comintern official Alfred Kurella reflect a peculiar self-awareness of the strange trajectory he was on: headlong into the abyss between the modern extremes of the colony and the metropolis.[51] The year is 1933, the very year that will separate his interwar experience into a "before" and an "after" (IV: 382). Reflecting back from his last days on this critical year, Benjamin mentions first his travels (Italy, the Scandinavian countries, Russia, and Spain) and then the fact that he left Germany in March, just after the Nazi declaration of a state of emergency and the quick consolidation of totalitarian rule. As Eiland and Jennings recognize in their biography, the very thought of travel had long been Benjamin's favorite psychological "poison"; now travel itself would bring spells of elemental melancholy punctuated by crystalline insights transferred to small notebooks and typewritten pages in a seemingly unending *peripateia* leading to a drug-induced suicide.[52] After his divorce, the proceedings of which left him bereft of his family inheritance by the judge's order, and after the rejection of his *Habilitationsschrift* on *The Origins of German Tragic Drama* (*Trauerspiel*), travel served to distract his mind from his ever shrinking prospects. Once Benjamin and his like were being reduced to human trash and rid from German soil by National Socialist operations—approximately 100,000 Germans fled Hitler's Germany between 1933 and 1935—Benjamin embarked on a journey through a series of makeshift situations that would lead him to the outer edges of modernity. He washed up on the pristine shores of Ibiza as the human refuse of a Europe that was ceasing to exist. He was now the bearer of a cultural tradition and language that had little place left for him. He was now, as the locals of Ibiza came to know him, "el misérable." Here the everyday experience of a distended temporality offered by underdevelopment mixed with the occasional experiments with hashish and opium to open distinct spheres of inquiry for Benjamin. To conclude this chapter, I will touch on how the quasi-colonial otherness of Ibiza left traces in Benjamin's inquiries into epic as a form, especially into its distinct temporality, and how the imbibing of exotic substances from the colonial hinterlands allowed "for the loosening of the self through intoxication" and the articulation of new kinds of collective agency on the basis of the revolutionary energies slumbering in the world of everyday things and the crowds forming from the refuse of modern society, in which the flâneur is exemplary as "l'homme des foules" (II: 208; IV: 27).

The circumstances that brought Benjamin to Ibiza in 1932 and 1933 have been recounted in greatest detail in Eiland and Jennings's recent biography, including descriptions of Benjamin's peculiar, if not penurious living conditions, and need not be rehearsed here. Vicente Valero's *Experiencia y pobreza: Walter Benjamin en Ibiza, 1932–1933* (Experience and Poverty: Walter Benjamin in Ibiza, 1932–1933) provides a nearly exhaustive account of conditions on the island at that time and portrays the key personalities who congregated there and who, like the art collector and drug enthusiast Jean Selz, shaped Benjamin's experiences over these years.[53] Yet it is worth observing how these journeys into the peripheries of the imperial world economies occurred just at the moment, Benjamin realized, when "the colonizing atmosphere"—the "most hateful of atmospheres" for him—had begun to swallow and slowly dissolve the ages-old ways of life of the island and the wider region.[54] The abruptness of the transformation he was witnessing lent a peculiar poignancy to his observations, for Ibiza was dissolving every day now under the spatiotemporal pressures of imperial capitalism. Travel had allowed for his attunement to undergo modification. "This time I wanted to explore the epic vein," he writes in "Spain, 1932." Reflected in the writings of the Ibiza period is a new attunement to the waning of the life-world that had given birth to forms such as the epic and a sharp awareness of the causes and consequences of the slow erosion of once seemingly spontaneous skills such as storytelling and narrative as such. For instance, in "The Handkerchief," a short *Denkbild* laced with explicit references to his own journey by steamship to Spain, Benjamin writes of one Captain O. as "the first and perhaps the last storyteller I ever met in my life" (II: 658). These observations and insights, once "purified of all vague impressions" left from travel, culminated in the classic essay "The Storyteller" and discussions around Brecht's epic theater.

What becomes apparent in many of Benjamin's writings over the last years of his life is just how catalytic the experience in Ibiza was for bringing his thoughts about narrative, memory, time, and revolution into sharp focus and penetrating formulation. The world of Ibiza contrasted so sharply with the entirety of Benjamin's rather typical bourgeois upbringing as to practically negate it. "It was a place removed from all civilization," he wrote to Gretel Adorno in 1933, meaning removed from all modern normativity. Of course Benjamin recognized that Ibiza had its own alluring economy, sociality, and expressive forms. As with others new to the island at this point in its history, he was thoroughly taken by the archaic quality that inhered in each. Here were to be found the seals of a primordial existence still active in nearly every facet of the island, for Ibiza remained a "place where antiquity could still be contemplated as a living object and not as a pile of ruins," Valero writes.[55] The radical alterity of Ibiza impressed upon Benjamin many prescient (and ever more relevant) *Weltanshauungen* that find their way into his conceptualization of epic form. The island virtually gave wider scope to his already pronounced commitments to the temporality of transience, critique of modernity, and theorization of natural history. Thus, against the reified divide between the modern subject and object, which allows for the domination of nature, animals, and humans to emerge as the normative measure of progress, Benjamin counterposits the immanent and internally harmonious measure of the pathway through the Ibizan countryside: "There are no highways or mail routes leading here, but neither were these just paths made by animals. Instead, here in the open countryside converged the pathways on which farmers and their wives and children and herds, through the centuries, had moved from field to field, from house to house, from pasture to pasture, rarely in such a way that they did not return to sleep under their own roof at night" (II: 664). The sense of distended time reaching into the infinite past in these reflections—"Things change, and trade places; nothing remains and nothing disappears"—opens a creaturely interface between the human and animal, between transience and permanence, culture and materiality (II: 664). (This is exactly the quality of creaturely or epic time that Benjamin will attempt through the medium of "The Storyteller.") Benjamin wrote often of feeling at a zero point in historical time in Ibiza, as if before the threshold of the original moment of naming and historical becoming. "The farmer . . . has the key" to this eternal code of the original names. "He knows their names" in silence, whereas the modern observer, with his cornucopia of language, "has only knowledge without the names" (II: 662).

What dilates in the silence of the farmer are the possibilities offered to the imagination by boredom; the temporality of boredom spurs the human skill for improvisation and endless self-potentiation. As consumerist distraction—perhaps Benjamin's most prescient of categories for the study of modern culture—colonizes the space once given to boredom, so does it vanquish the skill for storytelling, for "people who are not bored cannot tell stories" (II: 658). In various sketches of this period, such as the seminal "Experience and Poverty" (1933), Benjamin paints a picture of bourgeois civilization submerging all of nature and all immediate interaction with nature under the onus of artificiality, severing itself thus from experience in a fundamental sense—"poverty of human experience in general" (II: 732). The distance Ibiza afforded Benjamin from the habits of the typical German bourgeois—"habits that do more justice to the interior he is living in than to himself," unfortunately—made for experiences that often defied the encodings of his language (II: 734). One instance will help illustrate what is a leitmotif in his writings on Ibiza: a sense of his language's inadequacy in conveying the rawness of the Ibizan experience. In a letter to Gretel Adorno, he describes an encounter with local women on a procession along a deserted beach where he and Paul Gauguin (*petit-fils* of the painter) had disembarked after a long dreary outing for lobsters on the sea. It is as if Benjamin feels himself at that unrepresentable zero point of temporal experience: "And there we were presented with an image of such immutable perfection that something strange but not incomprehensible took place within me: namely, I actually did not see it at all; it made no impression on me; because of its perfection, it existed at the very brink of the invisible." The imaginary "historical indicator" of which he speaks sporadically in his correspondences was, "as it were . . . on zero and I did not notice a thing."[56]

Far from seeking to avoid the content of such apparently unrepresentable areas in his midst, Benjamin wished to delve into their veiled potentialities. From his early metaphysical writings, he questioned the limits of the egoistic "Ich" of bourgeois society in youthful thought experiments with sublime landscapes. This questioning implicated as well the normativity of "developmental time" within Western imperialist hegemony, as we glimpsed in the first section of this chapter. Before arriving in Ibiza, Benjamin had already experimented with hashish, opium, and other drugs in unofficial protocols and had already worked out various writing strategies to mimic the experience of intoxication, as in the short story "Myslovice—Braunschweig—Marseilles."

Moreover, in "Surrealism," he underscored not only "the propaedeutic function of intoxicants in achieving a 'profane illumination' of the revolutionary energies slumbering in the world of everyday things," as Eiland and Jennings recognize, but also the fact that the "image space to which profane illumination initiates us" marks a profound rupture with the normative image space of collectivity fostered in bourgeois centers of European society (something Eiland and Jennings fail to see, as do nearly all Euro-American Benjamin scholars; II: 217). It was as if the intoxication purified oneself for a futural collectivity that appeared veiled without it or revealed only through it. Selz, with whom Benjamin continued his drug experiments while in Ibiza, makes a revealing remark in "An Experiment by Walter Benjamin": "We then observed that *the opium was divesting us of the country in which we were living.* Benjamin added the humorous remark that we were engaging in 'curtainology' [*rideaulogie*]."[57] Whether or not drug-induced, this "curtainology" appears in Benjamin's Ibiza writings to have involved allowing oneself to dissolve into the elements, freeing the imagination to exist independently of one's subjectivity, and to lend voice, however tangentially, to cosmological creatureliness, or to the elements themselves. Through her keen observations of several allusions in Benjamin's "Myslovice—Braunschweig—Marseille," Carol Jacobs gives insight into how Benjamin repotentiates subjectivity through the destruction of the authorial name. "If Benjamin speaks in the name of another, writes in the name of the 'poison,' metaphorical source of the intoxication itself, it is also in the name of that most famous poison of all, hemlock (*Schierling*)," for it is not Benjamin (or whoever the narrator may be) who is the author of the story, but a so-called Eduard Scherlinger, whose surname is a play on the German word for "hemlock" and from whom an unending slippage of names and references begins.[58] Whoever the author of this tale is, by the end he is one transformed, for the "rhythm of the prose is such that we slip from name to name: names of authors, storytellers, artists, cities."[59] In his intoxication, Scherlinger (or is it Benjamin now?) mentions, "My gaze fell on the creases in my white beach trousers—I recognized them, the creases of a burnous. My gaze fell on my hand—I recognized it, a brown, Ethiopian hand. And while my lips stayed firmly sealed, refusing drink and speech in equal measure, from within me a smile rose up to them—a supercilious, African, Sardanapoline smile, the smile of a man about to see through the world and its destinies and for whom nothing remains a mystery anymore, either in objects or in names."[60] These figurative excursions on the loosening effects of intoxication on the bourgeois self were furthered in Ibiza to purify oneself of one's European self as a reciprocation of Europe's ridding of one's actual physical being from its delimited collectivities and demarcations of earth. This is the abyss between the extremes of the imperial order that intoxication (*Rausch*) figuralizes. *Rausch* thus became for Benjamin a medium through which one can access the primordial sense of time and its varying durations. Elemental time is summoned to speak in the medium of an element that deteriorates the centrality of the "I" in Benjamin's work. What emerges through the intoxicating substance is the distended temporality that Benjamin will associate with the epic form and some grasping for the futural collectivity upon the grounds of a new technologically reworked and thoroughly phantasmatic landscape—the natural territory of that exemplar of modernity, the flâneur, one of the masses, standing on any street corner.

The countersubject emerging as the progenitor of another beginning on the plain of modernity will, like the flâneur, itself be generated from the refuse of modernity. This subject will reoccupy the space of boredom, whose destruction by distraction and endless chatter eviscerates the ground for storytelling and cripples the transmission of experience. Its form will be a reconfiguration of what is destroyed with storytelling: the epic, whose emergence in the new conditions breaks with the taboo on didacticism in art. The epic asserts its usefulness for teaching experience just when this category is dissolving under the pressures of reification. As the vehicle for a new evolving collective, the epic now appears as much a medium connecting the near and the distant through collective, even creaturely memory as a discursive web drawing together all the various subjects strewn between the imperial metropolis and the colonial backwater into one shame economy, as we glimpsed in the *Denkbild* "Marseilles." The epic had already been asserted as the renewal of the collective subject in Alfred Döblin's *Berlin Alexanderplatz* and the programmatic essay that accompanied it, "Der Bau des epischen Werks" (The Construction of the Epic Work), both published in 1929. For Benjamin, Brecht (who considered Döblin his "illegitimate father") is the fulfilled theorist of the neo-epic, for he is "a specialist in starting from the beginning," and that is "what makes him a dialectician" (III: 330). With him, older models of temporal experience are salvaged from the endless, hellish replay of consumer fashions. Modernity, the "time of hell," is challenged with the distended time of epic.

The picture of the epic that will be adequate for the new collective Benjamin wishes to awaken from the dream worlds of the commodity-fetish is found in no single work of his and must be constructed or derived from the constellational pattern his last projects left behind. If "The Storyteller" had a nostalgic, even romantic ring, with all its evocations of a vanishing *Lebenswelt* of infinite continuity through the preservation of memory, itself the medium that blurs the distinction between distance and proximity, Benjamin's writings on Brecht demonstrate the application of the epic for contemporary situations. The epic will serve to widen and strengthen the new collective agencies that Döblin and Brecht were already beginning to detect within the wide ambit of imperial capitalism. This is because it is a medium in which old presences summoned by the storyteller (or epic dramatist) are replenished with his new energy, and he himself is enhanced by the experiences he is able to relive and recapture for the present. The direct participation and expertise of the audience is essential for the neo-epic, for the position of the storyteller and the listener may be switched instantly, as will be essential for the carrying of the lesson forward into the future. Narrative itself is generative of new possibilities: far from expending itself, it "is like those seeds of grain that have lain for centuries in the airtight chambers of the pyramids and have retained their germinative power to this day" (III: 148). As the medium of the absolute subject, the epic reestablishes the "old coordination among soul, eye, and hand," but now on the scale of time, space, and world (III: 162). It is the home of all of that has been and all that is to come. Allowing for the inhabitation of the totality by all, without any limits as to what kinds of times, spaces, and dwellings can be established in the future, drawing together the near and the distant into one plentitudinous present: the epic is the medium through which the messianic force existing within the present can awaken and find its natural-historical home.

PART II

Neo-Epic Constellation

Out of British India

CHAPTER 4

Hali's Transvaluation of Modernity

Allegories of Marsiya

I. MODERNITY'S WAY IN A COLONIAL LAND

It is irresistible to imagine that on the night the young Altaf Hussain (1837–1914) abandoned his traditionally arranged marriage and extended family in the provincial Punjabi *qasbah* of Panipat and set off for the legendary capital of the Mughal Empire, Delhi, he was already destined to be modern. It would take some decades yet before he would adopt the nom de plume by which he would thereafter be known: Hali, or "man of the times," the "contemporary," or even "the modern one." Yet on that night in 1854, the difficult, recursive, jagged journey had already begun. It would take him from escaping the clutches of tradition to taking recourse to it, if only to brace against the force of imperial power. To retrace the zigzags of his path and to analyze the works that marked his progress is to revisit the ambivalences and ambiguities that the movement toward modern times (*jadidiyat*) often provoked in colonial settings. In this case, these very ambivalences and ambiguities generated the particular energies that ultimately gave rise to a self-conscious and increasingly critical romanticism in the decades after his death in 1914.

As the details of Hali's trajectory have been discussed on several scholarly occasions,[1] I need point out only those moments of his life history most salient for the kinds of ambivalences and paradoxes I will explore here. Aside from the prescient quality of his pronouncements and the pregnant nature of his experiments with the Urdu language, what is noteworthy about his course is that it bridges the historical divide between the ancien régime of the Mughals and the new British colonial dispensation. From the moment he absconded to Delhi, Hali served as a mediating agent between provincial and metropolitan centers at various moments in his life. This was the case not merely at the subcontinental level but on an imperial plane as well, as Christopher Shackle and Javed Majeed observe penetratingly in their critical writings on this figure.[2] Between 1854 and 1869, Hali moved back and forth between Delhi and rural Punjab, bringing a taste of one to the other. Furthermore, over the first half of the 1870s, he edited Urdu translations of English textbooks on literary and historical matters for the British at the Government Book Depot in Lahore. This position allowed for the transmission of hegemonic aesthetic ideologies to find their way into colonial educational institutions. Being a conduit in this transmission, Hali acquired a Victorian aesthetic education that was itself a response to the Indian cultural forms that had slowly penetrated the chain of imperial command to the queen herself. As one who seconds the imperial morality as a refugee from the old regime, Hali embodies the shift from traditionalist mentoring toward the uneasy inculcation of modern science.

The passing of the old was marked in Hali's gradual turn away from the organic intellectuals of the classical order, such as Nawab Mustafa Khan Shefta and Mirza Asadullah Khan Ghalib, and the gravitational pull of Sir Sayyid Ahmad Khan, the loyalist Muslim modernist. However innovative the former may have been within the contexts and confines of classical forms, it was with Sir Sayyid that Hali sided and from whom he received support and guidance from the late 1870s until the end of his active life three decades later. It is telling how Hali depicts Sir Sayyid in his most celebrated and influential work, the neo-epic *Musaddas: Madd o Jazr-e Islam* (Musaddas: The Flow and Ebb of Islam, 1879). Here, in a work apparently motivated to convey "an exactly accurate picture of the present state of the community" and thus to render a rationally oriented reformist message, Hali cannot help reverting to classical mythopoetic images, for Sir Sayyid is "a servant of the Lord" (*khuda ka banda*), the "magic" of whose glance is so powerful that "whoever he looked at would close his eyes and go along with him."[3] Over the course of these years under the influence of Sir Sayyid, Hali became, despite the religious overtones of some of his language, one of the most prominent advocates of secular learning, the scientific worldview, and rationalist reformism in the Indo-Muslim community.

This potential—and potentially paradoxical—mismatch between medium and message characterizes much of Hali's most important works, especially *Musaddas*. Such mismatch brings to the fore his own underlying ambivalences regarding the processes of modernization under duress. The compulsion to conform to the Victorian ethos and to adapt the aesthetic code of the colonizer finds confused and contradictory response in his writings. As he had witnessed with his own eyes the scintillating glow of the last flame of Delhi's courtly culture, according to legend the ultimate effusion of all the aesthetic powers of Indo-Islamic civilization, could he really have been a cheerful follower of the British colonizers who had extinguished it? Is there not a tinge of nostalgia in the very subjects he took up for his literary critical efforts, such as *Yadgar-e Ghalib* (Memento of Ghalib, 1897) or *Hayat-e Sa'adi* (The Life of Sa'adi, 1886), toward the end of his life?[4] There is little doubt that Hali appreciated the challenges presented by the new rulers of the West, especially the manner in which they prodded one and all to experiment, innovate, and revolutionize the ways of old. "When I beheld the new pattern of the age [*zamana ka naya thath*]," he confesses in the first preface to *Musaddas*, "my heart became sick of the old poetry, and I began to feel ashamed of stringing together empty fabrications."[5] But was he willing or even able to break with the deeply entrenched Islamic Weltanschauung in order to imitate his Western masters? Did he not seek to find solutions to the new challenges and ways to accommodate the new dispensation by revisiting and renewing the origins of Islamic civilization? Was there not, he seems to have wondered, a way to reconnect with the energies that propelled Islamic civilization to its glorious heights of geopolitical hegemony and technological supremacy in the classical age? Was there not a way to rechannel those same energies to overcome the abject state in which Indian Muslims especially found themselves under British colonialism? Was not British supremacy the world over the result of their better emulation of the model advanced by Islam? Had not contemporary Muslims failed at this, their own authentic task? Such questions are meant to delineate the pressures Hali felt to become simultaneously modern and Muslim, to become scientific but not at the cost of faith, to push for progress yet not leave behind the animating spirit of the classical Islamic past, to absorb the aesthetic lessons of the Western overlords without abandoning the entirety of received Indo-Islamic traditions.

Hali's predicament seeks rhetorical resolution, and in hopes of that, he orients himself to the classical epic.

Shackle and Majeed have noted the ambiguities and ambivalences arising from Hali's experiences in the colonial milieu in their magisterial study of his *Musaddas*.[6] My reading aims to complement their work by delineating the discursive choices Hali made and their implications for grasping the cultural modes by which modernity was made inhabitable by its subjects in Victorian India. Of central significance will be the aesthetic form—in this case, the neo-epic—that was advanced as a way to imaginarily frame what was historically impossible at the moment, leaving in its wake apocalyptic imagery. Deeply structuring *Musaddas* and the object of some theoretical reflection in his *Muqaddamah-e Sh'er o Sha'iri* (Prolegomena to Poetry and Poetics) is the figure of allegory.[7] The work of allegory in *Musaddas* takes one beyond Hali's explicit intentions. By manifesting the underlying ambivalences about the colonial dispensation and revealing the logic of a late colonial sublimity, allegory traces the contours of a counternormative modernity.

II. AMBIVALENCES ON THE WAY TO HALI'S *MUSADDAS*

In their richly detailed and nuanced analysis of Hali's *Musaddas*, Shackle and Majeed lead the way to the contradictory valences concentrated in the allegorical figure. They reveal just how internally complicated and deeply vexed is what appears on the surface as a simple yet sweeping narrative of the rise and fall of Islamic civilization. Embedded within this work of criticism and blame meant to prod the Indo-Muslim public toward higher ideals—toward progress—are a number of perplexing inconsistencies. Beginning with the very materiality of the book itself, there are very tangible ways in which the work breaks with existing tradition intentionally and yet marks uncanny continuities at another. Shackle and Majeed observe that the very design of the book captures all at once an ambivalent movement. In forgoing the usual calligraphic embellishments and the simulacra of embroidery common in works of literary entertainment at the time, the printing style of Hali's *Musaddas* diverges from the conventions of poetry books.[8] Yet, while breaking with those conventions, it seems to resemble in its modest size and austere look works of Islamic popular devotion, on the one hand, and the streamlined quality of an Urdu textbook in the new Victorian style, on the other. The production is "unassuming, disciplined, and prosy."[9] Shackle and Majeed describe the tension embedded in the very design between traditional devotionalism, especially Shi'a *marsiya*, and the secularizing imperative of modern, especially Victorian, education. The contrast is "between a poetic format powerfully suggesting a rather long established genre designed to move its audience to public tears and a physical format modestly suggesting the utilitarian functions of an educational text of a kind only recently introduced into the vernacular languages of India."[10] These mutually opposing tendencies bring out potentialities of modernity often at odds with the normative tale of progression. It is as if, whenever Hali ventures to take a step forward toward a rather uncertain future, he matches it with an allegorizing step back upon familiar Islamicate tropes. These now operate in a historical temporality with which they are at odds.

These rhetorical tensions are symptomatic of more basic ambivalences at the level of the work's melancholic affect. The abject condition to which Hali attributes the genesis of his work reveals the very strong affinity that, *pace* Benjamin, melancholy has toward the allegorical form. Shackle and Majeed uncover, layer after layer, the thematic tensions and ambiguities that obtain on account of such a self-flagellating and self-paralyzing state of decline. Such a process of laying bare ultimately casts doubt upon Hali's commitment to the idea of progress, to a notion of human agency able to enact it, and to the project of modernity itself, normatively understood. First, there is the problem of whether one is encouraged to go historically backward or forward after the moment of awakening. Is regaining the classical spontaneity of Islam's founding really the best way to move forward? It becomes obvious in Hali's account of the founding of Islam that the kind of agency involved in that seismic shift was beyond the scope of the human: it is, by his own reckoning, unapproachable. Further, though later figures believe the classical moment of Islam is the ultimate model to emulate—for during that period, a genuine inner piety was supposedly mirrored by a just external polity—the prospect of actualizing such a state of affairs in the present seems next to nil without divine intervention.[11] Thus, even if the movement toward the classical is meant to remind the Muslim community of its past greatness and the strides it made to advance all of humanity, it is moot whether such an example will do anything other than make this community despair of its present capacities. Second, the very image of history that emerges over the course of this neo-epic seems to be guided more by abstract, inscrutable metaphysical principles than anything localizable as merely human. Thus the metaphor of tidal forces—"the flow and ebb of Islam"—connected to stellar movements in the heavens evokes the circularity of the seasons and the numinal, mysterious workings of a supernatural force.[12] Such abstract structuring tropes of the work suggest, Shackle and Majeed note, "a natural, cyclical process over which we have no power."[13] This cyclical and quasi-natural temporality overwhelms the linearity upon which the notion of progress depends. This entire quandary regarding the status of linear time helps to explain the fraught and vexed role of the notion of progress within the entire poem. It is on this question that Shackle and Majeed's analysis proves most compelling, bringing into the open the mixed feelings Hali has about modernity as a whole. Despite the explicit embrace of "the new pattern of the age" and the intention to awaken within the Muslim community an enthusiasm for the modern, it turns out that Hali has a less than sanguine attitude about progress. "We still do not have even the slightest idea as to what sort of carrion bitch progress is" (M 138). Such is the force modernity exerts upon diverse subject peoples that they are rewarded only if they are willing to completely mold themselves to its contours: "They let themselves be poured into every mould. Where things have changed, they change too. / They know the demands of every occasion. They recognize the expressions of the age" (M 137). Such demands give non-compliance cachet, if not great appeal. Considering how little human effort counts ultimately in a process moved by quasi-natural forces, and considering too the morbid undertones of progress itself, it should be no surprise that the rather carefree, ludic qualities of traditional society become alluring. Thus, in spite of Hali's moral condemnations, Shackle and Majeed observe, there is "a festive energy to the picture of young blades roaming around fairs, visiting wrestling pits and taverns, indulging in the sports of quail-fighting and pigeon-racing, loitering around affecting the pose of languorous lovers, and uttering curses in the 'gatherings of the base.'"[14]

I will return to the figuralization of these ambivalences to argue that allegory is the form that best accommodates so many divergent drives and best suits such pathos. Before turning to the allegorical polarities of Hali's neo-epic, it is interesting to note a peculiar convention of literary-historical periodization in Urdu studies. Despite all the hesitations I have mentioned, Hali is a modernist, and his innovations within the Victorian imperium testify to a denigration of the classical tradition, especially that of the *ghazal*. The point of my analysis is to account for the kinds of rhetorical strategies that were embraced to accommodate colonial power. Further, it is best not to equate a melancholy rhetoric regarding the decline of Urdu when it was on the cusp of becoming the lingua franca on the silver screens of the Bombay film industry. Yet if Hali is modern, as conventional understanding has it, then what does that say of modernity in the Victorian milieu, and in late colonial India more generally? What kind of modernity, then, does the *Musaddas* express? The question is pertinent because the sublime force that is beseeched—what one is asked to reckon with—does not accord well with the usual expectations of modernity: disenchantment and secularization. There appears in this instance to be no future in which human beings will realize they are the real authors of their present condition. The abject state seems the least able to come to such a healthy understanding of itself. For the melancholic state of mind, lost in its own ruins, the immediate world presents merely oracular encodings of heavenly intentions. In this state, one reconciles with the shortcomings of human existence and the fallen world through the allegorical mode.[15]

III. ALLEGORICAL POLARITIES

Downfall (*pasti*), ruin (*barbadi*), and sickness (*bimari*) weigh upon the psyche simultaneously presented and reflected in the *Musaddas*. Considering the abrupt downfall of the Mughal Empire in the wake of the 1857 Mutiny, the precipitous demotion and increasing vulnerability of the Muslim community under the British Raj, and the devastating famines that wracked northern India on an unprecedented scale over the decades in which Hali was most active, such sentiments are fitting. The vision presented in the poem is at one with such ruin. Indeed, the world it surveys is one of disorder on a vast scale, wherein the distinction between natural landscape and cultural artifact is increasingly wanting and historical time melds with the movement of natural forces. Likewise, the vision of the poem itself shifts abruptly from a social to a natural plane, drawing analogies between the immediate human wreckage and the inscrutable might of God and nature beyond human reckoning. This kind of allegorical vision penetrates the entire work and is signaled by the opening *ruba'i* (or quatrain) of the poem: "If anyone sees the way our downfall passes all bounds, the way that Islam, once fallen, does not rise [*ubharna*] again, / He will never believe that the tide flows after every ebb, once he sees the way our sea has gone out."[16] Verbs generally used for natural phenomena, such as *ubharna*, here with its thermodynamic and agricultural undertones, are deployed for sociohistorical categories such as Islam. Further, the correlation drawn between historical experience and an eternal order beyond normal human capacity altogether is ventured in these instances. It is as if the dark humor associated with the melancholic state serves as a catalyst of vision, making perceptible what generally lies outside the scope of human sight, as Benjamin once conjectured in a comparable context. The vision that forms belittles and mortifies mundane concerns. This vision informs what Shackle and Majeed understand to be a central aim of the poem: "to rescue that inner faith from the steady historical decline of Islam," what amounts, in other words, to "carving out a realm immune from the forces of history."[17]

Affinity for the figure of allegory in Hali's work takes hold from two opposed directions. On the one hand, a world orientation fixated upon the eternal order beyond the veil of phenomenal reality is naturally attracted to the allegorical mode. A melancholic attitude like Hali's is compelled by thick humor to interpret mundane ruin as justification for past moral violation and seeks within the wreckage signs of moral renewal and redemption. The classical Shi'a genre *marsiya*, composed to publicly commemorate the slaying of Ali Hussain in the Battle of Karbala of 680, is indissociable from the melancholic indignation at worldly injustice and tearful longing for future redemption through the coming of the *mahdi*. The genre also cannot be dissociated from the *musaddas* form that Hali expropriates and deploys to great allegorical effect. Thus, a peculiarly messianic affect finds in allegory a particularly effective means of communication.

However, the work of allegory at various moments in Hali's oeuvre takes on the opposite burden: that of modern secularization. As a member of the modernist Aligarh school, led by the influential educationist Sir Sayyid, Hali came quickly to realize the challenges that Enlightenment, the scientific worldview, and the new generally instrumentalist rationality presented to traditional Islamic belief structures. Like Sir Sayyid, Hali wrote a number of critical essays on the religious dimension of this problematic, often justifying the secularizing and metaphorizing hermeneutics of his intellectual guide. For Sir Sayyid, "the only touchstone of a true religion can be this: If that religion is in conformity with human nature or with Nature in general, then it is true."[18] Sir Sayyid's naturalist (*necari*) Islam is devoid of miracles, as Majeed has acutely recognized.[19] This desacralizing tendency of

Aligarh's *necari 'ilm-e kalam* (naturalistic theology) obviously set it apart from more traditionalist authorities of the community as well as emergent revivalist schools, such as the Deobandis and Barelwis.[20] The destabilizing impact of the modern dispensation was not restricted to theological questions but affected the entire traditional worldview and everyday practice.[21] The most succinct recognition of the problem occurs in a key passage of Hali's treatise on poetry, *Muqaddamah-yi Sh'er o Sha'iri* (Prolegomena to Poetry and Poetics). Criticizing the worldview embedded in traditional poetry and specifying the potentials for renewal pregnant within modernity, Hali comes yet again upon allegory as a solution.

The passage in question is worth citing in full for the complications of its very language reveal the destabilizing effect of the new challenges. Hali struggles all at once to address the modern, incorporate its force within the traditional structures of the old, and revitalize the received conventions and tropes through a radically altering process of allegorization:

> It is possible that an advance and broadening of the mind of a people occurs, and yet a corresponding broadening cannot occur in language. Nevertheless in an unconscious way the various styles of description [*bayan ke aslub*] slowly expand [*izafa kiye jate hain*] and they gradually become familiar to the ears of the public. Yet the old styles that have settled in the ears are kept in use according to custom. So much so that even if many classical poetic notions are proven to be simply false by the progress of knowledge, the words by means of which the old notions were expressed are not abandoned.

Referring to a handful of Islamicate tropes of the supernatural, Hali asks the reader:

> Just think: that the sky is alive and rotating, the earth rests, that water and air extend infinitely, that the elements [of the world] are basically reducible to four, that the fountain of eternal life is hidden in darkness, and that the golden falcon, devils, and fairies all exist, and so many other phenomena of the like, are proven to be utterly false by the advances of the sciences of man, still the poet's task is not to completely rid himself of those ideas, but rather his skill is to capture realities, actualities, and true and natural concepts through the ornament of those very

> false and groundless ideas, and to not allow the spell cast by the ancients to ever break. Otherwise he will realize that by the power of his very own mantras he has forgotten the spells that captivated hearts.

The idea is not to abandon the old forms but to redeploy them in such a way that they become the vehicles for the expression of new historical, social, and cultural contents. Hali continues to drive home the point:

> In any case, those people who want to advance Urdu poetry or, let us say, want to keep it based on the daily paper [*safaha-e rozgar*], it is their duty that when it comes to the genres of poetry [*isnaf-e sukhan*] generally and in the *ghazal* especially, that they consider, to the degree that it is possible, to adopt as little as possible the new styles, and that they not employ unfamiliar words, but rather go on enlarging the scope in an unconscious manner the [known genres], and for the most part keep the ancient styles, ordinary words and sayings as the basis of poetic composition. Yet, the duty is not to remain content with the metaphysical meanings [*haqiqi ma'non par*] of the words but instead to employ them only sometimes in their denotative meaning, and sometimes in their profane [*majazi*] sense, sometimes metaphorically or metonymically [*iste'are aur kinaye ke taur par*], or sometimes through the ornament of simile [*tamsil*].[22]

The passage is indicative of the manifold transformations under the British Raj at the cultural level and the strategies that were formulated for facing them head-on by so-called modernists such as Hali. It signals how precipitously had fallen the metaphysical grounds upon which the entire superstructure of the old culture had rested. Further, Hali's words incidentally indicate the inception of fiction in the Urdu—and by extension the Indo-Islamicate—sphere, for now the practice of suspending disbelief in light of a scientific worldview had supplanted what Hali takes to be a more giving classical belief structure. Yet, closer to the central matters at hand, the passage is remarkable for the kind of optimism it expresses about the flexibility of the traditional cultural forms, especially in being able to accommodate new social contents and an altered worldview. There seems to be little concern that the modern outlook may actually either render obsolete the old tropes or slowly deteriorate their expressive potentials. Further, the confidence in the classical structures and the expectation that past traditions could find a way to renovate themselves and survive the onslaught of a rather foreign and utterly destabilizing dispensation such as that of modernity under colonial command is hardly shaken in these lines. On the contrary, the sense is that modernity can be incorporated into the moral economy of traditional forms, digested, as it were, by the figure of allegory.

And thus the figure of allegory is meant to resolve what appear to be rather intractable contradictions of the moment. Hali seems to have thought that through the allegorical mode, it would be possible to maintain tradition and yet incorporate the force of the modern. But in hindsight, the lesson of the *Musaddas* remains quite contrary when it comes to the potentials of allegorization. There the traditional resonances of the *musaddas* form do not serve the imperatives of modernity so much as turn them on their head. The weight of the *marsiya* and the kind of attitude induced by melancholic or abject existence shield the tradition from the force of modernity, making it impervious to the new, to agency, to transformation. But for all that the tradition does not stay the same. Nor do the confines of the modern.

IV. MODERNITY THROUGH *MARSIYA*

I turn now to the sublimity of the *marsiya* as a form and the effect to which it was allegorized in Hali's *Musaddas*. A poetic stanza made up of six lines with an a a-a-a-b-b rhyme scheme, the *musaddas* is reserved almost exclusively for the Shi'a tradition of *marsiya*. Hali's *Musaddas* evokes this tradition not merely with its deployment of this stanza or with the dominant affect of indignation pushed to lamentation, but also in the fact that it begins with a *ruba'i* (quatrain), the convention with which the marsiya established a specific mood or theme for a particular composition. Generally speaking, the *marsiya* as a genre had one primary theme—the unjust suffering and execution of the grandson of the Prophet Muhammad in the Battle of Karbala in 680 C.E.—and one purpose: public commemoration through poetic recital, especially during Muharram. In the Indian subcontinent, Shi'as were generally a marginalized though tolerated minority. Only in one locality, Lucknow and the Avadh countryside, did Shi'ism have a solid enough footing that cultural forms such as the *marsiya* could be publicly performed and thus flourish. The association of this genre with Lucknow cannot be underestimated, nor should the association of Lucknow with the start of the 1857 Mutiny against the British. Though examples of *marsiya* can be found in the Deccan, especially around Hyderabad, from earlier centuries, it was only in Lucknow that the tradition attained a high privilege in literary spheres and generous patronage by high court officials. Credit for the efflorescence of this genre may be given to the ruling nawabs of the region. Having slowly attained independence from the Mughal Empire over the course of the eighteenth century, the nawabs of Avadh made Shi'ism the official religion of the state. By the middle of the nineteenth century, two patronized poets, Mir Babar 'Ali Anis (1802–1874) and Mir Salamat 'Ali Dabir (1803–1875), became celebrated as virtuosi of the *marsiya* form. Both concentrated their poetic energies on capturing in each moment of the Battle of Karbala a poignancy, especially a sense of tragic doom in which worldly events are given cosmological resonance and a millenarian longing for divine recompense is encouraged. Over the course of Anis's and Dabir's long careers as composers of *marsiya*, each legendary event of the Battle of Karbala received treatment. Eventually a full epic narrative could be strung together. Though each short *marsiya* composition concentrated on one moment of the battle narrative, each evoked the totality of the tale and a cosmological vision of its setting. Thus, the short concentrated emotion-images of both Dabir and Anis could be drawn together into coherent war epics. (In more recent times, the compositions of both have been edited, concatenated, and published as *Razm-namah-e Anis* and *Razm-namah-e Dabir*.)[23] By the time Hali adopted the *musaddas* stanza and drafted the opening *ruba'i*, the *marsiya* had already become a model ripe for emulation. Its advantage was that it was a form already laden with theological gravity, melancholic poignancy, and epic grandeur. In sum, the *marsiya* had taken shape in such a way that it could become allegorized for the discussion of conditions under colonial domination, and by deploying it as a form, Hali could sidestep entirely the more usual genres of popular entertainment such as *ghazal*, *dastan*, or *qissah*.

Now some questions need to be asked to clarify somewhat that other plane of signification to which the immediate contents of the poem are referring. This is that other higher plane of meaning to which the form itself points, but in the most subtle and elusive of ways. What is to be made of a message invested in setting a community in ruins on the path toward a healthy future within modernity when that very message and that very vision of modernity are undermined by the force of the discursive medium? Considering how heavily weighted this discursive medium is by a sublimity that renders human effort futile, what message about modernity is conveyed by it? These questions are consequential for grasping the dimension of modernity that attains expression in these ambiguities, ambivalences, and mismatches between medium and message. The discursive form that allegorizes the contents enacts a shift from the disenchanted world of science and progress toward that realm of eternal mystery embedded in the mute givenness of nature. It imputes supreme authority in fate, expressed by the movement of heavenly constellations, which themselves govern the ebb and flow of oceanic tides. Again, what is revealed about the logic of modernity as such when viewed through the allegorical frame from a colonial location?

To get some handle on these questions, it would be helpful first to briefly survey the image that appears of modernity in *Musaddas* and to then take into account the countervailing force produced by the choice of allegorical frame. As will become apparent, there is a certain sense of precariousness within the overarching hierarchical structure erected in this work, a precariousness that produces, Shackle and Majeed note, a peculiar frisson in the act of reading.[24] That is, there is a peculiar sense of disquiet, a feeling that everything is on the verge of breaking or being overturned. For these critics, this sublime affect "emerges from the intertwining of moral disapprobation with the fecund possibilities of pleasure in the text."[25] Nowhere is this sense of immanent slippage more tangible than in the picture presented of the new modern dispensation, which is either praised or given underhanded compliments. Efficiency, mobility, measure, industriousness, and health all characterize the Western paragons of modern life. The Europeans are generous benefactors for all, abiding by a commitment to liberalism that proscribes discrimination between the various subjects of the empire. Further, the British have secured the peace that allows for commerce to flourish, travel to proceed unimpeded, and technology to develop at an ever-faster rate. Yet at times the praise Hali bestows upon the colonial purveyors of modernity is so lavish that it strikes one as slightly sarcastic, and the fantasy of modern existence, with its proper measures for everything and instrumental attitude toward nature, becomes somewhat deflated. For instance, modern progress is depicted as a tiring race without end: "They are racing so fast along the way of searching as if they still had very far to go" (M 131). Life in these conditions, though productive of so many creature comforts, itself seems rather toilsome and miserable:

They never sleep their fill, they are never sated by hard work,
They do not squander their substance, they do not waste an instant uselessly,
They do not tire or get weary of going long. They have advanced a long way and keep on advancing. (M 132)

The race toward an ever-receding modernity appears to have lost its purpose along the way. Modernity itself appears to be just such a never-ending race. The implicit lesson is that though vanquished communities in the colony such as the Muslims of India have much to learn from European mastery, ultimately one must not lose one's own cultural bearings. There are ways to borrow and lessons about power to be taken seriously—and Hali's own poetic language exemplifies just one such invigorating borrowing from what he imagines to be the qualities of English literature. But such borrowings should not come at the cost of faith or ruin of the central pillars of the community.

There is a tinge of melancholic *ressentiment* in this imperative, and such *ressentiment* motivates, again, the choice of *marsiya* as allegorical form. It is strikingly naive to imagine that modern technologies, for instance, could be selectively espoused and that the worldview embedded in them could be staved off indefinitely. That is, it is naive to think that underlying presuppositions of modern science would not ultimately destabilize traditional, generally faith-based society. Yet it is this very view Hali seems blithely to adopt, for this is the view that best accords with the *ressentiment* of the defeated. The defeated can rest assured that they still have faith, that they are the truly righteous, and that if there is a God, then God will surely eventually set all aright once again for them. They can look upon the victors as ultimately lost in their own self-adulation. They do not realize that things will turn once again, just as the tide flows after an ebb. The central aim is "to rescue that inner faith from the steady historical decline of Islam" by carving out within the subject a "realm immune from the forces of history."[26] The melancholic vision finds solace in an eternal sphere just beyond the realm of the empirical and finds in allegory, as Benjamin recognized, a means to break through the stream of time and intimate a comforting temporality of eternity. The enveloping framework of the *marsiya* provides Hali with just such means for encompassing the current historical impasse of the Muslim community and, by extension, colonial India within a redeeming symbolic totality. What is most powerful is not science but the alchemical might wielded by the Prophet Muhammad:

"He came down from Hira and drew near his people, and brought with him an alchemical formula" (M 24); "The one turned crude copper into gold, and clearly separated the counterfeit from the pure" (M 25). The *marsiya* form forges an implicit allegory of apocalyptic correction. In this vision of cosmological unity, the normally mute natural realm is animated with a divine voice: "Such clamour was caused on all sides by God's message that desert and mountain echoed with His name" (M 30). Thus, the allegorical dimension helps maintain the notion that the force of faith will ultimately win the day.

V. MODERNITY AT SEA

Hali's traversals under the imperial horizon at high noon underscore just how much the process of modernization and progress generated simultaneously, even dialectically, desecularization and melancholic retrenchment. In this way a counternormative logic of modernity initially appears: the shadow of a doubt on the path of progress, as it were; the weight of allegory in the abject mode gives it form. It attains expression in Hali's work often as a scream for survival, as if by natural bodily instinct. If not sickness unto death, then images of collective drowning in shipwreck recur in the poem from early on:

> Precisely this is the condition in the world of that community,
> whose ship has entered the whirlpool and is surrounded by it.
> The shore is far away, and a storm is raging. At every moment there is the apprehension that it is just about to sink.
> But the people in the boat do not even turn over, as they lie asleep and unconscious. (M 3)

The scream is the natural response to the spiral downward to death. It participates in the permanent necessity of nature according to the command of God: "The life of God alone will never wane, this world's uniquely worthy Suzerain" (M 294); "For life eternal others hope in vane: not one has yet, nor ever will remain" (M 207). The instinctual scream confounds the distinction between human agency and natural necessity, marks a point of intersection between history and the structure of bodily finitude. It thus narrows the distance considerably between nature and culture. The scream's primordial nature, evoked in absentia in Hali's work, marks the interconnection between ephemeral human nature and a sublime eternal image of divinity. It is the point at which, according to Shackle and Majeed, "the final release into a transcendental realm beyond the temporal cycles of decay and renewal" is realized.[27] This sublime rhetoric manifested through melancholic allegory. In these mediations can be glimpsed, it appears, the struggle for brute survival in late colonial India—conditions unmitigated by Independence.

Countermodernity arrived thus with a dialectical, negative charge. It is the internally generated negation laboring in the mode of brute survival. What is deadly is nothing less than modernity itself, in Hali's eyes, appositely depicted as a flood that "doesn't just sweep over the banks of the Ganga and Yamuna rivers, but is rather an overflowing of the ocean, which lets water wash over all parts of the earth's surface."[28] These ebbs and tides of modern reifying powers—whirlpools—created the conditions for romanticism's own *Sturm und Drang* in the Urdu literary scene, as in the work of Muhammad Iqbal, one of Hali's literary scions. In various guises, but especially in the epic register, a late romanticism emerged from the grave doubts about the imposition of colonial power's reason. Simultaneously, as if instinctually, in the mode of an undercurrent, aesthetic movements against modernity began to take hold. They experimented with ways of disabusing oneself of imperialism's conceits, such as "progress" itself, groping for a path beyond its colonial circumference. Such experiments were oftentimes coterminous with attempts to salvage one's culture in a moment of danger and thus intermeshed all at once with logics of neotraditionalism and some strains of postcolonialism avant la lettre. The following chapters explore key moments in such experimentations and delineate their particular cultural logics.

CHAPTER 5

Iqbal, or the *Sturm und Drang* of Late Colonial India

Resemblances of Pure Content

I. INTRODUCTION

The following is an indirect meditation on Benjamin's understanding that the "past carries with it a secret index by which it is referred to redemption."[1] The pasts from which Muhammad Iqbal's visions appear to us now are in pieces, and one must work from stray fragments to evoke possibilities of redemption for other times. Three such fragments are offered here. By revealing the entanglement of visions of Islam in Goethe, late romanticism in Iqbal, and the elaboration of critiques of modernity across the metropolitan-colonial divide, the first fragment gives an account of how Iqbal's engagement with Goethe made possible experiments with subject formation in the modality of infinite reflection that still index an unreached futurity. The second fragment retraces Iqbal's conflicted political trajectory that eventuated in his neo-epic *Javid Nama* (1932). In seeking to reveal the Bergsonian premises of Iqbal's *Reconstruction of Religious Thought in Islam* (1934), this fragment discovers as well the ramifications pure duration had for his late literary style, as decoded through Faiz Ahmad Faiz's subtle observations. The third and final fragment enters into Iqbal's rhetoric of pure content, laying out the implicit conceptual source of *Javid Nama*'s sublimity.

II. FRAGMENT I. UNCANNY AFFINITIES: IQBAL REFLECTING GOETHE REFLECTING IQBAL AD INFINITUM

As Iqbal's oeuvre is exhumed and reexamined today in the light of postnational energies and under imaginary postcolonial constellations,[2] it reveals itself to be illuminated by futures *passé* to which recent times have been more often than not simply blind. The decades since Iqbal's death in 1938 have not served his intellectual legacy well. If the body of his work lay strewn under the rubble of a single sovereign left on the subcontinent at the end of British imperial rule, then perhaps it could have been more easily reassembled and favorably received than has been its destiny. Instead, his legacy fell through the chasms of a fragmenting world whose categories have been unable to adequately encompass his imaginary horizons or ways of inhabiting worlds. Iqbal's literary corpus will thus have to overcome the nationalist appropriation to which it has been subjected in his posthumous Pakistan. His spiritual autonomy is frayed by its usurpation by the nation-state, belied and betrayed by the challenges that fall upon Pakistan's sovereignty with the regularity of drone missiles today. The gushing praise of *Iqbaliyat*—as the industry around this conscripted spirit is known in Pakistan—often drowns the alternative fields of possibility that Iqbal explored. On the Indian side, he has faired no better. The unending ostracization and oblivion that has been meted out to his legacy with the rise of the Hindu-majority state have left only an enigmatic ghostly presence, for a fragment of his Urdu *kalam* continues to serve there, ironically enough, as an unofficial and ever-popular national anthem.

To the list of obstacles that Iqbal's poetic imagination and political flourish have had to endure can be added several others. There is the fact that he wrote most of his poetic masterpieces in a language, Persian, which itself became reduced to a national language that celebrated its own to the general exclusion and demotion of those deceased bearers of the august tradition who fell far beyond Iran's official borders. Moreover Persian itself waned dramatically over the twentieth century in the subcontinent. The traditional Islamicate idioms, genres, and styles Iqbal maintained were challenged, if not overwhelmed, by other languages, forms, and media and the general pressures of commerce, massification, plebianization, and homogenization that characterize the incivility of contemporary capital. In appearing now across an epochal rift, Iqbal uncovers for us a different, partially submerged set of spatial and temporal coordinates of the modern imagination, especially theories and practices of an infinite subjectivity and antagonistic form. An instance of this poetic and political practice is encapsulated in his engagement with the Eastern *Vorstellung* of the *West-östlicher Divan* (West-Eastern Divan, 1819) of the commanding European mind of Goethe. Indeed, the uncanny mixture of distance and proximity, the infinite reflection of the self's other self in the othered self of the other,[3] the echo of one's own spirit in the letter of the foreign tongue—all produce a peculiar affinity with contemporary affects, to the extent that these affects can be characterized as increasingly jaded or unenthused by imperial jingoism, national chauvinism, ethnic particularism, and religious complacency, or even a politics grounded in such accidents of birth as body and territory.

From within the fissures of a fragmented world can come to light fossilized fragments that seem to address new futures better than old pasts. Iqbal's *Payam-e Mashriq* (Message of the East, 1922), especially his preface in Urdu to this collection of Persian poems intended as an answer to Goethe's *West-östlicher Divan*, testifies openly to Iqbal's attempt to forge a new future through an elaboration—indeed, an innovative translation and infinite reflection—of a distant place and time. "There are certainly resemblances," Iqbal offers in the preface, "between the Germany of a hundred years ago and the state of the contemporary East" (see appendix A). His discovery of these resemblances between the Germany of Goethe's time and the colonized domains of the early twentieth century, between a secularizing West and Islamic awakening in the East depended upon a particular historical conjuncture that is disclosed through the manner in which he encountered the great German (post)romantic, delineating a process of transmission and translation of key concepts into new cultural frontiers. How did the specific historical conjuncture in which Iqbal find himself—if not the colonial world to which he sought to give voice in fashioning this missive—inflect his reading of Goethe? What was it about Goethe's work that lent itself to such theoretical travel in the distant world of the colonized East, especially in its Islamic spheres?

These rather simple yet consequential philological questions are key to any precise translation of the text (see appendix A). They are also meant to establish the ground for the more demanding inquiries of a concept-history (*Begriffsgeschichte*) focused on the elaboration of romanticism as a framework for an antagonistic, postcolonial critique of modernity. In both of these cases, Iqbal proves decisive. As someone concerned with articulating a universalist romantic imaginary and with reanimating Creation to construct "from the ashes of [the contemporary] culture and society" and "within the depths of Life" a "new Adam and new world for him to live in," he marks an instructive moment in reconfiguring romanticism and in distilling a postmodernist vision—avant la lettre, to be sure—of a possible future (see appendix A). In this context the central questions are: What light does this interaction between a thinker who inspired Islamic revivalism in the subcontinent and beyond and the German theorist of the determinate limits of European Enlightenment shed in *Nachträglichkeit* on contradictory patterns of modernity, and what speculations or aspirations does this interaction help encourage for the future? What lessons can be learned from this obscured moment of encounter and relay for our own times, especially in fostering a postcolonial future? What possible futures are to be found only in translation? These queries broach again the question of political subjectivity premised on infinite reflection, the very question with which Iqbal experimented as if in immediate response to a desperate situation of a minority, just one facet of late colonial aporia.

Long stretches and significant dimensions of Iqbal's life remain hazy to this day. Among the dimmest and least researched moments of his experience is the one of greatest relevance to the genesis of *Payam-e Mashriq*: his voyage west, especially the period spent in Germany. At the encouragement of his philosophy professor at Government College in Lahore, the well-connected and influential Islamicist Thomas W. Arnold, Iqbal sailed from Bombay on September 7, 1905, not to set foot in India again until 1908. Over the course of these years, he received training in a somewhat anomalous version of German idealism and metaphysics at the hands of the Cambridge philosophers John McTaggert and F. H. Bradley and immersed himself in German language, literature, and philosophy in Heidelberg and Munich. In the final year of his sojourn in the West, he attained a doctorate from the Ludwig-Maximilians-Universität in Munich upon submitting his dissertation, "The Development of Metaphysics in Persia," under the supervision of the Orientalist Fritz Hommel. From the fragments that remain from his time in Germany, the stray comments that appear in his letters, the recorded observations of others, and the points that can be surmised from statements such as his preface to the *Payam-e Mashriq*, one attains an impression of just how deep and lasting the impact was of this journey west. Indeed, the internal unrest he experienced upon his return to India, which lingered for years, suggests a mind-set emboldened by exposure to the value systems, notions of romance, conceptions of liberty, languages of selfhood, and experiences of mobility, exchange, and perhaps even love that occasionally betray a European tinge and would continue to color, one way or another, his modes of expression and inflect his understanding of the Islamic, colonial, and non-European worlds for the remaining decades of his life. It is not surprising, then, to read of his internal tumult and discomfort with traditional social conventions after his return home. For instance, in a letter addressed to the famous Atiya Fayzee, dated April 9, 1909, Iqbal writes:

> My life is extremely miserable. They force my wife upon me. I have written to my father that he had no right to arrange my marriage especially when I had refused to enter into any alliance of that sort. I am quite willing to support her, but I am not prepared to make my life miserable by keeping her with me. As a human being I have a right to happiness—if society or nature deny that to me, I defy both. The only cure is that I should leave this wretched country forever, or take refuge in liquor which makes suicide easier. Those dead barren leaves of books cannot yield happiness; I have got sufficient fire in my soul to burn them up and social conventions as well. A good God created all this, you say. Maybe. The facts of life, however, tend to a different conclusion. It is intellectually easier to believe in an eternal omnipotent Devil rather than a good God.[4]

The fact that the entirety of the quoted passage is excised from the Urdu translation and publication of this same letter in *Ruh-e Makatib-e Iqbal* (The Essence of Iqbal's Correspondence) is telling of just how transgressive were and continue to be the sentiments he expresses.[5]

Though these sentiments need not be reduced to an exposure to a European experience of liberalism and modern practices of romance alone—Iqbal himself would most certainly not have considered his feelings to derive strictly from the cultural spheres of the metropolitan powers—it is instructive to gather from the historical scraps of his time just what were his activities, especially amorous and intellectual, in Germany. For what Iqbal made of Western, especially German, thought at this early moment helps to situate his reading of figures such as Goethe and sheds light on the imperatives Iqbal came to espouse later in his life regarding Islamic culture, imperial politics, and the relations between the metropolitan West and the colonized East. Though these historical artifacts remain fragmentary and the allusions in his literary oeuvre figurative, they can nonetheless be read in revealing ways. For instance, there seems to have always been an integral connection between the libidinal and the intellectual for Iqbal during his stay in Germany. His greatest confidant of this era, Atiya Faiyzee, describes his time in Munich thus: "Of all places in Germany Iqbal liked Munich best, partly because he had his first lesson there under the direction of the beautiful and charming daughter of Herr Professor Rann. . . . We went to the home of Professor Rann and after a few words, the young beauty Fraulein Rann started examining Iqbal to find what deeper studies he was engaged in. . . . Iqbal was completely lost in front of her. . . . She seemed perfect in every branch of learning—apart from being a perfect piece of creation."[6] The introduction to young educated women went hand in hand with an introduction to physical training of the body, dance, and music. Faiyzee's descriptions give the impression that the periods of long study and philosophical discussion followed by spontaneous dancing, singing, and poetry made for a totally exhilarating experience for Iqbal. He would write nostalgically, even whimsically of these days in his letters to Faiyzee—"Ah, the days which will never come again"—after his return home, where he faced the challenge of living once again in a culture that had very different expectations for what a woman ought to think and do.[7] Just as his experiences in the West connected the libidinal to the intellectual, so did the struggle he wished to wage on the home front. His letters testify to a serious engagement with the emergent German scholarship on Islam, especially the works of Alfred von Kremer and Theodor Nödelke. We read as well of his desire to translate passages to upset the authority of the ruling *'ulama*, despite averring that his own views do not accord completely with those of the European scholars.[8] Over the course of the decades leading to the composition of the *Payam-e Mashriq*, Iqbal would continue to aesthetically cultivate the exilic perspective and emotional turmoil that the years abroad and a world in constant tumult had wrought. He would define himself against the norms of the Urdu tradition, employing the tropes of its literary landscape, especially the garden, in countervailing ways; conversely, he would promulgate an antagonistic conception of selfhood, refuting in this instance the static conceptions of colonial, including Muslim subjects, pushed by imperial ideology and often authorized by Orientalist scholarship.[9] This sense of exile within his own tradition only exacerbated his longing for a homeland, leading him eventually to toy with the extreme options of communalist nationalism and fascist attempts to overcome modernity. Perhaps it was the location of the colonial backwater that put these options closest to hand.

Iqbal seems to have found his own condition mirrored in that of Goethe, who had found his reflection in the *Vorstellungsbild* of the Persian tradition. Throughout the preface to *Payam-e Mashriq*, Iqbal emphasizes especially those dimensions of the German tradition of Orientalist poetry in which an acute sensation of exilic longing is given expression. "In the elegant melodies of the nightingale of Sheraz," goes the passage Iqbal translates and cites from German, referring to the Persian poet Hafiz, "Goethe discovered his very own image. From time to time even the sensation came over him such that he began to think, 'Perhaps my own soul has inhabited Hafiz's body and passed a lifetime in the lands of the East'" (see appendix A). Further, Heinrich Heine's own imaginary excursions along these lines complement those of Goethe. Iqbal notes that Heine fashioned himself in *Neue Gedichte* (New Poems, 1844) as an Iranian poet exiled to Germany, crying out "Oh Firdausi! Oh Jami! Oh Sa'adi! Your brother is a prisoner in the cell of melancholia, longing for the flowers of Shiraz." Several different reasons could be advanced for accounting for the appeal of such imagery for Iqbal. Foremost among them, I would like to suggest, is that what Iqbal saw reflected in the figure of the exiled or displaced European intellectual was a resemblance of his own imaginary exiled self. And what is generated in such instances, implicitly as well as explicitly, is the possibility for an infinitely dispersive and ever universalizing subjectivity disclosed through a poetic technique of infinite reflection. For someone who had already expressed the conceit in *Rumuz-e Bekhudi* (The Mysteries of Selflessness) that he is "trained to fashion mirrors out of words," such potentials of mirroring can be imagined as a mystery buried like a treasure in his own poetry.[10] Iqbal sought to capture explicitly this very subjectivity through his elaborations on the concept of *khudi* (selfhood), yet more than his peripatetic and excursive formulations on such concepts, it is his poetic practice that mediates uncanny affinities. It is the practice of infinite mirroring of self and other that he finds in Goethe's own reflexive praxis.

The grounds for Iqbal's turn toward Goethe are symbolically laid out in *Payam-e Mashriq*. Though it is possible to draw out the underlying rationales for his affinity for Goethe from implicit observations, tangential allusions, and associational assemblages strewn across his entire oeuvre, the most noteworthy indexes are given in the preface as well as in the body of *Payam-e Mashriq* itself. For instance, in the penultimate section of this work, "Images of Europeans," Iqbal depicts an encounter between Goethe and Rumi in heaven.[11] Goethe, alluded to as "the German sage" (*nukta-dan-e almani*), is greeted by Rumi, who obviously has preceded him to such an exalted station. Goethe is praised by his Persian predecessor and is told to refashion the old world afresh, as he is privy to the potentials of the old. The aphoristic and paratactic nature of the poem allows it to suggest that integral to such a reconstruction of the world is the revelation of the secrets Goethe had acquired through his aesthetic and philosophical efforts. Embedded centrally within is the aphorism, the meaning of which is not known by all: *zer ki'z 'iblis o 'ishq az adam ast* (Knowledge is of Satan come, of Adam love). Goethe seems to have discovered independently the truths to which Rumi had ascended by his own efforts. Further light is shed on the association between Rumi and Goethe here in the footnote Iqbal wrote to accompany this poem in Urdu: "By '*nukta-dan-e almani*' is meant Goethe, whose dramatic work *Faust* is renowned. Through the classical trope of the pact between the scientist and Satan, the poet expressed all the levels of potential human development with such virtuosity that one cannot imagine any work of art surpassing it."[12] This praise coincides nicely with Goethe's parallel status alongside Rumi in heaven, for the image of the two in conversation establishes for Iqbal's own work a singular aesthetic telos. As Rumi will play the role of guide for Iqbal in a journey toward self-realization through the heavens in the neo-epic *Javid Nama*, composed a decade later, Goethe can be seen as an equal yet invisible guide for Iqbal. The point of such a telos is the disclosure through careful artistic practice underlying realities beyond the phenomenal constraints of identities. That is, heaven here as well as elsewhere in Iqbal's oeuvre symbolizes the space where an absolute subjectivity—*khudi* in his lexicon—is able to manifest itself and existential secrets are revealed as constitutive realities. As in Rumi's discourse in the poem, the message of the one is freed through the other. And not simply meaning, but the potentials for freedom enter into a process of actualization through a specific configuration: mediation by reflection. Though Rumi has preceded Goethe to this exalted station and is thus the one who speaks, it is through the presence there of Goethe that Rumi attains a measure of his own self. The other mediates the self-realization of the one. If we take the image of the two in heaven as a model of reflection and uncanny affinity in Iqbal's own relationship to Goethe, then we may say that Rumi is able to disclose the message deep within the other's work to the extent that Goethe himself was exploring an otherness of his own self in his explorations of Eastern, Persian traditions. For the self and the other together in reflective relationship mediate freedom as such.

To understand Goethe's presence as an invisible counterpart to Rumi in Iqbal's work, to grasp in what way Goethe served too as a guide toward a particular politically inflected aesthetic telos, it is worth retracing the history that led Goethe to Islam, to his way of imagining the Orient and especially the Persian literary tradition. For the way Goethe opened himself to the *Unheimlichkeit* of Islam held magnetic attraction for Iqbal's own *unheimlich* Muslim Indian self. Iqbal would realize new ways of conceptualizing and valorizing Islam significantly beyond the mere narcissisms of identity and beyond the confines of traditional Muslim authorities.[13] From his early twenties, Goethe consistently engaged himself in one way or another with the intellectual underpinnings of Islam, ultimately absorbing what he considered to be its major spiritual message within his letters, poetry, and worldview, whether or not he was talking about Eastern or Western themes. In sharp contradistinction to our times, Islam appeared to Goethe's eighteenth-century predecessors as the faith of reason. Though the austere *Gestalt* of Muhammad could be deployed as a guise for the critique of the existing Christian Church, as in Voltaire's influential play *Le fanaticisme, ou Mohamet le prophete*, for the most part the founder of Islam and the religion itself were defended as bearers of reason and tolerance, even by Voltaire himself. Goethe's own views on Islam and Muhammad were somewhat more nuanced and multidimensional. As the tragedy of *Faust* allegorizes the predicament of a culture that seeks infinite knowledge only to discover that such science comes at the cost of its most vaunted traditions and most stabilizing beliefs, it should come as no surprise that toward the end of his life Goethe experimented with exits out of such a predicament and seemed to find them in the most unlikely of places. In Goethe's eyes, Islam seems to have exemplified the perfect balance for ultimately overcoming contradictory forces: the infinite extension of God and the spatial and temporal limits of humans; the militant striving of Muhammad and the spiritual lesson of submission to one's own destiny; the unfathomable content of God's universal message and the mediation of such a message through the particularities of languages, figures, symbols, however iconoclastic these may be configured. The role of the poet as the one who urges and prods his community to attain its potential gave inspiration and orientation to Goethe's own poetic practice. Yet at the same time, Goethe's expressions of a hard embrace of stoicism generally come with an Islamic flourish. Thus, Goethe had these words to address the grave illness of a daughter-in-law: "Weiter kann ich nichts sagen, als dass ich auch hier mich im Islam zu halten suche" (I can say no more than that here too I seek to maintain myself in Islam).[14] Other examples abound. He even employed Islam as a standard by which to judge the efforts and goals of contemporary reformism within Christianity. By the time he was composing advertisements for the *West-östlicher Divan*, Goethe claimed astonishingly that the composer of the volume would not dismiss "the suspicion that he is himself a Muslim."[15]

Iqbal picked up on key potentials of Goethe's engagement with Islam and the imagination of the Orient and sought to actualize them for his own times. He discovered in this uncanny past the grounds for anticipating a world beyond the categorical divisions and constricting identities characteristic of modernity, an anticipatory world in which a reconfigured Islam could be activated as the vehicle for arriving at a deracialized, postnational, and truly post-Enlightenment world. The telos of Islam for him would be a new universalizing subjectivity premised on a shared acknowledgment of social and spiritual totalities. This post-Enlightenment dispensation would, in its best formulation, be made possible by a truce between reason, technology, and human freedom, on the one hand, and nature, tradition, and the unknowable, on the other. As the logic of destruction wrought by the West on the colonies had reached the core of the metropolitan sphere, Iqbal imagined vast cultural reversals to be in the offing. Thus he writes toward the end of the preface, "Europe has seen with its very own eyes the dreadful results of her own scientific, moral, and political vision. . . . But it is regrettable that her clever yet conservative ministers were unable to accurately grasp this overwhelming revolution that is currently taking place in the heart of humanity [*insani zamir*]" (see appendix A). Though the revolution (*inqilab*) is given no name, the cumulative sum of his statements in the preface indicates what he anticipates as well as reveals, as if in hindsight, the rationale of his interest in the Orientalist streak in German *Geistsgeschichte*. A retrospective glance at all that has led up to this point in the preface provides clues to the nature of this revolution-to-come. The revolution would shatter the hierarchy of the imperial relationship and leave its pieces scattered. The pains to which Iqbal goes to demonstrate the indebtedness of high metropolitan culture to the colonial domains of his times unsettles the most dominant ideology buttressing imperialism: the civilizing mission. Iqbal's account may be taken to be an allegory of the dependence of Western wealth on the resources of the East, and thus an attempt to undo the immediacy of understanding and to tend to the countervailing force of underlying realities.[16] And perhaps most important, in projecting a future beyond Europe, all that which is constitutively foreclosed as possible forms of subjectivity within *bürgerliche Gesellschaft* can be reconstituted and reconfigured. As "Islam" operates as an anticipatory, multiply determined category in Iqbal's work and not simply as a traditional form, it aids in imagining all that is excluded, unthought, and impossible within the governing terms of European society. In reflecting back what Goethe himself had sought to reflect of the East in *West-östlicher Divan*, a particular technique is set into motion for freeing an infinite or absolute subjectivity against the norms, barriers, and divides of the imperial order: infinite reflection.[17]

The possibility of a future hangs, Iqbal remarks in passing at the conclusion of the preface, upon a mode of apperception and cultural becoming that would thrive through the creative elaboration of Eastern and Western qualities, colonial and metropolitan experiences, concretizations and abstractions. The physical location in which that future will unfold is a matter of conjecture. Yet his very own practice, one may surmise, is what is to be taken as a technique for forging a future beyond the warfare, destruction, and ruin of modern imperialism and entrenched belief in the West. The practice in question—the purposeful play with the trope of reflection to manifest, if not free, an absolute subject—is perhaps his most unique and most radically consequential contribution to the aesthetics of romanticism understood widely. Whether he is conscious of the matter or merely embodies its contents in his rhetorical gestures here and elsewhere, there is little doubt that the perspective he brings to the question of the colonial present and postcolonial future concretizes the disturbing energies of the subordinate within the realm of metropolitan society. As mentioned earlier, the overriding force of Iqbal's preface is to reverse the commonsensical understanding that the East is dependent upon the West, and equally, that the West is sui generis, autonomous, and complete in itself. Goethe's self-abandonment to uncanny affinities symbolizes for Iqbal the most open recognition to just such reversals. In attracting uncanny reciprocities (for example, Iqbal's visual self-portraits in the Western romantic fashion),[18] such experimental abandonments of reified selfhood bring out veiled truths. Such reciprocal reflections remind one of the degree to which true freedom is dependent upon being with oneself in another. The self that comes into being in the other through reflection is the absolute self: the total social self that enters into a relation with the infinite and only ever comes into its own by freely dispersing and receiving intimately political energies to and from the other and the self up to and beyond the point where these lose all definition. Iqbal reflected in Goethe and vice versa just how essential the overcoming of imperial and national divides was and continues to be for the experience of freedom.

III. FRAGMENT 2. METAPHYSICS AND POLITICAL IDENTITY, OR THE SOUND OF PAN-ISLAMIC FORM

However much certain facets of Iqbal's poetic oeuvre may strike one as possible material for imagining ways out of reified identitarian debacles of our present, this may be a measure of the concrete impossibilities of his late colonial moment. That is, what finds expression in his masterpieces is the flip side of certain sociopolitical impasses, if not sheer contradictions, that characterized the crisis-ridden politics of British colonial rule, especially over its last decades on the subcontinent. I will discuss some key dimensions of this crisis, for they lent a negative shape to Iqbal's poetic form, as if whatever the political crisis was unable to furnish in actuality found a foothold in his aesthetics. This becomes most apparent in his neo-epic *Javid Nama*. Conceived and composed over the years that witnessed a nearly ubiquitous attempt to firm up communal identities, this spiritual narrative indexes the vast extent to which a rhetoric of metaphysics intermeshed with British colonial negotiations over the shape of a future polity and the hegemonic structure that would be assumed within it. The crisis of political agency that the new experiments with political power-sharing were producing in British India culminated in events that involved Iqbal immediately: the Lucknow Pact of 1916; the round table conferences, in the second of which he participated; and the Communal Award of 1932, to mention but a few. While he was in London as a member of the Muslim delegation for a round of charged meetings with the likes of Mohandas K. Gandhi, B. R. Ambedkar, and Muhammad Ali Jinnah, news had already leaked regarding the impending publication of *Javid Nama*. It was the content of this very work that N. M. Khan, reporting for the

Morning News of Calcutta, became privy to. At Khan's urging, Iqbal dictated to him the entire plot of *Javid Nama*, the story of the poet himself being led by Rumi through the heavenly spheres to a vision of God. By the end of the recitation, Khan reports, Iqbal broke into tears, and "it was not until fifteen minutes later that he came to his normal self."[19] Though this is not the first nor the last time that pious tears would well up during Iqbal's poetic performances, it is possible to read this affect as indicative of the especially potent relationship forming between an increasingly turbulent political field and an unmistakably sublime aesthetics.

In regard to Iqbal, this relationship had been evolving for some decades. More scholarly attention must surely be brought to the interconnection between the evolution of Iqbal's literary aesthetics and the political predicaments the Muslim community faced over the last decades of British colonial rule. Yet enough insightful commentary and details have been furnished over the decades since Iqbal's passing in 1938 to allow for the faint retracing of sharply contradictory trajectories in his thought. Extant scholarship, especially from the period immediately after his death, demonstrates that Iqbal himself mediated aesthetic form and political affairs, shaping public emotions and attitudes with the sway of his words and bringing his accumulated cultural clout to bear on his negotiations on behalf of the Indo-Muslim community he immediately addressed in his work. The pervasive sense of political insecurity mounted among the minority populations in the years the dominant contestant to British power, the Indian National Congress, took on an unmistakably Hindu character in terms of dominant groups and corresponding political visions of the future. Despite doubts about the secularization of Islam and hesitations about seeing it down the path of a disenchanted West, Iqbal as well as several other prominent Muslim intellectuals of his generation could not help getting drawn into the processes of colonially devised communal politics. "He attacked traditional Islam and nationalism," writes Wilfred Cantwell Smith in his classic work, *Modern Islam in India*, "and yet advocated an ardent nationalism for the traditionally Islamic community."[20] Likewise the Urdu scholar C. M. Naim makes the sharp observation that Iqbal, "depending solely on his faith . . . Janus like, had one face toward the past—a recovery of the pristine nature of Islam—and another toward the future—a society fully assonant with modern times. Such a posture," Naim goes on to remark, "is easy in the realm of ideals, where all contradictions melt away in the heat of one's vision."[21] The "romantic streak" that Naim recognizes in Iqbal's political gestures appears to become all the more acute as the kind of subjectivity and agency Iqbal envisioned for a pan-Islamic future meets historical impasse, that is, when local attempts at securing Islamic sovereignty became conflated with and ultimately indistinguishable from a modern territorial nation-state. Nonetheless, this romantic streak was catalytic in producing an Islam commensurate with modernity in Iqbal's late oeuvre. In seeking to maintain Islam and the possibility of a religious as well as political identification with it, Iqbal had to recast this religious inheritance in such a way as to make it consonant with modern imperatives: scientific epistemology, individualistic aspiration, socially transformative agency, and, in ways that ultimately troubled him, national sovereignty. A medley of these modern elements comes to light in *The Reconstruction of Religious Thought in Islam*, based on a series of lectures Iqbal gave under the auspices of the nizam of Hyderabad in 1930, later revised and published in 1934. A lexical commitment to Islam is duly maintained, yet its substantial core is reconfigured. This paradoxical relationship is analogized in Iqbal's public denigration of the Sufi master of the *ghazal*, Hafiz, a canonical poet of fourteenth-century Persia, on the one hand, yet adherence to and even elaboration of the very forms stemming from classical Persian literature, on the other.[22] Thus the very topos of Islam in Iqbal's oeuvre is dynamic, internally torn by competing crosscurrents: the force of modernity in its contents, yet intransigence in the formal patterns deployed.

This is most obviously in evidence in *Javid Nama*, but to know how, we must retrace, even if cursorily, the political course that mediated its existence, which is to say, Iqbal's career through the British imperial bureaucracy. Conquered in the Second Sikh War by the English East India Company in 1849, the Punjab had been under British administration for a quarter of a century by the time Iqbal was born. Though notoriously halting in its elaboration of a bureaucratic structure in this region, the penetration of British colonial power into the quotidian life-worlds of its new subjects is in evidence at every instance of Iqbal's career, whether as a student or as a political agent enmeshed in the British colonial apparatus.[23] Iqbal was steeped in the loyalism that characterized colonial Punjab under the tutelage of Sayyid Mir Hasan (1844–1929), a distinguished scholar of Islamic theology and Arabic, Persian, and Urdu literatures who happened to espouse the modernist reformist agenda of the great loyalist, Sir Sayyid Ahmad Khan (1817–1898). After instructing Iqbal in the local madrasa, Mir

Hasan persuaded Iqbal's father to matriculate him in Sialkot's Scotch Mission College, where Mir Hasan held a professorship in Arabic. A Faculty of Arts diploma from that institution in 1895 paved the way to Lahore's well-established Government College. While in Lahore, Iqbal continued to straddle British education under Sir Thomas Arnold (1864–1930) and Islamic reformism with scintillating poetic performances at the Anjuman-i Himayat-i Islam (Society for the Support of Islam). With Arnold's guidance and patronage, Iqbal would go on to the highest institutions of learning in England and Germany, encountering and absorbing strands of philosophical thought into a steadily evolving Islamic framework. With the Anjuman-i Himayat-i Islam, Iqbal came into contact with the prominent provincial politician Fazl-i Husain, who later collaborated with the British in establishing the Unionist Party, the very pillar of the loyalist establishment that would uphold Iqbal for the Provincial Legislative Council in 1926. From then on, he would never be distant from the machinery of colonial governance or far from the minds of those who manned it.

The political and ethical complications that almost immediately began to engulf Iqbal cannot be covered here in anything approaching their entirety; all that need be indexed for present purposes are the ever-constricting set of possibilities permitted by colonial machinations and the ambivalences these engendered in Iqbal. Indeed, the biographer Iqbal Singh conjectures that over the course of Iqbal's political career certain deep-set ambivalences regarding colonial power (stemming, for instance, from his unfair rejection from the Provincial Civil Service in 1901) began to surface. In the wake of his exposure to self-assertion and independence in the West and stimulated especially by romanticism, Iqbal passed into a complex crisis that was for Singh a microcosm of the Muslim community as a whole: to maintain the tradition of Muslim loyalism reflective of Sir Sayyid and the proponents of the Aligarh movement and to join the chorus of protest against the patent injustices of the colonial power. According to Singh, Iqbal's years in the Provincial Legislative Council betray "a certain degree of opportunistic equivocation and ambivalence right at the very centre of will and purpose."[24] His ambition-driven compromises with colonial authorities were essential in bringing him into the court of power, as when he recited a poem in celebration of Michael O'Dwyer, the lieutenant-governor of Punjab responsible just a year later for the Jallianwala Bagh Massacre of 1919. Despite such atrocities, there is little evidence in his published letters that Iqbal had any qualms about accepting the knighthood just a few years after this otherwise galvanizing event for anticolonial movements in Punjab, if not the subcontinent as a whole. His political experience would bring into relief just how improbable fulfilling idealist intentions under colonial circumstances would be, no matter how much Iqbal spun out "cerebral sublimities," as Singh puts it, in his literary creations. Yet it is possible that Singh is unable to distinguish a peculiar political-ideological dynamic, though one must take into account his dismissive asides. It is, in other words, not insignificant that a particularly charged political atmosphere prompted ever more desperate, however unrealizable, visions of an open future. "It is now perfectly clear," stated a panicked Iqbal to Fazl-i Husain in a letter dated June 13, 1927, "that it is part of the Hindu programme to overawe Muslims by physical force, and thus to bring about a civil war in the country."[25] This impending sense of crisis certainly informed Iqbal's vision of a future polity for an undiluted Muslim majority in the subcontinent, expressed in his famous Presidential Address to the Annual Session of the All-India Muslim League in 1930. Over the course of his own lifetime, however, Iqbal would find even this vision improbable given that, according to him, it was being appropriated beyond recognition by advocates for Pakistan. Thus in a controversial letter to Edward Thompson on March 4, 1934, Iqbal wrote, "Now Pakistan is not my scheme."[26]

The vexed political situation never let up. Rather it placed tighter constraints on the political future of the Muslims, Untouchables, and other minority communities of the subcontinent. As this history of the endgame of empire on the subcontinent is now relatively well researched, we may simply ask: In what ways did Iqbal maintain a peculiar intransigence in the literary forms and philosophical worldviews to the logic of reification, particularization, and subordination of minority figures? How is it that the formal choices Iqbal made, especially in his Persian corpus culminating in *Javid Nama*, come to stand in sharp contrast to the rigid categorical schemes of colonial politics? Is it possible that one finds resistance to its identitarian reifications and sharp relativisms in the very invocation and attempts to theorize a notion of the absolute against the fragmenting logic of modern power? This last question brings us to the crux of a twofold problematic at the very core of Iqbal's late work. The first is the burden placed on religion—Islam in particular—in refashioning a modality of the absolute that would reconcile the divisions of modernity, especially science and faith, without reverting to traditionally inherited habits of thought. This problematic will involve retracing certain strands of Bergson's vitalist philosophy that Iqbal wove through *The Reconstruction of Religious Thought in Islam* in order to forge a notion of the absolute consonant with modern political exigencies. The second, and related, problematic involves fathoming the impact this very grappling with a modern mode of the absolute would have on Iqbal's late style, which the renowned poet Faiz Ahmad Faiz described once as "austere, precise, unadorned, almost without imagery and without the general poetic frills, almost epigrammatic with the lucidity and expressiveness of the great classics."[27] I will take each of these problematics in turn.

The annotated edition of the *Reconstruction* lays bare Iqbal's deep indebtedness to Bergson in his articulation of a new modality of the absolute. Whether discussing intuition, experience, temporality, infinity, or the ego, all of which play a huge role in projecting a newly reconfigured Islam, fragments of Bergson's philosophical oeuvre surface repeatedly throughout the lectures. This indicates just how immensely catalytic Bergson's theoretical vocabulary was for producing a notion of the absolute for modern Islam that departed radically from that of long-running Sufi doctrines. Just as Islam in this work is itself absolutized—that is, made to encompass the totality of the cosmos and the human's place within it—the Bergsonian insights must themselves be attributed to an Islamic predecessor, which happens in this case to be embodied by Ibn Khaldun, who, according to Iqbal, "in view of the nature of his conception of time . . . may fairly be regarded as a forerunner of Bergson."[28] While my focus will be on specifying what Bergson offered Iqbal for his endeavor of religious reconstruction, an irony must be noted in passing: while Ibn Khaldun is valorized for overcoming classical Islam's indebtedness to ancient Greek philosophy, Iqbal simultaneously betrays dependence on Bergson, and thus an inability to completely absolutize Islam. These ambiguities, if not paradoxes, reveal the extent to which "Islam" in Iqbal's work was itself losing traditional anchoring and becoming a figure charged with all the tensions of the late colonial (dis)order. Such ambivalences abound in the *Reconstruction*, a work abiding less by structured arguments, as Majeed has noted, than "evocative analogies," being "a self-consciously visionary book that is stylistically distinctive, even idiosyncratic."[29]

The appeal of Bergson in colonial contexts has been evinced in recent scholarship, bringing into its broad sweep even observations regarding Iqbal's engagement with this luminary of fin de siècle Paris from a French perspective.[30] Bergson was critical for Iqbal's agenda of religious reconstruction. Iqbal eagerly paid his respects to the philosopher on a visit to France in 1931, between giving his lectures and the initial publication of the *Reconstruction*. Bergson's philosophical emphasis on pure temporal duration, experienced in its full immediacy and not subject to spatial abstractions, allowed Iqbal to privilege mystical experience—a long-standing feature of Islam—as a source for overcoming divisions characteristic of modernity. Mystical experience rooted in "deeper insight into our conscious experience" where "beneath the appearance of serial duration there is true duration."[31] This temporal movement, experienced as deeper, is for Iqbal, citing Bergson, "the fundamental Reality" of which the Absolute Ego becomes a part by opening itself up to immediate intuition, for "intuition, as Bergson rightly says, is only a higher kind of intellect."[32] Iqbal is pointing out how, by constructing a philosophical method on the immediacy of intuition, Bergson was able to challenge Kant's sharp distinction between the noumenal "thing-in-itself" and the human mind, with its innate forms shaping perception. (This very division between dimensions of objective reality to which the human mind is not privy and the innate formal structures through which mental perception occurs may be considered the *Urtrennung* of modernity.)[33] Thus in *Creative Evolution*, the English translation of Bergson's work cited most in the newly annotated *Reconstruction*, a chapter is devoted to finding a way "beyond the noumenal." Bergson urges, "We must appeal to experience—an experience purified, or, in other words, released, where necessary, from the moulds that our intellect has formed in the degree and proportion of the progress of our action on things. An experience of this kind is not a non-temporal experience. It only seeks, beyond spatialised time in which we believe we see continual rearrangements between the parts, that concrete duration in which a radical recasting of the whole is always going on."[34] The exhilarating encounter with this "true duration" in the immediacy of experience was enough to awaken Iqbal from what he calls "our intellectual stupor."[35] This Bergsonian vitality is ubiquitous in the *Reconstruction*, giving it an ecstatic quality. Bergson's vitalism aided Iqbal in rediscovering a path toward a new vocabulary for the absolute: the "Absolute Ego," the "immanent Infinite," the "ceaseless creative activity" in which the new Islamic selfhood will participate spontaneously, renewing itself and the world simultaneously. With selective appropriations of Bergson's vitalism, Iqbal was able to secure Islam on new premises. In spite of the communal impasses that conditioned his times, Iqbal reconstructed Islam to be infinitely generative. Mystical and scientific all at once—with all the contradictions of the late colonial moment vanishing in an immediate experience indistinguishable from Islamic mysticism—the newly reconstructed Islam furnished visions that far exceeded the realm of political possibility. Its vaunted telos in fact coalesced with traditionalism in the present.

The sublimity of Iqbal's late style did not fail to move the vast middle strata of the Indo-Muslim public, for as Faiz recognizes in an essay on Iqbal, "his work is popular among progressives and reactionaries alike" and "contributed a great deal to the rise of the progressive movement in the Urdu language, firstly because its high and purposeful seriousness demolished many decadent notions regarding the function of poetry as trivial" and held up in their stead "great human ideals of freedom, justice, progress and social equality."[36] Faiz's commentaries on Iqbal capture the transfer of the Bergsonian absolute—with its emphasis on the pure duration over spatialization—into a literary register. The absolute finds its register in "a deliberate sound spectrum, " resonant most of all, paradoxically, with Hafiz. With full awareness of Iqbal's public dismissal of Hafiz early in his career, Faiz writes, the "only other poet who does it in that way is, as far as I know, Hafiz."[37] Faiz's subtle examination of the formal features of Iqbal's late style, with its "sense of unfamiliarity by unfamiliar metres," draws attention to the uncanny interplay of proximity and distance in Iqbal's choice of classical Persian, with its nearly lost lexicon of all the proper names from a vanishing landscape.[38] This intermixture of old and new results in an inner dynamism: the modern vernacular is infused with innovative charms, yet with the irony that this occurs through an incorporation of classical meters: "He has used at least half a dozen metres which were not used in Urdu poetry before and which he introduced for the first time," recognizes Faiz.[39] Stripping temporality of its serial divisions and creating a medium in which distinctions of past and future dissolve in sound—what could be a more appropriate formal quality for the translation of the creative vitality of pure duration?

IV. FRAGMENT 3. RESEMBLANCES OF PURE CONTENT

Mimetic behavior does not imitate something but assimilates itself to [*sich selbst gleichmacht*] that thing.

—Theodor W. Adorno, *Aesthetic Theory*

Tumultuous love, indifferent to the city—
for in the city's clangour its flame dies—
seeks solitude in desert and mountain-range
or on the shore of an unbounded sea.[40]

Thus confides Iqbal in the "Prelude on Earth" of his epically stylized magnum opus, *Javid Nama* (Book of Eternity, 1932). This movement to the edge of a landmass is at one with a departure from the traditional topoi of Indo-Islamicate poetry.[41] The Urdu tradition of lyric in which Iqbal is a pioneer of the far horizon found its emotional center of gravity almost exclusively within an urban complex of palace, court, alleyway, tavern, market, temple, mosque, and the gateway marking the threshold to the beloved. Enclosed within the gambit of such locations was, of course, the garden. Maintained with the subtle care appropriate for an entity replicating the symmetry and harmony of the cosmos, the garden sustained the natural entities, such as roses and nightingales, that reconciled the separation between mundane existence and heavenly mystery. Beyond the city and the cultivated pleasures of the garden was the deserted wasteland. Here the bereaved lover was free enough of civilizational constraints to tear apart the collar of his shirt with unbridled, delirious energy. Yet the beyond of this conventional beyond—the ocean—appears rarely in the lyrical landscape of the Urdu tradition. The fact that this entity, marking the beyond of terrestrial existence and the obverse of the sky, figures so centrally in Iqbal's most aesthetically accomplished and far-reaching oeuvre is worthy of some interpretive effort. For the very paradoxical location in which Iqbal finds himself—"on the shore of an unbounded sea"—may contain the key to the central problematic of the entire work: expressing the nature of the ineffable, finding the adequate form for the uncontainable notion of pure content, releasing the sublime energy embedded within mundane existence to reconfigure the limit between human agency and nature.

Iqbal's radical departure from the Indo-Islamic poetic tradition, albeit expressed in the very idiom of this tradition, is part and parcel of the dialectical tension between form and content captured and thematized throughout *Javid Nama*. Such a definitive move beyond the traditional topoi was already adumbrated in his early Urdu composition *Shikva* (Complaint, 1909) through the devastation of the garden. This locus classicus of the tradition is devoid of all the alluring charms with which it is normally associated: "Ahd-e gul khatm hua, tut gaya saz-e chaman" (The era of the rose is finished, the instrument of the garden is broken).[42] All that lingers within the desolation and silence that the combination of Western imperialism and Islamic decline have left the garden is the memory of days that may never return. So radically has the ground shifted that the old implements may no longer be adequate to the task; what is needed are symbols other than the rose of yesteryear. Yet, as Majeed has remarked, the disrepair of the garden "is suggestive of a de-linking which is necessary for the enactment of Iqbal's own radicalised and modernised aesthetic."[43] By the time Iqbal was composing *Javid Nama*, such an aesthetic had come to mean a freeing of the content of the old tradition beyond its conventional constraints. Now the classical tropes themselves are waning and dispersing, releasing a dynamic movement underlying the old steady symbolism:

You say that these roses and tulips are permanent here;
no, they are travelers all, like the wave of the breeze.
Where is the new truth which we seek, and do not find?
Mosque, school, tavern, all alike are barren. (*JN*, 70)

Considering this rather altered situation, the minimalist response is simply to ask: What are the new forms by which the content of this tradition can attain proper expression? Yet Iqbal takes a maximalist perspective on the matter. He takes what on first blush may appear to be simply a local problem involving a particular literary tradition and turns it into a question with social, political, and religious—indeed, apocalyptic—resonance: How can the sublimity of pure content ever attain expression?

The rhetoric by which emphasis is given to content over form in Iqbal's *kalam* is initially disarming, yet the problem itself demanded innovative, discursively overwhelming design. The chiseled expression Iqbal espoused early on partook in the movement of Urdu modernism to untie the ornate intricacies of traditional court poetry and convey socially transformative messages for ever larger collectives. Thus in

Secrets of the Self (Asrar-e Khudi, 1915), we find verses as humble as these:

Poetising is not the aim of this masnavi,
Beauty-worshipping and love-making is not its aim.
. . . .
Do not seek from me charm of style in composition
. . . .
O Reader, do not find fault with the wine-cup,
But consider attentively the taste of the wine.[44]

What first appears to be merely a mismatch between the aims of the poet and the expectations of the tradition, or between the mother tongue of the composer and the conventional language of the genre, develops by the time of *Javid Nama* into a general problem of incommensurability between human language as such and the sublime objective order eluding the cognitive apparatus of human perception.

Surpass the talisman, the scent and colour,
bid farewell to the form, gaze only upon the meaning.
Though it is difficult to descry the inward death,
call not that a rose which in truth is clay. (*JN*, 57)

And yet what language or representational mode would ever allow for adequate resemblance of what does not give itself to perception—to that rose which is not in truth apprehensible substance or visible form? For language is more revealing in this instance in what it cannot say than in what it can.

Human capacities are thus the dependents of this noumenal entity; they do not have the wherewithal to fully grasp, let alone master, this impalpable presence, to see this invisible image. "The beings of light from its reflected glory derive vision" (*JN*, 125). And yet Iqbal, taking a key lesson from the ocean, will assert that it is possible to reconfigure the line distinguishing the realm of pure content and the dimensioned realm of quantity and quality to which human experience is subject. "Happy is the wave that has transgressed the shore" (*JN*, 121). It is, after all, to this effort that Iqbal gives voice as much as momentum itself. His poetry thus comes to instantiate an absolute unity of theory and practice, actualizing what it is hypostasizing. But what is this realm of the so-called eternal, this realm of pure sublime nature, which challenges human agency to defy it, which makes defiance the key to self-formation? Before uncovering the quasi-natural—which is to say, narrative—strategies that are deployed to release in a spontaneous way the pure content that itself may be nothing other than the givenness of pure nature, it may be instructive to review the different ways in which pure content is conceptualized in *Javid Nama*. This will certainly help one grasp what defiance means in this context, as well as what it requires.

Within the overall loose narrative structure of *Javid Nama* hang figurations of the grandeur of what is to be overcome, figurations that stand at one and the same time as mystery and clue. For instance, toward the end of the journey that constitutes the central motif of the poem, structured as an elaboration of the *mir'aj* of the Qur'an, but with Iqbal being led by Rumi rather than Muhammad by the Angel Gabriel, through the spheres to a virtual vision of the sublime mystery beyond being and nonbeing, Iqbal enters the threshold of the divine palace:

My words and voice are immature, my thought imperfect:
how can I hope to describe that place?
The beings of light from its reflected glory derive vision,
a palace whose walls and gates are of turquoise
holding in its bosom the whole azure sky;
soaring beyond the bounds of quantity and quality,
it reduces thought to mean impotence. (*JN*, 125)

The disorientation and despair such an experience provokes result from the arrival within the absolutes of transcendence and radical departure from the relativities that condition everyday nonecstatic experience. The collapse of measure within this sphere of the absolutes tests the coordinates of perspective and reverses the terms of subject and object: "timeless it is, and yesterday and tomorrow spring from it, / priceless it is, and under and over spring from it" (*JN*, 32). The pressures that are thus placed on Iqbal's language fashion paradox: the thing is delineated in a language that is admittedly inadequate for such a task. For only paradox manages to give some shape to the supremacy of the object over the subject and reveal the temporal and spatial frames that limit human perception of noumenal nature as well as the subjection of human phenomenology to succession, measure, quantity, and quality. All of these are inevitable artifices that block the manifestation of content in its purity. It is thus no surprise that Iqbal had always aimed to give expression in a language that effaced form to the content of this pure content. For instance, in *Secrets of the Self*, the absolutes that are integral to the nature of pure content are given expression as the disorienting fluctuation of sizes that faith makes possible:

[Faith] sowed an atom and reaped a sun
. . . .
Driven onward by resolve with sublime concerns
My pen cast abroad the secret of this veil,
That the drop may become co-equal with the sea
And the grain of sand grow into a Sahara.[45]

These figural depictions of the fluctuations of natural entities from the absolutely small to the absolutely large capture the total machinery of nature as a single entity. The fragment—the drop of rain, for instance—makes sense only in the context of the whole: the ocean as well as the thermal dynamics of transfer and movement. The grain of sand encodes its total environment and the conditions that produced it. What matters is the total force underlying any single manifestation. In the framework of the total powers of nature, which demonstrate an ever-extending formal dynamism, proximity and distance themselves are maintained, but disaggregated from physical extension: "Even so the pure spirit rises from the dust, / the pure spirit flees towards whither towards is not" (*JN*, 72). As indicated here, what initially appeared an abstracted realm above and beyond the earth is embedded within certain human states, especially love, and is present within certain material substances, such as dust here, but especially water. Such absolutes are, in other words, immanent, but they require a step removed from everyday common sense: "Love knows nothing of months and years, / late and soon, near and far upon the road" (*JN*, 32).

I will return to the ecstatic modes of existence and the metaphoric powers of the ocean to grasp the kinds of collective human energies they encode. But first we must examine the discursive strategy Iqbal fashions to spontaneously release the pure content his poetic language succeeds in capturing only when it fails.

For a sense of this discursive strategy, one must attend to what appears most natural in this work: narration, and specifically the form *masnavi*, which accorded most with the innate desire to narrate in the Persianate world. For the form that works best to reveal content in its purity is the one that is hardly detectable as such, the form that is oftentimes so self-effacing as to appear almost at one with the nature of the content depicted, or even at one with the nature of the one doing the depicting. "To raise the question of the nature of narrative is to invite reflection on the very nature of culture and, possibly, even the nature of humanity itself," writes Hayden White, elaborating on Roland Barthes's conjecture that narrative "is simply there like life itself . . . international, transhistorical, transcultural."[46] With its rhyming couplets extending out in open fashion—aa bb cc dd, and so forth—the *masnavi* is simple and flexible. Unlike other, more restrictive meters required for genres such as the *ghazal*—aa ba ca da, and so forth[47]—the *masnavi* lends itself to clear didactic expression, shifting emphasis from the form of expression to the thing itself. The traditional exemplar of the form, Rumi, Iqbal's paragon and guide in *Javid Nama*, composed much of his famous *Masnavi* spontaneously, in the midst of a circle of disciples.[48] This kind of spontaneity accords with the quasi-natural disposition toward narration in human beings. For narrative produces a form of temporal belonging distinct from natural time, manifesting thus almost from within a specific world appropriate for a distinct species experience. As White writes, "narrative might well be considered a solution to a problem of general human concern, namely, the problem of how to translate knowing into telling, the problem of fashioning human experience into a form assimilable to structures of meaning that are generally human rather than culture-specific."[49]

All of these dimensions manifest themselves in Iqbal's choice of this form (and the *ramal* meter) for engaging with pure content. His words are sometimes direct citations of Rumi: "I wandered with the zephyr in Nishat / chanting as I roved, 'Listen to the reed'" (*JN*, 118). The commingling of Iqbal's words in the midst of this loose narrative indexes the deep common origins of narrative. The spontaneous eruption of the song with which Iqbal begins his narration anchors the movement of the work within quasi-animal, almost nonhuman origins: a quasi-instinctual longing whose source remains dark to human inquiry. Yet, in a very relevant aspect, Iqbal's own discursive mode presents an innovative elaboration, for in *Javid Nama* the form most apt for simple narration separates itself from narrative. It is as if narrative time stops and the form most conventional for narration purifies itself of storytelling and engages in rapturous song. In these moments, the pure content defies the form of narrative. It is released by the pure form that is the voice of nature. In other words, rather than narrative being the expedient means for the teaching of a spiritual lesson—as is the case in Rumi's *Masnavi*—in the context of *Javid Nama*, the conventional form for narration is overcome by a nontemporality of the lesson in its purity: the lesson of the eternal.

The submergence of narration and narrative temporality under the eternal sublimity of the pure content becomes palpable at various moments of *Javid Nama*. The way the narrative flow of the work gets overwhelmed by the eternality of pure content is evident in the very discontinuity, even episodic quality of the work. The epic quest for the beatific vision is interspersed with glimpses of the life of total satisfaction redolent of the romantic, revolutionary idyll. It is as if Iqbal has put us in the interstitial space of the radical Kantian divide between the noumenon and the phenomenon, the very divide the Hegelian labor of the negative seeks to overcome. The lyric interludes of angelic song, *ghazal*, and epiphany slow the journey of Rumi and Iqbal repeatedly, displacing its primacy. Furthermore, the figures Iqbal and Rumi encounter and the dialogues that occur between historical personages bear no relationship to the successive temporality of history. This logic of anachronous juxtaposition—where Nietzsche precedes, for instance, the meeting with Bhartrihari—makes it appear as if we are at a remove from serial time altogether. It is as if everything occurs simultaneously within one *Augenblick*. (Indeed the multi- and nondimensionality of the spaces traversed—a sort of defiance of measure in space—would appear to be make *Javid Nama* incommensurate with Dante's *Commedia*, though the comparison is often made.)

I will return to the intellectual-historical coordinates of the temporality of the *Augenblick* and the spatiality of measurelessness, that is, the temporal and spatial correlates of pure content. For the meantime, let me compile the disparate ideational fragments strewn across the spheres through which Rumi and Iqbal travel to grasp the nature of the earthly existence that struggles with this transcendent order of things. For here one is exhorted to "transcend the unseen, for this doubt and surmise are nothing; / to be in the world and to escape from the world—that is something!" (*JN*, 46).

Such exhortations are scattered across *Javid Nama* like a secret code awaiting decipherment. Iqbal's urgings suggest the entire ideational edifice of the transcendental realm that he has constructed negatively by demarcating the limitations of human language has a counterpart within worldly domains. This counterpart is not akin to the noumenal and thus inaccessible dimension of subjectivity in Kant. Unlike the soul in Kant, this force appears as an immanent yet somewhat abstracted moment of subjectivity requiring de-alienation: a force embedded within collective humanity which just the right conceptualization, symbolization, and practice can unlock, releasing simultaneously unrealized powers and clarity of vision. Over the course of *Javid Nama*, a fragile interdependence thus slowly begins to take hold between love, the ocean, and active struggle against the givenness of natural entities and reified social hierarchies. Thus we finds verse like "Man's reason is making assault on the world, / but his love makes assault on the Infinite" (*JN*, 26) or "Life is to attain one's own station, / life is to see the Essence without a veil" (*JN*, 30) and, in the "Tahsin of Zoroaster," "My breast is swarming with restless waves; / what should the torrent do but devastate the shore?" (*JN*, 48). This faint sense of the possibility embedded in actuality reflects Iqbal's preoccupation with preconceptual states of being, such as love, as well as the derivation of the proper metaphors for overcoming modernity's delimitation of human collectivity to the mean substances of dirt and body, the essential categories of nationalism. Here the conceptualization of pure content attains political traction. As an embedded natural force channeled through human being, pure content is meant to overcome such delimitations. Essential to the lesson is to realize that "when love is companioned by intelligence / it has the power to design another world" (*JN*, 58).

The divorcing of reason from love is part and parcel of the breakup of the supreme subject into the petty individualized subjectivities of liberalism, which in turn is part and parcel of the *bellum omnium contra omnes* of the market and nations. To counter this logic—which Iqbal detests and associates in this work with the sublime selfishness and divisiveness of Satan—he proposes throughout the preconception of love as a dynamic overcoming of the distance between self and other, the vehicle by which the contradiction of the one and the whole is overcome. Love wells within as a natural force; it thus has as its natural metaphor the ocean. Consequently we find Said Halim Pasha's parable of the waves:

Do you know what one day a wave
said to another wave in Lake Wular?
"How long shall we strike at each other in this sea?
Rise up, let us break together against the shore." (*JN*, 121)

Water as the worldly element symbolizing pure content in always overflooding formal spaces and overcoming boundaries, the ocean as the medium of a collective subaltern existence on the other side of an imperial order dominated by the terrestrially entrenched powers of liberalism and imperial nationalism,[50] love as the force of union of the submerged constituents beyond the shores (the waves of the ocean), forging the possibilities of struggle: the associations are manifold. It is worth noting in passing Iqbal's untimely prescience in construing the internal contradiction of modernity in elemental terms: the countervailing forces of land and water are an apt analogy of the way capital generates an uncontainable and collectively alarming logic of environmental destruction. What was yesteryear imagined to be the work of a proletarian upsurge becomes in the age of posthumanist and postpolitical hegemony—when people care more for their pets than they do fellow human beings—the task of floods of contaminated water, the precipitation of toxic rain, the uncontrollable rise of ocean levels.

There is perhaps no better way to conclude than to elaborate on these kinds of political potentials of Iqbal's work that extend beyond his own entrenched chauvinisms. It is certain that the very force of the concepts he expounds so powerfully cannot be contained by his personal preferences, and there is no telling what valences this force may pick up in the future, or whether it even has an explicit future. Yet it is possible to begin to delineate this concept's somewhat subterranean trajectory through modernity, that is, from early to late romanticism. We may thus begin to grasp the figures that were its vehicles, the locations in which they appear, and the political resonances this romantic concept had over various times and spaces. Considering the immense esteem in which Iqbal held Goethe over his adult life, it is not surprising to glimpse certain resemblances between the thematics of his own work and that of the German genius. Indeed, we may see concentrated in Goethe an effort to release the sublimity of pure content from its conventional religious containments—in other words, an effort to distill the concept of uncontainable feeling:

Nenn es dann, wie du willst,
Nenn's Glück! Herz! Liebe! Gott!
Ich habe keinen Namen
Dafür! Gefühl ist alles;
Name ist Schall und Rauch,
Umnebelnd Himmelsglut.

Call it then as you will,
Call it bliss! heart! love! God!

I do not have a name
For this. Feeling is all;
Names are but sound and smoke
Befogging heaven's blazes.[51]

This all-pervasive feeling defies space, and itself has no physical form. *Gefühl* is in many ways a despatialized correlate of the *Augenblicklichkeit* of certain moments in *Faust*. Faust's striving aims for ultimate fulfillment, which would gather all the temporal and experiential process of struggle within one single moment, thereby transcending time. Faust's movement in the second part of the epic through different moments of history prefigures this worldly fulfillment: the entire expanse of human history is concentrated in one ideational configuration.

Whereas Goethe sought to break into a nebulous spiritual zone beyond the constraints of established faith, Benjamin brought the Goethean aesthetic model to desecularize history with the messianic fullness of *Jetztzeit*. Just as revelation for Benjamin is the "highest mental region of religion," it is "at the same time the only one that does not know the inexpressible"; likewise *Jetzzeit* contains all historically determinate moments in its present but admits of no further movement.[52] The lead-up to such conceptions of full time can be detected in earlier fragments, such as "The Currently Effective Messianic Elements":

> The currently effective messianic elements of the work of art manifest themselves as its content; the retarding elements, as its form. Content makes its way toward us. Form holds back, permits us to approach. The retarding (formal) elements of music probably dwell in the memory, where listening forms an accumulation. In any case, art of every kind and every work of art contain something that causes perception to accumulate, and this is the essence of the artwork's form.[53]

Iqbal took the same conceptual apparatus into the colonial realm, as I have shown, to construct a subaltern aesthetic to counter the dominance of modernist irony and formalist solipsism in the metropolitan zones. To reconstruct the interlinkages of such manifestations of pure content is beyond the scope of this chapter. In the meantime, one is left waiting to know if the internal unity of our globalized condition will reveal itself in some manifestation as a quasi-Goethean *Urphänomen*—a bursting of latent agential powers—or if we will be drowning instead in a boundless sea.

CHAPTER 6

Utility and Culture

Modern Subjectivity and Neotraditional Aesthetics

I. TOWARD THE NEO-EPIC: "A SUBLIME, A SOLEMN, A GRAND, A WONDEROUS DRAMA"

Michael Madhusudana Datta's 1854 essay, "The Anglo-Saxon and the Hindu," frames the predicament through which the Indian neo-epic was forged over the course of the late nineteenth and early twentieth centuries. At the heart of this rhetorically rich essay appears an unresolved contradiction presented in terms of an antinomy. This antinomy is best captured in the dueling metaphors Datta employs for grasping the relation between the colonizer and the colonized as "a sublime, a solemn, a grand, a wonderous Drama they are destined to act."[1] This real-life drama between the Anglo-Saxon and the Hindu is allegorized as the relation between Virgil's epic hero, Aeneas, and the Carthaginian queen Dido, destined to self-immolation on account of her all-consuming passion for her absconding conqueror.[2] But instead of self-immolation and death at the hands of the Anglo-Saxon, Datta exclaims, "it is the glorious mission of the Anglo-Saxon to regenerate, to renovate the Hindu race!"[3] Self-nullifying ravishment or self-affirming regeneration: this antinomian structure is left to stand in Datta's essay. It finds only further elaboration and ornate complication in "The Anglo-Saxon and the Hindu," leaving for its resolution, however partial, only the aesthetic forms that Datta and others would later devise, including most prominently his 1861 neo-epic, *Meghanadvadh-Kavya* (The Slaying of Meghanad).

Crucial for understanding the kind of reconciliatory work the neo-epic aesthetic attempts to perform is the contradictory colonial milieu fashioned by nineteenth-century British liberalism and empire. Andrew Sartori's *Bengal in Global Concept History: Culturalism in the Age of Capital* explains the sociopolitical backdrop for the drama of Hindu death and/or regeneration in Datta's work. On the one hand, the themes of regeneration and rejuvenation of the Hindu find their grounding in potentials of the liberal-imperial dispensation extending alongside commercialization and commodification at various levels. The potentials of the liberal order were best instantiated in the reconfiguration of Advaita Vedanta as a doctrine of liberal egalitarianism in the hands of Rammohan Roy. The idea was that Indians could join the liberal project without having to give up, at least on the surface, their cultural particularities. Such a process was thought to parallel Roman incorporation and assimilation of colonized subjects into the empire. On the other hand, the very limited possibilities for actualizing liberal society in a colonial milieu threatened to turn admiration for the Anglo-Saxon into the very kind of idol worship to which Datta attributed India's downfall. The following question from Datta's essay poses the problem of this immanent potential for regression: "Who is this stranger that has bound us, as it were, with chains of adamant, and whose bright sword gleams before our eyes like a fiery meteor—terrifying us into submission and humbling us to the dust?"[4] As Sartori remarks in the context of Bengali Babu satires, some of which Datta himself composed, the "Babu's embrace of Western learning and reformism" smacked not of "any genuine engagement with the substantial content of those [liberal] ideals, but rather [of] the desperate desire for social or professional advancement and for the approval of the colonial Master."[5]

The neo-epic as an aesthetic form slowly evolved to harmonize these untenable contradictions as they amassed over the high noon and cloudy dusk of the British Empire. What we find taking inchoate expression in Datta's work got further elaborated as his writings spread and especially when his neo-epic *Meghanadvadh-Kavya* was translated into Hindi in 1923 and became a model for generating neo-epics in the colonial hinterland over the last decades of colonial rule. Yet a penetrating look into the "The Anglo-Saxon and the Hindu" will help us envision some of the main historical impulses behind the neo-epic as well as the most salient features of this form. This works helps to delineate the interrelations between modern imperial space and cultural form (that is to say, how the neo-epic presumes a specifically imperial spatiality).

Datta's essay also helps one grasp the immense force required to establish imperial space and the violence needed to forge its concomitant subjectivity. Further, the essay lays bare the strange combination of an indelibly modern form (the new dimension of epic) and the ways it helped maintain a traditionalized subjectivity (that is, the work the neo-epic does in modernizing tradition and traditionalizing emergent subjectivity). I will take up each of these briefly.

Referring to the Anglo-Saxon conquerors of India, Datta writes, "These men were like rivers, which suck their mother-clouds on their rocky cradles; acquire strength and then journey on; sometimes with impetuosity, felling down wide forests; subduing obstinate hills; sometimes, gently, warbling liquid melody, loving flowery meads, watering golden cornfields; and at last they melt away and vanish in the embrace of Ocean, their father."[6] What Datta's Anglo-Saxon leaves behind in the wake of such a violent clearing of natural impediments and his own vanishing is imperial space: an unmarked spatial homogeneity that has as its counterpart the liberal universalism in which unimpeded exchange can take place. Datta gives vivid expression in his poetic musings to the new spatiality of commodity exchange imposed by imperial capitalism. This kind of spatiality had become symbolized, if not enjoined, by the perspectival form that Erwin Panofsky compellingly laid out in his classic 1927 essay, "Perspective as Symbolic Form."[7] It is a zone of open exchange dependent upon establishing a continuum before filling it up with objects; it establishes the perfect sphere for the exchangeability of those objects as commodities, and it has as its correlate "the freely chosen position of a subjective 'point of view'" characteristic of liberal ideals.[8] It is this very spatiality that is presumed by Datta's neo-epic imagination in colonial India. It allows for the exchangeability of epic forms from different historical, linguistic, cultural, and geographic contexts and presumes a comparability and even equality of authorial subjects across these differences. Thus in Datta's letters we find comparisons between his *Meghanadvadh-Kavya* and epics in the Western as well as Indian traditions and comparisons between himself and all the authors of these epics: "The poem is rising into splendid popularity. Some say it is better than Milton—but that is all bosh—nothing can be better than Milton; many say it licks Kalidasa; I have no objection to that. I don't think it impossible to equal Virgil, Kalidasa and Tasso. Though glorious, still they are mortal poets."[9] (See appendix B for more examples of this literary seriality and equivalence in the Hindi sphere.)

In this chapter I will explore the kinds of checks, scrutiny, skepticism, and compromises modern subjectivity undergoes in Datta's immediate environs and especially in the colonial hinterland. The *desh*, the Hindi belt stretching from contemporary Bihar across Uttar Pradesh and into Rajasthan, as C. A. Bayly has recently observed in *Recovering Liberties*, was somewhat impenetrable to the modern liberalism sweeping over other spheres of the Indian world. For instance, with respect to the controversial figure of late colonial politics, Madan Mohan Malaviya, Bayly observes "the continuous eruption into Malaviya's discourse of Hindu language, tradition and 'prejudice,' in Gadamer's sense." Though Malaviya and his supporters accepted several liberal principles, Bayly says "their liberalism was inflected with concepts of karma, rebirth and the language and 'faith of our fathers.'"[10] I would like to suggest that the neo-epic seemed suited to modifying, if not muting, this subjective thrust of modernity while maintaining, even promoting its spatial and ideological conditions of possibility. In other words, as this form evolved in the Hindi *desh* under the auspices especially of *Chayavad*, it sought to reconcile dueling imperatives bequeathed to Indian subjects of colonial rule: traditional prejudice, in which little of liberal subjectivity is imaginable, and the modern bureaucracy premised on utilitarianism, in which only the liberal subject is presumed. The very process of reconfiguring traditions in nontraditional media made possible new political agendas such as nationalization, which inevitably alienated forms from their traditional grounding. This has been argued to be emphatically the case with the seminal Hindi writer Bharatendu Harishchandra.[11] In making of tradition a select series of increasingly manipulated and manipulating symbols, the literary and cultural actors I explore here were in the process of uncovering the manifold possibilities of culture once it had become an object of considerable political utility. Sumitranandan Pant's aptly titled "The Usefulness [*Upayogyata*] of the Epic Form in the Present Age," translated in full in appendix B, brings into perspective the turn toward epic by the likes of Jayashankar Prasad and other Chayavadi writers. Further, Pant's title alone alerts one to the predicaments that befall culture once utility is universalized in tandem with commodification: now all things must perforce be affirmed for their utility, or otherwise abandoned.[12]

II. MODERNITY AFTER UTILITY IN COLONIAL CALCUTTA: A BRIEF HISTORY

Before Datta composed "The Anglo-Saxon and the Hindu," he had famously converted to Christianity in 1842 and gotten expelled from Calcutta's most prestigious institution of learning, Hindu College, the following year for that very act. The conversion to Christianity was meant to serve two purposes: to break a marriage engagement with his father's pick of eligible brides among the nouveau riche Bengali landlord set and to secure travel to England, for as he urged upon his dear friend Gourdas Basak at midnight on November 27, 1842, "Depend upon it—in the course of a year or two more—I must either be in England or cease to be at all;—*one of these must be done*!"[13] In another letter to Basak, he fantasizes about himself as a poet on the order of Lord Byron, whose famous biography by Thomas Moore he believes should serve as a model for his own, "if I happen to be a great poet—which I am almost sure I shall be, if I can go to England."[14] Datta's yearning to reach England—despite the weight of imperial hierarchy and against the tide of established patterns of mobility—overrode all other concerns. As if taking the ethos of utilitarianism introduced by the British colonial establishment and adopted by ever-widening Bengali circles to its utmost logic, Datta instrumentalized the faith and sacred rites of the imperial authorities to the end of reaching "Albion's distant shore": "And, oh! I sigh for Albion's strand / As if she were my native-land!"[15] The rhyming words, each signifying different kinds of cultural rootedness and spatial trajectories under the imperial fold, express identification with radical liberalism and the free movement it implied. The famous Christian convert of Calcutta with whom Datta discussed his plans for conversion, Rev. K. M. Banerjee, remarked, "I was impressed with the belief that his desire of becoming a Christian was, scarcely, greater than his desire of a voyage to England."[16] The attitude Datta displays in this act of conversion and later took to both classical Sanskritic and Greco-Roman phenomena illuminates the utilitarian ethos permeating both the British imperial establishment and Indian intellectual milieus such as that of Hindu College. Datta's attitude toward his conversion to Christianity—more than the conversion itself, it can be argued—embodied the new utilitarian ethos that emerged in tandem with the wider establishment of imperial commerce in colonial Bengal.

While the impact of this ethos on British administrators has been worked over since Eric Stoke's seminal account, *The English*

Utilitarians and India (1959), relatively little attention has been given to how this philosophy was adopted by Bengali intellectuals, how it was adapted to the vernacular scene, and to what effect. How did the shifts in the institutional structure of imperial rule emanate outward into the wider Bengali and Hindi hinterland, remolding educational desires and provoking challenges to the interests vested in the Indian status quo? While this question hints at wider horizons than I will survey in this section, it does help situate the process of transmission I will cover. The relay of utilitarianism extends from the metropolitan centers of control under the tutelage, if not direct management, of Jeremy Bentham and James and John Stuart Mill, to the governments of Lord William Bentinck and the policies of Lord Thomas Babington Macaulay, to the reform efforts of Bengali authorities such as Raja Rammohan Roy, to the cultural rebellions of the New Bengal, such as that of our cynical convert, the newly christened Michael Madhusudana Datta. With respect to Datta's magnum opus, the *Meghanadvadh-Kavya*, Clinton Seely points out, "Bengali literary historians even today mark with his text and its year of publication the divide between the so-called premodern and modern eras of Bangla literature."[17] In retracing this line of transmission, some sharper light may be shed on the underlying rationale for this standard judgment of this work as marking a radical point of no return in vernacular Indian culture.

To see Datta's magnum opus as the culminating symbol of a transformative process, we must investigate the institutional connection between utilitarianism and imperial institution-building. What affinity was there between the two? What connected "[the legal reformer] Bentham's calm philosophic brow" to "James Mill's stern eyes of authority," to cite Stokes's memorable concluding image of a British Indian Leviathan?[18] How did the doctrine of maximizing self-interest, understood as "pleasure" or "happiness," get exported from London and become the basis for imperial law radiating out from Calcutta into the colonial hinterland? To grasp the connection, however schematically, we must turn initially to recent scholarship on Bentham, Mill *père*, and his famous son, the philosopher Mill *fils*. All three of these men exercised a profound impact on the way modernity was fashioned in colonial Bengal, and all happened to be the most influential exponents of utilitarian thought, bringing it to a political crescendo within the British Empire over the very years Datta and other members of the Bengal Renaissance were coming of age and finding their bearings in a new imperial dispensation.

Though none of these three figureheads ever set foot on the Indian subcontinent, Bentham and Mill *père et fils* had their hands on key levers of power over the British administration on both ends of the empire and, indeed, over the multitude of Indian subjects deemed incapable of self-governance. While Bentham's influence was the most indirect, it was by no means less powerful than the others'. As early as the 1780s, Bentham had begun focusing his attention on British India, figuring out how his system of legal codes would require modification in order to be transplanted successfully in Bengal and toying with the idea of constructing an Indian constitutional code from scratch. With the rise of his protégé Mill *père* in the British imperial bureaucracy from 1819 onward and the subsequent employment of Mill *fils* in the Examiner's Office in 1823, the Benthamite legacy for the subcontinent was sealed by the time Lord Bentinck departed for India in 1827. At his send-off dinner he famously feasted on "the pure milk of the Benthamite word," and before an audience including Mill *père* he uttered the oft-quoted line "I am going to British India, but I shall not be Governor-General. It is you that will be Governor-General."[19] While Bentham was the teacher of the teachers of colonial officials, Mill *père et fils*, as mentioned, were both directly involved in imperial governance. As Bentinck's line suggests, Mill the elder had already imbibed Bentham's doctrine and was proving successful in propagating it among his peers and the public at large. About a year after embarking on his monumental *History of British India*, published in 1818 after twelve years of hard judgment and destined to become a standard work for East India Company officials and a textbook for the Indian civil service, Mill *père* met Bentham. This proved "the most important political and philosophical alliance of his life."[20] The impact the elder Mill's encounter had with the reclusive fountainhead of modern utilitarianism was tremendous. It led to the radicalization of this doctrine and its propagation as a new militant faith intended "to define," as Majeed has argued, "an idiom for the British empire as a whole which would replace the dominant conservative one" that had arisen in reaction to the French Revolution.[21] Elie Halévy, the French historian of this brand of philosophical radicalism, quipped, "Bentham gave Mill a doctrine, and Mill gave Bentham a school."[22] He, in a sense, gave to Bentham his eldest son's mind for indoctrination and his vast network of contacts and administrative clout for building a movement. With the son, he secured for the promotion of utilitarianism one of Britain's leading philosophical minds; with his official clout, he established utilitarianism as a normative code of empire.

There is no way to grasp the process of transmission of the utilitarian ethos into colonial Bengal (and beyond) without knowing what utilitarianism amounted to as a vector of British imperial policy at this historical moment. What characterized utilitarian thought within the empire specifically? In order to answer this seemingly simple question, it is important to disaggregate a phenomenon of as much complexity as utilitarianism if not least because recent scholarship has pointed out how Bentham distanced himself from the pro-imperial policies of his otherwise keen disciple Mill *père*. Furthermore, in its emphasis on individualism, especially the rescue of the individual from superstition, idolatry, and priestly bondage, utilitarianism overlapped other strains of the British imperial apparatus that were coming to the fore by the early nineteenth century, especially Christian evangelicalism and a moderate liberalism.[23] Yet, as Stokes recognized, what set the utilitarians apart as a radical sect within the imperial establishment was an authoritarianism that emphasized the "immense and indefinite influence" of the power of law and government as levers of progressive reform.[24] This was best expressed in the elder Mill's view that "even the utmost abuse of European power, is better, we are persuaded, than the most temperate exercise of Oriental despotism," or that a "simple form of arbitrary government, tempered by European honour and European intelligence, is the only form which is now fit for Hindustan."[25] Such views were thought sound for Mill the elder and his followers for "exactly in proportion as Utility is the object of every pursuit, may we regard a nation as civilized." And, as a logical corollary, "exactly in proportion as its ingenuity is wasted on contemptible and mischievous objects," such as idols and other products of a pernicious superstition pervading India, "the nation may safely be denominated barbarous."[26]

We come finally to the principle of utility itself, what Bentham later called "the greatest-happiness principle," and its patent usefulness for the justification of imperial consolidation. Bentham and later Mill *père et fils* asserted the universal applicability of the principle of utility: "every action whatsoever" is to be judged, in the words of Bentham, "according to the tendency which it appears to have to augment or diminish the happiness of the party whose interest is in question."[27] Having become the sole standard for judging all action and for assessing the civilizational level of all social formations regardless of historical circumstances, the principle of utility gave pithy expression to the normalization of self-interest in a society dominated by commerce. It is no mere coincidence that utilitarian doctrines rose to prominence in tandem with the rise of the commercial sector within an expanding British imperial order. Marx observes that "with the dryest naïveté," Bentham "assumes that the modern petty bourgeois, especially the English petty bourgeois, is the normal man. Whatever is useful to this peculiar kind of normal man, and to his world, is useful in and for itself. He applies this yardstick to the past, the present and the future."[28] Making reference to the English shopkeeper as much as to the big industrialist, Mill *fils* recognized that "Bentham gave voice to those interests and instincts" that had grown in strength and prosperity since the revolutions of the seventeenth century.[29] The arrival of Lord Bentinck in Bengal in 1828 was thus a watershed moment. Now these very commercial interests and instincts could enjoy a freedom to experiment with radical reformist policies and agendas that would have been kept in check by competing interests in metropolitan arenas. Colonial India was thus the open testing ground for the "assault on ancient institutions," which, as Mill *fils* recognized, "has been, and is, carried on for the most part with [Bentham's] weapons."[30]

The penetration of the utilitarian ethos into the fabric of Indian sociocultural forms was remarkably fast, noticeable, and generative. The radical agenda of the legislators produced major controversies around the abolition of widow self-immolation, among other reforms. The utilitarian doctrine gave rise to new kinds of Indian authority, such as Rammohan Roy, "the bright morning star of the new India," who, according to Stokes, had long been "catechized" in Bentham's principle of utility.[31] And with the evolution of modern educational institutions and agendas, this overpowering principle virtually reconfigured the entirety of cultural forms inherited from classical antiquity. The most evident case for this kind of transfiguration of inherited codes is *Meghanadvadh-Kavya*. To elaborate, I would like to briefly outline how the new educational apparatus founded on utilitarian principles gave immediate rise to the new rebellious cultural ethos of the Young Bengal. Embodied by Datta and instantiated in acts like his conversion to Christianity, the new ethos reduced sacred rites to mere secular springs for launching a more felicitous life under imperial horizons and making progress toward Albion's distant shore. That is to say, the transformations within the Indian world were premised on a solid identification with the principles of liberalism embedded in commercial norms and palpable in doctrines of philosophical radicalism breaking upon the shore in India.

An indication of the profound impact the utilitarian ethos had on the making of a modern Indian educational system appears in the obituary for John Stuart Mill composed by Bankimchandra Chatterjee in 1873. The most influential Bengali man of letters of the late nineteenth century claimed, "In the field of education the path [Mill] elucidated is now followed everywhere by everyone." Its significance for the making of modern Indian subjects is also indicated: "Regarding the individual and society, Mill considered that if the individual was held to be of prime importance, society would flourish; otherwise, civilization would become enfeebled."[32] The first experiments with the implementation of an individualist liberal agenda occurred in Calcutta, where Hindu College was established with a larger utilitarian blueprint in mind. Whatever the designs prescribed by the combination of colonial and local powers, it became obvious that they were exceeded by the students they created. That is, such designs were themselves utilized in unexpected ways—and more often than not, on the basis of the very progressive values of this institution.

Founded in 1817 by a group of wealthy Bengalis under the auspices of the British imperial establishment, Hindu College set its cornerstone firmly on the premises of utilitarian thought. Not only does the rhetoric of the founding tracts betray Benthamite flourishes, but the college's very curriculum and the teachers it employed delivered on the radical premises of the institution almost immediately. *A Biographical Sketch of David Hare* (1877), written by Peary Chand Mittra, provides precious glimpses into the founders' ideas about the institution, especially their concern with happiness, efficiency, individualism, science, and reason. The work is replete with primary documents reproduced verbatim, including letters of the founder, David Hare. A Scottish freethinker and nonconformist, Hare took to education soon after arriving in Calcutta in 1807, abandoning his original profession of watchmaker along the way. "A few years after my arrival in this country," he recalls, "I was enabled to discover during my intercourse with several native gentlemen, that nothing but education was requisite to render the Hindoos happy, and I exerted my humble abilities to further the interests of India."[33] Foremost among these "native gentlemen" was Rammohan Roy. Mittra locates the genesis of an idea for the college in conversations Hare had with Roy in 1815. Whereas Roy believed that the founding of voluntary societies such as his own Atmiya Sabha (Friends Society) and the propagation of neo-Vedanta philosophy were the best means for lifting "society from the swamp of idolatry and superstition to a higher moral plane," for Hare the "education of native youths in Western literature and science would be a far more effective means of enlightening their understanding and purging their minds from pernicious cants."[34] The conviction that the new education had to be useful was sharply expressed in the letter Roy addressed to Lord Amherst in 1819 concerning the drawbacks of promoting traditional Sanskritic learning in British India. Such a program "can only be expected to load the minds of youth with grammatical niceties and metaphysical distinctions of little or no practical use to the possessors or to society." This is a matter of concern for Roy, for "every well-wisher of the human race must be desirous that the efforts made to promote it . . . should be guided by the most enlightened principles, so that the stream of intelligence may flow in the most useful channels."[35]

The consequences of the new educational programs quickly outstripped the limits of the founders' vision. Datta was not the first to convert to Christianity or to incite outrage among the school's authorities; he was following the path of rebellion carved by his predecessors, all in accordance with the riveting lessons of the college's most legendary, if not notorious, teacher, Henry Derozio. Young Bengal came of age under the tutelage of this inspired pedagogue, who took the liberal, secular, and utilitarian ethos of the day to logical extremes: radical equality against the norms of imperial hierarchy, atheism as the logical outcome of empiricism, and blasphemy as a new rite of passage beyond the constraints of traditional Hindu doxa. "Orthodox society was deeply alarmed. It was rumoured that some Hindu College boys, when required to utter mantras at prayers, would repeat lines from the *Iliad* instead; that one student, asked to bow down before the goddess Kali, greeted the image with a 'good morning, madam.'"[36] These inanities turned out to be the least of the authorities' worries. Derozio was forced to resign in 1831, after only five years at the lectern, and many of his pupils were expelled then and in subsequent years, so great was the "public alarm arising from the very unwarranted arrangements and misconduct" of Derozio, "who, it appears, has materially injured [his students'] morals, and introduced some strange system, the tendency of which is destructive to their moral character and to the peace of society."[37] In "Sonnet to My Pupils," published in 1829, Derozio offered his vision of what was spiritually coming to fruition:

Expanding, like the petals of young flowers
I watch the opening of your infant minds,

And the sweet loosening of the spell that binds
Your intellectual energies and powers,
That stretch, like young birds in soft summer hours,
Their wings to try their strength. O! how the winds
Of circumstance, and gentle April showers
Of early knowledge, and unnumbered kinds
Of new perceptions shed their influence;
And how you worship Truth's omnipotence![38]

To retrace more precisely the cultural forms forged by the force of this new Truth, we must return to Datta and his engagement with classical epic forms.

III. *THE SLAYING OF MEGHANAD*, OR THE MANIPULABILITY OF CLASSICAL TRADITIONS

When Datta realized that the doors of Hindu College were closed to him on account of his conversion to Christianity, he found himself in a difficult situation. He was unwilling to return to Hindu society, despite the pull of filial ties, and equally uncertain about his connection to his new faith, for even after taking up study in Bishop's College, on the outskirts of Calcutta, he took umbrage whenever a correspondent addressed him as a Christian. "I do not like 'My dear Christian Friend M. etc.,'" he writes in one letter; in another he clarifies, "'M. Dutt Esqr. or Baboo' (if you please), Bishop's College; and nothing more."[39] His self-fashioning as a Christian convert and his erstwhile aspiration to become a missionary were always alloyed with the desire for mobility and self-advancement. The wishes of his new masters to send him off as a fully credentialed Christian missionary on the peripheries of the empire went unfulfilled when Datta left Bishop's College without submitting to the final exams, perhaps a reflection of lingering ambivalences about his adopted faith. Whether the education he received at Bishop's College settled questions of religious faith for him remains unclear, given how moot historical records on the matter appear. What is indisputable, however, is how unusually formative the training in classical Greek and Latin languages and literatures was for Datta in developing a secular counterpoint to the religious education at Bishop's. It was not so much that a religious orientation was altogether lacking in Datta; school reports suggest otherwise.[40] Rather, his previous exposure to English romanticism allowed him to channel his spiritual energy toward the worldly domain of aesthetic affect, popular appeal, and political allegory—in other words, toward a domain free from the censures and sanctimony of biblical studies. His advancement in Greek and Latin during his years at Bishop's, uncommon then and increasingly prohibitive over the course of the nineteenth century, opened up a dialogical interplay with Sanskrit epics under the rubric of the Indo-European paradigm, recently generated by romantic Orientalists such as Sir William Jones. The effect of this dialogue between Indian and Western antiquity was the enactment of a kind of "resistance through classics," as Alexander Riddiford has suggested in his rich study, *Madly after the Muses: Bengali Poet Michael Madhusudan Datta and His Reception of the Graeco-Roman Classics*.[41] Here I want to suggest that any sound conception of Datta's neo-epic experimentations will have to grapple with the interchangeability of Indian and Western epic motifs and Datta's overarching commitment to bitextualism (modern-day *shlesha*), in which two narratives are told simultaneously, one Sanskritic and the other Greco-Roman, one implicit and the other explicit. In their simultaneous retelling, both are mutually transformed in subversive ways, revealing the embedded potentialities of a liberal and perhaps even postliberal conception of imperial space.

In order to get a sense of what uses could be made of Western classics in colonial Bengal, I turn to Riddiford's recent findings, for these reveal the politico-allegorical inflections of Datta's neo-epic works. As a trained classicist, Riddiford extends his hermeneutical reach beyond the gambit of nearly all previous interpretations of Datta, premised as these have been on either a Bengali provincialism or a constricted geocultural imagination deeply embedded in some versions of South Asian studies.[42] By using a classicist's lens on Datta's neo-epic musings, Riddiford is able to uncover a Greco-Roman stratum, that is, a subterranean layer of Greco-Roman references under the neotraditional Indian contents of his epic-based storylines. "If the [*Meghanadvadh-Kavya*] is Indian in subject matter," Riddiford writes, "then it is above all Greek in form and style: Valmiki's *Ramayana*, or an episode taken from it, recast in an Iliadic mould." Some of the details will be spelled out later. Here it is worth reiterating Riddiford's central claims and pointing out what some of their underexplored ramifications might be. First, there is the secularization thesis: "The British Orientalists, by comparing Hindu mythology and theology with those of Greece and Rome, indicated a new way of reading Sanskrit poetry and epic, not as a part of the living Hindu religion but as texts of secular interest." Riddiford understands that Datta's work draws from the secular worldviews of Orientalist scholarship, grasping within it a dimension of classical Indian tradition that could now be turned against Hindu orthodoxy or, as Riddiford more bluntly puts it, "a tool to resist and undermine the hegemony of elite Hindu culture." Though Riddiford does not make this connection explicitly, it is nevertheless plausible to see his secularization thesis working in tandem with the normalization of a vision attuned to utility. Second, Riddiford grasps the catalyzing effect of Datta's training in classics on his literary production, especially in terms of formal strategies for overcoming the implicit hierarchies of British imperialism. Whereas "the withholding of Graeco-Roman knowledge from most Indians effectively imposed a glass ceiling on their careers prospects within the British colonial system," especially considering how knowledge of Greek and Latin was "necessary at that time for advancement in almost every elite British profession," Datta was caught within the competing imperatives of liberal equality and imperial hierarchy.[43] That is, he was made privy to a proper English education (and not merely an education in English, like nearly all of his elite counterparts), but within the constraints of the colony. Furthermore, his training at Bishop's was taking place at the very moment when the liberal reformist underpinnings of what has been called "a short-lived early modern antiabsolutist formation" in colonial Bengal were slowly giving way.[44] These agonistic circumstances lead Riddiford to a recognition of Datta's "multifarious subversiveness," his third major claim: "In almost all cases his readings of the Graeco-Roman classics went against the grain of contemporary British tastes."[45] Both his incorporation of Western classical elements into his works and his incursions into restricted metropolitan spaces were often in service of the erosion of the British ordering of people, places, and things.[46]

Riddiford's insights suggest a way of giving conceptual weight to what generally amounts to a common yet unsubstantiated assertion in Bengali literary history, namely that Datta's *Meghanadvadh-Kavya* marks a fundamental step into the modern. What gives this work this privileged position, I want to suggest, is how it brings to culmination the utilitarian ethos that had begun to pervade and reconfigure large sectors of colonial Bengal. This culminating point is characterized by the peculiarly modern possibilities for manipulating—even turning upside down—long-stable cultural forms, symbols, and motifs. The uses to which Datta subjects different classical traditions dislodges them from their former semantic fields, whether from Hinduism, in the case of the Sanskritic epic inheritance, or from imperial ideology, in the context of Greco-Roman classics. He resituates these forms within new spatiotemporal coordinates established by commodity exchange in imperial space. These utilitarian transformations are attended by threats to the very intrinsic or nonutilitarian values associated with the realm of culture. Datta was aware of these lurking dangers and reflects on them in his poem "Atma-Bilap" ("Self-Sorrow" or perhaps "Lament of the Self"), with which I will conclude this section. The *Meghanadvadh-Kavya* thus marks a limit. It marks what the imperial dispensation made possible—the disaggregation, recombination, and modulation of cultural forms, alienating them from their earlier significations through a sharp grasp of their utility—as well as what this same imperial-capitalist formation makes increasingly impossible: the justification of cultural forms on the basis of a nonutilitarian orientation. This duality of horizons reflected from deep within this work's contradictions is the ultimate sign of its modernity.

Yet the newness of *Meghanadvadh-Kavya* was not so recondite as to be impalpable upon its release in 1861. The first instance of newness came in the very foreignness of the verse form Datta chose, for blank verse broke radically from the traditional Bengali meter employed for narrative works known as *payar*. Datta recognized the challenge his choice would pose for his readership, yet he considered its indefinite extension in the Indian world to be immanent: "The fact is, my dear fellow, that the prevalence of Blank-verse in this country, is simply a question of time. Let your friends guide their voices by the pause (as in English Blank-verse) and they will soon swear that this is the noblest measure in the Language. My advice is Read, Read, Read. Teach your ears the new tune and then you will find out what it is."[47] One gets a finer sense of what blank verse was encoding by seeing its development in Bengali in light of the history of this form in early modern English epic. It was Milton's *Paradise Lost* that provided Datta with a profound example of the potentialities of blank verse. By grasping what Milton himself had ventured as epic by dropping the traditional rhyming couplet, still employed for epic narrative by Dryden and other contemporaries, it becomes possible to gauge what was breaking into the Indian cultural world through blank verse. Two main thrusts of this verse form come to the fore immediately in Milton's own justification of it in *Paradise Lost*: "This neglect then of rhyme so little is to be taken for a defect, though it may seem so perhaps to vulgar readers, that it rather is to be esteemed an example set, the first in English, of ancient liberty recovered to heroic poem from the troublesome and modern bondage of rhyming."[48] The rupturing of the binds of enduring custom becomes for Milton a means for renewing the ancient legacy of the epic form as well as for reclaiming the rights of individualistic expression. Milton's own experimentations with the relationship between lineation and syntax—exactly what blank verse made possible—has been seen as "highly distinctive and unusual."[49] The insertion of his individuality into the poem marked *Paradise Lost*'s newness, for this was merely an analogue of his preference for internality and direct experience, the progenitors of modern subjectivity. These markers of individuality were adopted by Datta, who then took them as the universal criterion of the "true poet." Thus, in one of his letters, Datta writes, "Blank verse is the best suited for Poetry in every language. A true poet will always succeed best in Blank verse as a bad one in Rhyme. The grace and beauty of the former's thoughts will claim attention, as the melody of the latter will conceal the poverty of his mind."[50]

If blank verse was the vehicle for modern subjectivity in the colonial sphere, the multifarious, overlapping legacies of the ancient Indo-European epic traditions of Sanskrit, Greek, and Latin to which Datta now had immediate access became the fungible raw materials for fashioning a new chapter of world literary history. What marked this newness was the immediate translatability and exchangeability of motifs, tropes, themes, styles, and narrative forms of distinct epic traditions. This new expanse of interchangeable traditions, each uprooted from their original semantic fields and thus always already translated and translatable into the other, was the specific cultural mode through which the new spatiality of imperial capitalism took expression. As Riddiford has recognized, Datta made particularly subversive uses of this radically altered cultural sphere with his "ongoing project to combine and reconcile the Graeco-Roman and Hindu traditions in the creation of a new cosmopolitan aesthetic."[51] Subversion was implicit in the assertion of commensurability, if not equality, between the traditions of the colonizer and the colonized. Rather than being moribund, traditional Indian culture now has the potential to become reanimated and generative of a new ethos partaking of classical counterparts. "It is my ambition," writes Datta in the midst of composing *Meghanadvadh-Kavya*, "to engraft the exquisite graces of the Greek mythology on our own; in the present poem I mean to give free scope to my inventing Powers (such as they are) and to borrow as little as I can from Valmiki.

Do not let this startle you. You shan't have to complain again of the un-Hindu character of the Poem. I shall not borrow Greek stories but write, rather try to write, as a Greek would have done."[52] Considering how thoroughly the classical Valmiki *Ramayana* narrative is reworked in Datta's hand in light of Western models, and how traditional Indian forms are consequently made amenable to modern norms of subjectivity and spatiality, what Datta produced was a modern *shlesha*: a bitextual work in which the narratives of the Greco-Roman and Sanskritic epic could be retold simultaneously. This was the objective counterpart to the new subjectivity Datta was ushering in: the imaginary world in which radical liberalism could find a home in colonial India.

The real costs of fashioning this world in the utilitarian mold outlined earlier come to light in Datta's poem "Atmap-Bilap," in which the consequentialist logic of utilitarian practice leaves all activity bereft of any intrinsic significance. All time has become a secular empty extension in which one makes investments for future self-happiness and can be considered wasted if desired results do not obtain, and nothing but a mere means if they have. "To whom shall I speak of the years you have wasted / In pursuit of fame?" asks Datta repeatedly.

The fisherman troubles to dive into deep water
To bring up pearls—
But you have thrown your years worth a hundred
times more
Into the sea of death, you sinner!
Who will give you back your lost jewel, O foolish mind,
Dazed, alas, by all the magic tricks of hope![53]

We shall return to this mise-en-abyme through which the vacuity of the utilitarian world gapes. But it must be noted here that reflecting back to Datta is a mind bedazzled by the lure of time as linear and nonrecursive, the mere container of actions and their consequences. The source of sorrow is the trap of living in times that are themselves bereft of intrinsic meaning. This exile is the measure of Datta's modernity. The value of time is to be quantified only by the extent to which it has been employed to maximize any given utility for the sake of future happiness. Time itself has no value, nor does anything else, including tradition.

IV. FRANCIS BACON IN BENARES, OR TRADITIONAL AUTHORITY AND COMPETING TELEOLOGIES OF UTILITY

We leave our sorrowful Michael Madhusudana Datta to his travails through empire, racial discrimination, and the bouts of impoverishment and alcoholism that ended his life, all of which has been covered by his biographers.[54] But before proceeding, one caveat is in order that applies to Datta's case and helps situate what follows. It must be kept in mind that the radical liberalism-cum-utilitarianism Datta had imbibed was always mollified by a romantic sentimentalism. The edges of a doctrine that lent itself so easily to social atomism, individualistic hedonism, and cold calculation of all action could be mitigated only by the formation of a secular cultural order premised on maintaining social cohesion, as John Stuart Mill himself pointed out in his essay "Coleridge" (1842).[55] This appeared to be the case as much in the metropolitan as in the colonial sphere. Whereas Bentham was "pressing the new doctrines to their utmost consequences," Coleridge was "asserting the best meaning and purposes of the old."[56] Likewise in the milieu of Hindu College under Derozio's tutelage, as Rosinka Chaudhuri has recently pointed out, there arrived a new secular high culture into the colonial sphere "with an almost Arnoldian support for the self-consciously literary" and a "fearless enthusiasm in the cause . . . considered the most sacred upon earth, the improvement of the moral and physical state of mankind."[57] The agonism expressed here between crude utility and secular spirituality, contraries held together by the emergent social order, help situate the role the sacred city of Benares and the surrounding Hindi belt would play in the mutual remolding of modern and traditional thought, especially in the age of the famous Bharatendu Harishchandra and his successor, Mahavir Prasad Dvivedi. Benares acted as epicenter and interface of long-standing traditions of the subcontinent: over the late nineteenth and early twentieth centuries, this ancient city on the banks of the venerated Ganges was a dramatic locus for the interaction of the modern ethos of the British colonial power and the aura of long-standing religious traditions. As such, the Benares of Bharatendu revealed the malleability of ancient rites for the fostering of modern political programs and, in doing so, opened the potential for the hollowing out of the sacred from ancient traditions in the very process of instrumentalization.[58] Yet the city still proved capable of absorbing, integrating, and neutralizing new doctrines, including radical ones, such as the notion of utility, which by the Dvivedi era was considered increasingly indispensable for overcoming colonial subjection. This interrelation between useful knowledge and the forging of a Hindu political bloc powerful enough to contest the colonial power and establish wide hegemony over the diverse Indian populations requires some retracing.

Dubbed by the influential art historian E. B. Havell "the Rome of Hinduism," Benares had been extolled repeatedly in Sanskrit puranic literature for well over a millennium by the time the British began establishing their presence within its sacred confines at the end of the eighteenth century. Yet, unlike Rome, Benares had little weight historically as a site of political administration. Instead, canonical depictions of the city, such as those found in the *Kashikhanda*, placed it above the vagaries of mundane affairs, balancing as Benares was on the tip of Shiva's trident, where it encompassed the triple world but itself remained unencompassed. Similarly, tradition held that Benares was not merely one among the seven most venerated pilgrimage sites of Hinduism, but the one that contained all the rest within itself. This otherworldly authority remained unparalleled and combined with Benares's antiquity to produce distinct opportunities and challenges for the self-legitimating agendas of improvement, progress, and utility prized by the British. Resecuring it as the uncontestable center of Hindu tradition, the British, as Vasudha Dalmia has recognized, "wished explicitly to derive benefit from the authority generated by [Benares] and co-opt and integrate in one way or another the bearers of this tradition," most notably the Brahmin pandits.[59] Just as much as Benares provided the lever with which to organize and direct the Hindu masses, it also seemed to concentrate the larger Hindi hinterland's intransigence to the liberal utilitarian agenda (often in consonance with Christian proselytizing tendencies) of the British. "The special sanctity and influence of Benares constitute a gigantic obstacle to all religious changes within it," wrote the senior Anglican missionary M. A. Sherring in *The History of Protestant Missions in India, from Their Commencement in 1706 to 1871*.[60] For Sherring, the Hindi *desh* represented by Benares was "the last tract in India which will submit to the Gospel" and was "not changeable and progressive in the same way, and to the same extent, as in Bengal," referencing the colonial origins of the latter.[61] Likewise, for British educationists such as John Muir and James R. Ballantyne, "it was apparent . . . that in Benares, unlike in Calcutta, there was little prospect of quickly creating an English-speaking middle class."[62]

Though the broad interaction and dynamism between modern instrumental rationality and the apparently intractable inertia of Indian, specifically Sanskritic, culture is not containable within Benares, a short survey of strategies that were adopted to normalize utility (or "useful knowledge") within that city will be instructive for grasping the consequences that ensued in the cultural sphere more generally. I thus turn to key moments in Michael S. Dodson's fascinating *Orientalism, Empire, and National Culture* and Dalmia's magisterial tome on Bharatendu Harishcandra and nineteenth-century Benares, *The Nationalization of Hindu Traditions.*

In juxtaposing the relevant insights of these two scholars regarding the promotion of "useful knowledge" within influential media and educational institutions in Benares over the nineteenth century, it becomes possible to discern just how contrasting the ends were to which utilitarian doctrines could be put and just how crucial was the allegiance of Benares elites, the bearers of cultural authority, for validating competing agendas. Dodson's analyses of the curriculum of Benares College under the superintendence of Muir and Ballantyne reveal the pedagogical measures taken to further the aims spelled out famously in Thomas Babington Macaulay's 1835 "Minute on Education": "to form a class who may be interpreters between us [British] and the millions whom we govern; a class of persons, Indian in blood and colour, but English in taste, in opinion, in morals, and in intellect." For, Macaulay elaborates, "to that class we may leave it to refine the vernacular dialects of the country, to enrich those dialects with terms of science borrowed from the Western nomenclature, and to render them by degrees fit vehicles for conveying knowledge to the great mass of the population."[63] Dodson's research has brought to light the degree to which the project of "constructive orientalism"—characterized by the "engraftment" of Western scientific knowledge onto long-standing Indian idioms of authoritative learning (especially Sanskrit *shastra*) with emphasis on a "universal developmental framework"—arose as the Orientalist's response to the liberal-utilitarian push for English as the medium of modern education in India.[64] Further, "constructive orientalism," Dodson notes, was not inconsonant with the ultimate aim of bringing about "the eventual spread of Christianity in India."[65] With the enlistment and redirection of Benares's traditional intelligentsia, not only would Enlightenment-cum–instrumental rationality be secured within long-standing Indian idioms of authority, but "useful knowledge" would spread outward, to the Indian masses, as it got recapitulated in revamped vernaculars, all the while opening for these masses a path to Christian salvation and thereby ultimately vindicating imperial rule.

Leaving aside for the moment what ensued on the basis of this imperial teleology—something Dalmia's work on Bharatendu will help gauge—I shall examine the techniques employed at Benares College over the middle decades of the nineteenth century for bringing about the intended transformations. Dodson's research illuminates the strategies becoming increasingly available through print media and the colonial educational apparatuses for bringing into effect a top-down hegemony with the aid of the traditional intelligentsia. Not only was it increasingly possible to reorganize classical traditions, such as Sanskrit *shastra*, and put them to new ends, such as natural science and technical know-how, but the very ends of "useful knowledge" assumed by the British were themselves not inevitable. In other words, there was no necessary logical step from the empirical rationalism of Bacon's *Novum Organum* to the adoption of Christian faith, as some colonial officials presumed.

The manner in which colonial officials furnished Benares College with Sanskrit textbooks that engrafted the scientific methods of the early modern English philosopher Francis Bacon onto the philosophical doctrines of Sanskrit *shastra* is illustrative of the new possible configurations. Having celebrated the modern technologies oriented toward the "conquest of the works of nature," Bacon also made the new "useful knowledge" the basis of a new kind of religious mission in the seventeenth century. The point of the new knowledge was to "cultivate truth in charity." That is to say, it was morally imperative that the new science be disseminated "for the benefit and use of life."[66] Leading liberal utilitarians espoused this mission readily. Macaulay, for instance, saw in Bacon's *Novum Organum* a revolutionizing turn from Aristotelian syllogism toward a new object: "the accumulation of truth" for the purpose of "increasing the power and ameliorating the condition of man."[67] Likewise, for the educationists at Benares College, the value of Bacon's philosophy was patent: though already outdated in the West, it would put India on a similar path toward the cultivation of a rational scientific methodology oriented toward the manipulation of nature for the amelioration of the material condition of mankind as such. Such a move would lead inevitably, it was thought, to the obsolescence of "unfruitful" speculating that characterized much of classical Indian thought for British officials. For instance, John Muir wrote in

1838 of the relevance of Bacon's works for the education of the Indian: "The truth and common sense of Bacon's philosophy has commended it to the learned of Europe; and with what splendid results everyone knows. The command of nature, and the material benefits resulting to men, are there sought after with adequate zeal and energy. The application to India is obvious."[68] The experiments applying "useful knowledge" began that same year when George Nicholls, the headmaster of the Benares English Seminary, informally introduced the geometry of Euclid to Benares College. A decade later, Ballantyne's *Lectures on the Sub-Divisions of Knowledge*, "a preliminary outline of the totality of Western knowledge," appeared in print. While this work was later translated into Sanskrit prose, his *Synopsis of the Science* adopted, as Dodson recognizes, "an 'oriental guise' to facilitate its acceptance by the pandits, as it is framed into aphorisms and commentary, in accordance with the general style of *shastrik* literature."[69] The stance influential Benarasi pandits took on the utilitarian curriculum and its ideological premises provides cues for the larger project of reframing and assimilating utilitarian norms in vernacular spheres. Dodson writes that the formidable pandits Vitthala Sastri and Bapudeva Sastri "did not accept the 'new knowledge' of Europe wholly within the ideological/cultural superstructure with which it was presented." Instead, in mediating their new learning for a broader Indian audience, they opened a "critique [of] the claims made on behalf of Europe's knowledge and religion, including their inherent rationality and consistency," in order "to unravel the colonial assumption that the 'modern' scientific endeavor was tied solely to a specific European intellectual genealogy."[70]

Considering that the teaching of scientific principles went hand in hand with proclamations of Christian miracle in British colonial pedagogy—and leaving aside momentarily how mutually contradictory these two doctrines could prove to be—it should come as little surprise that elite intelligentsia of the sacred city and intellectual leaders within the emergent Hindi sphere could easily pry "useful knowledge" from imperial teleology. Yet any number of questions immediately arise: How should rational scientific principles and new technological capacities be framed? With what kinds of theological commitments, Indian or otherwise, could modern science possibly be coupled? Which language would be adequate for the conveyance of empirical method to the Indian mass, and what consequences would follow for this language? Could the new "useful knowledge" be abstracted from its Western imperial agency, and if so, could it be adopted without deteriorating or fully undermining the grounds of traditional Indian society, let alone British imperial hierarchy? Dalmia's research on Bharatendu and the Hindi milieu he indelibly fashioned captures the salience of these very questions as well as the political pressures that shaped the complex, even contradictory responses to utilitarian norms and colonial pedagogy in the vernacular sphere. By decoupling "useful knowledge" from Christian soteriology and making it instead coextensive with the project of Hindu political awakening and majoritarian assertion, Bharatendu introduced new problems into the Hindi world without, it seems, being fully aware of the consequences.

This was primarily because he was fashioning a public realm and persona for himself that remained inchoate. Under his stewardship, though, a particular edge was given to the Hindi sphere. After his loyalist rival, Raja Shiva Prasad had been awarded the title Sitara-i Hindi (Star of India) by the British, Harishchandra's followers named him Bharatendu, or "Moon of India," apparently in irreverent jest.[71] As an emerging public persona, Bharatendu encompassed a motley, increasingly unlikely, gamut: "a nagarika, a townsman, a Benarasi rasika, a connoisseur of the particular brand of the city," "a renegade who, even while he shared in the power and privileges enjoyed by his own social groups, challenged it at the same time," a "figure not easily classifiable as traditional or modern, communal or nationalist, loyalist or anti-British," one "who retained one foot in the premodern 'traditional' world of maharajas, mahants and mahajans, in order to plant the other all the more firmly in the world of new learning."[72] Such descriptions suggest not just an individual but the publicity center of an entire movement, as Ramvilas Sharma conceptualized Bharatendu.[73] Just as wide-ranging were the Hindi responses to the questions generated by the new knowledge. When seen in tandem, they likewise betoken a cultural world on the brink of slow fragmentation and mutual sundering. Cultural authority in Benares's vernacular realm did not merely stretch itself back into the city's vaunted antiquity but also incorporated or sutured unexpected repertoires. What Bharatendu's famous self-introduction—"I am a Sanskrit, Hindi, and Urdu poet, and have composed many works in verse and prose"—suggests now is an ensemble that would quickly fall apart largely on account of the very agendas he and his successors would put into motion. Much of this fragmentation, in other words, could be attributed to the Hindi sphere's experiments with "useful knowledge." As "useful knowledge" was becoming increasingly crucial for any effort at sheer survival, let alone assertion of autonomy, within the British imperium, its catalytic power was becoming increasingly manifest and productive of paradoxical effects. This is not the place for an extended cataloging of the riches Dalmia gleaned while examining the clashes and controversies of nineteenth-century Benares. I will restrict my survey to the manner in which Bharatendu's strategies for revamping Hindi made difficult the preservation of continuities with the past and analogies with other languages, such as Urdu. Just as there was an impending fragmentation of Bharatendu's initially wide mediating role and multiply alloyed persona, the incorporation of Enlightenment qua utilitarian normativity (i.e., "useful knowledge") produced intractable contradictions that are worth retracing, for these contradictions later became embedded in the very medium of modern Hindi and were thus conveyed ineluctably to successive generations, such as Chayavad or Hindi romanticism.

"The principle which ought to guide us in our exertions should be such as is calculated to render our vernacular, by whatever name you may call it, *useful* and *intelligible* to all," wrote Bharatendu in an English editorial in 1873.[74] Though his stance on language matters would evolve over the last decade of his life and the strategies employed to modernize the vernacular would shift over time, the aim of making it the means for conveying modern knowledge to a wide audience remained constant. Dalmia is correct in seeing this orientation as, "if not revolutionary, at least innovatory." It nonetheless triggered ambivalence, especially with respect to the English language and Christian theology. Rather than inherited rank and name as the basis for social mobility, "the new criterion for social betterment was *vidya*, learning." This new learning leveled the grounds of authority, which could now be debated openly in numerous periodicals, including those of Bharatendu himself. The new *vidya* crystallized what was implicit within the emergent public media: an amalgam of liberalism and instrumental rationality—the ethos of the commodity-form as introduced under the colonial aegis. *Vidya*, Dalmia explains, "was now to have practical functions as well (the useful knowledge of the Utilitarians); how to support your family, how to educate your child, how to work for the welfare of the country, how to administer the state, how to get on in the world, in social intercourse, in short, how to look to your welfare and advantage." The competitive undertones of "useful knowledge" were spelled out in regional terms in Bharatendu's essay. For all practical purposes Hindi was to be modernized "in the mould of English," as English "did not hesitate to plunder the treasures of other languages, and thus extend its frontiers." Increasingly acquiring "a model function" with "its immense functionality and the power it commanded," did not English, as a metonym of the superior military might and general sociopolitical organization of the British, ultimately reflect the superior efficacy of Western ideals and values, that is, Christian theology? It is on this point that a significant qualification is made, one mediating a new modal shift that might be called the *svadeshi* turn, for it is "the svadesi aspect," Dalmia notes, "which validates one's own tradition as the only truly acceptable one."[75]

The ramifications of the fact that "one's own tradition" was now mediated by the ideological force of British imperialism were manifold. For one, the newness that was produced—even if only by the reorganization of the contents of precolonial traditions, though the changes did not end there—undercut the fundamental desiderata of Bharatendu and his allies: to maintain continuity with antiquity, especially the Sanskrit tradition, and to bring about a supervening unity to the diverse local and regional languages, channeling thereby the collective energies pent up by imperial indifference and ineptitude. "If there is any language, therefore, which deserves to be called common, it is the Hindi," asserted an anonymous editorial in *Harishchandra's Magazine*. "And it is the language which the British Government has done and is still doing its best to smother and stifle."[76] Dalmia asserts that "at no stage did Harischandra, unlike the new iconoclasts such as the Brahmo and Arya Samaj, maintain that there was a break in tradition," and "though time and again he criticized the misuse of sacral authority by the Brahmans, nowhere in his writings did he challenge the caste system as a formation."[77] Yet the price of success in making Hindi modern and national would always be the severing of the emergent idiom standardized for "useful knowledge" from the premodern traditions through which it sought to authenticate itself.

The fissures that formed were often subtle but rarely insignificant. The issues that led to the promotion of the Devanagari script over Urdu and Persian's Nastal'iq cut Hindi off from the Indo-Islamic culture that had shaped courtly and popular tastes over at least three centuries. A sharp divide began to form between the written and the oral forms of Hindi itself, especially as the standardized form began to bring into sharp relief local dialectic variation. Such linguistic incongruencies were mapped palpably onto the divide between private and public spheres, as Francesca Orsini has found, marking in many ways the artificiality of official Hindi.[78] The distinction between modern standard Hindi and Sanskrit became inevitably starker as well. Formed as Hindi was in the mold of English at Bharatendu's urging for the sake of *vidya*, its new premises and general orientation marked a radical shift from the organic vernacular evolutions of classical Sanskrit, such as Braj Bhasha's ubiquitous eroticism and little concerted interest in secular matters—now the source of Victorian Indian shame. The ruin of the traditional aura—that is, the noticeable withering of the link and thus the marking of incongruence between the past and present within the same phenomenon—required urgent redress, besieged as the Hindi sphere was by Christian missionaries and the exigency of "self-strengthening" to meet the tests of colonial domination. A measure of how far utility had become normalized over the nineteenth century is, in hindsight, the extent to which the instrumentalization of past tradition for national-hegemonic ends was now a ubiquitous given—a featured shared by all resurgent religious movements.

The posited origin of the new literary canon was the epic. The relinking of Hindi to the distant precolonial or pre–Indo-Islamic past was essential, for "it was the linkage to the ancient and the classical which endowed the language with history, respectability and ancestry." This was best accomplished by locating for Hindi the epic origins that would capture the widest possible collective in the present.[79] The epic would reestablish continuity where it was most completely severed. For this purpose, the role of Chand, the medieval bard extolled in James Todd's influential *Annals* for his *Prithviraj-Raso*, becomes central.[80] "Prithviraj, as the last Hindu king, had been immortalized in the heroic poem of the epic poet Chand," notes Dalmia, "and it was this poem with which Hindi literature could be said to commence, and this through the near thousand years of the 'Muslim' period."[81] A trend was thus set for an uncertain coupling of utilitarian norms with a newly fashioned modern mythos—tradition by untraditional means, as it were. The tensions that arose on account of this coupling best come to light in the interactions between two overlapping formations in the early twentieth century: Mahavir Prasad Dvivedi and his circle, on the one hand, and the literary movement nearly always referred to as Hindi romanticism (Chayavad), on the other.

V. UTILITY AND FREEDOM: SOVEREIGNTY AND AESTHETIC EXPRESSION IN THE MOON'S SHADOW

If the period immediately after the 1857 Mutiny somehow allowed disparate cultural elements to cohere and round out the celestial figure of Bharatendu as the "Moon of India" for his generation, the two succeeding eras of Hindi literary culture conventionally referred to as Dvivediyug, or the era of Mahavir Prasad Dvivedi, and Chayavad, or Hindi romanticism, brought to a breaking point underlying fractures and distinctions. The debates between these two overlapping yet generationally distinct cultural formations—the Dvivedi circle, followed roughly two decades later by Chayavad—would cleave the Hindi cultural sphere in the wake of Bharatendu, leaving auratic, even uncanny, reflections of that celebrated "Moon of India" on the future of a transformed Hindi language, memory, canon, and literary forms, especially epic. At its core was the question of utility. Having witnessed firsthand the calamitous results of colonial policies on his rural Uttar Pradesh and the peasantry it once sustained, Dvivedi could not but equate the new utilitarian principles underlying the post-Mutiny colonial dispensation with sheer survival.[82] By the early twentieth century, when Dvivedi took on the editorship of the hegemonic Hindi periodical *Sarasvati*, too many artificial famines of unfathomable size had brought into question the paternalistic principles putatively guiding official policy, and too much cavalier disregard for liberal fairness on the part of the new, more pragmatic officialdom made earnest pleading unseemly, if not humiliating.[83] Thus for Dvivedi, as expressed in nearly every line of his writing, only that which proved useful now, immediately, for the *unnati* (uplift) of those subjugated most by the patently illiberal colonial juggernaut deserved consideration. He not only included but put first the vast roiling peasantry and the small, yet stunted industrial sector. In his magnum opus, *Sampatti Shastra* (Treatise on Wealth, 1916), Dvivedi imagined the unity of these two productive forces as critical for increasing and retaining the wealth of the emergent Indian nation. Affairs had to be taken into one's own hands. Pressing cultural questions of the day such as those concerning language (Which dialect and lexicon are to serve as the standard?), traditional knowledge (Could the materialist and logical currents of the distant past be revived for the needs of the present?), or literary form (Which models from the past or present will prove most conducive to collective self-strengthening?) were adjudicated regularly on the scale of utility. In direct challenge to the suborning of aesthetic sovereignty to external moral or political ends, Chayavad opened up the question of sovereignty to aesthetic freedom. For instance, when Suryakant Tripathi Nirala, foremost among the Chayavadi poets, prided himself in contradistinction to Dvivedi's norms for never writing "edifying epigrams or poems preaching a message" and stated his conviction that "preachiness is a sign of weakness in a poet," he was asserting nothing other than a subjectivity free of utilitarian normativity.[84]

To grasp the tensions that had surfaced along the fault line between sovereignty (*svadhinata*) and freedom (*svachandata*), one must reconstruct the distinct transformations that allowed instrumental rationality to be a source of self-empowerment—in fact, the most obvious means for wresting nation-based sovereignty from imperial control—as well as a fetter on various ways of imagining and actualizing freedom. Whereas Chayavadi cultural practices often raised the specter of expressive forms untethered to concrete political ends, for Dvivedi the imperative of sheer survival justified the instrumentalization of all existing resources, including cultural ones, for the project of self-strengthening and political independence. Dvivedi's views on such matters were forged in direct contact with the countryside and its immiserated peasantry around his bucolic residence. The seat from which he edited *Sarasvati* from 1903 to 1920 was the rural village of Juhi, near the industrial center of Kanpur. Yet far from taking him away from the new quotidian rhythms palpable in urban centers, the countryside led Dvivedi to the literal root of the colonial mediation of modern time: the punctuality commanded by the colonial power according to what the eminent historian Ranajit Guha has described as "a blunt and rigid fiscal routine based on what seemed to be an altogether alien sense of time to the natives." For, according to Guha, "rural society was the first to be seriously affected by the East India Company's mercantile time and its fiscal timetable."[85] A discussion of *Sampatti Shastra*, Dvivedi's treatise on agrarian economy under colonial rule, and his writings on the temporal constraints that forced peasants to auction their land under fiscal duress would take us far afield. Moreover, some excellent scholarship, in Hindi especially, already provides the general background on Dvivedi and the sociohistorical tendencies of the Hindi Renaissance under his stewardship.[86] Here I wish merely to sketch out some key developments that characterize the Dvivedi circle to help contrast it with Chayavad, for it is the contradictory field that emerges between these two countercurrents that sets the scene for Jayashankar Prasad's famous neo-epic, *Kamayani*, a short discussion of which serves as a coda to this chapter. It is on the field of epic that the two cultural currents, the Dvivedi and Chayavadi, meet.

If the transformations unleashed on the agricultural front continued apace after the 1857 Mutiny, sending shockwaves across the land and fits of instability up the colonial system, the picture that emerges from vernacular sources is one of deep historical rupture. The prevalent sentiment in the vernacular realm, as Shackle notes, was one of "immediate shock of abrupt displacement rather than any confidence in some new future order."[87] The son of a soldier who joined the sepoys in the 1857 revolt, Dvivedi got his bearings under the crisis-ridden high noon of British imperialism by familiarizing himself with the principles and protocols mediating the rhythms of reified time emanating in tandem with commodification. Dvivedi's rise from telegraph signaler to head clerk with the District Traffic Superintendent testified to his successful adoption of punctuality and efficient time management.[88] He later brought these newly acquired habits to the mission inaugurated by Bharatendu for making Hindi the vehicle for national self-empowerment to counter a colonial power that, in the wake of the 1857 Mutiny, only grudgingly accorded it any official status. In fact, it was as if Dvivedi had taken his cue directly from Bharatendu's 1877 address to the Hindi Vardhini Sabha (Society for the Advancement of Hindi), which urged, "Get together and cleanse your own language" in the image of a standard English and "Appropriate all the sciences, power, intelligence, and knowledge / Do away with mutual discord, unite, be the mine of all virtue."[89] As editor, Dvivedi took up the charge with alacrity, and *Sarasvati* soon became a successful commercial enterprise for the dissemination of "useful knowledge" and "useful literature." Indeed, Dvivedi translated and in many ways "Indianized" the doctrines of Francis Bacon, John Stuart Mill, and Herbert Spencer for a Hindi public, providing a model for future work to be done originally in that language, such as his own *Sampatti Shastra*.

Yet in merely "purifying" or standardizing Hindi to serve as the medium that could absorb and disseminate modern thought, Dvivedi risked actualizing a sharp rift between the customary ways of reproducing past traditions and the contemporary exigencies that were shaping tradition anew in the image of modern utility. What were loosely sutured realms in the Bharatendu era had now become untethered. For Dvivedi was inevitably creating sharp distinctions between the values that still governed everyday colloquial expression and the language he was instrumentalizing as a vehicle for social reform and technological catch-up. His choice of translations from Sanskrit into Hindi prose all at once moored the modern vernacular to this classical past while potentiating radical displacements as well.[90] In looking over the fifteen volumes of Dvivedi's collected writings, a peculiar economy of movement becomes discernible: for every step forward in incorporating modern utilitarian and technoscientific thought into Hindi, another had to find footing in the classical canon. It is as if the more he pressed forward in this uncertain direction, the more he realized that resecuring an Indian past became necessary. In the process, a more serviceable notion of the Indian intellectual past was being discovered and marshaled to counter the otherworldly spiritualism that had taken shape under broadly Orientalist auspices. What Dvivedi had uncovered through his efforts to exhume and resuscitate the rationalist, materialist, and, indeed, atheistic elements of past traditions was an Indian modernist counterpoint, for once recovered, these elements could be joined to the neotraditionalist literary canon the Dvivedi circle was also eagerly establishing. Central here was Datta's *Meghanadvadh-Kavya*, which Dvivedi's associate Maithilisharan Gupta translated into Hindi soon after Dvivedi himself extolled this work in his 1911 address "The Present State of Hindi" as a model worth emulating. With its balanced economy of traditional contents and familiar figures, on the one hand, and unprecedented meters and form, on the other, the neo-epic captured all at once the freedom of experimentation and self-imposed constraint within canonical materials and edifying tales that the Dvivedi circle advocated. It is striking the extent to which the major models, figures, and ideals the Dvivedi circle dredged up and wedded to the service of national progress derived from the Sanskrit corpus. In being found "useful" for the particular end of forging a Hindu-centric national sovereignty, this canon had attained its value, yet it also betrayed the radical penetration of utilitarian norms into the recesses of vernacular culture.

For the iconoclastic Chayavadi Nirala, it was "as if Sarasvati," meaning the goddess of literature, learning, and the arts but perhaps also alluding to the journal, "were a slave to politics."[91] Nirala's sardonic analogy was made in reference to the 1937 Hindi Literature Conference (Hindi Sahitya Sammelan), in which Prakash Tandon, a political figure in his own right but also the longtime chair of the Hindi Sahitya Sammelan and a member of the Dvivedi circle, argued for the subordination of literature to political imperatives. The quip bespeaks a sharp rift that had begun to unsettle the Hindi world since the advent of Chayavad, a literary formation that ushered in "a radically new aesthetic universe," to cite Karine Schomer.[92] Schomer's survey of the controversies that erupted over Chayavad in her enduring work *Mahadevi Varma and the Chhayavad Age of Modern Hindi Poetry*, will prove instructive, as will Francesca Orsini's *The Hindi Public Sphere*, for tracing the fault lines between the Dvivedi circle and this newfangled and somewhat mysterious cultural tendency. Dubbed dismissively "shadow-play" and later translated as "romanticism," this new formation was beginning to cast a disconcerting shadow on the literary scene, not least for bringing out the potential mismatch between aesthetic and political ends. Whereas the Dvivedi circle recognized that utility—or mastery over natural forces and accumulation of technological know-how—was indispensable for securing political freedom, for Chayavad, as Nirala's comment suggests, freedom proved equally indispensable for literature to have any aesthetic value. The divide that opened between the utilitarian norms maintained by the Dvivedi circle and those of aesthetic freedom introduced by Chayavad demonstrated how the very notion of freedom (*svadhinata*) opened up vistas of self-fashioning and forms of self-expression that were little imaginable, let alone hoped for, by those who initially pushed for it. The prospect of aesthetic freedom and individualist self-fashioning threatened to undermine the very notion of Indianness that was the ground for national political action. Seeing that Chayavadis were not constrained by his sanctioned canon, Dvivedi called into question their authenticity in his quip "Perhaps what is meant by Chayavad is poetry that is the shadow of poetry being written elsewhere."[93]

That Chayavadis like Sumitranandan Pant appreciated English romanticism and the early Nirala often betrayed an affinity to the poetic style of the Nobel laureate Tagore, as Dvivedi was referencing wryly earlier, should not to be taken to suggest that Chayavad was merely some quaint late-colonial regurgitation of an already elaborated cosmopolitan aesthetic. Rather, what Dvivedi's remark captures is a peculiarly pervasive anxiety regarding the formal experimentalism and individualistic self-fashioning of the Chayavadis as well as the following the movement was gaining among a newly educated generation of young Indians. The entire movement heeded little the canonical restrictions the Dvivedi circle had instituted in their journals. Shyamsundar Das, a longtime member of this circle, betrayed such anxieties in his realization:

> If poetry in English and Bengali can be moulded in arbitrary metres, why shouldn't graceless *raginis* start in Hindi, too? Nowadays high poetry is only that which has a very contorted descriptive style, which searches the whole universe to say the simplest thing, and which worships supernatural feelings that defy description. Chayavad and *samasya-purtis* are doing great harm to Hindi poetry. Our youth favours Chayavad and they only have to hum something and jot down a couple of verses straight away in order to consider themselves poets! To understand their poems is no easy task either. . . . This is the disgrace that is happening in Hindi by aping the venerable Rabindranath.[94]

The satirist Vishvambharnath Sharma Kaushik, also aligned with Dvivedi, revealed an organic, if troubling, modernist streak within Chayavad when he opined that "to compose a Chayavad poem was as easy as to cook khichri: all you needed was to open a dictionary, choose 5 to 10 kilograms of words, add some verbs without caring for metre or rhyme, and there was your poem ready."[95] If the Dvivedi circle decried the vagueness of the resulting poetry, it was primarily because it broke out of the canonical constraints they had in mind for Hindi's future literature. Indeed, the cavalier treatment of the rules of Hindi grammar and experimentation with new meters signaled Chayavadis' break with prescribed sociality and marked the tortured arrival of liberal subjectivity within the wider Hindi sphere. "What the new Chayavadi poets vindicated," writes Orsini, "was the poet's individual right to experiment and break existing norms."[96] The potentially destructive sweep of such experimentation exposed Chayavad to the charge that it was lacking in social conscience—"more interested in sitting on the bank of the triveni [the confluence of the rivers at Allahabad] and gazing out at infinity"—and therefore "useless" in that little of didactic or practical value could be expected of it.

The quandary between aesthetic freedom and political sovereignty expressed itself in distinct, even mutually contradictory ways in the careers of the four major Chayavadis: Nirala, Pant, Varma, and Prasad. All were committed to an anticolonial nationalism, yet their individual trajectories and diverging contributions to Hindi literary culture suggest improvisatory and often clashing ways of securing a link or finding reconciliation between national culture and liberal self-fashioning. Such reconciliation proved most difficult for Nirala, whose radical departure from his brahmanical caste norms, nationalist dogmas, and the constraints of the Hindi canon—as in his experiments with the *ghazal* form—was followed by a long onset of dementia, furthering his pariah status in the literary field. Pant ultimately found solace in the cult of Aurobindo after exploring a variety of modern spiritual and secular-cosmopolitan creeds, and Varma cultivated a connection with "the Vedic cultural layer," all the while shifting the semantics of *sadhana*, or "spiritual discipline," by elaborating "poetry as a means of self-perfection."[97] As the author of the neo-epic *Kamayani* (The Daughter of Kama), Prasad is of greatest relevance to the present discussion. Prasad is described by Dalmia as a "modernist who deliberately donned the mantle of tradition," and by Schomer as one who "insisted on his right to remain a totally private individual" within his ancestral city of Benares, all the while resurrecting and reformulating the Hindi collective's critical terminology by deriving from Sanskrit concepts such as *alamkara, rasa, and dhvani.*[98] For instance, Prasad's recasting of the classical aesthetic concept of *dhvani* to mean *svanubhutimayi abhivyakti*, "the expression of subjectively experienced truth," is but one example of the subtle transformations that ultimately allowed him to make the assertion "Chayavad already existed in our ancient literature."[99] Prasad's attention turned toward the epic, and in 1936 he published his famous *Kamayani.* An allegory of India's encounter with colonial modernity, this work is often considered the "culmination," or *nishpati*, of the entire Chayavadi formation. Composed in a style reminiscent of classical Sanskrit courtly epic (*mahakavya*) and engaging with materials from Vedic antiquity in a typically "lofty" (*uddat*) manner, yet thoroughly modern in its choice of the standard grammar (*khari boli*) as its medium from beginning to end, *Kamayani* sought to close the gap between itself and classical epics of the Sanskritic past.

VI. *KAMAYANI* AS HISTORICAL ALLEGORY: NEOTRADITIONALISM AS COUNTER-ENLIGHTENMENT

Kamayani opens with Manu, Hinduism's destined progenitor of each new age, seated alone on the peak of the Himalayas. He looks down upon a world drowning under a dazzling thunderstorm from which he was barely able to escape. Only with the guiding strokes of a gigantic fish was he led ashore. Repeated reflection on the quick dissipation of the old gods, despite their sheen of permanence, makes him shudder.

The neglectful sensuality and egotistical pleasures of the divine sovereigns have led to such calamity, Manu surmises. The prospect of living in a disenchanted world fills him with dread as night falls. Yet the rays of a new light the following morning bring him inspiration and hope as he witnesses nature's powers of regeneration all about him. Manu turns a cave into his dwelling and engages in austerities and animal sacrifices. In hopes of meeting a companion, he leaves the remains of a sacrifice outside his cave. Another survivor of the apocalypse, the Gandharvan princess Shraddha, sees the sacrificial remains while on a jaunt through the mountains and ventures to discover their source. Shraddha encounters a disheveled and somewhat despondent Manu in his cave and fills him with youthful energy with a sermon on the virtues of work and the offer to aid him in becoming more industrious and engaged. In a dream, the god Kama addresses Manu and informs him that Shraddha is his daughter and he needs to lead a fulfilling life with her and reestablish the world. A spirit of worldly engagement subsequently takes hold of Manu, and the couple eventually falls in love and establishes a household. Trouble lurks when Manu takes on two demons (*asura*) from the antediluvian world as his domestic chaplains (*purohita*) for performing animal sacrifices of even the beasts with which Shraddha has formed deep emotional bonds, possibly as an unconscious response to the jealousy this affectionate rapport provokes in Manu. Unable to bear the slaughter of her beloved beasts, Shraddha abandons the sacrificial grounds and lies despondent in the cave, wondering how Manu has become so violent. This initial rift is overcome when both partners imbibe soma juice and regain intimacy. Yet just when they are expecting their first child, Manu abandons Shraddha and their world of humdrum contentment and traditional observances, being unable to face the inevitable shift of Shraddha's loving devotion from himself to their son, Manava.

While this first narrative thrust of the neo-epic establishes a sharp diluvian divide, affording Manu an experience of individuated being in a momentarily disenchanted world, he nevertheless finds himself trapped within the confines of traditional social reproduction. What follows once Manu has escaped the clutches of domestic dissatisfaction and obscure religious observances is key for grasping *Kamayani* as a historical allegory in which neotraditionalism is explicitly articulated as a means for countering Enlightenment. In his escape, Manu eventually comes upon the ruins of the ancient city of Sarasvat, where Indra had slain the dragon Vritra. A vague swirl of emotions grips him, including remorse for abandoning his family, when he has a chance encounter with Ida, the embodiment of rational calculation and the empress of Sarasvat, where reason will now prevail. Having fallen under Ida's sway, Manu is inculcated in the ways of science and technological development, and before long Sarasvat is brimming with all the modern wonders of secular progress, including easily manipulated consumerist masses. Unable to curb his lust for total domination, Manu becomes tyrannical and forces himself on Ida. This attempted rape turns out to be the last straw of his tyranny. All the subjects of Sarasvat rise in rebellion against him. A battle, depicted as a chaotic class struggle, takes place in which Manu falls unconscious. Meanwhile, Shraddha, having glimpsed this entire sequence of events in a dream, departs to Sarasvat and finds her erstwhile husband in a wrecked state in the royal palace. Manu ruefully relates to her the course that led him to the heights of progress (*unnati*) and his ultimate fall. When Shraddha, Ida, and Manava are asleep, Manu again absconds. Deeply anguished, Shraddha meditates on the banks of the Sarasvati River, hoping for a sign of Manu. After her come Ida and Manava, whom she unites in marriage, seeing that Manava's deep cultivation of faith will ameliorate Ida's cold rationality. Shraddha boldly takes off to a deserted area, where she chances upon Manu in deep meditation. When he awakes to the sight of her, Manu has a brilliant vision of Shiva performing his dance of destruction on the Himalayan peaks. Manu is inspired to go to Mount Kailash to witness the full sublimity of Shiva's dance and asks Shraddha for her company. On their way up the mountain trails, they both come upon a vision of three spheres in the distance, representing desire (*iccha*), knowledge (*jnan*), and activity (*kriya*). After revealing the mystery (*rahasya*) behind these appearances, Shraddha bursts into laughter, which results in their uniting in one magnificent sphere and the world being flooded with bliss. The epic concludes with the couple accompanied on their pilgrimage by Manava, Ida, and the subjects of Sarasvat. All are now able to attain fulfillment and live in harmony since they have become absorbed and transformed by the overpowering force of the bliss promulgated in Shaiva theology.

Will this resolution hold, or will the explosive laughter that brings everything into a state of subjective bliss eventually dissipate? Will Manu run off again, and if so, will women be like Shraddha and Ida and keep pursuing him, or will they forge their own destiny with the use of their own rational faculties? If they pursue this last strategy, will Manu react in violence again, considering what an encounter with reason unleashed in him last time? Will he remain free to pursue his own way as a self-determining subject, or will the remnants of the antediluvian "traditionalism" hold his modernity in check and make it ultimately fantastical? These are only some of the most immediate questions that arise upon completion of the fifteen cantos (*sarga*) that make up this neo-epic, each of which is composed in a different meter in accordance with the generic norms of Sanskrit courtly epic, signaling a concerted effort to affirm continuities where they have been most ruptured. Here, in light of the dialectics of utility and culture retraced over this chapter, *Kamayani* can be read as venturing a cultural definition to the tension-ridden relationship between normative political ends and potentially transgressive aesthetic choices, attempting to enforce a lasting resolution where it is most likely to be ephemeral, unable to hold against contravening social logics. Given that Prasad's Manu is intended as an allegorical figure for the emerging masses of India, especially in the northern Hindi belt, is it not possible that whatever instabilities making up his social being are best understood as much within Prasad's neo-epic as within the social world of mass cultural politics itself?

I turn thus in the epilogue to the masses in Hindu India—that is, the mass Manu—and how they accrue a peculiarly melancholic ornament with the materials fashioned from classical epic, but now in the profane illumination of televisual dream kitsch.

EPILOGUE

Melancholic Ornament

TV Ramayana, *Nostalgia, and Kitsch as Counter-Enlightenment*

> Last evening they were there again, the hundreds of hired "devotees," young males, drunk, dancing obscenely to deafening disco music, piled into trucks and lorries, carrying garish painted idols of some sort of "Mata Rani" to the Yamuna River, blocking traffic for miles, threatening, obnoxious and aggressively "Hindu." Some sociologist needs to tell us what is happening to Delhi, overrun by "bhaktas" and "shraddhalus" of unknown gods and goddesses, one broken bottle or smashed vehicle away from a lynch mob.
>
> —Ananya Vajpeyi, New Delhi, Facebook post, September 18, 2014

I. HINDU MASSES AND THEIR AESTHETICS

Tinged with a mix of dread and fascination, Ananya Vajpeyi's comments on social media are striking for their candid sense of loss of language for grasping conceptually an increasingly perplexing phenomenon: the mobilization of masses and their movement beyond the frames of reference established for a modern secular India. Unlike the future imagined for India by an earlier generation of nationalists, the one Vajpeyi encounters on a regular, sometimes quotidian basis bodes the return of sacralized collective violence and the dissolution of modern institutional structures, ostensibly by the very dissatisfaction these have provoked in a restless public. The situation Vajpeyi describes, with its intimations of collective delirium, bacchanalian disregard, and imminent danger, contains in miniature the pulls and pushes that have fashioned a broad political crisis since India's first turn toward neoliberalism in the 1980s. This crisis periodically comes to a head in our current moment. Indeed, what Vajpeyi is tracking in her comments is merely the everyday fallout of events like of those of December 1992, when zealous Hindus unleashed upon the Babri Masjid a torrent of vengeful destruction for having putatively ruined and submerged the original birthplace of the Hindu deity Rama. This event revealed the fragility of legal structures established on the basis of India's Constitution, coming as it did in the wake of the phenomenally popular *Ramayana* serial broadcast on state-sponsored television, and caught in the broad majoritarian mobilization that precipitated anti-Muslim rioting across India. This event continues to cascade into an ever-extending horizon of destruction. Key electoral victories for the Hindu Right at the national and state levels have aided in undoing several impediments to the phantasmagoric restoration of a Hindu *rashtra*, especially the rights and legal protections of non-Hindu minorities, as attested most dramatically in the pogroms that erupted in Gujarat in 2002 and ricocheted across the country. The dismantling of the Nehruvian legacy has resulted all at once in the restitution of British colonial law for the neoliberal appropriation of common lands and a sharp departure from the secular-national narrative of the nation in favor of modern Hindu mythology. The debris from these violent shifts has only mounted since the election of Narendra Modi in 2014. The sum total has led to the reconfiguration of local, national, and international powers over the past decade, allowing the newfangled Hindu polity of today to enter into closer alliance with the neoliberal core of the United States while forging a righteously restored state ideology fashioned by nostalgic melancholia, and thereby departing from any recognizable modernity, a fact to which Vajpeyi's description is alert. Capturing the casual yet potentially explosive mix of political violence and devotional atmospherics by juxtaposing the instrumental rationality of party bosses with the masses' own propensity for self-sacrifice and self-transformation into instruments of religious violence, Vajpeyi brings into focus a core tension in the history of mass formation in modern India. Though their constitution may vary greatly, masses are at once means and ends: fabricated initially by the instrumentalization of lower orders for securing the representative capacity of Indian elites, the masses also appear rhetorically as the ultimate purpose or telos for which political mobilization is undertaken. As the concentration point of the countervailing tendencies of instrumental and noninstrumental relationality, the masses in contemporary India have redoubtable volatility. Through it all, the question surfaces: Can the masses in modernity become subject, that is, self-reflective as much as agential?

"Some sociologist needs to tell us what is happening to Delhi," urges Vajpeyi, "overrun by 'bhaktas' and 'shraddhalus' of unknown gods and goddesses, one broken bottle or smashed vehicle away from a lynch mob."[1] In response, it is to the unlikely social theorist and keen observer of the flotsam and jetsam of Weimar Germany in social crisis, Siegfried Kracauer, I turn for some cues for grasping a fundamental dimension of the TV *Ramayana* phenomenon that most eludes current social science on the matter: the aesthetic, ornamental—which is to say, affect-wise, the vast melancholic—dimension. Just as Kracauer himself turned his attention to the neglected surface sheen of Weimar's mass culture and discovered concentrated there the dream worlds that were devouring German realities, he helps one pick up where social science on the contemporary Indian scene leaves off. One finds in the mass phenomenon of the TV *Ramayana* not so much a representative or exhaustive case of the mass culture in postcolonial India but rather an indication of the power of the mass-produced dream image to summon the masses' desires and powers and its capacity to fashion the masses into an ornament that spells both deadly and utopian possibilities simultaneously. As the vehicle of mass ornament-formation in postcolonial India, the long-standing narrative tradition of the *Ramayana*, I suggest, was being pumped over the 1980s and 1990s for its deeply embedded themes of melancholia and nostalgia, allowing these to fashion the materiality of video into a recognizable neotraditional medium. By following the aesthetic dimension embedded in the dream kitsch that the video medium widely engendered, the relation between neotraditional sheen and communal violence in India becomes intelligible. And yet, as I will venture, the offerings of commodified dream kitsch are not necessarily exhausted in mass violence but indicate futurities little fathomable in our current debacle.

II. MASSES AND MASSIFICATION IN MODERN INDIA: A CONDENSED HISTORY

That the terms "mass" and "masses" had entered the lexicon of British colonial politics in India as early as the eighteenth century should come as no surprise considering that they were accruing a wider range of meanings and usages in the English language. Raymond Williams's entry for "masses" in his invaluable guide to the vocabulary of British imperial culture and society, *Keywords* (1976), reveals the peculiar dualities that accrued to the term "mass" and have remained salient in post-Independence India. Williams notes an ambivalence in the very usage of the words "mass" and "masses." They are at once neutral and partial, and when partial, the valences further bifurcate: "a term of contempt in much conservative thought, but a positive term in much socialist thought."[2] In Williams's short account, the English usages of "mass" have a prehistory of political contempt, such as "multitude," which often came with qualifiers such as "base," "giddy," "hydra-headed," and "headless," so monstrous were the lower social orders perceived to be over the early modern centuries. As "mass" evolved simultaneously over the early modern period to refer to "bulk," as in the physical sciences, painting, and everyday usage, Williams finds two alternate senses developing: something amorphous and indistinguishable, and a dense aggregate. These alternate senses have continued to inflect usages of the term into the twentieth and twenty-first centuries. Thus "mass" retained its second meaning "of a body of material that can be mould or cast (the root sense was probably of kneading dough)" whenever reference is made to the manipulation of masses by institutions such as the media or, conversely, the need for edifying programming, both of which were operative during the broadcast of the TV *Ramayana*.[3] The first meaning is operative whenever "a lack of necessary distinction or discrimination" allows for a sense of solidarity by the "avoidance of unnecessary division or fragmentation and thus an achievement of unity," thereby establishing a connection with the second meaning in phrases ranging from "the people" or "working people" all the way to the "saffron wave" into which one is invited and divested of individuating features, even if only momentarily, by idealized images of the Hindu *rashtra*.

It makes sense to begin this discussion with an examination of the English terminology for the very sociopolitical dynamics that precipitated a "mass politics" in India were unleashed by British rule. The dynamics in question involved a concerted struggle to determine the representational status of either colonial officials or Indian elites over the vast and motley populace of the subcontinent. The British imperial historian D. A. Low has traced how the British restructuration of Indian society and politics helped foster "emergent public bodies" (such as the Hindi Vardhini Sabha, discussed in chapter 6) but nevertheless stymied if not outright excluded these very political bodies from exercising any influence in their "neo-darbari" arrangement with non-official Indian notables. Instead stability and control over society, the

British believed, could best be maintained by the few petty princes and traditional elites included in their inner circles. The fact that the British did not concede that modern Indian elites represented the disfranchised subjects that made up the lower orders, and instead considered themselves stewards of the general interest, put the onus on these very elites to demonstrate just such a political status. By the end of the nineteenth century, the most prominent of these emergent public bodies, the Indian National Congress, itself composed of the new liberal elites, departed radically from the "neo-darbari" framework of colonial rule. In order to meet the British challenge and assert the legitimacy of their nationalist claims, Indian elites began to mobilize select sectors of the disfranchised and stage agitations against British policies over the early decades of the twentieth century. Three major phases of nationalist agitation led by Mohandas K. Gandhi (1917–23, 1927–34, and 1939–46) reveal a distinct political logic of massification. "Each [mass *satyagraha*, or act of collective disobedience]," observes Low, "began with a fairly protracted agitational run-up, especially propelled on each occasion by some great affront to Indian feelings," such as the appointing of the "all-white" Simon Commission in 1927 to determine India's future or Viceroy Lord Linlithgow's declaring in 1939 that India was at war without consulting one Indian public body.[4] The image of Gandhi himself as well as the mass-produced imagery allegorizing political hurt that accompanied nationalist agitations were especially effective in nonelite environments characterized overwhelmingly by illiteracy.

Instigated by British policies and later embedded into the grain of Indian politics with the constitutional guarantee of universal adult franchise following Independence in 1947, the imperative to mobilize the Indian populace into masses large enough for political effect has come with obvious opportunities and risks. Christopher Pinney's research into the politics of popular images over the late colonial period touches on the "affective intensities" provoked by mass-produced imagery allegorizing political hurt.[5] The controversies that were being generated by the dissemination of inflammatory imagery, often depicting symbols such as the sacred cow threatened by the dietary practices of non-Hindus, sounded alarms in official channels of the colonial government. For the colonial authorities, the affective charge of mass-produced images and syndicated media triggered recurrent paranoia about political stability and racist fantasies regarding the rational capacities of the subject population, leading to the rescindment of press freedom and further exacerbation of political crisis on several occasions over the climactic decades from 1917 to 1947.

For the nationalists, the political necessity of amassing an Indian public was received with both aplomb and wariness. Those, like Gandhi, who were willing to organize in nonelite arenas such as rural Uttar Pradesh learned quickly that masses could easily erupt into violence and offset the nationalist program. This was the lesson that resonated over the course of the nationalist struggle from Chauri Chaura, where in 1922 peasant "rioters" burned down the police precinct to the cry of "Victory to Mahatma Gandhi," despite the fact that for Gandhi only complete self-sacrifice and nonviolence were legitimate strategies for forcing the British hand.[6] Mass agitation had its risks; for nationalist elites, this meant that it could be deployed only selectively as a political strategy. Furthermore, the incorporation of aspiring merchant communities and budding industrialists into elite echelons of Congress proved a great deterrent to mass mobilization on social revolutionary grounds. Gandhi, as the Gujarati industrialist Ambalal Sarabhai once recognized, was the best guarantee against communism that India possessed.[7] The sacrifice of radical labor politics to the elite nationalist cause went hand in hand with a selective program of "nationalization" of local struggles. Emphasis fell inevitably on majoritarian buildup, characterized by opportunistic exploitation of popular deities and much mythmaking around *Ramarajya* (The Kingdom of Rama). Such political necessities made inevitable a particularly precarious balancing act between minority communities and majoritarian radicals. The assassination of Gandhi soon after Independence by a Hindu fundamentalist signaled the risks of mass mobilization for the very liberal-secular principles undergirding the new nation-state.

This problematic tension between the political imperative to mobilize masses and the costs such mobilization may entail for the structures of liberal-secular governance have only been further exacerbated since Independence, and especially since the simultaneous expansion, diversification, and liberalization of the media since the 1980s. The media historian Robin Jeffrey sees the end of Prime Minister Indira Gandhi's Emergency in 1977 as the "landmark for the burgeoning of mass culture" in India.[8] The dramatic ascent of media capitalism in the wake of the liberalization favored by Sanjay Gandhi and slowly implemented over the 1980s and early 1990s cleared the field alongside film and radio for the ascent of audio cassettes, video, and television. Some recent studies in the social sciences especially have explored the political ramifications of this new media environment. The venerable political scientist Lloyd Rudolph notes two striking effects in "Media and Cultural Politics" in the edited volume *India Votes*: new possibilities of massification and the impersonal production of a "standardized civilizational grammar" that supplants local customs, styles, and linguistic resources. The very fact that the new electronic media "makes less relevant the distinction between literates and illiterates" suggests new modalities of massification tethered less to *dal-roti* politics than to collective fantasy, desire, fear, *ressentiment*, and self-assertion. Epic megaseries like the TV *Ramayana* promote "the potential for weakening the pluralist toleration and inclusiveness of pre-TV religious identity and esteem."[9] In a similar vein, the anthropologist Stanley Tambiah, analyzing "Hindu nationalism, the Ayodhya campaign, and the Babri Masjid," has emphasized how a mass-produced "national standard" may transform "diverse local places, where it explodes like a cluster bomb in multiple context-bound ways."[10] Jeffrey likewise describes transformed localities operating under new media auspices, including the "tendency and capacity of individuals—'the people'—to worship themselves and their individuality" as a form of collective solace-seeking and the simultaneous expression of a "need to assemble (or be assembled) as a mass—'the people'—and to be consulted, sold things and entertained."[11] At just these moments social scientific accounts of India's mass phenomena such as the TV *Ramayana* meet their contemporary limits. They neglect to explore what might be socially encoded in the immediate, material, and superficial level. Instead mass aesthetics are dismissed outright. For Arvind Rajagopal, the TV *Ramayana* is rejected as "low-grade kitsch."[12] With such dismissals an entire domain of Indian vernacular modernism is refused adequate sociological engagement.

But is it not possible that kitsch, rather than being so fallen as to deserve little concerted mental effort, may actually put us, as Benjamin might have suggested, "on the track of things"? Might not kitsch bear "the last mask of the banal, the one with which we adorn ourselves, in dream and conversation, so as to take in the energies of an outlived world of things"?[13] Benjamin's "last mask" captures something of the imminent departure from reified temporality announced, as it were, in dream kitsch. For Kracauer, Benjamin's fellow traveler through the phantasmagorias of Weimar, kitsch retained a peculiar idealism and expressed through its hieroglyphics the dream images of mass society. Rather than dismissing mass ornaments Kracauer deciphered displaced social potentials as well as future promises within them: "No kitsch can be discovered that cannot be excelled by life itself."[14] For a more promising approach to Indian mass ornaments and dream kitsch—that is, the aesthetic dimension of mass society—we take our cues from Weimar, especially Kracauer's penetrating theorization of the mass ornament as this was fashioned by the pulls and pushes of an incredibly volatile political contest over higher spheres of meaning when idealism had already eroded under the hegemony of utility and religions remained mere vestiges of a noninstrumental spirit. In his arresting engagements with the at once ordinary and oneiric dimensions of kitsch and mass assemblies, Kracauer provides glimpses into how "the entrance into the truth is now in the profane," or, as the British sociologist David Frisby once remarked, how "even in a world robbed of higher meaning, this 'higher sphere' has been displaced" for Kracauer. It "is now located in the superficial phenomena of the everyday world."[15]

III. CUES FROM WEIMAR: SIMMEL, KRACAUER, AND A SOCIOLOGY OF MASS AESTHETICS

When Jeffrey makes fleeting reference to the increasing tendency and capacity of people in postcolonial India "to worship themselves" through the mediation of mass forms of consumption, he touches on the sphere of the aesthetic. By assembling or being assembled, the new masses demand "to be consulted, sold things and entertained," Jeffrey remarks.[16] In the evanescent fulfillment of this demand, I suggest, the Indian masses form a dream image. This takes the form of an aesthetic performance of a projected self-sufficiency that does not obtain in actuality. The ornament, or *alamkara*, cannot take hold in the workaday world, burdened as this realm is with everyday material needs and governed by the "asocial sociality" of market competition, profit, and individualistic survival at all costs. Rather, to take hold, this ephemeral phantasm requires makeshift departures from the quotidian realm. The way toward new media dreamscapes in India is paved with the mass ornament. Kitsch affords the requisite distraction toward the collective embodiment of nonfunctionality. Through the ornament, mass culture in India gives concrete aesthetic form to its widely dispersed yet integrated sociality, anticipating the harmonization of social antagonisms in one form or another. Being an end in itself, the ornament alludes to the finishing touch on a possible social self-sufficiency. All that which is impeded in actuality takes hard mute shape in the ornament. On occasions such as the TV *Ramayana* phenomenon of the late 1980s, the Indian masses are either summoned by aesthetic ornaments or constitute in themselves a spectacle. In seeing and being seen all at once, they form an end unto themselves, departing thereby radically, if only momentarily, from the utilitarian constraints that otherwise condition a hardening neoliberal objectivity. In the Hindi belt, the mass appeal of the TV serial bespeaks the perforation of political boundaries resulting from the "rise of the OBC at the expense of the upper castes," giving salience to what the political scientist Christophe Jaffrelot has called "the plebeianization of the Indian political class."[17] The political potency of the mass ornament is unmistakable, yet the social order to which it ultimately leads—utopian or dystopian—remains a matter of sharp contestation in the present crisis.

Not least among the many features Kracauer's sociology of mass aesthetics has to recommend itself to contemporary India—apart from the pervasive instability and impending doom of Weimar—is its thematization of just these spectacles through which newly formed masses discover themselves in concrete figuration or embodiment. Mass production on the assembly lines of the factory had generated its own aesthetic in the form of the Tiller Girls, Kracauer muses: "These products of American distraction factories are no longer individual girls, but indissoluble girl clusters whose movements are demonstrations of mathematics." Laying waste to the humanist inheritance in their machine-like tempo and abstract patterns, the expansion of mass culture could also render obsolete the cult of the organic "Aryan" community, offering in its stead an ever-expanding collectivity equipped with the technological capacities for radical self-transformation and social renewal. "As they condense into figures in the revues, performances of the same geometric precision are taking place in what is always the same packed stadium, be it in Australia or India, not to mention America. The tiniest village, which they have not yet reached, learns about them through the weekly newsreels. One need only glance at the screen to learn that the ornaments are composed of thousands of bodies, sexless bodies in bathing suits. The regularity of their patterns is cheered by the masses, themselves arranged by the stands in tier upon ordered tier."[18] The rub is that the base materiality of kitsch and the libidinal pleasures of collective performance fuel the critical power of the mass ornament, paving a ready retreat from the reason needed to fulfill the promises of such centrifugal massification. "Reason is impeded when the masses into which it should penetrate yield to emotions provided by the godless mythological cult," such as that of the Aryan (or "Hindu") *Volk*.[19] The ornament's opacity is as much a lever for reaffirming the troubled status quo as it is an index of a just reason to come. In Weimar, the mass ornament embodied all of the technological capacities requisite for radical social change on a mass scale, yet easily served as a means for thwarting social transformation and prolonging the passive revolution. (Similar ambivalences characterize contemporary Hindutva in India, which the social anthropologist Thomas Blom Hansen has correctly dubbed a "conservative revolution," as it is "premised upon yet reacting against a broader democratic transformation of both the political field and the public culture in postcolonial India.")[20]

Kracauer's innovative forays into the cityscape of vernacular modernism—picture palaces, best sellers, advertisements, fashion—partook in the widely emergent sociology of the urban masses and registered the political volatility of Weimar in its key terms: consumer culture, the white-collar set, ideological homelessness, pleasure barracks. Many of the troubles of Germany's exuberant experiment with democracy were concentrated in the newly evolving masses, which embodied in themselves the uncertainties, uprootedness, and flux of modernity. Indeed, as several intellectual historians of the period have found, the erosion of the long customary social fabric that inevitably resulted from the extraordinarily speedy industrialization of Germany gave rise to new forms of sociality and a need to understand the origins and possible futures of the radical social dynamism of industrial capitalism. This need informed the making of sociology as an autonomous discipline by the late nineteenth century. By 1920, with nearly twenty chairs in sociology secured in the German academy, the field turned its attention to the origins and possible futures of the very mass society that had established its raison d'être.[21] Having taken his cues most closely from Georg Simmel, whose sociological engagements with form lent themselves to a critical notion of the aesthetic, Kracauer turned to the everyday world of things as if they embodied this critical charge.[22] He did so, as Miriam Hansen has noted, with the insistence on "finding the antidote to modern mass culture within mass culture itself."[23] Over a series of studies, foremost among which are *Die Angestellten: Aus dem neuesten Deuschland* (The White-Collar Set: Out of the Newest Germany, 1930; translated as *The Salaried Masses: Duty and Distraction in Weimar Germany*) and *Das Ornamente der Masse* (The Mass Ornament, 1963; based on Weimar-era writings), Kracauer diagnosed the spiritual homelessness that ailed the rationally managed masses of Weimar, as well as the fantasies that fueled their spontaneous assemblage. By immersing himself in mass corporeality, he became acquainted directly with the new rhythms of consumer capitalism's psychosexual machinery. And, as the Jewish outsider who would have to undertake exile in the United States, he was aware of the monstrosities that attended the promises embedded in Weimar's phantasmagoria: "Like the pattern in the stadium, the organization stands above the masses, a monstrous figure whose creator withdraws it from the eyes of its bearers, and barely even observes it himself."[24]

What Kracauer presents of greatest relevance for grasping mass social dynamics in India today is not so much a ready-made theory that can be applied as a strategy for arresting and registering the flux of new phenomena whose meanings do not map directly on to established categories. By adopting the open-ended playfulness of the essay form in which nothing need be resolved and contradictory currents enter freely and encounter each other, Kracauer demonstrated his debt to Simmel's essayistic adventurousness. He also furnished an original take on a fundamental question posed in Baudelaire's notion of modernity as "the ephemeral, the fugitive, the contingent, the half of art whose other half is the eternal and the immutable."[25] Embedded within Simmel's unsystematic, restless, and ever shifting focal points, whether the new primacy of a money-mediated material objectivity in the urban sphere or the ever-changing appearances of fashion, was "a metaphysics of life." Transposed onto contemporary phenomena, this metaphysics facilitated the uncovering of ultimate values beneath banal surfaces by exploring their formal characteristics. Whereas for Simmel, modernity took on the guise of an eternal present and all sociological snapshots were viewed *sub specie aeternitatis*, according to Frisby—exposing thereby capitalist reification—for Kracauer, modernity presented a temporal rut that could be overcome only through immersion into the mass ornament. That is, the very critical dimension Simmel had posited in the aesthetic register was in Kracauer available for redeeming reason in the manner anticipated by fairy tales. The daydreams of society deposited in kitsch and embodied in mass ornaments were the hieroglyphs of new future possibilities.

We need not concern ourselves here with whether there is "a set of core issues that beat like a pulse through [Simmel's] entire corpus," or whether his focal point is ever-shifting and thereby only in conformity with the protean surface nature of the modernity it seeks to capture.[26]

More decisive is the manner in which questions of form are given methodological primacy in Simmel's oeuvre. As Frisby asserts, "Simmel viewed the aesthetic perspective as a legitimate one for acquiring insights into social reality."[27] Simmel's sociological aesthetics attained its methodological focus by rejecting a naive empiricism unable to recognize that the "ever fragmentary contents of positive knowledge" could never add up to any total picture, especially in conditions of endless social flux. Likewise, more rigorous sciences left a divide between empirical findings and the forms tacitly giving coherence to the positive bits of knowledge: "Science always finds itself on the path towards the absolute unity of the conception of the world but can never reach it; regardless of the point from which it starts, it always requires from that point a leap into another mode of thought—of a religious, metaphysical, moral or aesthetic nature—in order to expand and integrate the inevitably fragmentary nature of its results into a complete unity."[28]

Conversely, Simmel turned away from any abstract philosophizing on the totality of being, aiming to ground his schemata in immediate concrete social realities. Such formal philosophizing endlessly deferred engagement with the social details imprinted on surfaces of modern life. It was, after all, sociology's task to relate the surface level to "the ultimate values and things of importance in all that is human." Art here becomes crucial as a mode of apprehension of a historically arrived unity between individuals and society that is not perceivable immediately otherwise. The *wissenschaftliche* value of art, in other words, "lies in its being able to form an autonomous totality, a self-sufficient microcosm out of a fortuitous fragment of reality that is tied with a thousand threads to this reality."[29] Having analogies in the adventure and dream, the work of art obtains its essence when "it cuts out a piece of the endlessly continuous sequence of perceived experience, detaching it from all connections with one side or the other, giving it a self-sufficient form as though defined and held together by an inner core."[30] The work of art can thus prove to be exemplary of those "forms of human experience which can capture the fleeting nature of inner experiences in order that we can recognize them and temporarily at least hold them constant."[31] Because the work of art for Simmel "exists entirely beyond life as a reality," it is able to "stand over against life" and is thus "analogous to the totality of life itself, even as this totality presents itself in the brief summary and crowdedness of a dream experience."[32] By providing a concrete form from which all of society could be cognitively mapped, art responds to a characteristic longing of the modern experience—a longing to secure a stable area "beyond all the oscillations and fragmentariness of empirical existence" in order to escape from "life's complexity and constant unrest."[33] Many people, writes Simmel, "find in the artistic conception of things a release from the fragmentary and painful in real life. . . . The transcendental impulse, disillusioned by a fragmentary science that is silent as to everything final, and by a social-altruistic activity that neglects the inner, self-centred completion of spiritual development, has sought an outlet for itself in the aesthetic."[34] Through the fortuitous fragment of reality that is given form in the aesthetic dimension, a recurring break from the flatness of reified time and space is afforded. In posing a sharp contradiction between itself as an elevated autonomy in which all things exist in a timeless realm and the monotonous flux of everyday life, art plays an increasingly critical role.

In *Das Ornamente der Masse*, Kracauer writes, "Simmel is a born mediator between phenomena and ideas; using a net of relations of analogy and of essential homogeneity, he advances from the surface of things to their spiritual substrata everywhere he looks."[35] Kracauer's indebtedness to Simmel is implicit in every one of his readings of social space and urban design, for it was Simmel who pointed out (as, for instance, in his 1908 essay, "The Stranger") that "spatial relations not only are determining conditions of relationships among men, but are also symbolic of those relationships."[36] Just one year after Simmel's death, Kracauer wrote an unpublished thesis on his mentor's sociological principles, a précis of which is given in *The Mass Ornament*, and later indexed his abiding interest in Simmel by publishing a review of his posthumously published *Zur Philosophie der Kunst* (Toward a Philosophy of Art).[37] Kracauer marveled at Simmel's fundamental askesis as a thinker when he speaks of the one who in "yearning for the absolute exhibits precisely those enduring elements within him that remain the same amid all changes."[38] It is an analogous spatiotemporal complex held together by mass-produced forms, yet placed over and above existing society, that Kracauer discovers in everyday mass culture. These are hieroglyphs tokening alternate times. The everyday contents of ephemeral best sellers always "resemble the stars, in that the light which emanates from them may reach us only decades later."[39] The critical aesthetic dimension that Simmel had theorized as the prerogative of the self-realizing individual had now become, under conditions of reification, the preserve of mass kitsch: "The human figure enlisted in the mass ornament has begun the *exodus* from lush organic splendor and the constitution of individuality toward the realm of anonymity to which it relinquishes itself when it stands in truth and when the knowledge radiating from the basis of man dissolves the contours of visual natural form."[40] Under the weight of capitalist *Ratio*—leaving the impress of reified order on the social totality—the source and site of social criticism shifts, Kracauer suggests, from the individual to the posthumanist mass, radically secularizing, if not mortifying Simmel's original transcendental impulse.

Formed from an "inchoate human mass" through the application of the "same economic logic that ever more rationally moulds the enterprise," the new salaried types (*die Angestellten*) were the flexible, disposable, insecure, "morally pink," and "ideologically homeless" manifestations of the newest extreme of German culture. "Uniform working relations and collective contracts condition their lifestyle," writes Kracauer, "which is also subject . . . to the standardizing influence of powerful ideological forces."[41] Kracauer's notion of the mass ornament traces the retreat into "mythological structures of meaning" and the vehement opposition to reason in the fascist cultism of Weimar and the immanent powers pulsing through the new technologies, unraveling customary sociality and furnishing in its stead the possibility of forging solidarities across classes, nations, and generations—or as Hansen puts it, "the possibility, ultimately, of a universal language of mimetic transformation that would make mass culture an imaginative horizon for people trying to live a life in the war zones of modernization."[42]

Kracauer's mass ornament condenses conflicting tendencies and reveals both utopian and dystopian aspects of a uniquely modern dispensation. "The structure of the mass ornament reflects that of the entire contemporary situation," he writes; "it is therefore "ambivalent." The ambivalence is attributable to the very vexed relationship the mass ornament bears to reason. That is to say, the mass ornament openly betrays its origins in the materials of a Taylorist assembly line and bears the stamp of a calculative *Ratio*, for now "only as parts of a mass, not as individuals who believe themselves to be formed from within, do people become fractions of a figure"; the "hands in the factory correspond to the legs of the Tiller Girls." Yet as an "aesthetic reflex" of society dominated by instrumental rationality, the ornament, Kracauer asserts, "is an end in itself." In its spontaneous nonfunctionality and hard materiality, the mass ornament resists "capitalist *Ratio*" even while embodying it. Further, in implying a critique of a distorted reason, the mass ornament anticipates its redemption.[43] Rid now of the encumbrances of organic substance and natural teleology and separated likewise from an obsolete humanist individualism or national spirit, the mass ornament opens itself to a legitimate aesthetic pleasure in that, for Kracauer, it harkens to the justice and reason that obtains in the fairy tale. (The fairy tale signifies "not stories about miracles but rather announcements of the miraculous advent of justice." For the truth of the fairy tale "can become reality only on the ruins of the natural unities," and "only with the mass itself can a sense of justice rise up that is really just.")[44] This is because "in the mass ornament nature is deprived of its substance, and it is just this that points to a condition in which the only elements of nature capable of surviving are those that do not resist illumination through reason." In the mass ornament the "organic center has been removed and the remaining unconnected parts are composed according to laws that are not those of nature but laws given by a knowledge of truth," which is to say that the social totality now has great potential for being infused with a redeemed reason.[45] Yet much depends on whether the artificial irreality of the ornament can be adopted and transformed into critique.

IV. MELANCHOLIC ORNAMENT: IMAGINARY UNITIES AND GENOCIDAL REALITIES IN INDIA TODAY

On August 9, 1988, shortly after the final broadcast of Ramanand Sagar's video serial of the Indian epic *Ramayana*, the Hindi daily *Jan Satta* ran an article with the headline "Without the TV 'Ramayana,' Sunday Mornings Feel Desolate."[46] Gone now were the days when the serialized video epic would unite the entire country in the image of Rama, or rather, make it entirely *rama-maya*—made up of or having the consistency of the deity Rama. The *Dainik Jagaran*'s article "The Ramayana Serial: The Heart's Thirst Is Still Unsatisfied" claimed that the series "had proved that from Kashmir to Kanyakumari our *Bharat* is one and the national language Hindi is its own language."[47] As exaggerated as these claims may appear, they nevertheless affirm what was widely perceived to be something on the order of a mass-media event extending for what seemed months on end. Only after the broadcast of the last episode—drawing the narrative rapidly to a close with the coronation of Vishnu's avatar upon his victorious return to Ayodhya—did it become clear that an absorbing spectacle had suddenly vanished and everyday life could return to normal. The Hindi press in particular had remained most attentive to the TV serial. In reflecting its emergence and tracking the pace of its popularity, the Hindi media extended the reach of this spectacle and further consolidated its commercial success. The attention it brought to the serial as an event revealed just how much the TV *Ramayana* marked a radical break from the everyday work of social reproduction and a movement into nonfunctional relationality embodied by wide-ranging motley masses, often gaudily ornamented for the occasion.

It will be wise to look into what is fueling this mass nostalgic sentimentality and why the *Ramayana* serves so readily as a vehicle for it. But for the moment, let us stay with the Hindi press, for one facet of this mass event that could sell papers was the TV *Ramayana*'s ephemeral yet transformative effect on quotidian patterns of collective existence. Many accounts remark on how the massive viewership, numbering some 80 million at the very least, collected at 9:30 A.M. on Sunday mornings, bringing all other activities to a virtual halt. One article in *Svatantra Bharat* in particular picked up on the ruinous effect this was having on day-to-day affairs, calling the serial "an opiate in the name of the *Ramayana*": "The popularity of the TV Ramayana is obvious from the fact that the streets are as if under curfew during each broadcast." The article goes on to lament the extent to which ordinary people relinquish all ties to their expected social function, reporting that a child with severe diarrhea was unable to hire rickshaw wallahs at the street corner since "unke liye larke ki jan se zyada kimiti tha ishvar darshan" (for them a vision of the Lord was more valuable than the life of a child). The author, Satyendra Srivastava, alleges that Sagar had cashed in on the empathy of the people. He laments that in order to watch the serial too many were willing to abandon the most necessary tasks: "zaruri se zaruri kam." "It is definitely worth considering how much time we wasted in this unproductive activity [*anutpadak karya*]."[48] The TV *Ramayana* could be more than unproductive; it could be destructive—especially if the electricity went out during a broadcast. Any abrupt return to mundane routine on account of electrical outage was met with collective rage. Short articles covering the mob-like outbursts whenever the electricity went out during a broadcast litter the papers: "Electricity Outage on Occasion of TV 'Ramayana' Leads to Stone-Throwing and Arson at the Electricity Plant"; "Rage Because of Electricity Outage at the Time of TV 'Ramayana'"; "Will the Residents of Ramanagar Not Be Able to Watch the 'Ramayana'?"[49]

In marking a radical departure from the workaday world, the masses donned the guise of an ornament and entered into an aesthetic imaginary realm by way of kitsch. "Before the TV 'Ramayana,' Television Is Sacralized," runs a headline from *Aaj* (Today), remarking on the apparently common practice of decorating television sets, invoking Hindu liturgy, and lighting incense before each broadcast.[50] This enactment of profane illumination granted to the "Sagarayana"—a neologism the mass appetite could not refuse—the sanctity of the original, the English-language *India Today* suggested.[51] In an interview, Sagar explained that for him television accorded most with the demands of the extensive narrative (*gatha*) of the classic epic. Having the temporal extension permitted by television, it was "as if the TV medium had come to fulfill this unsatisfied [*adhura*] dream" of giving full narrative scope to the epic as canonized in Sanskrit especially.[52] The fact that the video serial maintained its slow pace regardless of impending cuts—going according to "apni chal" (its own movement), as one commentator put it—gave the program a peculiarly distinct temporality. I will analyze how the visual idiom of the serial departs from secular forms, a matter of some controversy given India's liberal-secular Constitution. But it is worth first taking a glance at the references in the Hindi press to the atmosphere that the serial and the kitsch surrounding it produced. Reports from the Maccharhatta Gate in Varanasi convey that the "entire atmosphere became 'rama-maya' with all the decorations and rituals performed in anticipation of, during, and after the final Sunday broadcast, culminating in the distribution of 125 kilos of *prasad* sanctified by the electric rays of the TV set. Mass entry into the realm of the aesthetic allowed for a virtual mass-mediated "ornamental order" to take hold across India. It was a virtual reconstruction on a national televisual plane of what Daud Ali has culled from medieval courtly sources: "an ornamental order" consisting in "a great chain of being which linked all the elements of the universe into a coherent set of relationships."[53]

However coercive such a chain of being may appear in reality, within the world of dream kitsch it is a chain of being that the masses make up with their voluntary donning of its bond. The most popular display at the "Mini-Disneyland" on Marine Drive in Bombay was the costumes of the epic figures from the TV serial. Apart from the costumes, which were a huge commercial success (and ominously on display at various sites along L. K. Advani's *rathayatra* in the days leading up to the demolition of the Babri Masjid), one could find TV *Ramayana* "comics, key rings, wall clocks, stickers, and so forth stocked for sale."[54] Such costumes and trinkets acquire their figurative abstraction from the everyday through their sheen. In becoming gaudy, the masses themselves become a part of the expressive process of the ornament, unloosing a carnivalesque version of epic motifs into public arenas. It is essential in mass dream kitsch that such processes—whereby the mass becomes itself a finishing touch on the epic tradition it is celebrating—take hold willingly and even spontaneously. Sensing that the popularity of an ornamental order that celebrated the nation's becoming "ramamaya" would inevitably subordinate non-Hindu constituencies, the Hindi women's magazine *Suhag Bindiya* prolonged the mass oneiric vision. All of the Indian Muslim women interviewed for the article "The Ramayana Is Popular among People of All Religions" claimed to have grown a natural affinity to the serial. Rubi Naz of Allahabad explained that the "TV Ramayana had bound everyone with the thread of unity."[55] The editors provided standard Hindi glosses for the Urdu idiom of these women, suturing thereby their minority status to the majority Hindu community. Troubling questions about the fissures in the body politic are kept in abeyance with the comforting thought that even Muslim women assure the integrity of the majority Hindu nation-state by inculcating in their children the standardized ethical codes befitting a *ramarajya*, a dream vision elaborated periodically in the Hindi sphere since the era of Bharatendu Harishchandra.

Having come into sharp contrast with India's actual social realities in which minority presences fracture the cohesive image of a Hindu state and Hindus themselves threaten to fragment into irreconcilable diversity, the very dream image of Hindi mass culture crashes under what Arjun Appadurai calls an "anxiety of incompleteness": "Numerical majorities can become 'predatory' and ethnocidal with regard to 'small numbers' precisely when some minorities (and their small numbers) remind these majorities of the small gap that lies between their condition as majorities and the horizon of an unsullied national whole, a pure and untainted national ethnos."[56] With the excision of ethically troubling aspects of the epic narrative, the TV *Ramayana* presented a guiltless Hindu heritage on national television. In becoming a widely shared basis of a prideful image of the past—an instance of modern technologies rendering a past mythic—the serial served the interests of majoritarian mobilization, implicitly if not explicitly. The sense of cosmological, religious, ethnic, and moral closure achieved in the TV *Ramayana* clashed painfully against the uncertain realities unleashed by the erosion of national sovereignty under neoliberalism. Thus, as ornament, the TV *Ramayana* was always simultaneously saturated with a melancholic volatility: through it, the disturbance of the dream image opens the way toward mass genocide. "The melancholiacs' erotic cathexis of his object," writes Freud in "Mourning and Melancholia," thus undergoes a twofold fate: part of it regresses to identification, but the other part, under the influence of the conflict of ambivalence, is reduced to the stage of sadism."[57]

V. NOSTALGIC VEHICLE: *RAMAYANA* AS ORNAMENT OF LOST TIME

The sense of loss that accompanied the end of the TV *Ramayana* serial broadcast in July 1989 was merely a metonym of a larger, more complex, and deeply embedded melancholia regarding a mythical image of the past generated in modernity, especially, as I have noted, over the last decades of British imperial rule. Despite many insightful socio-psychological studies of mass violence in contemporary India, little concerted effort has been given to investigating the pervasive sense of loss that fuels much majoritarian mass formation and political mobilization. The very arduous research required to grasp the animus of mass melancholia precipitated by nostalgic reflections of an irretrievable past is beyond the scope of the current project. Yet some indication of the problematic is crucial for at least two pressing questions. By outlining what is asserted in the very notion of a modern mass melancholy, one is giving conceptual grounding to the kind of formal pattern to mass violence suggested by Appadurai and others, all the while modifying the original psychoanalytic contours of the category. Moreover, one is indicating the possible linkages—formal as well as affective—that undergird the strong affinity between nostalgia and the *Ramayana* narrative. So obvious is the connection that it, like so much else in this arena, defies investigation. Yet this analytical lapse occurs to the detriment of being able to delineate the possible release from the temporality of commodification embodied in the nonfunctionality of the mass ornament—the very "unproductivity" lamented in the popular press that was responsible for opening the mass spheres to the utopian ephemerality of kitsch. The myriad accounts of spontaneous abandonment of the workaday world to experience the transient imaginary unity provided by dream kitsch bespeaks what Benjamin, in a not-so-distant context, called "profane illumination" involving the destruction of a reified life-form for the sake of happiness. The destruction renders legible, however ephemerally, I would like to suggest, a history congealed in things.[58]

The melancholic rage of the Hindu majority, in spraying genocidal venom upon minority presences in postcolonial India, has its premise in nostalgic affect. The nostalgic image furnishes communities with guiltless heritages and idealized pasts through the new mass media. Coining the term "restorative nostalgia," which she saw as characterizing the sweep of nationalist revivals all over the late twentieth-century world, Svetlana Boym described in *The Future of Nostalgia* the prevalence of "antimodern myth-making of history by means of a return to national symbols and myths."[59] This urge to "rebuild the lost home and patch up the memory gaps" in the restorative nostalgic mode is fueled by a particularly complicated process of identification with a lost love-object that Freud sought to conceptualize in "Mourning and Melancholia" (Trauer und Melancholie, 1917) and which he further elaborated in *Group Psychology and the Analysis of the Ego* (Massenpsychologie und Ich-Analyse, 1921). Whereas the mourner succeeds in letting go of the love-object, regains a libidinal attachment to the world, and settles back into the routine of everyday reality, the melancholic reveals "a morbid pathological disposition" for being incapable of letting go and coming to terms with the lost object. Freud attributes this incapacity of the melancholic to a structuring ambivalence characterized by "an identification of the ego with the abandoned object" and a particularly sadistic tendency toward whatever substitutes for it or hinders its actualization. Narcissistic identification with an idealized love-object becomes the basis for a sadistic drive toward whatever does not match up or gets in the way, self or other: "The ego wishes to incorporate this object into itself, and the method by which it would do so, in this oral or cannibalistic stage, is by devouring it."[60] In the fluctuation between sadistic and masochistic aims, the self can be sacrificed to the lost love-object as a way of signifying undying devotion, just as any threatening obstacle can be eliminated.[61] Though Freud references melancholia only in passing in the course of his discussion of mass psychology, it can be surmised from his arguments around this phenomenon that ephemeral mass formations allow the relatively uninhibited working out of such violent fantasies. The volatility and violence embodied by mass melancholia cascades across the nation-state with a force that mutilates its modern political structures, threatening most the minority groups whose presence stands in the way of a fully integrated polity of Hindu purity.

There is undoubtedly much validity to the view that the TV *Ramayana* was part and parcel of a rightward turn in Indian politics, buttressing its worldview and thereby providing sacred and profane inflections for the violence that ensued over the early 1990s. Yet the serial and mass dream kitsch that accompanied it are not completely emptied of their potential meaning by this assignation. That is, the TV *Ramayana* cannot simply be dismissed as a blithe affirmation of a neotraditionalist worldview and *Machtpolitik*. To do so would be to neglect what might be encoded in its own internal materiality and formal logic. This is the very obvious struggle the masses, especially the lowest orders among them, wage daily against the temporality of modernity and the deep discomfort they display regarding a world secularized and reordered by the commodity-form. What is most obviously on display in the TV *Ramayana*'s mass ornament is the embodiment of a generally inarticulate desire to depart en masse from the historical moment, painfully conditioned as it is by clock time. The critical challenge vernacular mass culture poses is to attend to those dimensions of its tinseled universe that are nonsynchronous with the compulsions of the capitalist market and that carve out from within modernity's rapacity the sentimental core of an alternate, imaginary, and indeed utopian spatiality. Kracauer's work met this challenge by regularly refraining from dismissing the "sentimentality (devoid of literary form) that appeals to the anonymous masses": "Rather than expensive reserve, the middle class and the impoverished masses in general demand heart, which costs nothing. When people lack all else, feeling is everything. It humanizes tragedy without abolishing it and obscures any criticism that might threaten the preservation of outdated contents."[62]

I will conclude with some brief reflections on the TV *Ramayana*'s visual rhetoric of sentimentality as well as the spectral time to which it gives rise, for in these instances, the critical dimensions of the *Ramayana* aesthetic become most pronounced. Modernity's unapologetic uprooting of customary relations and ruthless imposition of instrumental normativity in their stead give a nostalgic, indeed sentimental tinge to traditional contents, investing them with a radically new aura. The most obvious superficial levels of the TV *Ramayana* phenomenon demand concerted attention, for, as I remarked earlier, the surface sheen often distracts analysis where it can be most radiant. Let us begin with the epic narrative itself, for the narrative tradition of the *Ramayana* offers a point of departure into a visual rhetoric intent on clutching and holding still, however ephemerally, the dials of capitalist clock time. The detemporalization of calculative time is dependent in part on the nostalgia that holds the mass audience together. Sagar's own version is filtered through the sentimentality of Tulsidas's *Ramacaritamanas*, which in part activates latent media dynamics of the *Ramayana* only, in a sense, to give them a contemporary modern finish. This takes the form of a televisual distention of time in a dialectical standstill.

Sagar's televisual rendition of the narrative amply explores classic epic themes, including love and war, attachment and loss, exile and homecoming, worldly evils and heroic uprightness, all obviously germane for the proliferation of nostalgic and sentimental contagion among the Indian masses. Indeed, the problematics the television series faced in giving closure to the epic narrative recalled the difficulties explored in Bhavabhuti's classic Sanskrit tragedy, *Uttararamacarita* (Rama's Last Act).[63] Of no less importance is the longue durée of the *Ramayana*'s medial history. This is activated by the very transmission of the narrative to video, opening another chapter in a long history of medial shifts. The celebrated Sanskritist Sheldon Pollock suggests in *The Language of the Gods in the World of Men* just how much nostalgic affect fostered in the Valmiki *Ramayana* may have been rooted in a fundamental shift from orality to writing. "When Valmiki is shown to compose his poem after meditating and to transmit it orally to two young singers, who learn and perform it exactly as he taught it to them, we are being given not a realist depiction but a sentimental 'fiction of written culture.'" For Pollock, it was only on account of the implementation of writing that a new cultural form, *kavya*, came to life and with it a retrospective, even wistful, valorization of orality along with the "desire to continue to share in its authenticity and authority."[64] Pollock's concern with the materiality of culture—especially with the particular media that became authoritative, such as Sanskrit—and the substratum through which they are manifested helps situate core thematics, such as nostalgia itself. That is, the shift from orality to literacy embeds the problematic of passing time—especially how one could preserve what was already fading away, if not already gone. By erecting its narrative structure on the foundation of temporality, the epic could then thematize loss and recovery and provide instances of secular transience and divine permanence. The *Ramayana* narrative could then become the vehicle for a collective meditation on temporal alterity, as much oriented toward a time long gone as a time yet to come.

It is just this notion of a time yet to come, or a "pregnant time," that has been detected as a characteristic element of mythological cultural production in India's modern media sphere. Marking a break in the *Ramayana*'s narrative time, the visual dimension of the TV serial takes on the qualities of "frontality," "iconicity," and "tableau" widely discussed by Indian critics (Geeta Kapur, Ravi Vasudevan, and Ashish Rajadyaksha most prominently), which have their roots in epic forms reinvented for theater and film by the likes of Brecht and Eisenstein, and which were later addressed conceptually by Roland Barthes, among others. For present purposes, just a few points need to be made regarding the TV *Ramayana*'s visual economy in light of these categories of neotraditional aesthetics, key among which is tableau. In "Diderot, Brecht, Eisenstein," Barthes explores the radical challenges of an epic aesthetic and distills some of the visual tropes that Indian critics find ubiquitous in the popular modernism of postcolonial India, especially mythologicals and works exploring religious devotionalism. Uncannily resonating with characteristics of the ornament, Barthes's notion of the tableau seeks to specify an aesthetic modality that dwells on "a perfect instant." For Barthes, the "tableau (pictorial, theatrical, literary) is a pure cut-out segment [*decoupage pur*] with clearly defined edges, irreversible and incorruptible; everything that surrounds it is banished into nothingness, remains unnamed, while everything that it admits within its field is promoted into essence, into light, into view."[65]

Like Rama's mystical smile in the TV serial, given excessive manifestation from beginning to end, the tableau backlights "a hieroglyph in which can be read at a single glance (at one grasp, if we think in terms of theatre and cinema) the present, the past, and the future [*l'avenir*]."[66] In giving rise thus to a "pregnant moment," epic visuality dilates on a single scene with no pressing need to necessarily continue with the narration. This temporal lapse is allowed by the fact that, Vasudevan explains, "in genres such as the mythological film, the narrative process assumes audience knowledge of the narrative totality it refers to, so that a fragmentary, episodic structure can be deployed."[67] This representational rupture with narrative time, itself radically at odds with the reified structure of clock time, is afforded to the masses through a posthumanist technology. They in turn virtually switch it off by stepping temporarily out of their workaday time frame. In finding themselves collectively on the threshold of spectral time—what is left after tradition's bottomless well of resources has been poisoned—the masses depart from the sociopolitical order premised on calculation but only

Figure 2. Rama gracing the screen with his mystical smile in Ramanand Sagar's TV *Ramayana* (1989).

on the unreal grounds of dream kitsch. They give again a possible life to the revolutionary energies that once inhabited outmoded forms. Like Benjamin's surrealists, they "bring the immense forces of 'atmosphere' concealed in these [mournful] things to the point of explosion. What form do you suppose a life would take that was determined at a decisive moment precisely by the street song last on everyone's lips?"[68] What form of life by the tableau last seen by everyone reflecting how, though empty, "they are in some sort sufficient to themselves"?[69] And so on for all the other senses and capacities.

APPENDIX A

Translation of Muhammad Iqbal's Preface to *Payam-e Mashriq* (Message of the East)

I. A NOTE ON THE TRANSLATION

A century marked by Western imperial expansion separates the publication of Goethe's *West-östlicher Divan* (West-Eastern Divan, 1819) and Muhammad Iqbal's *Payam-e Mashriq* (Message of the East, 1923). The social, political, and cultural upheavals wrought by Western imperial hegemony over much of the East by the beginning of the twentieth century mirrored for Iqbal the age of unrest unleashed by the French Revolution and captured by the illustrious German poet in his *Divan*. The very movement toward the East that Goethe initiated in this innovative work as a way to release himself and his contemporaries from Western disciplines and cultural forms by adopting and elaborating upon Islamicate images of repose and earthly fulfillment (found most especially in the recently translated poetry of Hafiz, the fourteenth-century Persian master of the *ghazal*) took on renewed salience and urgency in Iqbal's *Message*. Indeed it is possible to see in Iqbal's optimism regarding the East as an antidote to the malaise besetting the modern West a peculiar prophetic charge. This prophetic element is signaled by the central term in the title of his work, *payam*, which, apart from "message," means "news," "embassy," and "mission." With the addition of the suffix "bar," it is connected with the Persian term for prophecy and the prophet. (It is no less curious that the very term for "message" or "prophecy" in Persian and Urdu has two ways of being vocalized, one with the voice velar frictive consonant, *paigham*, and the other as given in Iqbal's title, with a smooth semivowel instead.)

Goethe's *Divan* and Iqbal's *Payam* are both internally complicated and richly interconnected literary works. The reader should refer to chapter 5 (especially the first fragment) for a more detailed analysis of the genesis of Iqbal's work and its relation to Goethe's. Here it is worth noting that both works present a menagerie of poetic specimens. In the case of Goethe, these include metered and unmetered poetry, rhymed and unrhymed verse, literal translations from the Qur'an and Persian masterpieces, as well as imaginary dialogues with past figures, including ones that exceed orthodox Islamic canons but have found an enduring place within Sufi orders, such as the legends of the evergreen Khizr. In the case of Iqbal, things are no less variegated. The *Payam* comprises three sections (the *Divan* has twelve). A series of *ruba'yat* (quatrains), including one that is nothing other than a translation of the *Divan*'s "Mahomets Gesang" (Muhammad's Song), are followed by a miniature epic, a miscellany of poetic forms, including *ghazal*s, and various reflections. These last are primarily poetic portraits of Western intellectuals and political figures. The question of translation and dialogue will be taken up later, but here it is worth pausing to note how Iqbal's engagement with Goethe and early German romanticism in general opened already toward a remaking of the epic in an Indo-Persian idiom. The narrative poem "Conquest of Nature" (Taskhir-e Fitrat) coalesces within itself late romanticism and neo-epic. The Iqbal scholar Mustansir Mir remarks on how the story of the birth, fall, and redemption of Adam after his bout with Satan's allurements has "epic proportions" and is "future-oriented."[1]

Much of this futurity is premised on translation. As Adorno once wrote, "Treibt Liebe zu den Fremdwörtern" (Love drives us to foreign words).[2] The magnetic attraction to the foreign that both Iqbal and Goethe display in their works is powerfully alluring in itself. The translator has no sooner begun his task than he is drawn to survey the text as a multilayered ground of translation, recognizing that his own translation is an unearthing of certain deeply enclosed elements at the same time as it becomes another deposit upon a variegated surface. The rich underlying language complex that is produced by this to-and-fro and in-and-out movement is flagged by the foreign sign on the surface. This foreign element—the word *divan* in Goethe's title, for instance—reminds one that what one is translating is itself the product of the transfer of languages, ideas, and concepts. Capturing the movement outward of love and marking a striving against enclosure of one's being in the native tongue and other such accidents of birth, the switch to the foreign code works best, paradoxically, to convey the essential direction of the native motivation.

Unsurprisingly, the heteroglossic dimension of Iqbal's entire oeuvre, let alone the preface, presents several challenges. The referencing of works in German, English, Italian, Persian, and Arabic tests the breadth of one's own linguistic capacities and often demands an acquaintance with obscure fragments of the past. The total project is one of rescuing a charged sentiment from oblivion. What one grasps is just how much such a sentiment was produced by or within translation itself. Iqbal reconfigures Western thought within Islamicate terminology, interpreting Spinoza's monism, for instance, as part and parcel of the *vahdat ul-vaujud*, or "the unity of all existence," a central concept in Islamic, especially Sufi thought. I have attempted to keep intact this translational dimension of the work, drawing attention to the unexpected and somewhat unique turn of phrase in Iqbal's prose. This rendering was crosschecked with German and French translations and is meant to be an improvement on them by remaining more faithful to the stylistic choices that Iqbal made.[3] The impetus for this undertaking was provided by the realization that the preface was neglected or inadequately rendered in the translations of parts of *Payam-e Mashriq* into English. The lack of a scholarly apparatus for such a complex work, not to mention the want of accuracy and the obscurity of the venues in which these previous publications appeared, assured that the present exercise was not superfluous. It is offered as the definitive translation for the time being.

It is based on the *Payam-Mashriq* in the *Kulliyat-e Iqbal* (Farsi) (Lahore: Sheikh 'Ali aind Sanz, 1973).

II. TRANSLATION

Preface

The impetus for composing *Payam-e Mashriq* (Message of the East) was the *West-östlicher Divan* by the great German life-philosopher [*hakim-e hayat*] Goethe, in reference to which Germany's Jewish poet Heine writes, "This is a bouquet of trust [*'aqidat*] that the West has addressed to the East. . . . With this Divan, testimony obtains that the West became dissatisfied with its own flaccid and frigid spirituality and turned to the warmth at the breast of the East."[4]

This collection of verses, among the best of his compositions, and to which he himself gave the appellation "divan"—by which impressions was it shaped and in which conditions was it penned? To give a response to these questions, it is necessary to make brief mention of that movement which in the history of German letters is remembered as "Orientalism" [*tahrik-e mashriqi*]. It had been my intention to discourse upon the movement mentioned in sufficient detail, but sadly many of the sources which this task would require could not be availed of within Hindustan. Paul Horn, author of *History of the Literatures of Iran* [Geschichte der persischen Litteratur, 1901], has discussed in one of his essays the extent to which Goethe was indebted to the poets of Persia. But the issue of the journal *Nord und Süd* [North and South] in which the article mentioned was published could not be attained from any collections in Hindustan or in Germany.[5] Consequently I was forced to rely somewhat upon memory of previous study for the composition of this preface and somewhat upon Mr. Charles Remy's abridged yet extremely helpful and useful publication which he devoted to this matter.[6]

From the very beginnings of his youth, Goethe's all-embracing nature was inclined toward Eastern creativity. In Strasburg where he was immersed in legal studies he came into contact with the famous and admirable figure of German letters, Herder, the impact of whose company Goethe himself averred in his recollections. Herder did not know Persian, but because an ethical streak held sway over his nature, the works of Sa'adi were of the utmost interest to him. Thus, he even put into German several sections of the *Gulistan*. He was not much taken with Khavaja Hafiz. Directing attention toward Sa'adi, he writes, "We have sung the praises aplenty about the style [*rang*] of Hafiz. At this time, we require the delights of Sa'adi."[7] Yet, in spite of this interest of Herder's in Oriental literature, there is not a hint of Eastern literature in his poems or other works. Another great contemporary of Goethe's stature, Schiller, who died before the inception of Orientalism, was free of all Eastern influences. However, it should not be forgotten that the plot of his play *Turandot* was taken from Maulana Nizami's story "Daughter of the Emperor" (The Seven Princesses). Maulana began this work with this verse:

guft ki az jumlah-yi vilayat-e rus
bud shahari ba nikoi co 'urus

He said that across the country of Russia wide
Was a city with the peerless beauty of a bride.

In 1812, von Hammer published the complete translation of the *divan* of Khavaja Hafiz, and with this publication the Orientalist movement in German letters was inaugurated.[8] At that time, Goethe was forty-five, and this was the era when the decline of the German people had reached a nadir in all respects. Taking an active role in the political movements of the country did not suit Goethe's nature, and having become disgusted with the general tumult within Europe, the serene towering soul sought a homeland for himself in the peace and quiet of the Oriental ambience. The melodic voice [*tarannam*] of Hafiz set off an overwhelming rush of creativity within him. Ultimately this took lasting expression in the form of the *West-östlicher Divan*, but von Hammer's translation was not merely a motivating factor but also the source for his unique creativity. Time and again his poems appear to be free translations of the verses of Hafiz, and in several places his creative powers shed light on life's extremely subtle and grave problems on account of having come upon a new path through the influence of some specific poetic turn of phrase [*misr'a*] or other. Goethe's well-known biographer Bielschovsky writes:

> In the elegant melodies of the nightingale of Sheraz Goethe discovered his very own image. From time to time even the sensation came over him such that he began to think, "Perhaps my own soul has inhabited Hafiz's body and passed a lifetime in the lands of the East. That very earthly exhilaration [*masarrat*], that very heavenly rapture [*mohabbat*], that very simplicity, that very profundity, that very drive and passion, that very range of temperament, that very candidness, and that very freedom from restrictions and customs [*qaivud o rasum*]!" Simply put, in each phenomenon we discover a correspondence to Hafiz. Just as Hafiz is the oracular voice of the heavens and the interpreter of mysteries, so is Goethe, and just as a world of meaning resides in the apparent simplicity of Hafiz's lexicon, in this very way elemental being [*haqa'iq o asrar*] flashes through Goethe's spontaneity [*besakhtapan*]. They both garnered the acclamation of the wealthy and the poor alike. Both impressed the great emperors of their respective times (that is, Hafiz influenced Timur, and Goethe Napoleon), and they both maintained an inward peace and calm in an era of general destruction and ruin, thereby proving successful in keeping flowing the pourings of classical poetry.[9]

Aside from Khavaja Hafiz, Goethe was deeply indebted to Sheikh Attar, Sa'adi, Firdausi, and Islamicate literature in general for his own creative imaginings [*takhaiyulat*]. Here and there he even composed ghazals within the traditional mold of end rhyme [*radif*] and internal rhyme [*qafiya*]. He even employed with flair Persian tropes (such as "the substance of poetry" [*gauhar-e ashu'ar*], "the arrow of the eyelash" [*tir-e mazgan*], "conquering by the braided tresses" [*zulf-e girah-gir*]). In his passion for the Persianate, he did not abstain from making references to the adoration of boys. The names of different sections of the divan are in Persian, such as "Moganni Nameh" (Buch des Sängers), "Saki Nameh" (Das Schenkenbuch), "Uschk Nameh" (Buch der Liebe), "Timur Nameh" (Buch des Timur), "Hikmet Nameh" (Buch der Sprüche), and so forth. Despite all of this, Goethe was no imitator of any Persian poet, and his poetic nature is absolutely free. In the tulip gardens of the East, his melodic compositions [*nawa-paira'i*] are merely casual [*'arzi*]. He never wanted to abandon his Westernness, and his glance fell only on those Eastern elemental truths [*haqa'iq*] to which his Western nature could attract him. He had absolutely no interest in Iranian Sufism, and it was as if he knew that the poems of Hafiz were being interpreted through a Sufi lens. He was devoted to the literary absolute [*taghazzul-e mahz*] and had little sympathy for the Sufi exegesis of Hafiz's oeuvre. The philosophical ontology and gnosis [*haqa'iq o ma'aruf*] of Maulana Rumi struck him as vague. Though it may seem that he did not look deeply into Rumi's oeuvre it is not possible for one not to be a proponent of Rumi's who had become the eulogist of Spinoza (a philosopher of Holland who wrote on the problem of the unity of all existence [*vahdat-ul vajud*]) and who had raised his pen in support of [Giordano] Bruno (a pantheist [*vaujudi*] philosopher of Italy).

In brief, through the intervention of the *West-östlicher Divan* Goethe attempted to actualize the Eastern spirit [*'ajami ruh*] in German letters. The succeeding poets Platen, Rückert, and Bodenstedt brought to consummation the Orientalist movement which was begun by Goethe's divan. Platan learned Persian out of literary motives. He wrote ghazals not merely with the customary refrain and rhyme scheme [*qafiya radif*] but even according to the rules of Iranian prosody. He wrote quatrains [*ruba'iyan*] and a eulogy [*qasida*] for Napoleon. Like Goethe, he employed Persian tropes such as "bride of the rose" [*'urus-e gul*], "raven tresses" [*zulf-e mushkin*], and "tulip cheeks" [*lala 'uzar*], with flair even, and was committed to the literary absolute. Rückert was an adept at all three languages—Arabic, Persian, and Sanskrit.

He had great regard for Rumi's philosophy, and most of his ghazals were in imitation of Rumi's style. As he was an erudite Orientalist, he had a wider range of Eastern poetry at his disposal—*The Treasury of Secrets* [Makhzan ul-asrar] by Nizami, *The Spring Land* [Baharistan] by Jami, *The Compendium of Poetry* [Kulliyat] by Amir Khusrau, *The Rose Garden* [Gulistan] by Sa'adi, *The Wonders of the Enlightened* [Munaqib ul-'arafin] by 'Ayar Danish, *The Conference of the Birds* [Mantiq ul-tair], *The Seven Seas* [Haft qulzum], and so forth. He would note down the pearls of wisdom wherever they could be found. Indeed, Iran's pre-Islamic traditions and tales took his oeuvre to a zenith. He even poetically rendered several events of Islamic history, such as, for example, the death of Mahmud Ghaznavi, Mahmud's plunder of Somanath, the Empress Razia, and so forth. After Goethe, the most popular poet in the Oriental style was Bodenstedt,[10] who published his poems under the pseudonym "Mirza Shafi'." The small collection of poems became so popular that in a very short time 140 editions were printed. He was able to draw out the Eastern spirit so well that people in Germany believed for a long time that the poems of Shafi' were translated from Persian. Bodenstedt also gained much from Mirza Ma'azi and Anvari.

In this context I purposefully made no mention of Goethe's famous contemporary Heine. Although a Persian [*'ajami*] influence is evident in his collection of verses, titled *New Poems*,[11] and though he exquisitely put into poetry the tales of Mahmud and Firdausi, he did not have any major connection to the whole of Orientalism, and in his view, aside from Goethe's *West-östlicher Divan*, he did not give much weight to any other Eastern composition by a German writer. Yet the heart of this free spirit could not for long escape the clutches of the Eastern [*'ajami*] magic. Thus in one place, fashioning himself as an Iranian poet who has been exiled to Germany, he writes, "Oh Firdausi! Oh Jami! Oh Sa'adi! Your brother is a prisoner in the cell of melancholia [*gham*], longing for the flowers of Shiraz."

Daumer, Hermann Stahl, Löschke, Steiglitz, Leuthold, and von Schack are among the less noteworthy poets who were the imitators of Khvaja Hafiz.[12] The last among those mentioned ranked high in the intellectual milieu. His compositions "The Just Tale of Mahmud Ghaznavi" and "The Story of Marut and Harut" are well known, and on the whole of his oeuvre Omar Khayam's influence is estimable. To write a definitive history of the Orientalist Movement and to know the precise extent of Eastern influences on the basis of a rigorous [*tafsili*] comparison of German and Iranian poets, long study is required, for which neither the time nor the materials are available. Perhaps this rather brief sketch will give rise to the drive for investigation and fact-finding in the heart of some youth.

I have nothing more in particular to expound with respect to *Message of the East*, written some one hundred years after the *West-östlicher Divan*. Readers will realize for themselves that for the most part it seeks to bring into view ethical [*ikhlaqi*], spiritual [*mazhabi*], and political [*milli*] realities which bear upon the inner cultivation of the individual and the collective. There are certainly resemblances between the Germany of a hundred years ago and the state of the contemporary East. But the truth is that the innermost pressure of the collectivities of the world, the precise estimation of the importance of which it is difficult for us to estimate since we are ourselves shaped by this pressure, is the harbinger of a great spiritual and civilizational revolution. The Great War of Europe [World War I] was a calamity which annihilated the state of the old world in nearly every aspect, and now from the ashes of culture and society Creation [*fitrat*] is constructing within the depths of Life a new Adam and a new world for him to live in, the vague outlines of which obtain in the works of Dr. Einstein and Bergson. Europe has seen with her very own eyes the dreadful results of her own scientific, moral, and political vision and has heard the heartrending epic of *The Decadence of Europe* from Francesco Saverio Nitti (former prime minister of Italy).[13] But it is regrettable that her clever yet conservative ministers were unable to accurately grasp this overwhelming revolution that is currently taking place in the heart of humanity. Should one look at this from a purely literary perspective, after the pummeling of the Great War the vanishing of Europe's vitality was unfavorable for the development of a proper and firm literary vision. Rather there is the nagging doubt that the Eastern quality [*'ajamiyat*] which acts as an antidote to the withering, sluggishness, and difficulties of life, and which does not allow the feelings of the heart to be distinguished from the refulgence of the mind, will not hold sway over the natures of these nations. However, America seems to be just the right element among the elements of Western culture, and perhaps the reason for this is that this country is free from the bonds of ancient customs, and its collective rapture is able to adopt new ideas and influences.

The East, especially the Islamic East, has opened its eyes after centuries of perpetual sleep, but the nations of the East ought to feel that life cannot produce a revolution in its environs as long as first there is no revolution within its internal depths, as long as some new world cannot adopt external [*khariji*] existence, and as long as its being does not transform the inner spirit [*zamir*] of human beings. This firm law of Creation which the Qur'an expressed in these simple and eloquent terms, "God changes not what is in a people, until they / change what is in themselves,"[14] applies to both the individual as well as collective aspects of life, and I have endeavored to keep this truth in view in my Persian compositions.

At this moment, in the world and especially in the countries of the East every effort of this sort, whose purpose is to take the vision of individuated and collective subjects [*afrad o aqwam*] beyond geographical limits such that there be a growth and renewal of a proper and effective human Way, is worthy of respect. Upon this very basis, I have dedicated these few pages to the great sovereign of Afghanistan,[15] for on account of his natural sagacity and discernment he seems to be well apprised of his matter [*nukta*] and keeps his attention on the development of the Afghani people. May the Great Lord be his supporter and ally in this sublime task.

Finally I am grateful to my friend Chaudhuri Muhammad Husain, M.A., for he edited the drafts of *Message of the East* for publication. If he had not taken such troubles, then there would most likely have been much delay in the publication of this collection.

APPENDIX B

Translation of Sumitranandan Pant's "The Usefulness of the Epic Form in the Modern Age"

I. A NOTE ON THE TRANSLATION

Sumitranandan Pant (1900–1977) sealed his reputation as one of the four canonical Hindi Chayavadi poets by the mid-1930s, if not earlier. Though Pant wrote three *mahakavya* (narrative poems stylized in the tradition of Sanskrit courtly epic) and one epic narrative, *Lokayatan* (1964), poems in the early decades of Independent India, he is known most for allegorical nature poetry, celebrating the bucolic environs of his native Kasauni in the Himalayan foothills. Pant is held on a par with his fellow Chayavadis (Hindi romantic poets) for his innovations in meter, a powerful medium for the expression of the modern individualistic subjectivity that became nearly synonymous with the romantic strain of Hindi poetry in the early twentieth century. The gifted translator and scholar of modern Hindi, David Rubin, notes a tendency in Pant's poetry toward an overly abstract and "artificial romantic impulse." Accordingly, Rubin ventures that "despite his current vogue, it is possible that Pant will be best remembered not as a poet but as a brilliant prose stylist, essayist, and critic, surely one of the greatest of modern Hindi."[1]

The short essay translated here on the utility of the epic in an age that is described as dynamic through and through—"our age is essentially the age of the epic form"—sheds light on the norms that were penetrating Hindi literary and aesthetic spheres. It is worth noting right away that the key term in the title, "utility" (*upayogyata*), is most likely a neologism invented for capturing the newness of utilitarian thought in the late nineteenth century. The essay presents a wide global consciousness as emergent, requiring for its awesome breadth the epic form as a medium of reflection. The work presents as well the commonplace trope of establishing a seriality of canonical figures, in which Indians are interchangeable with Europeans, allowing for cosmopolitan egalitarianism to coincide with national belonging. The translation does not deny the prolixity of the original, nor does it shy away from presenting the extraordinary, however trite, leap into a fabricated pre-Muslim Indian memory of Aryan descent. No date is given in Pant's *Granthavali* for the publication of this essay, but its mention of Jayashankar Prasad's *Kamayani* (1936), discussed in chapter 6, helps to periodize in more ways than one. First, it signals that Pant's essay was composed much later, when it could be recognized that *Kamayani* had already signaled a distinctly new age. Indeed, Prasad's neo-epic is given centrality in Pant's notion of the contemporary in the Hindi literary sphere.

The translation is based on the republication of "Adhunik-yug men Mahakavya ki Upayogita" in volume 6 of *Sumitranandan Pant Granthavali* (Nayi Dilli: Rajkamal Prakashan, 2004).

II. TRANSLATION

Epic [*mahakavya*] becomes a symbol of an era's life, an era's intellect as well as an era's consciousness. It is the fluvial convergence of the entirety of human ways of life, struggles, ascents and declines, impediments as well as developments and advances. One can say of any canonical epic that it is the backbone of a life-world as well as a global consciousness. The flesh of human civilization and culture is supported by this skeletal structure. Because in the veins of epic flows the blood of species consciousness, one can hear in it the beating of the heart and the breathing of the life-breath of all political formations as well as humanity [*manavata*]. Whether one takes Vyas, Valmiki, Tulsidas or whether Homer, Dante, Virgil, or Milton or Goethe, one finds in their works the living reflection of an entire age; equally, a delineation of the life struggles of entire species beings, their ideals, their political perspectives, the rise and fall of fundamental values, as well as inherited wisdom and polymorphous development. The spiritual essence of epic transgresses the limits of space-time dimensions like a high mountain peak crested by a light piercing the heavens and, in its eternally sublime [*paratpar*] dignity, stands in indestructible glory regardless of the historical or cultural background of any particular narrative. From this peak to infinity flow perpetually rivers of diverse emotions, thoughts, inspirations, and intellectual surges, sprinkling with their nectar of immortality the landscapes of the imagination of innumerable generations, leading toward meritorious acts as well as enriching the aesthetics of life. Why look afar when you can take simply Tulsi's *Manas*, for the popular culture of all of India, especially the North, drank the eternally lasting devotional sap, became inspired, has come down over the ages well-nourished. The popular poet of the *Manas* churned within the human subject [*manav*] the sea of all of Indian life and Aryan culture and ornamented it with the new spiritual values, practical ethics and lived realities of the times. In it, we attain a unitary vision of all the perspectives and qualities of all the national religions, sects, doctrines and counterdoctrines, positions and counterpositions spread out from North to South and from East to West. Tulsidasji had purified Ram, the paragon of human virtue, in his sublime individuality for an Indian spirit lost in the blindness of differing opinions and in the mire of multifaceted medieval rituals and codes, as if he were propping him up again in the hearts and minds of the people. In this manner you will find the *Mahabharata* also to be a life mirror in the form of a huge mountain of Aryan civilization and culture, without which the understanding of Indian life and intellectual history is impossible. Thus the epics of the world stand like huge pillars of inextinguishable light amid an oceanic tumult of great times rocked high by the advance of consciousness and human life struggles as well as moved by cresting countercurrents, which radiate a light in distant directions and which advance the course of humanity, saving it in instances of danger, and helping it traverse obstacles.

It has been observed in world history that not all periods have the same significance. Several periods pass like nothing with their distinct rites and modes of life. They are either inactive or merely take advantage of the gains of the past in locally distinctive ways. In this manner some eras are ones of decline and ruin and some are eras of minor integration—such eras are incapable of giving birth to epic. In England the Victorian Age, known in India as the late middle period, remained just such an era. It remained ill-suited to giving voice to any great literary or artistic consciousness. In history, eras of intense creative stimulation have either been eras of awakening [*jagaran*]—in our country Kalidasa and Rabindranath Tagore were poets of such eras—or they have been eras like our own, in which global revolutionary spiritual as well as material transformations are under way. Science has brought such an epochal transformation [*yugantarakari parivartan*] to human conditions that even the human subject's perspective on life goes on changing. Past conceptions of time and space are changing down to the root. On account of the coming into dense and continuous contact with one another of peoples of different cultures, past spiritual and ethical beliefs are also in the process of development and expansion through mutual exchange. The topsy-turviness connected with political and economic struggles has changed the very conception of existence of terrestrial life. In a transitional period of such frightening reversals, innumerable kinds of situations, uncertainties, fears, and distortions occur in the subject's mind and wreak havoc on his mind. On the one hand the art of the declining age assembles received intellectual dispositions and desires to valorize them; on the other, extremely serious thinkers, audiences, and artists [*sarjak*] search for rays of a new light within the darkness of the present. And after having endeavored to understand what is behind this disintegration and tectonic shifting, after having organized human values within the framework of a global age, they are making efforts to tie human existence to a new global pattern and to establish a new spiritual ground. With this human beings [*manushya*] take the reins of future development in their own hands, put a human stamp on the manifold primary tendencies of nature, and become capable of turning them into a part of the new world culture. To study or meditate comprehensively upon such vast epochs is neither simple nor easily accomplished. For this reason, the creative tendency and artistic genius of today remain tied to random poetic expressions [*pragit*], abstract symbols, as well as intangible indistinct deep feelings reflecting the scant and sporadic inspirations, upsurges, and sympathies of the new shifts of the great era. They appear perpetually engrossed in giving expression to the subtle forces within the patterns of daily life [*antah kriyakalap*]. And having gathered together the aesthetics [*saundarya*]of the new great force [*mahapran*] of the present age [*yugjivan*] through innumerable visions, such creative tendency and artistic genius are attracting the attention of the consciousness of the age by going beyond the grounds of the false tracks, distortions, and ugliness of received thinking. It is only natural for poetic expression to attain greater success in depicting the multidimensional and mobile nature of this present age. In the time of such universal transformation the manifestation and indeed abundance of such poetic expression are easily comprehended. In their indomitable force, just as a sandy riverbank of meter is overwhelmed, they desire to give rhythmic expression to their momentary accomplishments as well as to their instinctively alert sense of existence.

However, despite all of this, this epoch of innumerable eras of transformations, once exposed on a worldwide film screen, a living, awoken, artistically inspired, aesthetically enlightened, sentiment-wise eloquent, imaginatively winged, heavens-embracing universally concrete symbol full of individuality, with all its forces, passions, ups and downs, creation and destruction, disorder, natures, limits, capabilities, material, political, economic, biological, emotional, intellectual, spiritual accomplishments, and potentials can be brought down to the level of the consciousness of the present age [*yug-jivan*]. This consciousness can indicate the path of future development toward universal existence for generations drowned in the mire of a dense swamp of the fleeting present. It can deliver the human mind from decline, destruction, and the darkness of faithlessness and open the cosmos of a new light before it. Having established a comprehensively new spirituality in mankind, inclusive of everything from the life of the senses to the life of the soul, and having given human life new meaning, new values, and new capabilities, it can grant the full attainment to the existence on earth. There is in this no doubt that our age is essentially the age of the epic form, which, surpassing the summits of the Vindhyas of contemporary creative processes, arising in the inexpressible [*avak*] and unsurpassable glory like the all-encompassing eternal and boundless Himalayas in the sky of the human consciousness, and binding the hundreds of narrow human dispositions to the fascination of the unconquerable godly greatness, can organize them in the new universal humanity, which is to become a vast crystal mountain mirror of the future fulfillment [*purnata*] of human consciousness excessively made imperfect by the particularity of place and people, which like *Kamayani* is to be the symbol of the coincidence of intellect and faith as well as the heavens-embracing auspiciousness of the radiant soul Prasad, of whom the meaning and speech are inseparable, established upon the truth and beauty of the inner life of the new Man and mankind. May it be thus.

Notes

INTRODUCTION

1. For the epigraph: Georg Lukács, *Theory of the Novel: A Historico-Philosophical Essay on the Forms of Great Epic Literature*, trans. Anna Bostock (Cambridge, Mass.: MIT Press, 1971), 62.

2. Christopher Shackle and Javed Majeed, trans., *Hali's Musaddas: The Flow and Ebb of Islam* (Delhi: Oxford University Press, 1997), 117.

3. Ibid., 109, 195.

4. Ibid., 151.

5. Ibid., 79.

6. Shackle and Majeed call the poem an "epic" pure and simple on the dust jacket and in their introduction as well.

7. Shackle and Majeed, *Hali's Musaddas*, 57, 149.

8. This distinction receives penetrating treatment in Moishe Postone, *Time, Labor and Social Domination: A Re-interpretation of Marx's Critical Theory* (Cambridge, U.K.: Cambridge University Press, 1993). This is discussed at greater length in chapter 1.

9. Shackle and Majeed, *Hali's Musaddas*, 56, 135, 203.

10. Ibid., 69, 76, 8.

11. Ibid., 89, 105, 61, 89.

12. For the epigraphs: "In der epischen Naivetät lebt die Kritik der bürgerlichen Vernunft," in Theodor W. Adorno, "Über epische Naivetät," in *Noten zur Literatur* (Frankfurt am Main: Suhrkamp, 1974), 36; Meenakshi Mukherjee, "Epic and Novel in India," in *The Novel*, vol. 1: *History, Geography, and Culture*, ed. Franco Moretti (Princeton, N.J.: Princeton University Press, 2006), 603.

13. Mukherjee, "Epic and Novel in India," 597.

14. For a critique of modernism, especially the ideological reduction of its purport to formalism, see Fredric Jameson, *A Singular Modernity: Essay on the Ontology of the Present* (New York: Verso, 2002).

15. Jürgen Habermas, "Modernity—An Incomplete Project," in *The Anti-Aesthetic: Essays on Postmodern Culture*, ed. Hal Foster (New York: New Press, 1998), 1–16. Habermas points out the "aporetischen Situation" that fundamentally characterizes Horkheimer and Adorno's *Dialektik der Aufklärung* in "Die Verschlingung von Mythos und Aufklärung: Horkheimer and Adorno," in *Der Philosophische Diskurs der Moderne: Zwölf Vorlesungen* (Frankfurt am Main: Suhrkamp, 1983), 130–57.

16. Phillipe Lacoue-Labarthe and Jean Luc-Nancy, *The Literary Absolute: The Theory of Literature in German Romanticism*, trans. Philip Barnard and Cheryl Lester (Albany: State University of New York Press, 1988), 5, 3, 7.

17. See Walter Benjamin, "Poliklinik" (1928) in *Einbahnstraße / Berliner Kindheit um Neunzehnhundert* (Frankfurt am Main: Fischer, 2011). For commentary, see Shierry Weber Nicholson, "Language: Its Murmurings, Its Darkness, and Its Silver Rib," in *Exact Imagination, Late Work: On Adorno's Aesthetics* (Cambridge, Mass.: MIT Press, 1997), 59–102.

18. Karl Marx and Friedrich Engels, *The German Ideology, Part 1 and Selections from Parts 2 and 3* (New York: International, 1970), 51.

19. See John Whittier Treat, *Writing Ground Zero: Japanese Literature and the Atomic Bomb* (Chicago: University of Chicago Press, 1995); see also Srinivas Aravamudan, "The Hindu Sublime, or Nuclearism Rendered Cultural," in *Guru English: South Asian Religion in a Cosmopolitan Language* (Princeton, N.J.: Princeton University Press, 2006).

20. *Bhagavad-Gita*, 11.32; R. C. Zaehner, trans., *The Bhagavad-Gita* (Oxford: Oxford University Press, 1973), 311. Oppenheimer's "Now I am become Death, Destroyer of Worlds" is an allusion to this verse of the *Gita*.

21. Homer, *Odyssey*, 332 (lines 440–41).

22. This is by no means to downplay the fascist tendencies within modern Indian culture, a topic that deserves sharper analysis lest it become reified and neutralized as mere "culture."

23. This very fact is given allegorical indication in Intizar Hussain's celebrated short story "The Unwritten Epic." See Muhammad Umar Memon, ed., *An Epic Unwritten: The Penguin Book of Partition Stories* (Delhi: Penguin, 1999).

24. On this point, see my critique of *The Modernist Papers* by Fredric Jameson in "Zero Figurality, or Imperialism and Form," *Bryn Mawr Review of Comparative Literature* 8, no. 1 (2010).

25. For the epigraph: Friedrich Schlegel, "Fragments on Literature and Poesy" (1791), in *Theory as Practice: A Critical Anthology of Early German Romantic Writings*, ed. Jochen Shulte-Sasse (Minneapolis: University of Minnesota Press, 1997), 333. For some powerful critiques, see Benita Parry, "Signs of Our Times: A Discussion of Homi Bhabha's *The Location of Culture*," in *Learning Places: The Afterlives of Area Studies*, ed. Masao Miyoshi and Harry Harootunian (Durham, N.C.: Duke University Press, 2002), 119–49; Timothy Brennan, *Wars of Position: The Cultural Politics of Left and Right* (New York:

Columbia University Press, 2006); Neil Larsen, *Determinations: Essays on Theory, Narrative and Nation in the Americas* (New York: Verso, 2001).

26. For historical context, see Ralph Russell and Khurshidul Islam, *Ghalib: Life and Letters* (New Delhi: Oxford University Press, 1994), 130, 149, passim.

27. See Ernst Bloch, "Nonsynchronism and the Obligation to Its Dialectics," *New German Critique*, no. 11 (Spring 1977): 22–38.

28. Walter Benjamin, *Selected Writings*, vol. 3, ed. Michael W. Jennings et al. (Cambridge, Mass.: Belknap Press, 2004), 148. All further citations from these volumes are given in the text, with the Roman numeral marking volume number and Arabic numerals page numbers.

29. For the epigraph: Schlegel. "Athenäum Fragments" (1798), in Schulte-Sasse, *Theory as Practice*, 321.

30. Walter Benjamin, *The Origin of German Tragic Drama*, trans. John Osborne (London: Verso, 2009), 36, 31.

31. This point is given further elaboration in the final section of chapter 1.

32. This is not to say that questions of gender and sexuality do not inevitably abound in the chapters ahead. It was not lost on me that the relationship established through reflections of otherness between Iqbal and Goethe may have homoerotic undertones, or that the scene of rape in Prasad's *Kamayani* may allegorize historical problematics of a mass sort in modern India. Delving further into these gender problems would have required a different, though not unrelated, theoretical architecture.

33. See Benjamin's "Notes on a Theory of Gambling" (II: 298).

34. Shackle and Majeed, *Hali's Musaddas*, 103.

35. Jameson, *A Singular Modernity*, 29. For the epigraph: Hamann, cited in Reinhart Koselleck, *The Practice of Conceptual History: Timing History, Spacing Concepts*, trans. Todd Presner et al. (Stanford: Stanford University Press, 2002), 131.

36. See Dipesh Chakrabarty, *Provincializing Europe: Postcolonial Thought and Historical Difference* (Princeton, N.J.: Princeton University Press, 2000). A return to historicization and an uncritical scheme of periodization underwrites his *The Calling of History: Sir Jadunath Sarkar and His Empire of Truth* (Chicago: University of Chicago Press, 2016).

37. Charles Bright and Michael Geyer, "Regimes of World Order: Global Integration and the Production of Difference in Twentieth-Century World History," in *Interactions: Transregional Perspectives on World History*, ed. Jerry H. Bentley, Renate Bridenthal, and Anand A. Yang (Honolulu: University of Hawai'i Press, 2005), 216. Another work that discusses the integrative spatial logic of British imperial development over this same period is Manu Goswami, *Producing India: From Colonial Economy to National Space* (Chicago: University of Chicago Press, 2004).

38. These developments are highlighted in Tirthankar Roy, *India in the World Economy: From Antiquity to the Present* (Cambridge, U.K.: Cambridge University Press, 2012), 183, passim.

39. Bright and Geyer, "Regimes of World Order," 217–18.

40. See Harish Damodaran, *India's New Capitalists: Caste, Business, and Industry in a Modern Nation* (New York: Palgrave, 2008).

41. Werner Hamacher, "'Now': Walter Benjamin on Historical Time," in *Walter Benjamin and History*, ed. Andrew Benjamin (London: Continuum, 2005), 38, 39.

CHAPTER 1

1. The shift in public discourse in the wake of the global Great Recession has been subtle yet unmistakable. See, for instance, Lisa W. Foderaro, "Colleges Turn the Economic Crisis into a Lesson Plan," *New York Times*, December 11, 2009. In this article, Sidney Plotkin, a professor of political science at Vassar College, is quoted as saying "Marx is the uninvited guest in the discussion."

2. Fredric Jameson, *Postmodernism, or The Cultural Logic of Late Capitalism* (Durham, N.C.: Duke University Press, 1991), xxi.

3. Karl Marx, *Capital: A Critique of Political Economy*, trans. Ben Fowkes (New York: Vintage, 1977), 1:163.

4. Walter Benjamin, *Ursprung des deutschen Trauerspiels* (Frankfurt am Main: Suhrkamp, 1974), 10. "Presentation is the inner-concept of the [work's] method."

5. Susan Buck-Morss, *The Dialectics of Seeing: Walter Benjamin and the Arcades Project* (London: MIT Press, 1989), 254.

6. Howard Eiland and Kevin McLaughlin, "Translators' Foreword," in Walter Benjamin, *The Arcades Project* (London: Belknap Press, 1999), x.

7. Walter Benjamin, *The Arcades Project*, trans. Howard Eiland and Kevin McLaughlin (London: Belknap Press, 1999)461.

8. Ranajit Guha, "The Advent of Punctuality," in *The Small Voice of History: Collected Essays*, ed. Partha Chatterjee (Delhi: Permanent Black, 2010), 396, 394, 407.

9. A useful bibliographic essay is included in David Arnold, *Famine: Social Crisis and Historical Change* (Oxford: Wiley-Blackwell, 1991); works on this controversial topic continue to surface and interrogate conventional wisdom regarding imperial beneficence.

10. Shackle and Majeed, *Hali's Musaddas*, 153.

11. Muhammad Iqbal, *Javid Nama*, in *Kulliyat-e Iqbal* (Farsi) (Lahore: Sheikh Ghulam Ali and Sons, 1983), 597.

12. Karl Marx, *Das Kapital: Kritik der politischen Ökonomie*, Erster Band, in Karl Marx und Friedrich Engels, *Werke*, Band 23 (Berlin: Dietz Verlag, 1962), 67, 52.

13. Étienne Balibar, *La philosophie de Marx* (Paris: Éditions La Découverte, 1993), 54, 5.

14. Marx, *Capital*, 1: 167–68. Subsequent citations appear in the text.

15. Private email correspondence, January 30, 2016.

16. Michael Heinrich, *Kritik der politischen Ökonomie: Eine Einfuhrung* (Stuttgart: Schmetterling Verlag, 2005), 38.

17. Fredric Jameson, *Representing Capital: A Reading of Volume One* (London: Verso, 2014), 19–20.

18. Ibid., 20.
19. Postone, *Time, Labour and Social Domination*, 152.
20. Ibid., 197.
21. Ibid., 202.
22. Ibid., 181.
23. See, for more details, Benita Parry, *Delusions and Discoveries: India in the British Imagination, 1880–1930* (New York: Verso, 1998).
24. Gillian Rose, *The Melancholy Science: An Introduction to the Thought of Theodor W. Adorno* (New York: Verso, 2014), 36.
25. See Timothy Bewes, *Reification: or The Anxiety of Late Capitalism* (London: Verso, 2002); Axel Honneth, *Reification: A New Look at an Old Idea* (New York: Oxford University Press, 2008).
26. Rose, *The Melancholy Science*, 36, passim.
27. Georg Lukács, *Selected Correspondence 1902–1920*, ed. Judith Marcus and Zoltán Tar (New York: Columbia University Press, 1986), 219.
28. Georg Lukács, *A Defence of* History and Class Consciousness: *Tailism and the Dialectic*, trans. Esther Leslie (New York: Verso, 2000), 11, 28.
29. Ibid., 157.
30. Ibid., 151.
31. Ibid., 79.
32. Georg Lukács, "Reification and the Consciousness of the Proletariat," in *History and Class Consciousness: Studies in Marxist Dialectics*, trans. Rodney Livingstone (New Delhi: Parrot Reads, 1971), 83.
33. Postone, *Time, Labor and Social Domination*, 79.
34. Lukács, "Reification," 91, 101.
35. Ibid., 135.
36. Postone, *Time, Labor and Social Domination*, 116.
37. Lukács, "Reification," 126.
38. Georg Lukács, "Preface to the New Edition (1967)," in *History and Class Consciousness*, xx.
39. Jameson, *Postmodernism*, 269.
40. Lukács, *Theory of the Novel*, 62.
41. For the epigraph: Adorno translated by Weber Nicholson, *Exact Imagination*, 90.
42. Weber Nicholson, *Exact Imagination*, 83–84, 96.
43. Gershom Scholem and Theodor W. Adorno, eds., *The Correspondence of Walter Benjamin*, trans. Manfred R. Jacobson and Evelyn M. Jacobson (Chicago: University of Chicago Press, 1994), 359.
44. The reference is not explicitly to capitalism in this instance, but becomes increasingly associated with that social form over the course of Benjamin's career.
45. Weber Nicholson, *Exact Imagination*, 91; Adorno, as cited on same page.
46. Beatrice Hanssen, *Walter Benjamin's Other History: Of Stones, Animals, Human Beings, and Angels* (Berkeley: University of California Press, 1998), 71.
47. Andrew Benjamin, "The Absolute as Translatability: Working through Walter Benjamin on Language," in *Walter Benjamin and Romanticism*, ed. Beatrice Hanssen and Andrew Benjamin (New York: Continuum, 2002), 112.

CHAPTER 2

1. W.H. Auden, *Enchafèd Flood; or, The Romantic Iconography of the Sea* (New York: Random House, 1950), 2.

2. Arthur O. Lovejoy, "On the Discrimination of Romanticisms," in *English Romantic Poetry: Modern Essays in Criticism*, ed. M. H. Abrams (New York: Oxford University Press, 1960), 3.

3. For the basis of this theory of ideology, see Marx, *Capital*, vol. 1, trans. Fowkes.

4. Joseph Conrad, *Lord Jim*, ed. Thomas C. Moser (New York: Norton, 1996), 135. All further citations are given in the text.

5. Max Horkheimer and Theodor W. Adorno, *Dialectic of Enlightenment: Philosophical Fragments*, trans. Edmund Jephcott (Stanford: Stanford University Press, 2002).

6. Benita Parry, *Conrad and Imperialism: Ideological Boundaries and Visionary Frontiers* (London: Macmillan, 1983), 76.

7. For pointers, see Fredric Jameson's "Romance and Reification: Plot Construction and Ideological Closure in Joseph Conrad" in his now classical work of sociohistorical hermeneutics, *The Political Unconscious: Narrative as a Socially Symbolic Act* (Ithaca, N.Y.: Cornell University Press, 1981), 206–80.

8. Of special interest is Pierre Lefranc, "Conradian Backgrounds and Contexts for *Lord Jim*," in Conrad, *Lord Jim*, 386–90.

9. Parry, *Conrad and Imperialism*, 36.

10. Joseph Conrad, *Heart of Darkness*, ed. Paul B. Armstrong (New York: Norton, 2006), 7.

11. Parry, *Conrad and Imperialism*, 23.

12. Ibid., 87.

13. Ibid., 97.

14. Horkheimer and Adorno, *Dialectic of Enlightenment*, 45.

15. For the epigraphs to the previous section: Benjamin, II: 299; Hesiod, *Works and Days*, ed. Glenn W. Most (Cambridge, Mass.: Harvard University Press, 2007), lines 648–49, 661–62; Charles Olson, "Call Me Ishmael," in *Collected Prose*, ed. Donald Allen and Benjamin Friedlander (Berkeley: University of California Press, 1997), 105; Christopher Connery, "Thalassophilia and Its Discontents," *Harvard Design Magazine*, no. 39 (Fall–Winter 2014): 156; Benjamin, IV: 35; II: 735; III: 340. For the epigraph to part II: Muhammad Iqbal, *The Development of Metaphysics in Persia* (1908; Whitefish, Mont.: Kessinger, 2005), 76.

16. Barbara Metcalf, "Iqbal's Imagined Geographies: The East, the West, the Nation, and Islam," in *A Wilderness of Possibilities: Urdu Studies in Transnational Perspective*, ed. Kathryn Hansen and David Lelyveld (New Delhi: Oxford University Press, 2005), 160.

17. See Xiaobing Tang and Michel Hockx, "The Creation Society (1921–1930)," in *Literary Societies of Republican China*, ed. Kirk A. Denton and Michel Hockx (New York: Lexington Books, 2008), 132n8.

18. Raymond Schwab, *La Renaissance orientale* (Paris: Payot, 1950), 504. See Edward Said, "Raymond Schwab and the Romance of Ideas," in *The*

World, the Text, and the Critic (Cambridge, Mass.: Harvard University Press, 1984), 248–67.

19. See Metcalf, "Iqbal's Imagined Geographies."

20. William Blake, "The Song of Los," in *Blake's Poetry and Designs*, ed. Mary Lynn Johnson and John E. Grant (New York: Norton, 1979), 136.

21. Wang Hui, *The End of the Revolution: China and the Limits of Modernity* (London: Verso, 2011), 77.

22. See, for instance, Oppenheimer's remarks in the introduction regarding the testing of the atomic bomb.

23. Raymond Williams, *Politics of Modernism: Against the New Conformists* (London: Verso, 1989), 33, 35, his italics.

24. Walter Benjamin, *Das Passagen-Werk*, in *Gesammelte Schriften*, vol. 5, ed. Rolf Tiedemann (Frankfurt am Main: Suhrkamp, 1982), 576.

25. See, for instance, the concluding section of *One-Way Street*, "To the Planetarium," in I: 486–87.

26. Winfried Menninghaus, "Walter Benjamin's Theory of Myth," in *On Walter Benjamin: Critical Essays and Recollections* (Cambridge, Mass: MIT Press, 1991), 296.

27. Theodor W. Adorno, *Prisms*, trans. Samuel Weber and Shierry Weber Nicholsen (Cambridge, Mass.: MIT Press, 1983), 234.

28. This is most succinctly expressed in his well-known letter to Max Horkheimer. See Walter Benjamin, *On Hashish*, trans. Howard Eiland et al. (Cambridge, Mass.: Belknap Press, 2006), 145–46.

29. Raymond Geuss, *Outside Ethics* (Princeton, N.J.: Princeton University Press, 2005), 235.

30. See Willem van Reijen and Jan Branson, "The Disappearance of Class History in *Dialectic of Enlightenment*: A Commentary on the Textual Variants (1944 and 1947)," in Horkheimer and Adorno, *Dialectic of Enlightenment*, 251.

31. Geuss, *Outside Ethics*, 164, passim.

32. Horkheimer and Adorno, *Dialectic of Enlightenment*, 3.

33. Ibid., 8.

34. Ibid., 13.

35. Theodor W. Adorno, "Culture Industry Reconsidered," in *The Culture Industry: Selected Essays on Mass Culture*, ed. J. M. Bernstein (London: Routledge, 1991), 100.

36. This is further argued in the following chapter.

37. The possibilities of *Sprengung* find their sharpest articulation in Benjamin's "On the Concept of History," in IV: 389–400.

38. Natsume Soseki, "The Civilization of Modern-Day Japan," trans. Jay Rubin, in *The Columbia Anthology of Modern Japanese Literature*, vol. 1: *From Restoration to Occupation, 1868–1945* (New York: Columbia University Press, 2005), 319.

39. Tapan Raychaudhuri, *Europe Reconsidered: Perceptions of the West in Nineteenth Century Bengal* (New Delhi: Oxford University Press, 1988), ix.

40. Wang, *End of the Revolution*, 155, 157.

41. Dipesh Chakrabarty, "Romantic Archives: Literature and the Politics of Identity in Bengal," *Critical Inquiry* 30, no. 3 (2004): 678.

42. For an extended summary of this essay's contents as well as a theorization of its meandering aesthetic, see Charles A. Laughlin, *The Literature of Leisure and Chinese Modernity* (Honolulu: University of Hawai'i Press, 2008), 55–59.

43. Kirk A. Denton, *Modern Chinese Literary Thought: Writings on Literature 1893–1945* (Stanford: Stanford University Press, 1996), 118.

44. Ibid.

45. Ibid.

46. Wang, *The End of the Revolution*, 196.

47. Lu Xun, "On Photography," trans. Kirk A. Denton, in Denton, *Modern Chinese Thought*, 196, 198.

48. Ibid., 200, 202.

49. This is not the only time Tagore's mere presence marks the historical senescence of romanticism. We return to Tagore anon.

50. Leo Ou-fan Lee, *The Romantic Generation of Modern Chinese Writers* (Cambridge, Mass.: Harvard University Press, 1973).

51. Stephanie Hemelryk Donald and Yi Zheng, "Chinese Modernisms," in *The Oxford Handbook of Modernisms*, ed. Peter Brooker et al. (Oxford: Oxford University Press, 2010), 982.

52. Ibid., 983–84.

53. Ibid., 984.

54. Guo Moruo, "Preface to *The Sorrows of Young Werther*," in Denton, *Modern Chinese Literary Thought*, 205, 206.

55. Tang and Hockx, "Creation Society," 107.

56. As cited ibid., 115.

57. Zhang Junmai, quoted in Wm. Theodore de Bary and Richard Lufrano, eds., *Sources of Chinese Tradition* (New York: Columbia University Press, 2001), 2:372.

58. Xiaobing Tang, *Origins of the Chinese Avant-Garde: The Modern Woodcut Movement* (Berkeley: University of California Press, 2008), 68, passim.

59. On this theme, see as well Lydia Liu, *The Clash of Empires: The Invention of China in Modern World Making* (Cambridge, Mass.: Harvard University Press, 2006), especially chapter 6, "The Sovereign Subject of Language."

60. Carl Schmitt, *Political Romanticism*, trans. Guy Oakes (Cambridge, Mass.: MIT Press, 2001), 18.

61. .

62. Jun'ichiro Tanizaki, *In Praise of Shadows*, trans. Thomas J. Harper and Edward G. Seidensticker (Sedgwick, Me.: Leete's Island Books, 1977), 36, 6, 7, 11, 40.

63. See "Appendix A. Members of the Japan Romantic School," in Kevin Michael Doak, *Dreams of Difference: The Japan Romantic School and the Crisis of Modernity* (Berkeley: University of California Press, 1994), 153–56.

64. As cited in Alan Tansman, *The Aesthetics of Japanese Fascism* (Berkeley: University of California Press, 2009), 49.

65. Tanizaki, *In Praise of Shadows*, 8, 9, 8.

66. Ibid., 13, 14, 22, 27–28.

67. Masakazu Yamazaki, "The Intellectual Community of the Showa Era," in *Showa: The Japan of Hirohito*, ed. Carol Gluck and Stephen R. Graubard (New York: Norton, 1992), 257.

68. Ibid., 258.

69. Harry Harootunian, *Overcome by Modernity: History, Culture, and Community in Interwar Japan* (Princeton, N.J.: Princeton University Press, 2000), 46.

70. See chapter 6 for a discussion of Chayavad; the Halqah-ye Arbab-e Zauq must be mentioned in conjunction with chapter 5.

71. Muhammad Ali Jinnah, "Hindus and Muslims: Two Separate Nations," in *Sources of Indian Tradition*, ed. Stephen Hay, 2nd ed. (New York: Columbia University Press, 1988), 2:230.

72. Krishna Dutta and Andrew Robinson, eds., *Selected Letters of Rabindranath Tagore* (Cambridge, U.K.: Cambridge University Press, 1997), 146–47, dated February 17, 1914.

73. Krishna Dutta and Andrew Robinson, *Rabindranath Tagore: The Myriad-Minded Man* (London: Bloomsbury, 1995), 266.

74. Dutta and Robinson, *Selected Letters of Rabindranath Tagore*, 332

75. Dutta and Robinson, *Rabindranath Tagore*, 271.

76. Ibid., 267.

77. Ibid., 269–70.

78. Tapan Raychaudhuri, *Perceptions, Emotions, Sensibilities: Essays on India's Colonial and Post-Colonial Experiences* (New Delhi: Oxford University Press, 1999), 62.

79. Ibid., 61.

80. Ibid., 82, 87.

81. Chakrabarty, "Romantic Archives," 666.

82. Andrew Sartori, *Bengal in Global Concept History: Culturalism in the Age of Capital* (Chicago: University of Chicago Press, 2008), especially chapter 4, "Hinduism as Culture."

83. Ibid., 190, passim.

84. Antonio Gramsci, "Lyons Thesis," in *The Antonio Gramsci Reader: Selected Writings 1916–1935*, ed. David Forgacs (New York: New York University Press, 2000), 147–48.

85. Dutta and Robinson, *Rabindranath Tagore*, 267–68.

86. Dutta and Robinson, *Selected Letters of Rabindranath Tagore*, 339.

87. Ibid., 340.

88. Ibid., 268.

89. Iqbal, *Javid Nama* (Farsi), 597; Muhammad Iqbal, *Javid Nama*, trans. A. J. Arberry (London: Allen and Unwin, 1966), 22.

90. Iqbal, *Javid Nama*, 22; Iqbal, *Javid Nama* (Farsi), 597.

91. See Barbara Metcalf, *Islamic Revival in British India: Deoband, 1860–1900* (Princeton, N.J.: Princeton University Press, 2014).

92. Christian Troll, *Sayyid Ahmad Khan: A Re-interpretation of Muslim Theology* (New Delhi: Vikas, 1978), 215.

93. Ibid., 325.

94. As cited ibid., 17.

95. See chapter 1 for a discussion of Benjamin's notion of nonsensuous similarity.

CHAPTER 3

1. For the epigraph: Walter Benjamin, *Gesammelte Schriften*, band VI, ed. Rolf Tiedemann et al. (Frankfurt am Main: Suhrkamp, 1985), 92.

2. Stéphane Mosès, *L'Ange de l'histoire: Rosenzweig, Benjamin, Scholem* (Paris: Gallimard, 1992), 49.

3. Gershom Scholem, *Walter Benjamin—die Geschichte einer Freundschaft* (Frankfurt am Main: Suhrkamp, 1975), 151.

4. Walter Benjamin, *The Work of Art in the Age of Its Technological Reproducibility, and Other Writings on Media*, ed. Michael Jennings et al. (Cambridge, Mass.: Belknap Press, 2008), 75.

5. Ibid., 76.

6. Walter Benjamin, *Early Writings 1910–1917*, trans. Howard Eiland et al. (Cambridge, Mass.: Belknap Press, 2011), 213. In this context, Benjamin makes reference to "sehnsuchtlos Erinnerung" (longingless memory).

7. Kris Manjapra, *Age of Entanglement: German and Indian Intellectuals across Empire* (Cambridge, Mass.: Harvard University Press, 2014), 63.

8. Judith Ryan, "Germany's Heart of Darkness," in *A New History of German Literature*, ed. David E. Wellbery et al. (Cambridge, Mass.: Belknap Press, 2004), 635.

9. See Benjamin, *Early Writings*, 70.

10. Ambivalences regarding the romantic inheritance would continue to abound in Benjamin's writings, prompting him to adopt new methods for writing literary history. See chapter 1 on the materialist literary-historical course he eventually adopted for the *Arcades Project* (*Das Passagen-Werk*). This project is sprinkled with critiques of romanticism. For instance, a variety of bohemianism is taken to be "a bastard scion of the old Romanticism" (in the cited words of Jules Levallois). Benjamin, *Arcades Project*, 773.

11. See Marc Cioc, *The Rhine: An Eco-Biography, 1815–2000* (Seattle: University of Washington Press, 2002); David Blackbourn, *The Conquest of Nature: Water, Landscape, and the Making of Modern Germany* (New York: Norton, 2006).

12. Benjamin, *Early Writings*, 47.

13. Ibid., 88–89.

14. Ibid., 153, 68, 234, 69, 154.

15. Blackbourn, *Conquest of Nature*, 173.

16. Benjamin, "Socrates," in *Early Writings*, 234.

17. Peter Fenves, *The Messianic Reduction: Walter Benjamin and the Shape of Time* (Stanford: Stanford University Press, 2011), 69.

18. Ibid., 73.

19. *The Correspondence of Walter Benjamin and Gershom Scholem, 1932–1940*, trans. Gary Smith and Andre Lefevere (New York: Schocken Books, 1989), 202, 203.

20. Eiland quoted in Benjamin, *Early Writings*, 33.

21. Benjamin, *Early Writings*, 117.

22. A more literal rendering of the original hints at even more: "Aber er is nicht tot, er ist ins Menschenschicksal einbezogen" (But he is not dead, he has been drawn into the destiny of humankind). Walter Benjamin, "Kapitalismus als Religion" in *Kairos*, ed. Ralf Konersmann (Frankfurt am Main: Suhrkamp, 2007), 111.

23. Howard Eiland, "Translator's Introduction," in Benjamin, *Early Writings*, iv.

24. Immanuel Kant, *Critique of Practical Reason* (1788), in *Practical Philosophy*, ed. Mary J. Gregor (Cambridge, U.K.: Cambridge University Press, 1996), 269, italics in original; 5:162, according to the standard Kantian referencing scheme (volume and paragraph number).

25. Henry E. Allison, *Kant's Theory of Taste: A Reading of the Critique of Aesthetic Judgment* (Cambridge, U.K.: Cambridge University Press, 2001), 303.

26. Allen W. Wood, *Kant* (Malden, MA: Blackwell, 2005) 162.

27. Allison, *Kant's Theory of Taste*, 336.

28. Ibid., 341.

29. Ibid., 343.

30. Benjamin, *Early Writings*, 151.

31. Ibid., 66.

32. Howard Eiland and Michael W. Jennings, *Walter Benjamin: A Critical Life* (Cambridge, Mass.: Belknap Press, 2014), 298.

33. Klaus Christian Köhnke, *Entstehung und Aufstieg des Neukantianismus: Die deutsche Universitätsphilosophie zwischen Idealismus und Positivismus* (Frankfurt am Main: Suhrkamp, 1986), 433.

34. Ibid., 17.

35. Gershom Scholem, *Walter Benjamin: The Story of a Friendship* (New York: NYRB Classics, 2003), 77.

36. Ibid., 60.

37. Benjamin, *Early Writings*, 109.

38. Hanssen, *Walter Benjamin's Other History*, 27.

39. Scholem, *Friendship*, 74.

40. This is the concise definition given in Gillian Rose, *Hegel contra Sociology* (1981; London: Verso, 2009), 1.

41. Scholem, *Freundschaft*, 77. "A philosophy that does not include the possibility of soothsaying from coffee grounds and cannot explicate it cannot be a true philosophy" (Scholem, *Friendship*, 73).

42. Scholem and Adorno, *The Correspondence of Walter Benjamin 1910–1940*, 79. It should be noted, though, that Benjamin revealed on occasion to Scholem that he had a deep veneration for Buber's language, especially in his work *Daniel.*

43. Ibid., 80.

44. Ibid.

45. Ibid.

46. See, for instance, Alfred Lord's influential *The Singer of Tales*, ed. Stephen Mitchell and Gregory Nagy (Cambridge, Mass.: Harvard University Press, 2000), especially the introduction.

47. See Margarete Kohlenbach, "Religion, Experience, Politics: On Erich Unger and Walter Benjamin," in *The Early Frankfurt School and Religion*, ed. Margarete Kohlenbach and Raymond Geuss (New York: Palgrave, 2005),82.

48. See Scholem, *Freundschaft*, 173; my translation of these phrases differs significantly from Eiland and Jennings's in *Walter Benjamin*, 284.

49. See Beatrice Hanssen, "Language and Mimesis in Walter Benjamin's Work," in *The Cambridge Companion to Walter Benjamin*, ed. David S. Ferris (New York: Cambridge University Press, 2004), 58.

50. Weber Nicholsen, *Exact Imagination*, 68.

51. Scholem and Adorno, *Correspondence of Walter Benjamin 1910–1940*, 393. For the epigraph: Walter Benjamin, *Gesammelte Briefe*, vol. 4, ed. Christophe Gödde and Henri Lonitz (Frankfurt am Main: Suhrkamp, 1998), 224.

52. Eiland and Jennings, *Walter Benjamin*, 240.

53. Vicente Valero, *Experiencia y pobreza: Walter Benjamin en Ibiza, 1932–1933* (Barcelona: Édiciones Penínsulas, 2001).

54. Scholem and Adorno, *Correspondence of Walter Benjamin 1910–1940*, 419.

55. Valero *Experiencia y pobreza*, 60.

56. Scholem and Adorno, *Correspondence of Walter Benjamin 1910–1940*, 420.

57. Jean Selz, "An Experiment with Walter Benjamin," in Benjamin, *On Hashish*, 152.

58. Carol Jacobs, *In the Language of Walter Benjamin* (Baltimore: Johns Hopkins University Press, 2000), 61.

59. Ibid., 13.

60. Benjamin, *On Hashish*, 115. Rarely, if ever, do the Europeanist versions on Benjamin capture or comment on such non-European dimensions of his work, including Jacobs, who apparently finds nothing to comment upon here.

CHAPTER 4

1. See the bibliography in Frances Pritchett, *Nets of Awareness: Urdu Poetry and Its Critics* (Berkeley: University of California Press, 1994), 225–30.

2. Shackle and Majeed, *Hali's Musaddas*, 61, passim.

3. Ibid., 97, 91, 93. Citations of the *musaddas* and the opening *ruba'i* (quatrain) are given in the text, followed by M or R accordingly.

4. Altaf Husain Hali, *Yadgar-e Ghalib* (Memento of Ghalib), Urdu and Farsi vols. (Delhi: Maktaba Jam'ia, 2002); Altaf Husain Hali, *Hayat-e Sa'adi* (Life of Sa'adi) (Delhi: Maktaba Jam'ia, 1992). See also Mirza Farhat Allah Beg Dehlvi, *Delhi ki akhiri Shama'* (Last Candle of Delhi), ed. Rashid Hasan Khan (Delhi: Anjuman-e Taraqqi-ye Urdu, 1992).

5. Shackle and Majeed, *Hali's Musaddas*, 93.

6. I expatiate upon these ambivalences and ambiguities in the following section and throughout the rest of this chapter.

7. Altaf Husain Hali, *Muqaddamah-e Sh'er o Sha'iri* (Prolegomena to Poetry and Poetics) (Delhi: Maktaba Jam'ia, 1998).

8. For a discussion of early Urdu printing conventions, see Ulrike Stark, *An Empire of Books: The Naval Kishore Press and the Diffusion of the Printed Word in Colonial India* (Delhi: Permanent Black, 2007).

9. Shackle and Majeed, *Hali's Musaddas*, 9.

10. Ibid.

11. On the long-standing tradition of reverting to the norms of the primitive caliphate, see Marshal G. S. Hodgson, *The Venture of Islam: Conscience and History in a World Civilization* (Chicago: University of Chicago Press, 1974), 1:252–56, passim.

12. Hodgson grasps this sense of "cosmic transcendence" in Islam and connects it to "efforts, practical or symbolical, to transcend the limits of the natural order of foreseeable life—that is, efforts based on hope from or struggle toward some sort of 'supernatural' realm" (ibid., 88).

13. Shackle and Majeed, *Hali's Musaddas*, 74.

14. Ibid., 79.

15. See Walter Benjamin, *Ursprung des deutschen Trauerspiels* (The Origin of German Tragic Drama) (Frankfurt am Main: Suhrkamp, 1955) for an engaged treatment of melancholia as allegory-inducing affect. Benjamin's work traces explicitly the counterlogic that modernity furnishes through the allegorical mode among its vanquished.

16. Shackle and Majeed, *Hali's Musaddas*, 103.

17. Ibid., 52, 51

18. As cited in Hay, *Sources of Indian Tradition*, 2:191.

19. Javed Majeed, "Nature, Hyperbole, and the Colonial State," in *Islam and Modernity: Muslim Intellectuals Respond*, ed. John Cooper et al. (London: I. B. Tauris, 2000), 10–37.

20. See Metcalf, *Islamic Revival in British India*.

21. Some of these questions are broached in Hali's essay "Quran-e Majid men ab nayi tafsir ki gunja'ish baqi hai ya nahin?" (Is There Any Remaining Possibility of a New Interpretation of the Holy Quran?), in *Kuliyat-e Nasr-e Hali*, ed. Sheikh Muhammad Ismael Panipati (Lahaur: Majlis-i Taraqqi-yi Adab 1967), 70–97.

22. Hali, *Muqaddamah*, 160–61.

23. Mirza Babbar 'Ali 'Anis', *Razm Namah-yi Anis*, ed. Mas'ud Hasan Rizvi Adib (Lucknow: Kitab Nagar, 1951); Mirza Salamat 'Ali 'Dabir', *Razm Nama-yi Dabir* (Lucknow: Nasim Buk Dipo, 1964).

24. Shackle and Majeed, *Hali's Musaddas*, 79.

25. Ibid.

26. Ibid., 52, 51

27. Ibid., 50.

28. Hali, *Muqaddamah*, 140.

CHAPTER 5

1. Walter Benjamin, "On the Concept of History" (Thesis II), in *Selected Writings*, IV: 390.

2. See Javed Majeed, *Muhammad Iqbal: Islam, Aesthetics and Postcolonialism* (London: Routledge, 2009).

3. See Winfried Menninghaus, *Unendliche Verdopplung: Drei frühromantische Grundlegung der Kunsttheorie im Begriff absoluter Selbstreflexion* (Frankfurt am Main: Suhrkamp, 1987).

4. B. A. Dar, ed., *Letters of Iqbal* (Lahore: Iqbal Academy Pakistan, 1978), 21–22.

5. Muhammad Abdullah Qureshi, ed., *Ruh-e Makatib-e Iqbal* (Lahore: Iqbal Academy Pakistan, 1977), 86. Iqbal's marriages to his second and third wives seem to have leavened this transgressive urge. See Iqbal Singh, *The Ardent Pilgrim: An Introduction to the Life and Work of Mohammad Iqbal* (Delhi: Oxford University Press, 1997), especially chapter 12.

6. Dar, *Letters of Iqbal*, 6–7. The entire letter as well as other writings by Faiyzee on Iqbal are reproduced in appendix 2 of Sunil Sharma and Siobhan Lambert-Hurley, *Atiya's Journey: A Muslim Woman from Colonial Bombay to Edwardian Britain* (Delhi: Oxford University Press, 2010), 271–82.

7. Dar, *Letters of Iqbal*, 24.

8. See, for instance, letter 37 in Qureshi, *Ruh-e Makatib-e Iqbal*, 86–87; letter 19 in Dar, *Letters of Iqbal*, 186–87.

9. This is a prominent thematic in Majeed, *Muhammad Iqbal*, especially chapter 4.

10. Muhammad Iqbal, *The Mysteries of Selflessness: A Philosophical Poem*, trans. Arthur J. Arberry (London: John Murray, 1953), 2. The original goes simply, "az sukhan a'ina sazam kardehand." See Muhammad Iqbal, *Rumuz-e Be-khudi*, in *Kulliyat-e Iqbal* (Farsi), 82.

11. Iqbal, *Javid Nama* (Farsi), 376–77. A useful, though slightly off translation in a Western language can be found in Muhammad Iqbal, *Botschaft des Ostens (als Antwort auf Goethes West-Östliche Divan)* (Wiesbaden: Otto Harrassowitz, 1963), 97.

12. Iqbal, *Javid Nama* (Farsi), 376.

13. See, for instance, the letter to the educationist Sahibzadad Aftab Ahmad Khan in Dar, *Letters of Iqbal*, 151–56.

14. As quoted in the richly researched and concise work by Katharina Mommsen, *Goethe und der Islam* (Stuttgart: Goethe Gesellschaft, 1964), 17.

15. As given in a passage by Mommsen: "Eine von Goethe verfaßte Ankündigung dieses Werkes enthält sogar den erstaunlich Satz: der Verfasser des Buches lehne 'den Verdacht nicht ab, daß er selbst ein Muselmann sei'" (ibid., 5).

16. See the gloss on "reification" in chapter 1.

17. This is a prominent theme in Benjamin's *Der Begriff der Kunstkritik in der deutschen Romantik*, incorporated in the penetrating collection of interrelated writings by Walter Benjamin, *Aura und Reflexion: Schriften zur Ästhetik und Kunstphilosophie*, ed. Hartmut Böhme and Yvonne Ehrenspeck

(Frankfurt am Main: Suhrkamp, 2007). See also Menninghaus, *Unendliche Verdopplung.*

18. See chapter 2 for a discussion of "romantic" photography in interwar Asia, including the image referred to here.

19. Syed Abdul Vahid, ed., *Thoughts and Reflections of Iqbal* (Lahore: Muhammad Ashraf, 1964), 226.

20. Wilfred Cantwell Smith, *Modern Islam in India: A Social Analysis* (Lahore: Sh. Muhammad Ashraf, 1946), 107.

21. C. M. Naim, *Ambiguities of Heritage: Fictions and Polemics* (Karachi: City Press, 1999), 112.

22. Singh in *The Ardent Pilgrim* makes the following acute observation in reference to Iqbal: "He broke no new ground in so far as poetic media are concerned. He was perfectly happy working within the framework of conventional patterns and rhythms. Though he had been influenced by the European Romantics and was temperamentally akin to them in many respects, he adhered to orthodox and traditional modes of poetry" (136).

23. On the making of the colonial bureaucracy and productive infrastructure in Punjab, see Ian Talbot, *Punjab and the Raj 1849–1947* (New Delhi: Manohar, 1988); see also Imran Ali, *The Punjab under Imperialism, 1885–1947* (Princeton, N.J.: Princeton University Press, 1988).

24. Singh, *Ardent Pilgrim*, 76.

25. Dar, *Letters of Iqbal*, 62.

26. As cited in Singh, *Ardent Pilgrim*, xiii.

27. Faiz Ahmad Faiz, "Iqbal," in *Culture and Identity: Selected English Writings of Faiz*, ed. Sheema Majeed (Karachi: Oxford University Press, 2005), 182.

28. Muhammad Iqbal, *The Reconstruction of Religious Thought in Islam* (1934; Stanford: Stanford University Press, 2013), 113.

29. Ibid., xvii, xvii–xviii.

30. See, for instance, Souleymane Bachir Diagne, *Bergson postcolonial: L'Élan vital dans la pensée de Léopold Sédar Senghor et de Mohamed Iqbal* (Paris: CNRS, 2011).

31. Ibid., 48.

32. Ibid., 2.

33. See Lukács, "Reification."

34. Henri Bergson, "Beyond the Noumenal," in *Henri Bergson: Key Writings*, ed. Keith Ansell and John Mullarkey (New York: Continuum, 2002), 291.

35. Iqbal, *Reconstruction*, 6.

36. Faiz, "Iqbal," 179, 182–83.

37. Faiz Ahmad Faiz, "Iqbal—The Poet," in Majeed, *Culture and Identity*, 176.

38. Ibid.

39. Ibid.

40. Iqbal, *Javid Nama*, trans. Arberry, 28. All further citations of this work are given in the text as *JN*. For the epigraph: Adorno, translated in Weber Nicholsen, *Exact Imagination*, 146. This appears to be based on a reconstructed

sentence fragment from Adorno's *Ästhetische Theorie* (Frankfurt am Main: Suhrkamp, 1970), 169: "Ahmt das mimetische Verhalten nicht etwas nach, sondern macht sich selbst gleich, so nehmen die Kunstwerke es auf sich, eben das zu vollziehen."

41. For a brief but relevant survey of these topoi, see the introduction in Mustansir Mir, *Tulip in the Desert: A Selection of Iqbal's Poetry* (Montreal: McGill-Queen's University Press, 2000).

42. See Muhammad Iqbal, *Kulliyat-e Iqbal* (Urdu) (New Delhi: Farid Book Depot, 2003), 140.

43. Majeed, *Muhammad Iqbal*, 5.

44. Muhammad Iqbal, *The Secrets of the Self: A Philosophical Poem*, trans. Reynold A. Nicholson (London: Macmillan, 1920), 16–17.

45. Ibid., 16, reworked translation.

46. Hayden White, *The Content of the Form: Narrative Discourse and Historical Representation* (Baltimore: Johns Hopkins University Press, 1987), 1.

47. See Agha Shahid Ali, "Basic Points about the Ghazal," in *Ravishing Disunities: Real Ghazals in English*, ed. Agha Shahid Ali (Hanover, N.H.: Wesleyan University Press, 2000), 183–84.

48. Jawid Mojaddedi, introduction to Rumi, *The Masnavi*, book 1, trans. Jawid Mojaddedi (New York: Oxford University Press, 2004), xxiii.

49. White, *Content of the Form*, 1.

50. See the reading of Conrad's *Lord Jim* in chapter 2 for an elaboration of this image.

51. *Goethe's Faust*, trans. Walter Kaufmann (New York: Anchor Books, 1961), 327; the lines from the original German are 3453–58.

52. Walter Benjamin, "On Language as Such and the Language of Man," in *Selected Writings*, I: 67.

53. Walter Benjamin, "The Currently Effective Messianic Elements," in *Selected Writings*, I: 213.

CHAPTER 6

1. Michael Madhusudana Datta, "The Anglo-Saxon and the Hindu," in *Madhusudana Racanabali*, ed. Kshetra Gupta (Calcutta: Sahitya Samsad, 1965), 525.

2. For a canonical translation of this episode, see book 4 in Virgil, *Aeneid*, trans. Robert Fitzgerald (New York: Vintage, 1990).

3. Datta, "Anglo-Saxon," 529.

4. Ibid., 520.

5. Sartori, *Bengal in Global Concept History*, 104.

6. Datta, "Anglo-Saxon," 521.

7. Erwin Panofsky, "Perspektiv als Symbolische Form," in *Aufsätze zu Grundfragen der Kunstwissenschaft*, ed. Hariolf Oberer and Egon Verheyen (Berlin: V Spiess, 1985), 99–167.

8. The original reads, "Die frei wählbare Lage eines subjektiven 'Blickpunktes'" (ibid., 123).

9. Ghulam Murshid, ed., *Heart of a Rebel Poet: Letters of Michael Madhusudan Dutt* (Oxford: Oxford University Press, 2004), 157.

10. C. A. Bayly, *Recovering Liberties: Indian Thought in the Age of Liberalism and Empire* (Cambridge, U.K.: Cambridge University Press, 2011), 222.

11. Vasudha Dalmia, *The Nationalization of Hindu Traditions: Bharatendu Harischandra and Nineteenth-Century Banaras* (Delhi: Oxford University Press, 1997).

12. See the gloss on "reification" in chapter 1.

13. Murshid, *Heart of a Rebel Poet*, 33.

14. Ibid., 29.

15. Gupta, *Madhusudana Racanabali*, 438.

16. Clinton Seely, introduction to his translation of Michael Madhusudan Datta, *The Slaying of Meghanad: A Ramayana from Colonial Bengal* (Oxford: Oxford University Press, 2004), 18.

17. Ibid., 3.

18. Eric Stokes, *The English Utilitarians and India* (Oxford: Clarendon Press, 1959), 322.

19. Ibid., 51.

20. Terence Ball, "Mill, James (1773–1836)," in *Oxford Dictionary of National Biography*, Oxford University Press, October 2007, http://www.oxforddnb.com/view/article/18709.

21. Javed Majeed, *Ungoverned Imaginings: James Mill's* The History of British India and Orientalism (Oxford: Clarendon Press, 1992), 7–8.

22. Elie Halévy, *The Growth of Philosophic Radicalism* (Boston: Beacon Press, 1955), 251.

23. See Thomas Metcalf, *The Aftermath of Revolt: India, 1857–1870* (Princeton, N.J.: Princeton University Press, 1964).

24. Stokes, *English Utilitarians*, 55.

25. Jennifer Pitt, *A Turn to Empire: The Rise of Imperial Liberalism in Britain and France* (Princeton, N.J.: Princeton University Press, 2005), 125, 126.

26. Majeed, *Ungoverned Imaginings*, 136.

27. Jeremy Bentham, "On the Principle of Utility," in *Selected Writings on Utilitarianism* (Ware, U.K.: Wordsworth Editions, 2000), 88.

28. Karl Marx, *Capital: A Critique of Political Economy* (1867), trans. Ben Fowkes (New York: Penguin Classics, 1992), 1:758–59.

29. J. S. Mill, "Bentham," in John Stuart Mill and Jeremy Bentham, *Utilitarianism and Other Essays*, ed. Alan Ryan (New York: Penguin Classics, 1987), 134.

30. Ibid.

31. Stokes, *English Utilitarians*, 52.

32. Bankim Chandra Chatterji, *Sociological Essays: Utilitarianism and Positivism in Bengal*, ed. S. N. Mukherjee and Marian Maddern (Calcutta: Rddhi, 1986), 203, 204.

33. Peary Chand Mittra, *A Biographical Sketch of David Hare*, ed. Gauranga Gopal Sengupta (Calcutta: Jijnasa, 1979), xvi.

34. Ibid., xii.

35. Rammohan Roy, "A Letter on English Education" (addressed to Lord Amherst, governor general in Council), in *The English Works of Raja Rammohun Roy*, ed. Jogendra Chuner Ghose (Calcutta: S. Roy, 1901), 471, 470.

36. Jagannatha Cakrabarti, *Studies in the Bengal Renaissance*, ed. Atulchandra Gupta (Calcutta: National Council of Education, 1977), 20.

37. Thomas Edwards, *Henry Derozio, the Eurasian, Poet, Teacher, and Journalist: With Appendices* (Calcutta: W. Newman, 1884), 74.

38. Rosinka Chaudhuri, ed., *Derozio, Poet of India: The Definitive Edition* (Oxford: Oxford University Press, 2008), 291.

39. Murshid, *Heart of a Rebel Poet*, 41, 43.

40. See Ghulam Murshid, *Lured by Hope: A Biography of Michael Madhusudan Dutt*, trans. Gopa Majumdar (New Delhi: Oxford University Press, 2003), 60–61, passim.

41. Alexander Riddiford, *Madly after the Muses: Bengali Poet Michael Madhusudan Datta and His Reception of the Graeco-Roman Classics* (Oxford: Oxford University Press, 2013), 54.

42. Take for instance Seely, trans. *Slaying of Meghanad.*

43. Riddiford, *Madly after the Muses*, 95, 29, 50, 20, 19.

44. Partha Chatterjee, *The Black Hole of Empire: History of a Global Practice of Power* (Princeton, N.J.: Princeton University Press, 2012), 153.

45. Riddiford, *Madly after the Muses*, 50.

46. Riddiford's claim that there was a proto-nationalist dimension to Datta's efforts is the least tenable of all, as it radically forecloses possible political potentials other than nationalism at this historical moment (ibid., 50, passim).

47. Murshid, *Heart of a RebelPoet*, 128.

48. John Milton, *Paradise Lost* (New York: Norton, 1993), 6.

49. Thomas N. Corns, ed., *A Companion to Milton* (Malden, Mass.: Blackwell, 2003), 91.

50. Murshid, *Heart of RebelPoet*, 114–15. See Michael Madhusudan Dutt, *The Poem of the Killing of Meghnad*, trans. William Radice (New Delhi: Penguin, 2010), xxxix.

51. Riddiford, *Madly after the Muses*, 90.

52. Murshid, *Heart of a Rebel Poet*, 125.

53. As translated in Dutt, *Poem of the Killing of Meghnad*, cxv–cxvi.

54. See Murshid, *Lured by Hope.*

55. John Stuart Mill, "Coleridge," in John Stuart Mill and Jeremy Bentham, *Utilitarianism and Other Essays*, ed. Alan Ryan (New York: Penguin, 1987), 177–227.

56. John Stuart Mill, "Utilitarianism," in Mill and Bentham, *Utilitarianism*, 206.

57. Chaudhuri, *Derozio*, xxxvi, xxxviii.

58. See Dalmia, *Nationalization of Hindu Traditions*, where this is a line of argument throughout.

59. Ibid., 58.

60. M. A. Sherring, *The History of Protestant Missions in India, from their Commencement in 1706 to 1871* (London: Trübner, 1875), 184.

61. Cited in Dalmia, *Nationalization of Hindu Traditions*, 114.

62. Michael S. Dodson, *Orientalism, Empire, and National Culture: India, 1770–1880* (New York: Palgrave Macmillan, 2007), 92.

63. Thomas Babington Macaulay, "Minute on Indian Education" (1835), in *Archives of Empire*, vol. 1: *From the East Indian Company to the Suez Canal*, ed. Mia Carter and Barbara Harlow (London: Duke University Press, 2003), 237.

64. Dodson, *Orientalism*, 80.

65. Ibid., 90.

66. Francis Bacon, *Selected Philosophical Works*, ed. Rose-Mary Sargent (New York: Hackett, 1999), 74, 75.

67. Dodson, *Orientalism*, 106.

68. Ibid., 107–8.

69. Ibid., 102.

70. Ibid., 172.

71. See C. A. Bayly, *Empire and Information: Intelligence Gathering and Social Communication in India, 1780–1870* (Cambridge, U.K.: Cambridge University Press, 2000), 347.

72. Dalmia, *Nationalization of Hindu Traditions*, 234, 235, 42, 226. The meanings of *nagarika* and *rasika* are glossed in the lines cited.

73. For the argument for Bharatendu as a publicity center, see Ram Vilas Sharma, *Bharatendu Harishchandra* (Dilli: Rajkamal Prakashan, 1966).

74. Dalmia, *Nationalization of Hindu Traditions*, 196–97.

75. Ibid., 197, 261, 207, 219, 375.

76. As translated by Dalmia, ibid., 198.

77. Ibid., 31, 236.

78. See Francesca Orsini, *The Hindi Public Sphere 1920–1940: Language and Literature in the Age of Nationalism* (New Delhi: Oxford University Press, 2002), 47, passim on "compartmentalization."

79. Dalmia, *Nationalization of Hindu Traditions*, 211.

80. For the textual history of this work, see the appendix in Cynthia Talbot, *The Last Hindu Emperor: Prithviraj Chauhan and the Indian Past 1200–2000* (Cambridge, U.K.: Cambridge University Press, 2016), 277–90.

81. Ibid., 194.

82. For details, see Nandakishor Naval, *Mahavir Prasad Dvivedi* (New Delhi: Sahitya Akademi, 1992), especially chapter 2.

83. The transition from pleading to imaginary fencing with the likes of Curzon is covered in Shobna Nijhawan, ed., *Nationalism in the Vernacular: Hindi, Urdu, and the Literature of Indian Freedom* (New Delhi: Permanent Black, 2010); see, for instance, Brij Narain Chakbast's "A Spat with Lord Curzon," trans. Mehr Farooqi.

84. As cited in Karine Schomer, *Mahadevi Varma and the Chhayavad Age of Modern Hindi Poetry* (New Delhi: Oxford University Press, 1998), 108.

85. Guha, "The Advent of Punctuality," 404, 409.

86. See, for instance, Ramavilas Sharma, *Mahavirprasad Dvivedi aur Hindi Navjagaran* (Nayi Dilli: Rajkamal Prakashan, 1977).

87. Christopher Shackle, introduction to Bullhe Shah, *Sufi Lyrics* (Cambridge, Mass.: Harvard University Press, 2015), 5.

88. Details regarding this moment in Dvivedi's life, including his spat with his British superior, are in Madan Gopal, "Mahavir Prasad Dvivedi, a Maker of Modern Hindi," *Indian Literature* 15, no. 1 (1972): 27–37.

89. See Bharatendu Harishchandra, "A Discourse on the Progress of Hindi," trans. Vasudha Dalmia, in Shobna, *Nationalism in the Vernacular*, 341.

90. Nearly all of the canonical Sanskrit poets of the *mahakavya* (courtly epic) tradition appear within Dvivedi's voluminous writings. This is a topic worthy of more scholarly attention.

91. Orsini, *Hindi Public Sphere*, 366.

92. Schomer, *Mahadevi Varma*, 94.

93. As translated by Schomer, ibid., 101.

94. As translated by Orsini, *Hindi Public Sphere*, 154. A *ragini* is a short poem or musical piece composed with a feminine inflection; a *samasya-purti* is a minor genre in which a part of a metrical composition is provided with the challenge to complete the rest of it according to the meter.

95. Ibid., 154.

96. Orsini, *Hindi Public Sphere*, 150.

97. Schomer, *Mahadevi Varma*, 121.

98. Vasudha Dalmia, "Title of Chapter on Prasad," in *Poetics, Plays, and Performances: The Politics of Modern Indian Theatre* (New Delhi: Oxford University Press, 2006), 88; Schomer *Mahadevi Varma*, 102.

99. Schomer, *Mahadevi Varma*, 113, passim.

EPILOGUE

1. *Bhakta* and *shraddalu* mean "the devoted" and "the pious," respectively.

2. Raymond Williams, *Keywords: A Vocabulary of Culture and Society* (Oxford: Oxford University Press, 1985), 192.

3. Ibid., 193.

4. D. A. Low, *Eclipse of Empire* (Cambridge, U.K.: Cambridge University Press, 1991), 67.

5. Christopher Pinney, *"Photos of the Gods": The Printed Image and Political Struggle in India* (New Delhi: Oxford University Press, 2004), 112.

6. Shahid Amin, *Event, Metaphor, Memory: Chauri Chaura 1922–1992* (Delhi: Oxford University Press, 1996), 2.

7. See Low, *Eclipse of Empire*, 80.

8. Robin Jeffrey, "Communications and Capitalism in India, 1750–2010," *South Asia—Journal of South Asia Studies* 25, no. 2 (2002): 70.

9. Lloyd I. Rudolph, "The Media and Cultural Politics," in *India Votes: Alliance Politics and Minority Governments in the Ninth and Tenth Elections*, ed. Harold A. Gould and Sumit Ganguly (Boulder, Colo.: Westview Press, 1993), 175.

10. In Stanley Tambiah, *Leveling Crowds: Ethnonationalist Conflicts and Collective Violence in South Asia* (Berkeley: University of California Press, 1996), 257.

11. Jeffrey, "Communications and Capitalism," 72.

12. Arvind Rajagopal, *Politics after Television: Religious Nationalism and the Reshaping of the Indian Public* (Cambridge, U.K.: Cambridge University Press, 2001), 136.

13. Walter Benjamin, "Dream Kitsch: Gloss on Surrealism," in *Selected Writings*, II: 4.

14. David Frisby, *Fragments of Modernity: Theories of Modernity in the Work of Simmel, Kracauer, and Benjamin* (Cambridge, Mass.: MIT Press, 1986), 133.

15. Martin Jay, *Permanent Exiles: Essays on the Intellectual Migration from Germany to America* (New York: Columbia University Press, 1985), 208; Frisby, *Fragments of Modernity*, 184.

16. Jeffrey, "Communication and Capitalism," 70.

17. Chrisophe Jaffrelot, "The Plebeianization of the Indian Political Class," in *Religion, Caste, and Politics in India* (New York: Oxford University Press, 2011), 421. OBC stands for "Other Backward Class," an Indian governmental category meant to classify castes deemed disadvantaged socially and educationally.

18. Siegfried Kracauer, *The Mass Ornament: Weimar Essays* (Cambridge, Mass.: Harvard University Press, 2005), 75–76. Originating in late nineteenth-century England, the Tiller Girls were a popular troupe known for high-kicking precision dancing resembling military drills and mechanical processes.

19. Frisby, *Fragments of Modernity*, 151.

20. Thomas Blom Hansen, *The Saffron Wave: Democracy and Hindu Nationalism in Modern India* (Princeton, N.J.: Princeton University Press, 1999), 4–5.

21. For a short account of the discipline, see the introduction in Uta Gerhardt, ed., *German Sociology* (New York: Continuum, 1998).

22. It should be noted that while Simmel only survived a little over a month into the Weimar Republic before his death in 1919, Kracauer and others, including Benjamin, extended his legacy into the new era.

23. Miriam Bratu Hansen, *Cinema and Experience: Siegfried Kracauer, Walter Benjamin, and Theodor W. Adorno* (Berkeley: University of California Press, 2011), 8.

24. Kracauer, *Mass Ornament*, 78.

25. Charles Baudelaire, *The Painter of Modern Life: And Other Essays*, trans. Jonathan Mayne (London: Phaidon, 1964), 13.

26. Donald N. Levine and Daniel Silver, introduction to Georg Simmel, *The View of Life: Four Metaphysical Essays with Journal Aphorisms* (Chicago: University of Chicago, 2015), ix.

27. Frisby, *Fragments of Modernity*, 53.

28. As cited ibid., 49.

29. As cited ibid.

30. Georg Simmel, "The Adventurer," in *Georg Simmel on Individuality and Social Forms*, ed. Donald N. Levine (1971; Chicago: University of Chicago, 2011), 189.

31. Frisby, *Fragments of Modernity*, 62.

32. Simmel, "The Adventurer," 189–90.

33. As cited in Frisby, *Fragments of Modernity*, 44.

34. As cited ibid., 45.

35. Kracauer, *Mass Ornament*, 252–53, translation modified.

36. Simmel, "The Stranger," in Levine, *Simmel on Individuality*, 143.

37. Siegfried Kracauer, "George Simmel: 'Zur Philosophie der Kunst,'" in *Aufzätze 1915–1926*, ed. Inka Mülder-Bach (Frankfurt am Main: Suhrkamp Verlag, 1990), 233–35.

38. Kracauer, "Georg Simmel," in *Mass Ornament*, 231.

39. Kracauer, "On Bestsellers and Their Audience," in *Mass Ornament*, 90.

40. Kracauer, "The Mass Ornament," in *Mass Ornament*, 83.

41. Siegfried Kracauer, *The Salaried Masses: Duty and Distraction in Weimar Germany*, trans. Quintin Hoare (New York: Verso, 1998), 35, 68.

42. Hansen, *Cinema and Experience*, 48.

43. Kracauer, "Mass Ornament," 78, 83, 76, 79, 86.

44. Ibid., 80, 81; Frisby, *Fragments of Modernity*, 147.

45. Kracauer, "Mass Ornament," 83.

46. "Bina 'Ramayan' Ravivar ki Subah Suni-Suni Si," *Jan Satta*, August 9, 1988.

47. "Dharavahik Ramayan: Hiy ki pyas bujhai na bujhaye" (The Ramayana Serial: The Heart's Thirst Is Still Unsatisfied), *Dainik Jagaran*, July 31, 1988.

48. "Ramayan ke Nam par Aphim" (An Opiate in the Name of the Ramayana), *Svatantra Bharat*, August 3, 1988.

49. "'Ramayan' ke Mauke par Bijli Jane se Upakendra par Pathrav, Agjani" (Electricity Outage on Occasion of TV "Ramayana" Leads to Stone-Throwing and Arson at the Electricity Plant), *Dainik Jagaran*, March 21, 1988; "Ramayan ke Samay Bijli Jane se Rosh" (Rage Because of Electricity Outage at the Time of TV "Ramayana"), *Aaj*, March 17, 1988; "Ramnagar Nivasi Aaj 'Ramayan' nahin Dekh Sakenge?" (Will the Residents of Ramanagar Not Be Able to Watch the "Ramayana"?), *Aaj*, June 12, 1988.

50. "'Ramayan' se pahle Telivijan ki Puja" (Before the "Ramayana" Broadcast Television Sets are Worshipped), *Aaj*, June 6, 1988.

51. Simran Bhargava, "Ramanand Sagar's Ramayan Is Being Awarded the Sanctity of the Original," *India Today*, April 30, 1987.

52. "Adcanon ke bavajud Ramayan saphal hai" (Despite Obstacles, *Ramayan* Is a Success; Interview with Ramanand Sagar), *Dainik Jagaran*, June 13, 1988.

53. Daud Ali, *Courtly Culture and Political Life in Early Medieval India* (Cambridge, U.K.: Cambridge University Press, 2004), 177.

54. "Kamai ka naya Dhandha 'Ramayan' ke Kastyum ki Pradarshini" (Displaying "Ramayana" Costumes Is a New Way to Earn a Living), *Dainik Jagaran*, July 13, 1988.

55. "Har Dharm ki Logon Men Lokpriya hai Ramayan" ("Ramayana" Is a Favorite among People of All Religions), *Suhag Bindiya*, July 1988.

56. Arjun Appadurai, *The Future as Cultural Fact: Essays on the Global Condition* (New York: Verso, 2013), 91–92.

57. Sigmund Freud, "Mourning and Melancholia," in *General Psychological Theory: Papers on Metapsychology*, ed. Philip Rieff (New York: Touchstone, 1963), 173.

58. Hanssen, *Walter Benjamin's Other History*, 18.

59. Svetlana Boym, *The Future of Nostalgia* (New York: Basic Books, 2001), 41.

60. Freud, "Mourning and Melancholia," 164, 170, 171.

61. "Where once the suffering of pain has been experienced as a masochistic aim, it can be carried back into the sadistic situation and result in a sadistic aim of *inflicting pain*, which will then be masochistically enjoyed by the subject while inflicting pain upon others, through this identification of himself with the suffering object" (Rief, *General Psychological Theory*, 93).

62. Kracauer, "Bestsellers," 96.

63. Bhavabhuti, *Rama's Last Act*, trans. Sheldon Pollock (New York: New York University Press, 2007).

64. Sheldon Pollock, *The Language of the Gods in the World of Men: Sanskrit, Culture, and Power in Premodern India* (Berkeley: University of California Press, 2006), 78.

65. Roland Barthes, "Diderot, Brecht, Eisenstein," in *L'obvie et l'obtus: Essais critiques III* (Paris: Éditions du Seuil, 1982), 87. The translation by Stephen Heath was consulted; see *Image, Music, Text* ed. Stephen Heath (New York: Hill and Wang, 1977), 70.

66. Ibid., 89 (73 in English translation).

67. Ravi Vasudevan, "Aesthetics and Politics in Popular Cinema," in *The Cambridge Companion to Modern Indian Culture*, ed. Vasudha Dalmia and Rashmi Sadana (Cambridge, U.K.: Cambridge University Press, 2012), 231.

68. Walter Benjamin, "Surrealism: The Last Snapshot of the European Intelligentsia," in *Selected Writings*, II: 210.

69. Barthes, "Diderot, Brecht, Eisenstein," 73–74.

APPENDIX A

1. Mustansir Mir, trans., *Tulip in the Desert: A Selection of the Poetry of Muhammad Iqbal* (Montreal: McGill-Queen's University Press, 1999), 24, 23.

2. Theodor W. Adorno, "Wörter aus der Fremde," in *Noten zur Literatur* (Frankfurt: Suhrkamp, 2003), 218.

3. Mohammad Iqbal, *Message de L'Orient*, trans. Eva Meyerovitch and Mohammad Achena (Paris: Société d'Édition "Les Belles Lettres," 1956); Sir Muhammad Iqbal, *Botschaft des Ostens (als Antwort auf Goethes West-Östlicher Divan)*, trans. Annemarie Schimmel (Wiesbaden: Otto Harrassowitz, 1963).

4. "Unbeschreiblich ist der Zauber dieses Buches: es ist ein Selam, den der Okzident dem Oriente geschickt hat, und es sind gar närrische Blumen darunter. . . . Dieser Selam aber bedeutet, daß der Okzident seines frierend mageren Spiritualismus überdrüssig geworden und an der gesunden Körperwelt des Orients sich wieder erlaben möchte." Heinrich Heine, *Die romantische Schule*, in *Werke und Briefe*, vol. 5, ed. Hans Kaufmann (Berlin: Aufbau Verlag, 1961), 57–58. I must thank my colleague Loisa Nygaard for her help in tracking down this source.

5. Paul Horn, "Was verdanken wir Persien?," *Nord und Süd* 94 (1900): 377–95.

6. A. J. F. Remy, "The Influence of India and Persia on the Poetry of Germany," Ph.D. diss., Columbia University, 1901. It is unclear how or why Iqbal gives him the name "Charles."

7. The original is pithier than Iqbal's rendition of it in Urdu: "An Hafyz Gesängen haven wir fast genug; Sa'adi ist uns lehrreicher gewesen." See Johann Gottfried Herder, *Adrastea* XI, in *Werke in zehn Bänden*, ed. Günter Arnold (Frankfurt am Main: Deutsche Klassiker Verlag, 2000), 862.

8. The reference is to Josef Freiherr von Hammer-Purgstall (1774–1856), an Orientalist and diplomat in the Balkans and Near East, and from 1847 to 1849 the president of the Wiener Akademie der Wissenschaften. Von Hammer was editor of the *Fundgruben des Orients* and translator of *Der Diwan des Mohammed Schemsed-din Hafis: Auf dem Persischen zum erstenmal ganz übersetzt von Joseph v. Hammer* (Stuttgart: J. G. Cotta'schen, 1812–13).

9. Albert Bielschowsky, *Goethe, sein Leben und seine Werke* (Munich: C. H. Beck, 1896–1906), 2:341–42. The original passage reads as follows: "Der Sänger von Schiras erschien wie sein leibhaftiges Ebenbild. Ob er vielleicht in der Persers Gestalt schon einmal auf Erden gewandelt? Dieselbe Erdenfreudigkeit und Himmelliebe, Einfachheit und Tiefe, Wahrheit und Gradheit, Glut und Leidenschaftlichkeit, und endlich dieselbe Offenheit und von keinerlei Satzung eingeschränkte Empfänglichkeit für alles Menschliche. Passte es nicht auch auf ihn, wenn die Perser ihren Dichter zugleich die mystische Zunge und den Dolmetsch der Geheimnisse nannten, wenn sie von seinen Gedichten sagten, sie wären dem Äusseren nach einfach und ungeschmückte, hätten aber tiefe, die Wahrheit ergründene Bedeutung und hoechste Vollendung? Und genoss nicht Hafis wie er die Gunst der Niederen und Grossen? Ja, erroberte er nich auch der Eroberer, den gewaltigen Timur? Und rettete er sich nicht aus allem Umsturz der Dinge seine heiterkeit und sang weiter wie vordem in Frieden, in den alten gewohnten Verhältnissen?—So wurde ihm Hafis ein geliebter Bruder aus der Urzeit, und gern trat er einmal in die verwandte Spuren und versuchte dem oestlichen Diwan einen westlichen entgegenzusetzen, der ein westoestlicher werden musste, da der westliche Dichter die Anschauungen und Formen des Ostens mit denen des Westens verschmolz und getrost die Maske des persischen Sängers anlagen konnte, ohne von der eigenen ausgeprängen Persoenlichkeit einen Deut aufzugeben. In dieser innerlichen angenommenen Maske reiste Goethe in Juli 1814 nach den Rhein-und Maingegenden. Das erste lakonische Wort des Reisetagesbuch ist: 'Hafis.'"

10. Friedrich Martin von Bodenstedt (1819–1892), German author and popularizer of the Persian poetry of Omar Khayam through his translations; composer of poetry in the Orientalizing vein in his pseudonymous work, *Die Lieder des Mirza-Schaffy* (Berlin: R. v. Decker, 1878).

11. The reference must be to Heinrich Heine, *Neue Gedichte*. For an accurate reprint see Heinrich Heine, *Neue Gedichte* (Stuttgart: Reclam, 1995).

12. Georg Friedrich Daumer (1800–1875), Heinrich Leuthold (1827–1879), Adolf Friedrich von Schack (1815–1894). The other figures referred to in this line have been difficult to trace and remain ambiguous.

13. Francesco Saverio Nitti, *La decadenza dell'Europa* (Firenze: R. Bemporad, 1922). The work appeared in English as *The Decadence of Europe: Paths of Reconstruction*, trans. F. Brittain (London: Unwin, 1923).

14. As translated by A. J. Arberry in *The Koran* (Oxford: Oxford University Press, 2008), 240 (Surah 13.12).

15. Amanullah Khan (1892–1960), ruler of the Emirate of Afghanistan from 1919 to 1929, succeeded in attaining the independence of Afghani foreign affairs from the United Kingdom.

APPENDIX B

1. David Rubin, trans., *The Return of Sarasvati: Four Hindi Poets* (New Delhi: Oxford University Press, 1998), 112, 117.

Index

Adorno, Gretel, 120
Adorno, Theodor W., 8, 13, 16, 48, 50, 73, 101, 105; "A Portrait of Walter Benjamin," 69
Adorno, Theodor, and Max Horkheimer, 16–17, 62; *Dialectic of Enlightenment*, 16, 68–75
Act for the Better Government of India (1858), 4–5
allegory, 58, 60, 133–137, 166–167, 188, 204–207; and melancholy, 131–132
Allison, Henry E., 107
Anis, Mir Babar 'Ali, 138
aporia, 7–8, 18, 67, 83, 196–197
Arberry, A. J., 92
Arnold, Thomas W., 146, 157
Auden, W.H., 54
aura, 6, 9, 78, 82–84, 95, 100, 106, 109, 189, 197, 198, 229

Bacon, Francis, 189, 192, 193, 200
Balibar, Étienne, 33
Barthes, Roland, 167, 231
Bäumler, Alfred, 105
Benjamin, Walter, 17, 30–31, 96–117, 131, 140, 171; "Announcement of the Journal *Angelus Novus*," 115; *Arcades Project*, 31–32; "Capitalism as Religion," 31; "Central Park," 31; "Dialogue on the Religiosity of the Present," 101; "Doctrine of the Similar," 52; "Experience and Poverty, 121; "Kaisarpanorama," 97; "Marseilles," 103–105, 123; "Moral Education," 110; "Myslovice—Braunschweig—Marseilles," 122; "On the Coming Philosophy," 111; "On the Concept of History," 26; "On Language as Such and the Language of Man," 114, 116; "On the Mimetic Faculty," 19; *One-Way Street*, 96–97; "Program for Literary Criticism," 49; "Spain, 1932," 119; "Surrealism: The Last Snapshot of the European Intelligentsia," 115, 122; "The Currently Effective Messianic Elements," 171; "The Handkerchief," 119; *The Origins of German Tragic Drama*, 118; "The Pan of Evening," 102; "The

Storyteller," 17, 119, 120, 124; "The Task of the Translator," 114; on Kant and neo-Kantianism, 105–111; on language and language-magic (*Sprachmagie*), 113; on the theory of the name, 115–117; on theory of the sublime, 21, 106
Bentham, Jeremy, 177–181, 189
Bentinck, Lord William, 177
Bergson, Henri, 10, 22, 143, 159–162, 240
Bewes, Timothy, 42
Bhagavad-Gita, 12
Bharatendu Harishchandra, 175, 189, 191–192, 194–198, 200, 226
Blackbourn, David, 101
Blake, William, 67
Bradley, F.H., 146
Brecht, Bertolt, 64, 101, 119, 123, 124
Bright, Charles, 25
British colonialism, 24–26, 156. *See also* colonialism
Buber, Martin, 112–113
Burton, Sir Richard, 66
Byron, Lord, 66, 176

Carnap, Rudolf, 105
Chakrabarty, Dipesh, 24, 75, 90
Chatterjee, Bankimchandra, 181
Chaudhuri, Rosinka, 189
Chayavad (Hindi romanticism), 10, 22, 23, 87, 175, 195–204, 242
Cioc, Mark, 101
Cohen, Hermann, 110
colonialism, 24–26, 32–33, 41–42, 70, 99–100, 118–119, 155–156, 176–180, 212–214; and shame, 104–105; and "constructive orientalism," 191–193
commodity-form, 7; commodification, 6, 34; as fetish, 36–37, 71, 73; and nonsensuous similarity, 49
Conrad, Joseph, ; *Lord Jim*, 54–63
constellation, 19, 48–51; as translational medium, 50; as method for literary history, 48–53
Creation Society, 65, 79, 95
Croce, Benedetto, 89

Dabir, Mir Salamat 'Ali, 138
Dalmia, Vasudha, 190–197, 204
Datta, Michael Madhusudan, 9, 13, 53, 172–177, 180, 182–189, 201; *Meghanadvadh Kavya*, 172–174, 177, 180, 184–187, 201; "The Anglo-Saxon and the Hindu," 172–174
Dazai Osamu, 82
Derozio, Henry, 182, 189
Doak, Kevin Michael, 85
Döblin, Alfred, 123
Dodson, Michael, 191–193
Donald, Stephanie Hemelryk, 79
dream kitsch, 13, 22, 25, 53, 207, 209, 211, 215–217, 219
Dvivedi, Mahavir Prasad, 53, 189–190, 197–203

Eiland, Howard, 31, 118, 122
English East India Company, 32–33
Enlightenment, 10, 16–17, 24, 34, 45, 62, 68–82, 90–95, 134, 146, 152, 191, 195, 205; and question of equality, 69, 75; as instrumental rationality, 4, 7, 8, 11, 13, 14, 18, 22, 25, 26, 36–46, 56, 67, 70–77, 94, 113, 117, 134, 153, 176, 189, 191, 195, 197, 199, 201, 210, 216, 229; as utilitarianism, 76, 131, 175–182, 185, 189, 191–199, 201–202, 217, 243. *See also* reification
epic, 11, 13–14 197–198; and temporality, 123; as visual idiom, 227–232

Faiz, Faiz Ahmad, 143, 159, 161
Fayzee, Atiya, 147–148
Feng Naichao, 81
Fontane, Theodor, 103
Frankfurt School (Institute for Social Research), 68, 70, 105

Gandhi, Mohandas K., 26, 154, 213–214
German Colonial Society, 99
Geyer, Michael, 25
Ghalib, Asadullah Khan, 15, 128, 129
Goethe, Johann Wolfgang, 23, 66, 143–154, 170–171, 233–239, 243, 249 n. 32; and *Faust*, 150, 151, 171; and *West-östlicher Divan*, 23, 145
Gramsci, Antonio, 91
Greater East Asia Co-Prosperity Sphere, 85
Guha, Ranajit, 32, 38, 41; "The Advent of Punctuality," 32–33
Guo, Moruo, 65–66, 79–80
Gupta, Maithilisharan, 201
Gutkind, Erich, 114

Habermas, Jürgen, 9
Hafiz, Khwaja Shams ud-Din Muhammad, 149, 156, 161, 233, 236–239
Hali, Altaf Husain, 3–8, 15, 33, 53, 127–142
Hayat-e Sa'adi, 129; *Muqaddamah-e Sh'er o Sha'iri*, 130; *Musaddas: The Ebb and Flow of Islam*, 3–8, 21, 128–142; *Yadgar-e Ghalib*, 129
Halqah-ye Arbab-e Zauq (Circle of Connoisseurs), 87
Hamacher, Werner, 26
Hamman, Johann Georg, 24, 26
Hansen, Thomas Blom, 218
Hanssen, Beatrice, 51, 110
Hare, David, 181–182
Harootunian, Harry, 85
Harper, Thomas J., 83
Havel, E.B., 190
Hegel, G.W.F., 50
Heine, Heinrich, 149
Heinrich, Michael, 35
Helmholtz, Hermann von, 103
Hommel, Fritz, 146
Honneth, Axel, 42
Husain, Fazl-i, 157, 158

imperialism. *See* colonialism
imperial space, 102, 173–174, 184; as landscape, 102–105, 148; as messianic, 103; and shame, 104–105
instrumental rationality. *See under* Enlightenment
Iqbal, Muhammad, 9, 22, 23, 53, 65, 92–95, 143–171; *Asrar-e Khudi*, 164, 166; "Conquest of Nature," 23; *Javid Nama*, 13, 22, 33, 92–94, 143, 150, 154–156, 158, 162–171; *Payam-e Mashriq*, 23, 145, 146, 149, 150; translation of preface to, 235–241; *Rumuz-e Bekhudi*, 149; *Shikva*, 163; "The Development of Metaphysics in Persia," 146; *The Reconstruction of Religious Thought in Islam*, 156
Islam in late colonial India, 92–95, 128–136, 140, 143–163, 196, 197, 234, 235

Jacobs, Carol, 122
Jaffrelot, Christophe, 217
Jameson, Fredric, 29; *Representing Capital*, 35
Japanese romantic school, 82–86, 95
Jeffrey, Robin, 214–216
Jennings, Michael, 118, 122
Jinnah, Muhammad Ali, 87
Jones, Sir William, 184

Kant, Immanuel, 106; *The Critique of Practical Reason*, 107; *Critique of the Power of Judgment*, 107
Kaushik, Vishvabharnath Sharma, 203
Khan, Sir Sayyid Ahmad, 92–94, 128, 156
Kipling, Rudyard, 42
Kobayashi, Hideo, 75
Köhnke, Klaus Christian, 109
Kracauer, Siegfried, 211, 215–223, 229

Kurella, Alfred, 118

Lacoue-Labarthe, Phillipe, 11
Lagarde, Paul de, 100
late colonial; periodization of, 24–26
League of Left-Wing Writers (China), 79
Lee, Leo Ou-fan, 78
Liebert, Arthur, 106
Lovejoy, Arthur O., 55
Lu Xun, 75–79; "On Photography," 75–78
Lukács, Georg, 30, 43–48; *History and Class Consciousness*, 43–48

Macaulay, Thomas Babington, 179, 191–192
Majeed, Javed, 4–5, 128, 130–132, 139, 163, 178
Manjapra, Kris, 100
Mao Dun, 80
marsiya, 7, 137–141
Marx, Karl, 33, 38–39, 48–49, 51; *Capital: A Critique of Political Economy* (vol. 1), 33, 50
Marx, Karl, and Friedrich Engels, *German Ideology*, 12
Masakazu Yamazaki, 85, 86
masses: in modern India, 211–216; as ornament, 216, 222, 225–226; theory of, 211–212; in Weimar Germany, 216–223;
materialist theology, 19, 47–48, 51–52, 117, 219–220. *See also* profane illumination
May Fourth Movement, 79–80
McLaughlin, Kevin, 31
McTaggert, John, 146
Menninghaus, Winfried, 69–70
Mill, James, 177–179
Mill, John Stuart, 42, 177–181, 189, 200
Milton, John, 186–187, 243
Mishima Yukio, 82
Modi, Narendra, 210
Moore, Thomas, 176
Moser, Thomas C., 59
Mukherjee, Meenakshi, 8

Nachtigal, Gustav, 99
Naim, C.M., 155
Nancy, Jean-Luc, 11
nature, 94, 134, 164
neo-epic, 5, 9, 175, 201; theory of, 13–14
neotraditionalism, 4, 9, 10, 12, 14, 22, 87, 90–91, 184, 201, 205, 211, 231
Nicholson, Sherry Weber, 49
Nirala, Suryakant Tripathi, 199, 201–203
Nietzsche, Friedrich, 42
nonsensuous similarity, 49, 99, 102

Oceanic, 57, 62–64, 141–142, 162, 170–171
Okakura Tenshin, 66
Oppenheimer, J. Robert, 12
Orsini, Francesca, 196, 202, 203

Pan-German League, 99
Pant, Sumitranandan, 9, 23, 175, 202–204, 242–243; "The Usefulness of the Epic Form in the Modern Age," 23; translation of, 243–246
Parry, Benita, 57
Peters, Carl, 99
Pinney, Christopher, 213
Prasad, Jayashankar, 9, 13, 21–22, 53, 175, 200, 203–204, 207, 225, 243, 246; and *Kamayani*, 13, 22, 23, 200, 204, 205, 207, 243, 246
Prophet Muhammad, 3, 137, 151, 165, 234
Postone, Moishe, 38, 39
profane illumination, 216, 225, 227–228

Queen Victoria, 5, 99

Raabe, Wilhelm, 100, 103
Rajagopal, Arvind, 215
Raychaudhuri, Tapan, 75
reification, 6, 42–48
Ricardo, David, 42
Riddiford, Alexander, 184, 184–185, 187

Rolland, Romain, 91
romanticism, 9–10, 90, 145–146, 153, 157; as Asian neoromanticism, 67 ; as critique of bourgeois society, 11; as critique of Western civilization, 95; late, 21, 91–92; theory of, 11
Rose, Gillian, 42
Ruckteschell, Walter von, 100
Rumi, Jalal ud-Din, 165, 167–168, 238, 239
Ryan, Judith, 100

Schiller, Friedrich, 66
Schlegel, Friedrich, 15, 18, 66
Scholem, Gershom, 49, 97, 105, 109, 114; *Walter Benjamin: The Story of a Friendship*, 110, 115
Schomer, Karine, 202, 204
Schmitt, Carl, 79, 81; *Political Romanticism*, 81
Schwab, Raymond, 66
Seidensticker, Edward G., 83
Shackle, Christopher, 4–5, 128, 130–132, 139
Shefta, Mustafa Khan, 128
Simmel, Georg, 42, 43, 216, 218–222
Sleeman, Captain William H.
Smith, Wilfred Cantwell, 155
Soseki, Natsume, 74
Stifter, Theodor, 103
Stokes, Eric, 177, 179–180
Storm, Theodor, 103
sublime, 16, 19, 21, 33, 38, 47, 52, 71, 82, 84, 89, 94, 100, 139, 164; and Kant, 106–113

Tagore, Rabindranath, 66, 78, 88–92, 95, 203, 245; in Beijing, 78; in Mussolini's Italy, 89–92
Takeuchi Yoshimi, 85
Tanizaki Jun'ichiro, 82–86; *In Praise of Shadows*, 82–86; and traditional sublime, 82–86
Tansman, Alan, 85
temporality: as abstract, 40–41; of boredom, 121; as clock time, 9–10, 13, 17, 22, 230; and colonialism, 120–121, 131; as "developmental time," 109, 121; and epic, 123; as futurity, 24, 26, 153; and intoxication (*Rausch*), 123; as messianic, 31; and modern work regimes, 4; as "pregnant time," 231; as standard measure in colonial India, 5
Tetsuo Najita, 85
Thompson, Edward, 158
Tian Han, 65–66, 80
Tod, James, 197
translation, 23, 50–51, 112–117; as silver rib, 11; and mimesis, 49; and name, 115–117
TV *Ramayana*, 22, 209–232

Unger, Erich, 114

Vajpeyi, Ananya, 209–211
Valero, Vicente, 119
value, 37, 41, 37–40; crisis of, 5–6
Varma, Mahadevi, 202–204
Victorianism in India, 1, 6–7

Wang Hui, 67, 75, 79
Weber, Max, 42, 43
White, Hayden, 167
Wilhelm II, 99
Williams, Raymond, 68–69, 211–212
Wood, Allen, 108
Wordsworth, William, 13
Wyneken, Gustav, 98

Xiao, Jun, 78
Xu Zhimo, 78

Yasuda Yojuro, 82, 83
Yi Zheng, 79
Yu Dafu, 78

Zhang Junmai, 81

FLASHPOINTS

1. *On Pain of Speech: Fantasies of the First Order and the Literary Rant,* Dina Al-Kassim
2. *Moses and Multiculturalism,* Barbara Johnson, with a foreword by Barbara Rietveld
3. *The Cosmic Time of Empire: Modern Britain and World Literature,* Adam Barrows
4. *Poetry in Pieces: César Vallejo and Lyric Modernity,* Michelle Clayton
5. *Disarming Words: Empire and the Seductions of Translation in Egypt,* Shaden M. Tageldin
6. *Wings for Our Courage: Gender, Erudition, and Republican Thought,* Stephanie H. Jed
7. *The Cultural Return,* Susan Hegeman
8. *English Heart, Hindi Heartland: The Political Life of Literature in India,* Rashmi Sadana
9. *The Cylinder: Kinematics of the Nineteenth Century,* Helmut Müller-Sievers
10. *Polymorphous Domesticities: Pets, Bodies, and Desire in Four Modern Writers,* Juliana Schiesari
11. *Flesh and Fish Blood: Postcolonialism, Translation, and the Vernacular,* S. Shankar
12. *The Fear of French Negroes: Transcolonial Collaboration in the Revolutionary Americas,* Sara E. Johnson
13. *Figurative Inquisitions: Conversion, Torture, and Truth in the Luso-Hispanic Atlantic,* Erin Graff Zivin
14. *Cosmopolitan Desires: Global Modernity and World Literature in Latin America,* Mariano Siskind
15. *Fiction Beyond Secularism,* Justin Neuman
16. *Periodizing Jameson: Dialectics, the University, and the Desire for Narrative,* Phillip E. Wegner
17. *The Practical Past,* Hayden White
18. *The Powers of the False: Reading, Writing, Thinking Beyond Truth and Fiction,* Doro Wiese
19. *The Object of the Atlantic: Concrete Aesthetics in Cuba, Brazil, and Spain, 1868–1968,* Rachel Price
20. *Epic and Exile: Novels of the German Popular Front, 1933–1945,* Hunter Bivens
21. *An Innocent Abroad: Lectures in China,* J. Hillis Miller
22. *Form and Instability: East Europe, Literature, Postimperial Difference,* Anita Starosta
23. *Bombay Modern: Arun Kolatkar and Bilingual Literary Culture,* Anjali Nerlekar
24. *Intimate Relations: Social Reform and the Late Nineteenth-Century South Asian Novel,* Krupa Shandilya
25. *Media Laboratories: Late Modernist Authorship in South America,* Sarah Ann Wells

26. *Acoustic Properties: Radio, Narrative, and the New Neighborhood of the Americas*, Tom McEnaney
27. *The New Woman: Literary Modernism, Queer Theory, and the Trans Feminine Allegory*, Emma Heaney
28. *Civilizing War: Imperial Politics and the Poetics of National Rupture*, Nasser Mufti
29. *Late Colonial Sublime: Neo-Epics and the End of Romanticism*, G. S. Sahota